STATESMEN, SCHOLARS
AND MERCHANTS

DAME LUCY SUTHERLAND

STATESMEN, SCHOLARS AND MERCHANTS

Essays in
Eighteenth-Century History
presented to
Dame Lucy Sutherland

Edited by
ANNE WHITEMAN, J. S. BROMLEY
and P. G. M. DICKSON

OXFORD
AT THE CLARENDON PRESS
1973

Oxford University Press, Ely House, London W. 1

GLASGOW   NEW YORK   TORONTO   MELBOURNE   WELLINGTON
CAPE TOWN   IBADAN   NAIROBI   DAR ES SALAAM   LUSAKA   ADDIS ABABA
DELHI   BOMBAY   CALCUTTA   MADRAS   KARACHI   LAHORE   DACCA
KUALA LUMPUR   SINGAPORE   HONG KONG   TOKYO

*Printed in Great Britain
at the University Press, Oxford
by Vivian Ridler
Printer to the University*

Foreword

THIS collection of essays, written by some of Dame Lucy Sutherland's pupils who have specialized in eighteenth-century studies, and by others whose research is closely allied to her own, is without the names of some who would gladly have made a contribution but were, for various reasons, unable to do so. The editors would like particularly to mention the late Romney Sedgwick, who had promised to write on 'The Duke of Newcastle's Income'.

The editors wish to express their gratitude to the Staff of the Clarendon Press for their care and efficiency in the production of this book, and to Rosemary J. Thomas for compiling the index.

Lucy Stuart Sutherland

THE world contains a large number of people—let us call them statesmen, scholars, or merchants, but they come from all walks of life and from half a dozen countries—who are not in a position to share Dame Lucy Sutherland's overriding interest in the University of Oxford. Yet none of them would care to visit that ancient seat of learning without seeking to get in touch with her. They might do so for advice, learned or otherwise, in which case they would not come empty away. More often, the object of the visit would simply be to renew contact with one of the liveliest minds and the most vivacious personality they had ever come across, who also happens to be a distinguished figure in British public life. In that case the visitor would depart with a sense of life enhanced, confident and convinced where before he had been uncertain and perhaps depressed.

During her long and memorable principate of Lady Margaret Hall from 1945 to 1971, the visitor would enter a long and airy room into which the light was reflected by the lawns and trees below. The flowers, often gathered from that part of the garden which was the Principal's special care, were always in noble abundance. Low along one wall, three shelves of books, including a complete run of Horace Walpole's letters. Above the fireplace, with its ample tools, a painting of some sun-splashed Mediterranean village; beside it, the Principal's black-and-white cat. High-backed armchairs of some luxury. A small Sheraton window-desk on which lay a silk-embroidered blotter, a pair of delicate eighteenth-century scissors, a silver paperknife and inkstand: but no papers and no photographs. This calm and spacious room faithfully corresponded with the character of its tenant. It had a country-house feeling, without the clutter. It was the sort of timeless interior which a Vermeer might have liked to record, a fitting place to receive a guest, were it a headmistress, a Director of the Bank, the Head of a House, or a student bearing an essay.

At the appropriate hour, drinks would be brought in on a salver with a small bucket of ice. The guest could then enjoy the illusion of keeping up with the pace of the Principal's conversation, and with the rising three-note laugh which runs like quicksilver through all her talk. On festal occasions the table in the adjoining library would be laid for a dinner party— a dozen covers in the candle-light, arranged with the elegance of that age which most of the books came from. Here the Works of Burke and memorials of the East India Company might be faintly glimpsed as one exquisite dish replaced another. The Principal might well have endorsed a saying of the eighteenth-century traveller, Joseph Townsend: 'No man is fit to govern an empire who cannot give a dinner to his friends.'

The Principal ruled her college with a strong but humorous hand. She knows her own mind and makes it up quickly, for she is speedy and economical in all she does; like most very able leaders, she may be suspected of preferring her own judge-ment and enjoying the victory in discussion. But her domain by the River Cherwell was run on strict cabinet principles. If it was not a loose government by departments, such as Lord North's ministry, neither was she an overbearing prime minister. In truth, she took the greatest pains to consult college opinion as well as to compromise with obvious interests. This came naturally because she liked the companionship of her colleagues and sought to encourage them. They, for their part, valued her supreme courage and good sense, her gay manner of taking the heat out of a situation, her serene indifference to all petti-ness. With a highly retentive memory and unusual powers of assimilating the details of any question, she was of course easily mistress of the business in hand, which she seemed to conduct with effortless ease, although she had always read the papers very carefully and thoughtfully. Since Lady Margaret Hall underwent a major change of face during her reign, it was as well she took immense pleasure in the planning of new buildings, and very fortunate that she possesses a practised eye for the intricacies of finance. She knew every inch of the property in her trust, just as she knew the biographies of all its members. If at first contact her brisk manner might seem daunting, the shyest student or servant soon discovered her immense kindness and resourcefulness. Her generosity, both to persons and causes, became a college legend. So, too, at receptions and on other occasions, her totally unselfconscious adaptability to people of different sorts, her eagle eye for any neglected guest. Her out-flowing, informal courtesy might be said to raise the tone of any company she is in. It has certainly won for her a host of devoted friends.

This quality, a dominant characteristic, springs as it must from deep and partly hidden sources. One of them is her un-obtrusive Christianity. No one exhibits fewer exterior marks of the *dévote*, or for that matter of the stereotyped academic spinster. But Lucy Sutherland was confirmed a member of the Church of England when she was already of adult years, and its worship has long provided a secret source of power and equilibrium which she would be quite unashamed to acknowledge; no doubt it also has something to do with her extreme humility and transparent unselfishness. As Principal of Lady Margaret Hall, she had always a strong sense of her obligation to guarantee the college chapel, in the future as well as the present. Sunday mornings are reserved for Christ Church cathedral.

So much energy, so much kindness, such an allergy to bore-dom. Dame Lucy's undiminished joy in living has made her an omnivorous reader and what might be called an omnivorous traveller, with a preference for southern climates and sea-bathing, for Italy and *antichità*, even for a modified form of safari. Lucy Stuart Sutherland was in fact brought up in South Africa, where her father, Alexander Charles Sutherland, was a mining engineer; he took her about with him on many of his journeys and endowed her with an enduring love of the opera. But both her parents were Australians by origin, both graduates of Melbourne. Lucy herself was born not at Johannesburg but at Geelong, on 21 June 1903. Her mother came of a family prominent in eighteenth-century London and her mother's father was born within the sound of Bow Bells. He married a Musgrave of Co. Fermanagh. Lucy's father was of Scottish Highland descent—one of her earliest memories is of hearing her Stuart grandmother sing Jacobite songs, with verses in them that never get into the printed versions. There was a brother, but he died in childhood. Dame Lucy still acknowledges a deep devotion to her parents, evidently remarkable people, who gave her the priceless advantage of a secure and happy youth. It was a comfortable home, where bronze dancing-shoes were ruled out as 'common'.

Lucy Sutherland's early formation, until she was 22, was entirely South African. At eight she went to Roedean School in Johannesburg, where some of her lifelong friendships took root, particularly with the painter Maud Sumner, who was later to do one of the portraits which Lady Margaret Hall has of her. In 1921 came the History and Economics courses, pregnant with destiny, at the University of Witwatersrand, where she owed much to the encouragement of Professor W. M. ('Pinkie') Macmillan. The first of her numerous degrees was acquired here in 1924, after an accomplished performance recognized by the award of the Herbert Ainsworth Research Scholarship, which she held for three years. Thus fortified, Miss Sutherland came up to Somerville College in 1925. It was a momentous transition, almost a marriage, for Oxford has remained essential to her, and she to it, ever since.

Somerville was her first Oxford home. Her early affection for it owed a great deal to two gifted medievalists, her tutor Maude Clarke and Miss Clarke's successor, May McKisack. In those days it was considered more profitable for a brilliant graduate from some other university to take one of Oxford's first-degree Schools rather than proceed at once to research. So one of Witwatersrand's new-vintage M.A.s set herself to become an Oxford B.A. in Modern History. Locally, this is the description given to all history from the fall of the Roman Empire. The young lady was in fact a passionate student of the Middle Ages—an indulgence that was to be reflected in her own early publications. When Maude Clarke died, it was Lucy Sutherland and May McKisack who in 1937 completed her last work for the press; and a year later appeared the results of a similar editorial collaboration with Helen Cam and Mary Coate, this time on Miss A. G. Levett's important but unfinished work in manorial history. By this date 'L. S. S.' had been two years a Fellow and Tutor of Somerville, in Economic History and Politics, which meant that she taught for the School of Modern Greats (P.P.E.) as well as Modern History. In 1927 this elevation had been foreshadowed in an unusual way by her election to an assistant tutorship before her Final Examination—a situation which did not tempt her examiners into denying her a First, but one which would severely have strained any ordinary candidate. It was fortunate perhaps that one of her tutors, J. R. H. Weaver (later President of Trinity), had warned her very sternly against the dangerous Oxford climate, which in those statelier years prohibited all work in the afternoons.

Apart from her early diversions into the Middle Ages— themselves as much as anything early examples of Lucy Sutherland's absolute loyalty to persons as well as to institutions— her career as historian has turned out to be all of a piece. The list of her publications at the end of this volume possesses an exceptional degree of coherence; they all spring from a single root. She chose the eighteenth century as soon as she turned to research of her own, and has stuck to it ever since. Not only that: her dominant interests in it proclaimed themselves at the outset. Her first article, nearly thirty years before her volume of Edmund Burke's correspondence appeared in Professor Copeland's definitive edition, was about Burke ('the ablest man of the eighteenth century') and the first Rockingham ministry. A year later, in 1933, with her first book—on William Braund—she declared her lifelong interest in the business and politics of the eighteenth-century City of London, on which she still has more to give the world. When war came in 1939 she was far enough forward with her classical study of the East India Company, published eventually in 1952, to lock the unfinished manuscript away while she went off to administer the Board of Trade's interest in the iron and steel industries.

It is odd now to realize that Dame Lucy's early work on the English eighteenth century met with initial discouragement. A well-known historian of the time is understood to have told her that virtually no further work was required on that period. A little later, in 1929, a certain Lewis Bernstein Namier published his epoch-making *The Structure of Politics at the Accession of George III*. No work has had a deeper influence on Dame Lucy's own studies; nor has she ever concealed what she owes to the encouragement and friendship of the late Sir Lewis Namier. But for this, it is possible that she would have remained primarily an economic historian. Many interests drew them together, not least a fascination with human nature, although, her sense of humour being richer than his, she has tended to see absurdity where he saw miching mallecho. Perhaps they were also drawn together by the fact that both were powerfully attracted to a British 'establishment', including the Church of England, into which neither of them had been born. At any rate, their close academic relationship, for over thirty years, is one of the fundamental data of contemporary British historiography. When Sir Lewis died, Dame Lucy was the natural choice for the British Academy Memoir of him.

There was another brilliant figure who shared their interests and who also became a power in his own right. A year before Lucy Sutherland came to Somerville, Richard Pares had been elected a Fellow of All Souls. They were almost the same age, strikingly similar in wit and intelligence, above all in their dedication to hard, technical history and what he called the historian's 'scientific conscience'. Although 'L. S. S.' never became what used to be called a colonial historian, Pares's work on the sugar trade came very close to her own interest in business history—then a much more esoteric genre than it is today. Later, he was to give his famous Ford Lectures on King George III in the very year that *The East India Company in Eighteenth-Century Politics* came out. She has always, rightly, thought of him as a very remarkable man. When, after his premature death in 1958, she wrote of his 'unwavering self-discipline for the perfection of his highly sophisticated and meticulously unspectacular art', she could also have been speaking for herself.

The fortunes of war sent them both into the Board of Trade— he in 1939, she in 1941. She was to leave it in 1945 as an Assistant Secretary. It is no secret that those were the years when most sectors of commerce and industry were to encounter, amid their other difficulties, the keen edge of female brains in a number of Whitehall's strategic posts. Encountering Miss Sutherland, as a provider of iron and steel in time of acute scarcity, must have entailed some readjustment of received ideas about the inequality of the sexes in the minds of many captains of industry. She herself greatly enjoyed the work, not least for the wide variety of non-academic friends it brought her. As other temporary civil-service dons were to find, Whitehall was a grand corrective of academic stiffness and pride. Lucy Sutherland's Oxford friends noted how much this experience had matured her, how much she had gained in humanity because of it. She was said to have become more keenly aware of the differences in people, more interested in dress and party-going. It was only then, they said, that she felt herself to belong wholly to the English scene.

The new Principal of Lady Margaret Hall did not contract out of national affairs when she left Whitehall. Indeed, one of her inestimable services to her colleagues was undoubtedly her continuing association with a wider world, besides the virtuoso demonstration of how members of their sex were now increasingly called upon to participate in its government. As early as 1946 the Principal found herself Chairman of the Lace Working Party, which really was about the lace industry and involved some study of its long history, not only in Britain. In 1949 she joined a Committee of Enquiry into the Distribution and Exhibition of Cinematograph Films, an exceptionally fecund source for the delight of her Senior Common Room. Then, from 1951 to 1955, the labours of the Royal Commission on Taxation of Profits and Income, followed in 1964–9 by the University Grants Committee.

This last, it must be supposed, would have challenged some of Dame Lucy's most cherished Oxonian assumptions, but she made the most of the opportunities it gave for setting foot in the red-brick and plate-glass universities. The University of North Staffordshire she knew from the start of its heroic period, as a member of its Academic Council; this connection brought her one of those uncovenanted surprises in which she delights, for making part of the journey to Keele by taxi, her driver inducted her, by origin a hockey-player, into the finer points of soccer. Later, she became a member of the Sponsoring Body of the University of Kent, and of its Promotion Committee; her summer examining has extended from Edinburgh to Southampton. Two other academic commitments that have been close to her heart outside Oxford were the presidency of the Girls' Public Day School Trust and a governorship of the Administrative Staff College at Henley.

Within Oxford itself she was a member of the Hebdomadal Council, the governing body of the university, from 1953 until her retirement in 1971, but with time to spare for the chairmanship of the Awards Board of the County Council. But for a change in the age-rules, she could have been Vice-Chancellor.

Instead, she was a Pro-Vice-Chancellor throughout the sixties, and for a time Vice-Chairman of the General Board, a notoriously taxing post.

By any test this is an outstanding record of public service combined with the pursuit of learning. It has been recognized by a sparkling series of public and academic honours: C.B.E. in 1947, F.B.A. in 1954, D.Litt. (Oxon.) in 1955, D.B.E. in 1969, not least D.C.L. (Oxon.) in 1972. In addition, Dame Lucy is a Foreign Honorary Member of the American Academy of Arts and Sciences and an Honorary LL.D. of Smith College, Massachusetts. She has been awarded so many honorary degrees, indeed, that some of her friends hesitate to congratulate her any more: besides those already mentioned, they number Cambridge (1963), Glasgow (1966), Kent (1967), Keele (1969), and the Queen's University, Belfast (1970). Before this process got seriously under way she was Creighton Lecturer in the University of London (1959), Raleigh Lecturer of the British Academy (1960), and a very active member of the History of Parliament Trust. But for the claims of L.M.H., it is hardly too much to assume that she would have been appointed to a Chair of History in Oxford.

Throughout this crowded career of public activity inside and outside Oxford, Dame Lucy never relinquished her loving guardianship of the college which was her home and where she could be free of 'greatness', where she has both lived simply and entertained lavishly. Even at the busiest times she managed to assist in the run-of-mill college teaching—eighteenth-century England, of course, but also Political Thought and the very successful Special Subject on Warren Hastings, for which she taught pupils from other colleges. She has had her full share in the direction of graduate research, as some of the contributions to this volume bear witness, though by no means completely so. If a price has had to be paid for her not hoarding her time to herself, it has been some slowing-down of her own scholarly output, and yet certainly not of scholarly effort; her Fellows were not infrequently alarmed when she would ask them, during full term, how their 'work' was getting on—a question which to her seemed perfectly natural. It is good to know that she is now editing the eighteenth-century volume of the projected history of the University of Oxford, on the launching of which hers was not the least decisive influence. Not surprisingly, it arouses her deepest enthusiasm.

Dame Lucy's historical and public careers have in a special sense run in harmony. Not for her the familiar complaint that teaching and research and administration compete to destroy each other. That is a legitimate cry from the heart in modern conditions, for few of us can hope to possess her extraordinary vitality. But of course she owes her triumphant survival in so many roles to a wholly personal amalgam. Jean-Jacques Rousseau acknowledged in his *Confessions* how suddenly the idea came to him that 'tout finit en politique'. To Dame Lucy it would always have seemed obvious that everything, even politics, ends in the service of humanity. Only, in her almost classical reserve, she would never pretend to use such language of herself.

Contents

Abbreviations

B.I.H.R.	*Bulletin of the Institute of Historical Research*
B.M.	British Museum
Bodl.	Bodleian Library, Oxford
Cal. S.P. Col.	*Calendar of State Papers Colonial Series*
Cal. S.P. Dom.	*Calendar of State Papers Domestic Series*
D.N.B.	*Dictionary of National Biography*
Econ. Hist.	*Economic History*
Econ. H. R.	*Economic History Review*
E.H.R.	*English Historical Review*
H.M.C.	Historical Manuscripts Commission
I.O.L.	India Office Library
I.O.R.	India Office Records
N.S.	New Style
O.E.D.	*Oxford English Dictionary*
O.S.	Old Style
P.R.O.	Public Record Office
R. Hist. Soc.	Royal Historical Society
S.P.	State Papers
T.L.S.	*Times Literary Supplement*
T.R.H.S.	*Transactions of the Royal Historical Society*
V.C.H.	*The Victoria History of the Counties of England*
W. & M. Qtly	*William and Mary College Quarterly*

The place of publication is omitted for books published in London.

I

The Census that Never Was:
A Problem in Authorship and Dating

W HEN he was preparing his *Memoirs of Great Britain and Ireland*, to be illustrated by state papers from Versailles and London, Sir John Dalrymple was granted access by George III 'to the cabinet of King William's private papers at Kensington', that selection of letters, papers, and memoranda which, now incorporated in the State Papers Domestic in the Public Record Office, goes under the name of King William's Chest.[1] Among the papers he published as an appendix to his work was one headed 'The Number of Freeholders in England'.[2] It has been frequently cited by historians and demographers as a guide to population at, or about the time of, the Glorious Revolution.

'The Number of Freeholders in England' gives totals of conformists, nonconformists, and papists for the province of Canterbury (2,123,362, 93,151, and 11,878) and for that of York (353,892, 15,525, and 1,978), followed by other totals including one for conformists, nonconformists, and papists for the whole of England (2,599,786), and a statement of the proportion of conformists to nonconformists, conformists to papists, and conformists and nonconformists together to papists. Then comes a list, showing the number of papists above the age of sixteen in the several dioceses (misnamed provinces) in Canterbury province, and an elaborate table, setting out for the same dioceses the number of conformists, nonconformists, and papists in each, with the proportions between the groups. A calculation follows of the number of male papists in Canterbury province capable of bearing arms, with a similar one for York province, which discloses the information that the figures for York had been

---

[1] *Memoirs of Great Britain and Ireland* (3 vols., Edinburgh and London, 1771–88; later edn., 1790), Appendix, Preface. See M. Jolliffe, *B.I.H.R.* xx (1943–5), 119–30, for an explanation of, and an index to, the contents of the *Memoirs*.

[2] Dalrymple, App., ii. 11–15.

worked out on the basis that the province bore a sixth part of the taxes of the kingdom and thus had a sixth part of the people that Canterbury province contained. In this way a total of the papists fit to bear arms in England [and Wales] (4,940) is arrived at, together with a calculation of the whole papist population in the country (23,740), based on the assumptions that everywhere there were as many under the age of sixteen as above it, that a seventh part of the population was over sixty, and that half the population were women. The paper concludes with some observations, entitled 'An Account of the Province of Canterbury', under nine heads.

The original in the Public Record Office consists of four sheets of paper (one wholly blank), roughly of foolscap size, with the writing entirely in the same (and at present unidentified) hand. Dalrymple transcribed it faithfully, keeping the layout substantially the same. It is neither endorsed nor dated, and there is nothing to show for what purpose the figures, calculations, and observations were drawn up.[3] Dalrymple himself annotated it thus: 'While King William was engaged in his project of reconciling the religious differences of England, he was at great pains to find out the proportions between churchmen, dissenters, and papists. In his chest there is the following curious report in consequence of an enquiry upon that head.'[4] For purposes of clarity, the document will be referred to below as Dalrymple's paper.

Although Dalrymple's *Memoirs* excited a certain amount of contemporary comment, largely because of the unflattering light they cast upon the conduct of some of the politicians of the Revolution period, this particular paper was not sufficiently sensational to attract much attention.[5] It was noted, however, by a fellow Scot, George Chalmers,[6] who in 1782 published *An Estimate of the Comparative Strength of [Great] Britain during the present and four preceding reigns*, reissued substantially altered in

³ P.R.O., S[tate] P[apers], 8/14, fos. 268–71. The volume contains papers of 1693, with a few undated ones.   ⁴ Dalrymple, App., ii. 11.

⁵ *D.N.B.*, s.v. Dalrymple, Sir John; cf., e.g., *Observations on a late Publication entitled 'Memoirs of Great Britain', by Sir John Dalrymple* (1773); *Letters of Lady Rachel Russell . . . To which is prefixed, An Introduction, Vindicating the Character of Lord Russell against Sir John Dalrymple* (1773).

⁶ See Grace A. Cockroft, 'The Public Life of George Chalmers' (Ph.D. thesis, Columbia University, N.Y., 1939). Dalrymple gave Chalmers valuable encouragement (ibid., pp. 48–50, 53).

1786, further revised and reset in 1794, and reprinted with minor changes several times later.[7] Chalmers was an indefatigable historian, biographer, and antiquarian, who combined the post of Chief Clerk of the Committee of the Privy Council for Trade with extensive reading, particularly in the British Museum. A man of strong opinions, who hated American rebels and renegade Whigs like Burke and Fox who supported them, he included among his interests the identification of Junius on the one hand and the early antiquities of Scotland on the other. His *Estimate*, of which George III ordered a copy, was an attempt to persuade Englishmen that the setbacks in America would not be permanently damaging to the country's interests; he sought to show that although wars in the past had led to a temporary trade depression, this was inevitably a short-lived phenomenon, since England had the population and industry needed for continuous expansion and progress.[8] The first edition of the book showed that Chalmers had gone to great pains to find figures to demonstrate changes in population from the Middle Ages onwards, and he made use of the work of Graunt, Petty, Davenant, Halley, and King. He also referred to Dalrymple's paper and added a critical footnote to it, which will be discussed later.[9] In the 1786 edition of the *Estimate* he recast much of the material he had used and added the results of further research. His reading in the Museum had revealed, in the Harleian Manuscripts, some of the Bishops' Certificates of 1563, giving returns of families, and the summary results of the 1603 survey of conformists, recusants, and non-communicants. He had also given more time to a study of Gregory King's 'Observations on the State of England in 1696', a manuscript of which he found in the Library and first printed in 1802 as an Appendix to a new edition of the *Estimate*.[10] Again

[7] For a list of the editions, see Cockroft, p. 216; cf. p. 63. Dr. Cockroft does not mention that two editions were published in 1794, the first virtually the same as that of 1786, the second reset and rearranged into chapters (cf. B.M. 959 c. 5 and 288 e. 9). The word 'Great' was omitted from the title of the first edition.

[8] Cockroft, pp. 80–9, 44–7, 66, 198–9, 210, 179–80, 201–4, 63–5.

[9] *Estimate* (1782 edn.), pp. 88–158; for the reference to Dalrymple, see pp. 117–18 n.

[10] *Estimate* (1786 edn.), esp. pp. 34–5 n., 43 n.; *Estimate* (1802 edn.), Appendix, with Life of Gregory King prefacing King's *Natural and Political Observations*. For the 1563 Bishops' Certificates and the 1603 inquiry, see T. H. Hollingsworth, *Historical Demography* (1969), p. 80.

he drew attention to Dalrymple's paper but, as we shall see later, with a rather different emphasis from what he had given it in 1782.[11] Chalmers's achievements have not always been rated very highly; but it is worth noting that a leading modern demographer, Fr. Roger Mols, has put it on record that Chalmers showed 'une clairvoyance statistique remarquable pour l'époque',[12] and, at least with respect to the paper whose history we are tracing, Chalmers applied stricter critical standards to the evidence at his disposal than have many modern historians.

The figures in Dalrymple's paper were given a much wider currency by Macaulay, who used them in his famous Third Chapter. 'King William', he wrote, 'was desirous to ascertain the comparative strength of the religious sects into which the community was divided. An inquiry was instituted; and reports were laid before him from all the dioceses of the realm.' The total population of England and Wales, Macaulay reckoned, was about 5,200,000 according to these figures; to arrive at this, he must have accepted the statement given in the paper that to double the figure given (2,599,786) would allow for those under sixteen. A footnote, exemplifying Macaulay's wide reading and splendid memory, drew attention to a passage in *Gulliver's Travels*, where Gulliver reported that the King of Brobdingnag 'laughed at my odd arithmetic, as he was pleased to call it, in reckoning the numbers of our people by a computation drawn from the several sects among us in religion and politics'. Macaulay thought well of the accuracy of the figures, which seemed to agree with Gregory King's estimate that the population in 1696 was 5,500,000, and with the 5,200,000, or slightly less, put forward for the end of the seventeenth century, on the basis of information from parish registers, in the Preface to the Census results of 1831.[13]

Dalrymple's paper might have been expected to excite re-

---

[11] *Estimate* (1786 edn.), p. 43 n.; see below, p. 9.

[12] R. Mols, S.J., *Introduction à la démographie historique des villes d'Europe du XIVe au XVIIIe siècle* (3 vols., Louvain, 1954-6), iii. 20. Cf. Cockroft, p. 65; Thomas Amyot, *Archaeologia*, xx (1824), 524-31; *D.N.B.*, s.v. Chalmers, George.

[13] *The History of England from the Accession of James II*, ed. C. H. Firth (6 vols., 1913-15), i. 273-4. For Macaulay's interest in population figures, see Sir G. O. Trevelyan, *The Life and Letters of Lord Macaulay* (2 vols., Oxford, 1961 edn.), ii. 156-7.

newed interest when it was partly reprinted in the *Calendar of State Papers Domestic* for 1693;[14] but it does not seem to have attracted immediate attention. One of the first historians to quote the figures from the *Calendar* was Sir George Clark, who concluded that the census of which they were a result had been carried out in 1693, but only in Canterbury province.[15] It was to Dalrymple's presentation, however, that Professor J. C. Russell referred in 1948; he attributed the figures to 1690, as did Dr. G. S. L. Tucker, writing on 'English Pre-Industrial Population Trends', in 1963.[16]

The latest commentary on the paper, in 1969, again quoted from Dalrymple's transcription, is that of Dr. T. H. Hollingsworth.[17] Whereas historians had assumed that the figures referred to a census taken under William III, Dr. Hollingsworth suggested that the enumeration upon which the totals were based had been carried out in 1688, by order of James II, but only drawn up into figures for dioceses and provinces in 1689 or 1690.[18] The information gained from the census was, he considered, fairly accurate as a count of the adult population, except for York province, for which he postulated a higher figure. He put forward the hypothesis that the results of the census, which he regarded as an official one, were secret. Gregory King, he suggested, may have been told of the totals, perhaps by Harley, though the source of them was kept from him; information given him that in 1688 the population of England and Wales was five and a half million would explain, he conjectured, why King gave a population estimate for 1688 instead of for 1690 (which might seem to be the date of his Hearth Tax data), and also why he worked round to his final total which Professor Glass, reviewing King's evidence, thought was too high. In order to get to the supposed total of 5,500,000, Dr. Hollingsworth had to conjecture that a lost survey for York

[14] *Cal. S.P. Dom. 1693*, ed. W. J. Hardy (1903), pp. 448–50; cf. Introduction, pp. xxxvi–xxxvii, where it is said, incorrectly, that Dalrymple did not print the paper in its entirety.

[15] *The Later Stuarts* (Oxford, 1934; 2nd edn., 1955), p. 26.

[16] *British Medieval Population* (Albuquerque, N. Mex., 1948), pp. 270, 279, 361; G. S. L. Tucker, *Econ. H. R.*, 2nd ser. xvi (1963), 212. Mols, i. 59 and iii. 22, also refers to the figures in Dalrymple's paper, which he dates 1690.

[17] *Historical Demography*, pp. 81–8.

[18] Ibid., p. 82. Dr. Hollingsworth suggests no reason why this task, which would have been very onerous, should have been undertaken.

province put up the adult figure for the whole country to 2,750,000, instead of the 2,123,362 arrived at when the figures for the northern province are taken as a sixth of those for Canterbury province. In a later stage of his argument he went on to wonder whether the figure King was given was 5,550,000, rather than 5,500,000, as he was anxious to discover whether Professor Glass's reworking of King's data, which produced a total population of 4,838,100 for 1695, was compatible with a reworking of the figures in Dalrymple's paper, and such an assumption would play its part in bringing both estimates closer together.[19] Dr. Hollingsworth's argument is not entirely easy to follow as he does not make it clear that King himself gave 5,550,000 as the figure for population in 1688 and 5,500,000 for 1695;[20] he also does not take into account that the Hearth Tax was abolished at the Revolution, so that the figures King used must in fact have been those of 1688/9, although he may not have collected them from the Hearth Tax Office till Lady Day 1690.[21] Nevertheless, his hypothesis that King knew of the results of a recent census would, if convincing, be important, as no trace of such an influence on his reasoning has so far been discovered.

At this point it is necessary to ask whether there is any evidence that a census of any kind was organized in 1688, 1693, or at any other date within a few years of the Revolution, of which the figures in question might be the result. The answer is that there is none. No trace of such an inquiry has come to light in either state or diocesan archives; even if we assume, with Dr. Hollingsworth, that the census was carried out secretly and its results closely guarded, it would be strange if no reference at all to it were to be found. What can be established without doubt, however, is that the figures Dalrymple and the editor of the *Calendar of State Papers Domestic* printed from the paper in

[19] *Historical Demography*, pp. 85–7; D. V. Glass, 'Two Papers on Gregory King', in *Population in History*, ed. D. V. Glass and D. E. C. Eversley (1965), pp. 159–220, esp. 202–4.

[20] G. E. Barnett (ed.), *Two Tracts by Gregory King* (Baltimore, 1936), pp. 26–7.

[21] The Hearth Tax was abolished by 1 W. and M., c. 10, with the proviso that nothing in the Act should hinder or prejudice the collection of taxes due on 25 March 1689 or of any arrears. King says that the basis of his calculations was the number of houses 'as charg'd in the Books of the Hearth Office at Lady Day 1690'. The returns for 1688/9 may not have been complete till the spring of 1690 (Barnett, p. 16; cf. Glass and Eversley, p. 217).

King William's Chest refer not to any enumeration at the time of the Glorious Revolution, but to the census of 1676, often called the 'Compton Census', after Henry Compton, Bishop of London, popularly accounted to have been the organizer of the inquiry.[22] That this is the case was shown long ago by C. H. Hull, the editor of *The Economic Writings of Sir William Petty*.[23] More recently, the late Andrew Browning recognized that the paper from the *Calendar of State Papers Domestic* in fact gave the results of the 1676 census.[24] The paper's table, with its figures for conformists, nonconformists, and papists, and the proportions between them, for all the dioceses in Canterbury province, has been accessible for over fifty years: it forms part of the great work of transcription undertaken by G. Lyon Turner for his *Original Records of Early Nonconformity*. Lyon Turner printed it from a copy, kept in Lambeth Palace Library, of the table which prefaces Salt MS. 33, in the William Salt Library at Stafford, which is the most complete record of the 1676 census for Canterbury province.[25] Complete figures for York province have never been found, although the census was certainly taken in York and Carlisle dioceses;[26] perhaps no returns were sent in for Chester and Durham. If this was the case, it is understandable that a rough calculation should have been made as early as 1676 to supply a figure for the northern province.[27]

Summaries of the figures for both provinces were already in circulation well before the Revolution, either in whole or in part. Joseph Glanvill commented on some of the figures for papists in Canterbury province as early as 1681; Sir William

---

[22] For accounts of the census, see G. Lyon Turner, *Original Records of Early Nonconformity* (3 vols., 1911–14), iii. 140–51; Thomas Richards, 'The Religious Census of 1676', supplement to the *Transactions of the Honourable Society of Cymmrodorion, 1925–6* (1927); C. W. Chalklin, 'The Compton Census of 1676: the dioceses of Canterbury and Rochester', *Kent Records*, xvii (1960), 153–74. I hope in the near future to publish a critical edition of the census.

[23] 2 vols. (paginated continuously), Cambridge, 1899, i, p. xxxi; ii. 460–1 n.

[24] A. Browning, *Thomas Osborne, Earl of Danby* (3 vols., Glasgow, 1951), i. 198 and n.; *English Historical Documents, 1660–1714*, ed. A. Browning (1953), pp. 413–16.

[25] Lyon Turner, iii. 140–2; Salt MS. 33, pp. 1–2. I am most grateful to the Trustees of the William Salt Library for allowing me to consult this manuscript.

[26] Bodl., MS. Tanner 150, fos. 27–38ᵛ, 129 (York diocese); MS. Tanner 144, fos. 1–4 (Carlisle diocese).

[27] B.M., Egerton MS. 3329 (Leeds Papers), fos. 120, 126ᵛ; see below, p. 10 and n. 37.

Petty observed, perhaps in the same year, that 'the Bishops late Numbring of the *Communicants*' pretty well agreed with the accounts of the Poll Tax and the Hearth Tax.[28] Sir Peter Pett, in *The Happy Future State of England*, published in 1688 but written probably in the early 1680s, discussed the results of the census in some detail.[29] The allegedly secret information was even so well known as to appear in the *Harlemse Courant* of 1 January N.S. 1688, from which John Locke copied it into one of his notebooks.[30] But to show that Dalrymple's paper gives figures which relate to the 1676 census is only to answer some of the questions to which it gives rise. Let us look at it more closely.

In the first place, the paper has a curious heading. Whatever the figures represent (and most people have assumed that they refer to communicants, i.e. those over sixteen),[31] they certainly can never have represented 'The Number of Freeholders'; indeed, the word *freeholders* does not appear anywhere in the Salt MS. or in any other contemporary, or nearly contemporary, report of the census. It occurs, however, with an even odder prefix, 'The Telling of Noses', on two papers which give exactly the same figures and proportions, in exactly the same form, as on the first page of Dalrymple's paper, one of them in Stowe MS. 322 and the other in MS. Tanner 28, where the prefix was added in the hand of no less a person than Archbishop Sancroft, who also put a date, 1688, to the paper. An endorsement on the version in Stowe MS. 322 runs, 'Calculation of the People of England. 1687'. What is more, both titles on these copies of the totals conclude with the words 'according to Sir W. P.', who cannot be anyone else but Sir William Petty.[32] Chalmers commented on the use of the word *freeholders* in a footnote in

[28] Glanvill, *The Zealous and Impartial Protestant* (1681), pp. 46–8; Petty, *Another Essay in Political Arithmetic* (1683), reprinted by C. H. Hull, [*The*] *Economic Writings of [Sir William] Petty*, ii. 460. Hull thinks that Petty's pamphlet was probably written in 1681 (ibid. ii. 452).

[29] Preface, D. 2–3 and pp. 104, 117–19, 140–2. Cf. below, n. 44.

[30] Bodl., MS. Locke f. 9, p. 318, entry for Saturday, 20 March N.S. 1688. I am indebted to the late Professor Rosalie L. Colie for this reference, and for her kindness in discussing certain aspects of this paper with me.

[31] e.g. Hollingsworth, p. 81; Chalklin, art. cit., p. 155.

[32] B.M., Stowe MS. 322, fos. 89–90, printed in *Economic Writings of . . . Petty*, ii. 461 n.; MS. Tanner 28, fo. 7. On the question of Petty's association with these two papers, see below, pp. 13–14.

the first edition of his *Estimate*; he compared a figure of 356,586 freeholders taken from King's calculations with the figure given in Dalrymple's paper, and pointed out that the latter would imply either that King's calculations were open to serious question, or that there must have been a much higher population than that conjectured by King, Davenant, or Halley, which he was discussing in the text of his book. By 1786, when the first revised edition of the *Estimate* appeared, Chalmers had altered his views. He dropped the footnote calling attention to the word *freeholders*, but added one comparing the figures printed by Dalrymple (which he dated 1689) with those for 1603, which he must have discovered meanwhile in the Harleian Manuscripts. A juxtaposition of the two sets of figures must have persuaded him that the information in the paper should be taken seriously, however misleading the title. It is much to his credit that he considered the problems it raised so carefully and critically.[33] The association of Sir William Petty's name with the two shorter papers will be considered later.

Secondly, the figures in Dalrymple's paper are not always in agreement with each other: for example, the total for papists in Canterbury province is given variously as 11,878, 11,867, and 11,876; the total for nonconformists for the same area as 93,151 and 93,104; the diocesan totals for papists differ in the case of Canterbury, Gloucester, and Peterborough. The table giving numbers of conformists, nonconformists, and papists in all the dioceses in Canterbury province, moreover, is not absolutely the same in all respects as that in Salt MS. 33.[34] Such differences, slight as most of them are, suggest that the various parts of the paper were either drawn from different versions of the figures or inaccurately copied, and that little trouble was taken to see that it was consistent in the information it provided.

Thirdly, the nine observations headed 'An Account of the Province of Canterbury', which conclude the paper, can be shown to relate not to the province but merely to the diocese of Canterbury. They are in fact identical with the observations appended to the 1676 figures for Canterbury diocese in

---

[33] *Estimate* (1782 edn.), pp. 117–18 n.; *Estimate* (1786 edn.), p. 43 n.; cf. pp. 34–5 n.

[34] Dalrymple, App. ii. 12–14; cf. Salt MS. 33, pp. 1–2.

Lambeth MS. 639, where they appear above the name of Samuel Parker, Archdeacon of Canterbury in 1676, and his Official. All the places mentioned are in Kent; the emphasis is almost entirely upon Protestant nonconformity; the references to 'the late Indulgence' and to 'the late Rebellion' make much better sense in the context of 1676 than in that of the Glorious Revolution.[35] They form an incongruous part of a paper which, in the main, shows a preoccupation with papist strength in England.

Lastly, attention has already been drawn to two sets of assumptions, clearly stated in the paper: first, that there were everywhere as many under the age of sixteen as above it, that a seventh part of the population was over sixty, and that half the population were women; second, that York province bore a sixth part of the taxes of the kingdom and had a sixth part of the people that Canterbury province contained.[36]

In order to discuss these problems further, we must ask who could have drawn up this strange hotch-potch of a paper, when, and for what purpose. How did it get into the collection known as King William's Chest? Definite answers to these questions are not known and perhaps cannot be discovered. An almost identical list of papists in each diocese in Canterbury province, and calculations based on the assumptions about the proportions of women in the population and of those under sixteen and over sixty, relating to both provinces, and worded almost exactly as in Dalrymple's paper, were in the hands of Lord Treasurer Danby some time in 1676; they have survived among the Leeds Papers, written in a minute hand on two playing cards.[37] In the same year the rest of the findings of the census became available to those authorized to know them; Salt MS. 33, with the elaborate table which appears in Dalrymple's paper, was probably compiled in the autumn.[38] What we have in Dalrymple's paper, however, is a selection of information from and about the census, and it is only in the works of Sir

[35] Lambeth MS. 639, fo. 168ᵛ; printed by Lyon Turner, i. 27.

[36] Dalrymple, App. ii. 14.

[37] Egerton MS. 3329, fos. 126–7; the list of papists on the recto, the calculations on the verso. The calculations on fo. 126ᵛ are difficult to read, but enough can be made out to show that figures for York province, based on the usual assumptions, are included. The cards are associated with correspondence of 1676, originally enclosed by a paper (fo. 120) endorsed 'The number of papists in the 2 Provinces of Canterbury & York as return'd in 76'.

[38] I hope to give a time-table of the census in my forthcoming edition.

Peter Pett, particularly in *The Happy Future State of England* (1688) and in *The Genuine Remains of . . . Thomas Barlow, late Bishop of Lincoln* (1693), that three of the five essential elements in it appear together. According to his own testimony, Pett had as early as September 1677 received from his friend Bishop Barlow

an account of the *Numbers* of the *Conformists, Nonconformists, Papists*; of the Age of *Communicants*: with the *Proportions* of their *Numbers*, to one another in the several *Dioceses*, in the *Province of Canterbury* . . . together with the *nine Paragraphs* of *Remarks*, made by some imploy'd in the *Survey*.

Pett published this information, with his comments, in *The Genuine Remains*, claiming that it had not previously appeared in print. Whether Barlow also sent him the separate list of papists over sixteen, and the calculations about the number of papists able to bear arms, based on the assumptions about the number of women, and of those over sixteen and over sixty, as they appear in the Leeds Papers, and to which he may have had access, cannot be established. Pett, at any rate, relied on the same assumptions, thinking fit, he wrote, 'to corroborate Dr. Glanvile's assertion of the inconsiderableness of the number of the Papists, by Calculation'.[39] In *The Happy Future State* he explains that according to what he called 'the currant Rule of *Calculation*', he doubled the total given for Canterbury province to get a total for the inhabitants of all ages. He reconstructed the figures for York province by reckoning that they should stand at a sixth of those in the southern province, because it paid a sixth part of the taxes and therefore might be presumed to contain a sixth part of the people; the figure he arrived at he doubled, to make allowance for those under sixteen. He made almost exactly the same calculations, more roughly but more extensively, in his comments in *The Genuine Remains*, where he also included the assumption that a seventh part of the population was over sixty.[40] He referred at least three times in *The Happy Future State* to the observations on Canterbury diocese, incorrectly related to Canterbury province, which make up the last part of Dalrymple's paper.[41] There are, it is true, a few

[39] *Genuine Remains*, pp. 312–15, 316–20; Epistle to the Reader, A. 4.
[40] *Happy Future State*, pp. 118, 149–50; *Genuine Remains*, pp. 320–2.
[41] *Happy Future State*, pp. 139, 147–8.

arithmetical differences between the figures in the paper and those Pett apparently received from Barlow, but these could be printer's or copyist's mistakes.[42] Pett was obviously fascinated by the census and mentions it frequently in all his books; he seems to have been allowed to examine the detailed returns and it may well have been the volume now known as Salt MS. 33 which he handled.[43]

Did Pett himself, then, draw up the paper Dalrymple printed? As a former Advocate-General for Ireland, and a close associate of Arthur Annesley, Earl of Anglesey, for whom *The Happy Future State* was ostensibly written, he was a man immersed in public affairs who had long been concerned with problems to do with toleration and recusancy.[44] He has himself left it on record that he discussed with one of James II's ministers the deficiencies in the count of nonconformists in the 1676 census;[45] he certainly had much of the material—perhaps all of it—to write the paper, either before or after the Revolution. The essential conclusion in it, that there were very few male papists in England of age to bear arms, is consonant with arguments in *The Happy Future State*, which Pett himself said he had written 'as perswasive against the Exclusion, & the growth of the

[42] There is a closer correspondence between the figures in *The Genuine Remains* and Salt MS. 33 than with the figures printed by Dalrymple, App. ii. 12–13.

[43] The appearance of certain mistranscriptions both in Pett's *Happy Future State*, p. 118, and in Salt MS. 33, pp. 20–36, suggests that he may have used this.

[44] For Pett's life, see *D.N.B.* and Anthony Wood, *Athenae Oxonienses*, ed. P. Bliss (4 vols., Oxford, 1813–20), iv. 576–80; for a genealogical table of the Pett family, see H. B. Wheatley, *Pepysiana* (1899), p. 177. The history of Pett's book *The Happy Future State*, both under its original title and under that of the reissue of 1689, *A Discourse of the Growth of England in Populousness and Trade*, is difficult to unravel. Page 1 of the text bears the date 27 Jan. 1680 [probably 1680/1]; Pett said in his Dedication (to the Earl of Sunderland) that it was 'almost wholly Printed long ago in the last Reign during the freedom of the Press' [sc. 1679–85]; there are references to 'this year 84' in the Preface to the Reader (C. 3, D. 2, K. 2). In *The Memoirs of the . . . Earl of Anglesey* (1693) Pett confirmed that the book was written before the death of Charles II and that Anglesey (in whose defence it was partly composed) had it 'by him in his Study, Printed and bound up long before he dyed' [in 1686] (Preface, A. 4; pp. 33–4). Pett presumably delayed its publication because some of the arguments in it, particularly the contention that there was little to be feared from papists and popery, were politically dangerous. His own account of the book and its reissue is to be found in his letter to Anthony Wood (Bodl., MS. Wood F. 43, fos. 211, 211ᵛ). I am grateful to Mr. J. S. G. Simmons, Librarian of the Codrington, for allowing me to make a study of *The Happy Future State* and *The Discourse of the Growth of England*; the Codrington Library's copy of the latter work was given by Pett himself to his old college.

[45] *Genuine Remains*, p. 321.

popular fears of Papists and Popery'.[46] Pett's opinion that the census gave an accurate count of recusants meant that he could prove his case no matter whether the figure for the whole population was correct or, as he argued, underestimated.[47] The paper could just as well date from the reign of James II—even from the latter years of Charles II—as from that of William III; indeed, the fact that the first part of it is exactly the same in form and detail as the two papers, dated 1687 and 1688, which are associated with the name of Sir William Petty points to the decade before the Revolution.

But two problems remain. First, does Petty come into the picture? His name is associated only with the titles of the two shorter papers; it does not occur in the title of Dalrymple's paper. What is more, neither the elaborate tables, nor the arguments which form an integral part of Dalrymple's paper, are to be found in Petty's published writings,[48] whereas they are part and parcel of Peter Pett's various works. On the other hand, Petty and Pett were friends who belonged to the same intellectual circle; both had early been elected to the Royal Society; both shared an interest in statistics; both came under some suspicion as crypto-papists, or as associates of crypto-papists.[49] We know that Petty, like Pett and Joseph Glanvill, was interested in the number of papists in England; Pett tells us that Petty thought there were 32,000 papists of all ages in the country in the reign of James II.[50] Petty's work was well known to Pett: 'He never writt any thing for the presse but what he informd Sir Robert [Southwell] & me of & gave us manuscript copys of', Pett told Anthony Wood.[51] Pett may have lent

[46] *Memoirs of the . . . Earl of Anglesey*, Epistle Dedicatory, a 2ᵛ; cf. *Happy Future State*, Preface, B. 2 and pp. 64, 122.

[47] Ibid., Preface, D. 2–3 and pp. 117–19, 139–42, 149.

[48] Cf. *Economic Writings of . . . Petty*, and *The Petty Papers*, ed. the Marquis of Lansdowne (2 vols., 1927).

[49] *Economic Writings of . . . Petty*, i, pp. xxxi, xliii–xlv, lxxvii; *D.N.B.*, s.v. Petty, Sir William; *Private Correspondence and Miscellaneous Papers of Samuel Pepys 1679–1703*, ed. J. R. Tanner (2 vols., 1926), i. 112–16; Pett, *Memoirs of the . . . Earl of Anglesey*, Epistle Dedicatory, a. 2, a. 2ᵛ; MS. Wood F. 43, fo. 212 (Pett to Wood, 13 Aug. 1691).

[50] *Genuine Remains*, pp. 321, 316–20; cf. T. Carte, *Life of James Duke of Ormond* (6 vols., Oxford, 1851), iv. 567.

[51] MS. Wood F. 43, fo. 217ᵛ (Pett to Wood, 10 Oct. 1691); *Economic Writings of . . . Petty*, i. 100, 124, 237; *Samuel Pepys's Naval Minutes*, ed. J. R. Tanner (Navy Records Society, lx, 1926), pp. 212–13. Pett frequently referred to the works of

Petty *The Happy Future State*, or let him see the papers he had received from Bishop Barlow, before he published them, which was of course after Petty's death in 1687. But whereas the case for associating the argumentative part of Dalrymple's paper with Pett is strong, that for connecting it with Petty is weak.[52] It is worth noting, moreover, that Petty was much better known as a practitioner in 'Political Arithmetic' than was Pett; and that if a name had been wanted to give conviction to the figures in the two shorter papers, or even to point up a joke in the title, Petty's would have come readily to mind. To establish who drew up the two shorter papers, which are exactly the same as the first part of the paper in Dalrymple, is impossible: Pett had been given the figures to do it (though perhaps with some minor differences), but many others must have had them too, since they merely summed up the final totals disclosed by the census, with the usual assumptions behind the figures supplied for York province.[53]

Secondly, why do all three papers purport to give the number of *freeholders*? Both Pett and Petty would have known how absurd the word was in this context; it seems unlikely that either of them would have used such a term of art frivolously. Chalmers had noted, in commenting on Dalrymple's paper in 1782, that 'there can be no dispute about the term *freeholder*, as there has been with respect to . . . *houses* and *families*'.[54] Pett, it is true, thought that the census had counted 'heads of Families or House-Keepers, i.e. Man and Wife' and 'but very few Servants, or Sons, and Daughters, or Lodgers, or Inmates of the people of several perswasions of Religion';[55] but householders were not all freeholders, nor were the words regarded

'Sir W. P.'; e.g. *Happy Future State*, Preface, A. 1, G. 3, O. 1, and pp. 92, 106, 116, 122, 192–3, 245.

[52] Hull (*Economic Writings of . . . Petty*, i, p. xxxi) accepted without question that Petty was the author of the paper in Stowe MS. 322, fo. 89. He drew attention to Pett's comments on the 1676 survey and printed some of his calculations and arguments as found in *The Happy Future State* (pp. 117–18), which are identical with those in Dalrymple's paper, but did not suggest that Pett was associated in any way with the paper itself (ibid. ii. 461 n.).

[53] Dalrymple and the two shorter papers give 93,151 and 11,878 for nonconformists and papists in Canterbury province, respectively, as against 93,154 and 11,870 in the table in *The Genuine Remains* and in Salt MS. 33 (Dalrymple, App., ii. 12, Stowe MS. 322, fo. 89, and MS. Tanner 28, fo. 7; *Genuine Remains*, p. 314, and Salt MS. 33, p. 1).

[54] *Estimate* (1782 edn.), p. 118 n.   [55] *Happy Future State*, pp. 117–18.

as interchangeable. Were it not for the title given to the longer paper, the hypothesis would be strong that Pett, drawing on the material Barlow had sent him, himself drew it up. As it is, some doubt must remain about his authorship, although his association with it in some form seems likely. While Pett's assertion, that copies of the Bishops' Survey were in the hands of many people, must not be overlooked,[56] it would be a strange coincidence if Dalrymple's paper, with a title so like those of the two shorter papers of 1687 and 1688, with parts of it identical with the appendix in *The Genuine Remains*, and with an argument so similar to that set out in *The Happy Future State*, were not in some way connected with the other two papers and with Pett himself. Such a line of reasoning does not establish the date of the paper, but makes it probable that it was written before the Revolution. It is a pity that we do not know why the editor of the *Calendar of State Papers Domestic* included the paper in the volume for 1693; he may have had some association for it which has not been passed on.

When, and why, the paper got into William III's hands is equally difficult to explain. The information in it might well, of course, have been of interest to the King, out of date though it was. It was a real matter of public concern to know how many papists there were in the country able to bear arms, in case James with French help should mount an invasion; and if the only available figures were at least twelve years old, they may have been regarded as a great deal better than nothing. But if William took note of the paper, he would not have learnt anything from it which the better-informed of his subjects did not know already, or could quite easily get to know.

Among all the conjectures, however, one thing is clear: there was no census in 1688, 1689, 1690, 1693, or in any other year immediately before or after the Revolution. Had there been one, it is inconceivable that it could have been kept secret; either King or Davenant would surely have referred to it somewhere in their writings. That both knew of the results of what their contemporaries called 'the Bishops' Survey' is to say the least likely; certainly a great many people did. Perhaps they paid little attention to the figures it disclosed because they thought them unreliable; or perhaps they considered them of

[56] Ibid., Preface, D. 3.

little interest when the Hearth Tax returns and the new levy, in the 1694 Act, on marriages, births, and burials seemed to open up statistical possibilities of more accurate and up-to-date calculations of population.[57] That a succession of later historians none the less assumed that the figures referred to some enumeration at the time of the Revolution is not surprising, for the results of the 1676 inquiry had passed into oblivion and the historians were not to know that what Dalrymple had brought to light was a sort of ghost. It is time now that the ghost should be laid.

[57] Glass and Eversley, pp. 168–71.

II

The Jacobite Privateers in the Nine Years War

AN effect, if only a side-effect, of recent studies of British politics during the generation after 1688 has been to reinstate the Jacobites, and not merely Jacobitism, as a counter-revolutionary force which William III and Walpole had to take more seriously than the Whig historians did. Yet historians have overlooked the brief but sensational career of the corsairs launched by James II in exile, in a war which ended without disproving Vauban's thesis that the correct strategy against the Maritime Powers at sea was to attack their commerce by means of 'une guerre de mer subtile et dérobée', waged for the King at private expense.[1] The commissioning of privateers was, of course, a demonstration of regal authority and as such had perplexing repercussions in the English courts. It was also potentially lucrative and we know that some Jacobite captains like Robert Dunbar took many prizes, though it is not yet possible to count them. A list of the armaments themselves has still to be compiled. In 1692 James commissioned a score of captains and in 1693 procured French commissions for as many more; after that the sources, always fragmentary, become more elusive, but leave no doubt that the Jacobite *course* continued till late in the war, on a diminishing scale. An attempt to piece the scattered evidence together, despite the loss of the Irish admiralty records, may shed a little light, not only on the behaviour of a shadow government and a by no means negligible aspect of its impact on the British public, but also on the seventeenth-century Irish migration, which has still to receive the study it deserves.

During the battle for Ireland James made only a late and hesitant use of the privateering weapon. Remembering the

[1] 'Mémoire sur la course', in R. d'Aiglun (ed.), *Vauban: sa famille et ses écrits* (2 vols., Paris–Grenoble, 1910), i. 457.

Dutch Wars as Lord High Admiral, he may have disliked it, as William III certainly did. At first, with an eye at this stage perhaps to English supplies or susceptibilities, he annoyed his French allies by discouraging the presence on Irish coasts of corsairs from St. Malo; at the end of 1689, a valuable French prize carried into Limerick and only partially condemned there was also a cause of friction. In a letter of 20 July N.S. to his representative d'Avaux,[2] Louis XIV implies that he had already had to urge James to commission privateers against the English and Dutch

et tirer d'eux par ce moyen une partie de sa subsistance; et si contre mon opinion il ne l'avoit pas encore fait, ne manquez pas de luy conseiller de ma part et de luy dire qu'il ne peut pas esperer de ramener ses sujets qu'en leur faisant ressentir tous les maux que la rebellion entraisne avec soy, et que c'est aussy le sentiment de tous ceux qui sont le plus affectionnez à ses interests.

About this time James did issue his commission to Peter Nagle, but he was already captain of a French frigate, 'given to the King of England', and was back in Brest by February 1690. On 30 April we have Tyrconnel writing to Queen Mary Beatrice from Dublin:[3]

I wonder why wee may not have half a score of frigats to attend this coast. I am sure they would not bee soe usefull any where else. Would to God wee had those frigats of St. Malo's, if wee can have noe others, for to see this Kingdome all surrounded with sea, without soe much as a cockboat to attend it, is somewhat extraordinary.

---

[2] J. Hogan (ed.), *Les Négociations de M. le comte d'Avaux en Irlande, 1689–90* (2 vols., Dublin, Irish Manuscripts Commission, 1934), i. 415; cf. ibid. 626–9, 640–1, 647–8. Dates in this chapter are given in Old Style unless otherwise indicated as N.S.; in both cases the year is taken to begin on 1 Jan.

[3] *Analecta Hibernica*, no. 4 (Oct. 1932), p. 121 (letter-book of Richard Talbot). Cf. Hogan, pp. 575, 641. Nagle did not return to Ireland. He was clearly in French service and his frigate had only been 'given' to James in the sense of being allocated to the Irish service. Louis XIV had promised three frigates 'qui navigueroient continüellement sur les costes d'Irlande', but there was difficulty in providing them. Archives du Port de Brest, 1 E 16, letters of Seignelay dated 18 Feb. and 5 March N.S. 1690; ibid., 1 E 426, fos. 163–4, 206, Desclouzeaux to Seignelay, 27 Feb. and 10 March, and 1 E 428, fos. 222–3, same to Pontchartrain, 13 and 27 Nov. N.S. 1690. I am much obliged for these references to M. Philippe Henrat, archivist of the port of Brest. Nagle's appointment to command the *Badine* frigate in Nov. 1690 was soon cancelled (ibid. 1 E 17, fos. 207, 227), but he was commissioned as captain of the *Marin* privateer on 23 Feb. 1695 by James II (H.M.C., *Stuart MSS.* i (1902), 97).

The Breton corsairs certainly needed no special encouragement to cruise off western Ireland, with so much Dutch shipping moving north-about Scotland and the American convoys coming home within sight of the Blaskets; the Irish campaign offered an opportunity, indeed, to gain a familiarity with the soundings and landmarks that enabled the Bretons in later years to come and go much as they liked there—d'Avaux reports them charting the Shannon estuary and bay of Galway. But St. George's Channel, of much more direct importance strategically in 1689–91, involved greater risk of capture. Pressure was needed before the authorities could engage private *armateurs* to fit out fifteen corsairs at Brest and St. Malo, in July 1690, for a month's cruise under naval command in St. George's Channel. The results were poor. One was captured; four did nothing on hearing of James's return to Brest after the Boyne; two others used the same excuse to indulge in some profitable Atlantic privateering; of those that got to Ireland, three merely took cargo to Limerick.[4] It is interesting, however, that four of the captains were later to cruise on James's account, and that two of them, Antoine and Raymond (Rémond, Redmond) Géraldin (Geraldine), belonged to 'the old and gentle family of Giraldin of Gurteen, County Kilkenny', long since established in Brittany and related to James Geraldine of Dunkirk, who himself hired a French frigate, the *Sorcière*, to cruise in St. George's Channel at this juncture, with instructions from the minister to pick up half her crew in Ireland.[5]

By 1691 fleeting traces of 'King James's privateers' begin to occur in the correspondence of the time, and a commission to one Nicholas Roche, given at St. Germain on 29 June N.S., has survived among the Admiralty prize papers.[6] A British

[4] [Paris, Archives Nationales,] Marine B³ 60, fos. 252, 263, 270, 308, 323–5 (Du Guay to Bonrepaus, 3 and 12 July, 22 Nov., 13 Dec. N.S. 1690); ibid., B² 73, fo. 615 (Seignelay to Louvigny, 27 June N.S. 1690).

[5] R. Hayes, *Biographical Dictionary of Irishmen in France* (Dublin, 1949), p. 106; Marine B² 73, fo. 612 (Seignelay to Patoulet, 24 June N.S. 1690). The *Sorcière* was diverted to Edinburgh and her captain's secret mission there is described in C. Bréard (ed.), *Journal du corsaire Jean Doublet de Honfleur* (Paris, 1883), pp. 155 sqq.

[6] Printed in R. G. Marsden (ed.), *Law and Custom of the Sea* (2 vols., Navy Records Society, 1915–16), ii. 139–40. It is short and vague, merely permitting Roche (of whom nothing else is known) 'to fitt out . . . in order to privatier and seaze the ships of all persons whatsoever, onely excepted the subjects of those who are in freindship and allyance with us, or of such as have our royal protection and passeport, or of the Duke of Tyreconnel, our lieuftenant general and general governor of our

prisoner of war at Port Louis mentions two months later that
he is boarding in the house of Walter Ding, lieutenant of 'a pinke
frigott of King James'.[7] Captain George St. Lo, himself a
prisoner at Brest and Angers in 1689–91, claimed in 1693 that
'there are three privateers belonging to King James that were
set out of Ireland when he was there, that are manned with
English and Irish'.[8] Although St. Lo makes this admission in
a context intended 'to confute a popular mistake among us,
that the French have abundance of our seamen in their service',
there is no evidence that he seriously underestimated the number of Jacobite privateers before 1692. What he overlooked was
'the flight of the wild geese' after the Capitulation of Limerick
on 3 October 1691.

The scenes following that treaty have been pitilessly described
by Macaulay, who allows that the great majority of Sarsfield's
army elected to depart for France, though some deserted on
the road to Ginkel's ships at Cork; he omits the additional
10,000 Irish taken off the Shannon in Châteaurenault's fleet.
The latest historian of the Irish campaign puts the number of
soldiers alone at 12,000 and remarks on the astonishing arrangement whereby an 'army in being . . . was to be transported at
William's expense to a hostile country where they were to be
used in an attempt to restore William's rival to the throne'.[9]
The terms of this honourable surrender were interpreted by
the refugees, intelligibly enough, to mean that they were as
free to serve their exiled king by sea as on land. Even of those
who belonged to the Irish regiments (which were not absorbed
by the French army until after 1697), not all were professional
soldiers; many were militiamen. For them the temptation to
fall sick—if indeed not really so—would have been especially
strong, as it was for James Drillan, a Kilkenny tailor who 'not

Kingdom of Ireland'. This may be compared with the more precise commission
issued in 1694 to Edmund French and printed in H.M.C., *Stuart MSS.* i. 92–3,
and with the official French translation of James's commission to John Jordan at
Morlaix in 1692, printed by H. Bourde de la Rogerie in *Collection des inventaires
sommaires des Archives départementales antérieures à 1790: Finistère*, t. iii (Paris, 1902),
pp. 261–2.
[7] Arundel Castle, Aylward Papers 19, Andrew Cratey to John Aylward, 1 Sept.
N.S. 1691. I am grateful to His Grace the Duke of Norfolk and to his archivist,
Mr. Francis W. Steer, for access to these papers (referred to below as AY).
[8] *England's Safety* (1693), reprinted in *Somers Tracts*, vol. ii (1814), pp. 53–4.
[9] J. G. Simms, *Jacobite Ireland 1685–91* (1969), p. 258.

being able to endure the Feild was received into the late King James's service at sea'. Hugh Stokes, a real soldier from Meath, procured his officers' leave after several months in the army to visit friends at St. Malo, who advised him to go to sea. In the circumstances, it is not difficult to recognize the truthfulness of William Daile of Dublin, even when under examination by an Admiralty advocate as a preliminary to indictment for high treason: he fell sick at Brest

whilst the Army marched up into Normandy, and after his Recovery the Examinate being very poor and not able to get his bread he did about the month of September last enter himselfe aboard a French Privateer called the St. Joseph.[10]

Since the privateers relied much on their musketry and always carried a high proportion of soldiers, such men made welcome recruits, and in any case there were also plenty of necessitous Irish seamen knocking about the Breton ports.

So long as the French navy continued to compete for men, as it did long after La Hogue, the corsairs faced a continuing crisis of recruitment. Needy immigrants, free of the conscription, were advised to address themselves to the local *commissaire de marine*, who could always put them in touch with a corsair captain if they had not already encountered one. Thus Constantine Doherty 'to get a Livelyhood applyed himselfe to the Sea Affaires', while James Lynch, finding himself in St. Malo 'without either money or friends', met with Thomas Tully, captain of the *Prince de Galles*, a privateer manned almost entirely by Irishmen when taken in 1693. Under examination for their liberty, however, prisoners were tempted to deny any initiative on their part. Francis Keagher, a boy from Galway, 'happened to get to St Maloes and there he met with some privateersmen who carried the Examinate on board . . . the Prince of Wales . . . to sweep the decks and to have only his victualls for his service'. Morris Dessett, a joiner of 24, claimed that he had been pressed on board, though 'the Examinate had never served at sea before', after Tully's men had made him drunk in a Nantes tavern.[11]

According to St. Lo, pressure was early brought on English prisoners at Dinan by the Duke of Berwick, Henry Fitz-James,

---

[10] P.R.O., H[igh] C[ourt of] A[dmiralty] (Oyer and Terminer examinations), 1/52, fo. 152; cf. ibid., fos. 150ᵛ, 158ᵛ.
[11] Ibid., fos. 154ᵛ–155, 159, 168, 175–6ᵛ.

and Sir William Jennings to join the French sea-service. St. Lo denies its efficacy, but we can certainly trust the admission of Roger Harding in 1694, if not that he was a genuine prisoner or that he was 'forced' on board the *Prince of Wales*, at any rate that he joined this privateer at the instance of 'one Mr. Stafford [*sic*] who is an Englishman and a Commissioner at St Maloes for the late King James . . .'[12] For Thomas Stratford, until his bankruptcy late in the war, was James's prize agent in Brittany. As both Jacobite prize agent and a leading promoter of privateers at Dunkirk, Sir James Geraldine told John Beer, a Dorset mariner who had somehow been driven to 'Callice Cliffe' and arrested as a spy, that he must be lieutenant of a privateer. In the same year, 1696, the naval commissary at St. Malo advised Francis Cavanagh, a discharged soldier anxious to go home with the English prisoners, 'that he had a double shallop fitting out for . . . two months and that if the Examinate would serve in her he would be very kind to him . . .'[13]

The immigrant in distress could easily approach one or other of the Franco-Irish business houses whose origins go back to the Cromwellian exodus.[14] They were already prominent in some French ports, it might be with an interest like John Aylward's in the historic export trade in Breton linens to Cadiz, or more likely in the Irish provision trade, which in turn was a cornerstone of the French West Indian economy; a few had already taken to banking operations, like Aylward himself and his brother-in-law John Porter of Rouen, named 'consul' there for the exiled James as early as 1689.[15] By the 1690s these families had forged numerous domestic and business links with the French as well as with one another. Already the same names occur in more than one centre: thus, besides their rela-

[12] St. Lo, p. 53; H.C.A. 1/52, fo. 167[v].
[13] H.C.A. 1/53, fos. 19–21. In 1692 Geraldine had been accused of embarking some Irish 'par force' on one of his own privateers, *Les Jeux*, and then of failing to pay them; two years later the naval intendant at Dunkirk had orders to arrest some Irish on passage for Holland, to serve in similar frigates (Marine B[3] 68, fo. 100[v], Patoulet to Pontchartrain, 13 Oct. N.S. 1692; Marine B[2] 99, fos. 497[v]–498, Pontchartrain to Patoulet, 1 Sept. N.S. 1694).
[14] See R. Hayes, *Old Irish Links with France* (Dublin, 1940), Appendix, for details from parish registers at Nantes, St. Malo, etc.
[15] AY 42 and 69; *Stuart MSS.* i. 46. I suspect that J.-B. Artus (Arthus), listed by H. Lüthy in *La Banque Protestante en France* (2 vols., Paris, 1959–61), i. 76, was a member of the Arthur family in Paris, who discounted bills for Aylward's circle: the deformation of foreign names in France is notorious.

tive in Dunkirk, the Geraldines of St. Malo had a branch in Nantes, where such compatriots as Luc O'Shiell and the Walsh dynasty were to create some of the great fortunes of the eighteenth century; the Walshes were already active in St. Malo and Bordeaux.[16] Something in the style of Herbert Lüthy's 'banque Protestante', in reverse and in miniature, the Franco-Irish operated a business network that embraced the Netherlands and Spanish Europe as well as the British Isles and West Indies. Family ties with Ireland itself, and also with London, of course did much to sustain a vigorous contraband trade, under French passports, in wartime; but family solidarity, as we know, long remained a major ingredient of commercial success in peace as well. It is harder to evaluate the sentimental ties which are of such significance for Jacobitism. At the time of the second migration the Franco-Irish still tended to marry within their own community, and there were Irish chapels transcending social distinctions.[17] John Aylward's correspondence refers more than once to inter-Irish litigation, but gives an overwhelming impression of warm hearts and some culture. In 1704, perhaps not for the first time, the Malouin Irish— 'parmi lesquels il y a beaucoup d'honnestes gens'—were to ask the French government to stop the pillage of Irish coasts by corsairs and to distinguish the Catholics from other prisoners.[18]

It has recently been stressed that the Malouin Irish were themselves among the first to arm corsairs on the outbreak of war in the eighteenth century, and it is legitimate to suppose that religious and dynastic fidelities were among their motives.[19] Privateering was almost a badge of the true Jacobite in St. Malo. This could well have been true of Nicolas Géraldin the younger, who in 1691 armed a medium-sized corsair, the *Soleil*, was knighted by James II in 1700, and was described by James III to Bolingbroke in 1715 as apprehending 'trouble on account of all the *mouvements* he has given himself on my account'.[20] His relatives, Raymond and Antoine, were among the ten captains commissioned at St. Malo in 1688; Richard

---

[16] For some of the more successful Irish families, cf. J. Meyer, *La Noblesse bretonne au XVIIIᵉ siècle* (2 vols., Paris, 1966), ii. 1034-49.

[17] Ibid., pp. 1039 and 1031 n.

[18] Marine B³ 123, fo. 544, Saint-Sulpice to Pontchartrain, 9 July N.S. 1704.

[19] Meyer, ii. 1035.   [20] *Stuart MSS.* i. 148, 466-7.

Géraldin appears as such in 1691, André in 1692.[21] Other Irish names—Butler, Murphy, Walsh, White, etc.—figure prominently among the Malouin captains of the Nine Years War, a few of them, like Patrice Lambert, doing well enough to become *armateurs*. The most frequent *armateurs* were François Browne, James's 'vice-consul' at Brest by 1695, and Georges Kennedy,[22] though neither was so audacious as Walter Cruice, another Irish Malouin, who in 1692 journeyed to Nantes to raise more money for three armaments all at once. One of these, the *Reyne Marie* of Brest (Capt. Richard Power), cost the unusually large sum of 56,000 *livres* and her total loss in December, after a four-hour engagement off the Scillies, must have contributed to the bankruptcy of Cruice and his partner Richard Morphy of Brest in 1693, when their second privateer, the *Prince de Galles* (Thomas Tully), surrendered off Île de Batz. In Nantes itself, much less of a corsair base and as yet less 'Irish' than St. Malo, we know of privateers commanded by Patrick Lincoln (*Le Lévrier*, 1693), who appears as one of Kennedy's captains in 1697, and Walter Harold (1695); the *Sarsfield*, for which Terence Dermott received a Jacobite commission in 1692, was armed by Dominique Knowles at Nantes in 1691; and Captain Jean Jourdan (*L'Espérance de Nantes*, 1695) is probably the John Jordan who registered James II's commission with the *amirauté* of Morlaix in 1692.[23]

Lists of shareholders are harder to come by, but we know that a substantial Irish one at Nantes was Edward Lucker, at least in 1692–3, while others invested in Malouin armaments: the sixteen owners of *Le Coëtquen* in 1693 included Géraldin father and son of Nantes as well as three of their family (and Patrick Fitzgerald) of St. Malo, not to mention the captain, Richard

[21] Anne Morel, *La Guerre de course à St-Malo, 1681–1715* (Paris, Académie de Marine, n.d.), pp. 106 sqq.

[22] *Stuart MSS.* i. 97. According to Mlle Morel's admittedly provisional list, Browne armed five times in 1693–7—more often than any other Franco-Irishman except Kennedy (7 armaments 1695–7). That Browne's privateering was successful is implied by his frequent armaments in 1702–9, compared with Kennedy's reappearance only in 1712.

[23] AY 69, John Porter to Aylward, 14 June N.S. 1693; H.C.A. 1 /52, fos. 154ᵛ–155, 179ᵛ; *Stuart MSS.* i. 69; Raoul Ottenhof, 'La Course et les prises à Nantes, 1688–1697' (thesis in typescript for Diplôme d'Études Supérieures, Rennes, 1961), pp. 26, 29, 74. I am grateful to the author and to Professor Jean Delumeau for allowing me to see this thesis. For Jordan at Morlaix, cf. B. de la Rogerie, iii. 2, 5, 261–2.

Géraldin.[24] We also have a list of shareholders in one of Browne's privateers, *L'Espion* of St. Malo (Jacques Walsh) in 1695, showing that Browne himself held a half-share, with the captain and Philippe Walsh each going one-sixteenth and Patrice Lambert one-thirty-second; the remainder was held by four French subscribers, including Nicolas Magon, constable of the city and *écuyer*, as to a quarter.[25] Did more such lists survive, it is hardly to be doubted that we should find, conversely, an Irish presence in armaments directed by native Frenchmen.

The only other French privateering base with a known and constant Jacobite interest was Dunkirk. Operations here had naturally more to do with Scotland, including the supply of the Jacobite garrison on Bass Rock in the Forth until its surrender in June 1694, after it had been weakened by the famine in France. As the reports of the Dunkirk captains massively demonstrate, the east coasts of Scotland and England were their habitual cruising-ground. They included one notable Scot, Robert Dunbar, the terror of coastal skippers between Leith and Moray Firth, who had escaped from Scotland while a prisoner on parole.[26] From July 1692 till June 1696 Dunbar sailed regularly for James Geraldine (Giraldin, Girardin), whose other captains included Dominique Masterson, Jean Cassgref, André Bryan, and Antoine Fitzgerald. Masterson, who came from the Aran Islands and had carried some of James's Scottish officers to Dunkirk after La Hogue, followed Dunbar's (indeed the Dunkirk) practice of taking prizes into Norwegian ports and was arrested by the governor of Bergen in the winter of

[24] Ottenhof, pp. 14 n., 29–30, 73–4. In 1693 Lucker and William Clear each held quarter-shares in *La Fidèle*, 80 tons. M. Ottenhof has drawn on two notarial *études* at Nantes, but there are none for St. Malo.

[25] Rennes, Archives départementales d'Ille-et-Vilaine, 9 B 167 (Actes de vente et de société), fos. 62ᵛ–64. I am deeply obliged to Mlle Anice Bellion for this reference. Unfortunately this series records only a limited number of privateering contracts.

[26] T. C. Smout, *Scottish Trade on the Eve of the Union* (Edinburgh, 1963), pp. 68–70, 208. For the capture and defence of the Bass Rock, see Sir Charles Petrie, *The Jacobite Movement* (1932), pp. 85–6; cf. *Stuart MSS.* i. 85–6, for James II to Captain Michael Middleton, 19 March N.S. 1694, lamenting the scarcity of provisions. The obligatory *déclarations des capitaines* registered by the Dunkirk *amirauté* for most of 1689, 1693–4, and 1696 are in Marine C⁴ 252, 258, 263. With two brief gaps down to June 1695 and a complete gap thereafter, the Dunkirk commissions are registered ibid. 252–3, 255, 257, and 259.

1692–3: his release under French diplomatic pressure led to strong but unavailing British protests.[27] He then took service at St. Malo, as Cassgref did more briefly—in his case with Nicolas Géraldin. Masterson's privateer, *La Roue de Fortune*, was driven by the weather into Galway early in 1695; Cassgref was captured by four Guernsey corsairs on an armed trading voyage from Bordeaux a little later. Nothing much is known of Fitzgerald, but Bryan took a number of prizes, usually in company with other Dunkirkers, sometimes including Dunbar, in 1695–7. Like Cassgref, however, he ended up in the employment of Jacques Pleits, the most outstanding Dunkirk *dépositaire* (*armateur*) of the period.[28] Before he died in June/July 1696, Geraldine himself was responsible for at least sixteen armaments, beginning with the celebrated Jean Doublet as captain of *La Princesse* in 1688. By 1693 he had received King James's knighthood. His financial success is clearly implied by his ability in January 1695 to arm a naval third-rate, *Le Fortuné* (56 guns), under another renowned corsair captain, Beaubriand Levesque of Granville. This he did in partnership with Nicolas Géraldin of St. Malo. Next month, off Cape Clear, *Le Fortuné* took part in a lucrative attack on an American convoy, sinking *England's Frigott* (54) with the loss of 130 lives.[29]

The *Fortuné*, though far the biggest, was not the only naval vessel armed by Geraldine of Dunkirk. In 1690 he had been concerned with two frigates of 24 guns, *La Serpente* and *La Sorcière*, commanded by Carel de Keyser and by Doublet and 'accorded for the service of the King of England'. Masterson's first privateer, *Les Jeux*, was a naval fifth of 30 guns, accorded in 1692 strictly for the relief of the Bass Rock, although the intendant Patoulet acknowledged that she could not be trusted to confine her privateering to opportunities arising on the direct route: 'L'espérance flatteuse de la course est trop

[27] O. A. Johnsen (ed.), *Innberetninger fra den franske legasjon i Kjøbenhavn* (correspondance consulaire) *vedrørende Norge 1670–1791*, vol. i (Oslo, 1934), pp. 88–9, 109; P.R.O., S.P. 75/23, fos. 28, 47, 321.

[28] Morel, pp. 128–9, 132–3, 138–9; H.C.A. 32/35 (1) and 32/44 (1); [Oxford, All Souls College, Codrington Library,] Wynne MS. LR. 2 E. 23; Marine C⁴ 263, fos. 5–6, 132ᵛ, 137ᵛ, 168ᵛ. Geraldine's recent death was mentioned by the intendant Ceberet to Pontchartrain on 11 July 1696 (ibid., B³ 93, fo. 148).

[29] Marine C⁴ 259; C. de la Morandière, *Histoire de Granville* (Bayeux, 1947), pp. 124–5; H.C.A. 1/53, fo. 3.

attrayante.'[30] *Le Sauvage* and *La Railleuse*, commanded by Dunbar in 1693–4, were both light frigates lent by the French Crown, the former remaining under Geraldine's direction when Dunbar transferred to *La Railleuse*. Geraldine's first agreement for the latter (28 April 1694), nominally for a single campaign, gave rise to some suspicion when in fact she made two; but he was allowed a second lease in October on somewhat onerous conditions.[31]

The new captain of *Le Sauvage* was neither Irish nor Scottish but a true Dunkirker, Ferdinando Danemberg.[31] Nevertheless, he cruised in 1694 on King James's 'account' and was not the only French captain to do so. Geraldine's strictly Jacobite commissions, whether issued by James II or Louis XIV or the Admiral of France, can be distinguished by the manner of their registration at the Dunkirk admiralty. Contrary to normal practice, he was required to produce neither a deposit nor anyone to 'certify' his solvency on these occasions. Such was not the case with Roger Hereford, the only other British name among the Dunkirk *dépositaires* in this war (from 1690) and a prominent one, concerned in at least a score of armaments, though more often as surety than *dépositaire*. In 1715 James III instructed Bolingbroke to address Ormonde's accounts to him under cover to Hereford, then described as a banker at Dunkirk.[32] Yet Hereford, who launched two privateers in August and November 1692, did not obtain James II's commissions even

<hr>

[30] Marine C⁴ 253. For *Les Jeux*, ibid., B² 83, fo. 542 (Pontchartrain to Brodeau, 15 March N.S. 1692) and B³ 68, fo. 17 (Patoulet to Pontchartrain, 5 April N.S. 1692).

[31] Marine C⁴ 259 and F² 14, fo. 472 (Pontchartrain to Jean Pottier de la Hestroye, 1 Dec. 1694). James's commissions to Peter Nagle and Philip Walsh on 23 Feb. N.S. 1695 seem to have involved two royal frigates, *Le Marin* (28) and *La Trompeuse* (12), for which Richard Géraldin and Andrew White respectively received his commission later in that year (*Stuart MSS.* i. 97, 103–4). The loan of naval ships to private *armateurs* was a common practice in France, though the contract terms vary; by the *Ordonnance* of 6 Oct. N.S. 1694 the Crown, in return for a fifth of the net prize proceeds, supplied the ship fully equipped, bore the cost of repairs and replacement of stores, and took the risk of losing it. Geraldine's (second) agreement of 4 Oct. N.S. 1694 allowed the French Crown a quarter of the net proceeds and he obliged himself to restore the ship (including 'provisions') in the same state as he found her; a copy of the notarial act is in Marine B³ 81, fo. 198. Naval warships accorded to the 'King of England' after 1691 implied such an arrangement, James merely receiving the Admiral's tenths.

[32] *Stuart MSS.* i. 466. Neither Geraldine nor Hereford is found arming at Dunkirk in the next war, when the name of Matthew Herries (or Harris) figures prominently.

while these were in vogue. Here, then, appears an ostensibly Jacobite privateering promoter who did not operate technically on King James's account. On the other hand, Geraldine's privilege of forgoing the usual deposit (15,000 *livres*) was explicitly related to the three commissions he obtained from St. Germain on 24 April and 3 July N.S. 1692; he had not enjoyed it previously, but he continued to do so when he took out French commissions later on, because his armaments were still 'pour le compte du Roy d'Angleterre'.[33]

This contrast between Geraldine and Hereford implies a fundamental distinction between Jacobite privateering *armateurs*, since it would be rash to assume that Hereford was the only one not to work on James's 'account'—a term which conveys the precise meaning that James was entitled to the prize tenths that were ordinarily a highly valued perquisite of the *Amiral de France*, at this time the Comte de Toulouse, one of Louis XIV's bastard sons. The correspondence between the Earls of Melfort and (from August 1694) Middleton with Phélypeaux de Pontchartrain, the naval minister and Controller-General, shows that the exiled court cared deeply when James's tenths were inadvertently assigned to Toulouse. They were no doubt regarded by Louis XIV himself as a potentially useful supplement to James's pension, for they were continued to him even when his privateers cruised under French commissions in 1693 and later. On 18 February N.S. 1692, a week after the short and simple letter giving James the power to commission privateers on French soil, all the Ponantine *amirautés* (for the Mediterranean ports were not involved) were instructed to allocate the *dixième* to James, unless he abandoned it to the *armateurs* themselves, on prizes legitimately taken under his commission.[34] Between 13 February and 20 March 1692 James granted nine commissions *en course*. On 13 February he had already commissioned Thomas Stratford to be his consul at Brest 'or any other port of Brittany, and also to be receiver of the tenths', at a salary of eighty *louis d'or* p.a. On 1 January N.S. 1694 (confirmed on 1 March N.S. 1695), evidently to

---

[33] The commissions were registered at Dunkirk (in English) on 16 May, 14 June, and 7 Oct. for Captains Nicholas Walsh (a further indication of Geraldine's links with St. Malo), Masterson, and Dunbar: Marine C⁴ 255. Only for *Le Fortuné* was there a surety.   [34] Marine F² 10, fos. 91ᵛ, 101ᵛ.

stimulate vigilance, Stratford was accorded 10 per cent of the king's tenths in lieu of salary and expenses. The Stuart papers preserve no trace of a comparable appointment at Dunkirk before June 1694, when John Constable was made agent and receiver under the direction of Sir James Geraldine, who was then commissioned comptroller of all prize accounts in Dunkirk and 'all other ports in Picardy and Normandy'.[35]

Geraldine's administration raised no eyebrows at St. Germain, but on 24 August N.S. 1695 Sir William Ellis was commissioned 'Comptroller General of the revenue from prizes' and instructed to require a sight of Stratford's books, comparing them with relevant prize inventories in St. Malo and elsewhere, examining all concerned with the produce of prize sales and reporting 'what arrears are due, and why not paid in [to the King's Treasurer], what part thereof is desperate, and how it came to be so . . .' Ellis quickly discovered a debt of 14,233 *livres*, for recovery of which a decree was obtained in the Châtelet of Paris, though James subsequently took pity on Stratford's indigent condition.[36] With so many ports to watch into which prizes might be brought, poor Stratford had a more difficult task than Geraldine, who had mainly only to keep himself in order and had taken care of the king's interest before his formal comptrollership, with which Ellis was expressly told not to meddle: by the time Ellis became James's receiver-general 'in any port of France', on 19 March 1697, Geraldine had been eight months in his grave.[37]

Stratford's revised instructions of 1 March N.S. 1695 reveal very clearly the interest of St. Germain in prizes. On the delivery of a commission, he was to take security for the tenths and for fulfilment of the instructions attached to it, which themselves make the usual stipulations about the custody of papers and cargo till lawful judgement in the French courts; Stratford was to nominate 'an inspector or écrivain' on board,

---

[35] *Stuart MSS.* i. 69, 88, 97–9. When Constable was made clerk of the kitchen in ordinary, in June 1695, he was replaced as prize agent by Louis Raulin, receiver for the Admiral of France: ibid. 102–3. Geraldine was described as 'agent there for the late King James' in a letter of July 1691 to Nottingham: H.M.C., *Finch MSS.* iii. 375. [36] *Stuart MSS.* i. 105–6, 122.
[37] Ibid. 122. As late as 12 March N.S. 1694 Stratford was ordered to receive some tenths at Boulogne (ibid. 85). Prizes were not necessarily brought into their captors' port of armament, although government and *armateurs* normally preferred this, for better control over the captains and crews.

giving each a seal, and to take further security if it was desired to transport prize goods coastwise, and to solicit inventories and appraisements from the *amirautés* of any perishable cargoes sold before adjudication. He could appoint 'fit deputies' (though he was to act with his vice-consuls at St. Malo and Brest) and make small presents to the French port officers, whom he was also to provide on demand with pilots for the English and Irish coasts—'not exceeding one person on each vessel'. He was of course to gain what intelligence he could from returning corsairs, sending it with any prints and papers to 'the Principal Ministers'. And he was to correspond constantly with one of James's Secretaries of State.[38]

Since their prizes had to be judged at Versailles or Fontaine-bleau, on the evidence of documents prepared by the local *amirautés*, King James's privateers were expected to conform with the steadily evolving rules governing the French *course*; it was in his interest that they should. Yet Jacobite practice followed its own path in certain respects. The tolerance allowed to Sir James Geraldine in the matter of his deposit has already been noticed. A more surprising variation, which caused confusion then as it does now, was the development of blank commissions at St. Germain. Those sent out early in 1692, together with a few others known to us from 1694–5, conform with French practice in stating the names of captain and ship; so do those which Melfort obtained from Pontchartrain in 1693. Late in 1694, however, ten blank commissions (with brief or more ample instructions as the case might be) were delivered at St. Germain to Robert Brent for dispatch to the ports, probably for use by Stratford, whose own instructions of 1694–5 ordered him to 'give from time to time an exact account of how the blanks in each commission are filled'. It looks as if Stratford was none too communicative, for in August 1695 Ellis was 'to require from him an exact account of how he has disposed of commissions, blank and others', as well as of 'what they have produced'.[39]

[38] *Stuart MSS.* i. 97–9. Cf. ibid. 93, for standing instructions to a Jacobite privateer (reprinted in Marsden, ii. 152–3).

[39] *Stuart MSS.* i. 93–4, 98, 105–6; cf. ibid. 92–3, 97, 103–4, 106 (giving names and on p. 104 noting a change in the *armateur*'s choice of captain). The last blank commission was dated 29 July N.S. 1696 (ibid. 118). In June 1693 Bonrepaus at Copenhagen had noted this defect in Jacobite commissions, but he may refer to the copies given to prizemasters: Johnsen, 89 n.

When James II 'agreed' to substitute French commissions for his own, in February 1693, Melfort would name both ship and captain to Pontchartrain, who unquestioningly transmitted the document within a few days to him.[40] It soon became necessary for Melfort to indicate the port of armament as well, for the admiralty of St. Malo made difficulties about registering commissions signed by Toulouse or his secretary, Valincour, the reason being that until March 1695 there was still an Admiral of Brittany in the person of the governor, Chaulnes, who drew a substantial income from prize tenths there. The difficulty was surmounted by commissions from Louis XIV himself, and these were duly recorded in Pontchartrain's entry-book as being 'pour le compte du Roy d'Angleterre'—that is, any tenths would be payable to James by private treaty with the promoters. In practice, even without allowing for the shortcomings of the prickly office-holders of the *sièges d'amirauté*, this arrangement was far less patent than the *dixièmes* derived from James's own commissions. In June 1693 Stratford was complaining about further obstruction at Brest and Morlaix, and in August all the admiralties had to be told to allow James's tenth. A list of his privateers was circulated and in future the prize sentences of the royal council were to make special mention of his right.[41] An apology to Middleton on 4 August N.S. 1694 shows that the council had omitted to do this on a number of occasions, however, and it would not reopen closed cases—'des affaires consommées qui ne méritent pas qu'on change la disposition des arrests'.[42] Pontchartrain promised better for the future, but in the following months the sentences of three important prizes taken by Dunbar and Danemberg reserved the tenths to Toulouse. This time the matter was put right on appeal, 'Sa Majesté estant informée que les frégates

[40] Pontchartrain to Valincour, 4 and 26 Feb., 11 and 25 March N.S. 1693, Marine F² 11, fos. 45ᵛ, 135ᵛ, 150ᵛ, 216.

[41] Ibid., fos. 213, 221ᵛ, 484ᵛ–485, and F² 12, fos. 85ᵛ–86: Pontchartrain to Melfort, 18 and 25 March, 17 June, 12 Aug. N.S. 1693. The commissions entered in Marine F² 11 and F² 12, *passim* are confined to Brittany and to 1693; by contrast, there are two exceptional Dunkirk entries (20 Jan. and 17 Feb. 1694) in ibid., F² 13, fos. 70ᵛ–71, 151, but no Breton ones. A slightly incomplete list of thirteen French commissions (all but one traceable to 1693) in the Royal Library at Windsor (Stuart MSS., Miscellaneous, vol. 18) was most kindly transcribed for me by Mr. Robert Mackworth-Young and has been used by gracious permission of Her Majesty the Queen: cf. *Stuart MSS.* i. 69.   [42] Marine F² 14, fos. 61ᵛ–62.

qui ont fait ces prises ont esté armées pour le compte du Roy d'Angleterre'.[43]

This disappointing experience was doubtless one reason, if not the main reason, why James reverted to his own *commissions en course*. Although Jacobite privateers remained free to cruise under French commissions, Pontchartrain's letter to Middleton of 4 August 1694 restored James II's power to issue his own. It was assumed, as always, that the crews would be 'uniquement formez d'Irlandois et autres ses sujets'. Evidently this condition was becoming difficult to fulfil, however, judging by a further letter to Middleton on 25 August N.S., allowing the crews to be composed 'd'autres étrangers que de ses sujets'—a gloss of more value at Dunkirk than elsewhere—and promising an order forbidding James's 'subjects' from serving other corsairs.[44] The High Court of Admiralty archives record no British capture of a Breton privateer after July 1694 with any large number of men whose enemy nationality could be seriously challenged, as had been the case with the *Prince de Galles* (Tully) in 1693, or with the *Soleil* (Robert Walsh) and the *Fortune* (Daniel Macdonald), taken in June–July 1694.[45] After that date, indeed, the only bunch of English-speaking privateersmen to fall into English hands was the crew of a 'two-and-twenty-oar barge', the *Loyal Clancarty* of Boulogne (Thomas Vaughan), seized after a chase over the Goodwin Sands in June 1695. The *Sainte-Marie* of Dunkirk, an open boat with two guns arrested in the Downs in June 1697, had an English captain and two other British subjects, but was armed by the sieur Marsilliac, a surgeon without apparent Jacobite associations.[46] The few other such cases

[43] *Arrêt* of 1 April N.S. 1695, ibid., F² 15, fo. 239, and C⁴ 259, fo. 242ᵛ: *Saint André de Stockholm, Pigeon Blanc,* and *Marie de Consbach.*

[44] Marine F² 14, fos. 107–8. 'Subject' was evidently a courtesy, for the navy's claim on some of James's subjects was expressly reserved. Conscription did not apply to Dunkirk, where there were many foreigners. Since the Jacobite privateers, like others, had to submit a crew-list before sailing, a study of the Malouin *rôles d'équipage* in the naval archives at Brest may throw further light on this point. The crew of Jordan's *Saint Nicolas* was almost entirely Irish (B. de la Rogerie, iii. 261). Much later, the French government was prepared openly to allow the recruitment of French seamen 'pour achever leurs équipages' (Pontchartrain to Middleton, 13 April N.S. 1695, Marine B² 107, fos. 110ᵛ–111).

[45] H.C.A. 1/52, fos. 154ᵛ–155, 177, 185–7.

[46] Vaughan's (French) Commission is in H.C.A. 1/13, fo. 110; cf. H.C.A. 1/53, fos. 4ᵛ–5, 30–1. For his trial see F. Hargrave, *A Complete Collection of State-Trials,* 4th edn., vol. v (1777), cols. 17–39.

examined by the High Court of Admiralty in the later years of the war only concerned individuals, one of whom, David Creagh, turned king's evidence against Vaughan. With this negative background[47] there is the fact that no more letters to James's Secretaries of State occur in Pontchartrain's prize entry-book after August 1694. The blank commissions that followed, together with the disorder in Stratford's affairs, also suggest that Jacobite privateering was now waning, despite Geraldine's activity at Dunkirk and the loan of two royal frigates in 1695 to Jacobites at St. Malo.[48]

Why did King James first abandon and then resume the commissioning of privateers? On neither occasion does he seem to have acted under pressure from the French court, although Bonrepaus at Copenhagen drew attention to the embarrassment created by the appearance of a Jacobite commission in the territorial waters of a state which recognized 'the prince of Orange' as king. James himself valued the power to commission, whether regiments or corsairs. It was a mark of his status and a means of rallying the morale of his supporters. He would have abandoned it for privateers, if not under French persuasion, then for good reasons of his own. That he had had one is hinted at in the very letter of August 1694 in which the power was restored. After observing darkly that his king perfectly well understood why his own commissions had been used, Pontchartrain adds these startling lines:[49]

. . . et pour empescher le prince d'Orange de continuer à faire punir comme rebelles ceux qui feront la course sous ses commissions et obliger à les traiter comme prisonniers de guerre Sa Majesté trouvera bon que le Roy d'Angleterre punisse aussy comme rebelles

---

[47] Ibid. and H.C.A. 1/53, fos. 3 (Creagh), 9 (John Murphy), 19–21 (John Beer, Francis Cavanagh). Creagh served on the Geraldine corsair, *Le Fortuné* (Levesque), and Murphy was a prizemaster from a privateer whose name he professed not to know: it was *La Notre-Dame des Bonnes Nouvelles*, Capt. Thomas Foramby of St. Malo, a successful corsair who cruised as far as Madeira; he may have been a Jacobite, for in 1697 he commanded *Le Chêne-Royal* (H.C.A. 1/14, fo. 62; B. de la Rogerie, p. 9; Morel, pp. 146–9, 158–9, 164–5). Beer was taken in the *Louis* of Dieppe, Cavanagh in the *Levrette* of St. Malo—neither of them Jacobite privateers. But the Irish evidence is negative only because it has been lost. As late as 1696 Nottingham mentions the capture of corsairs with James's commission: H.M.C., *Finch MSS.* iv. 446 (to Blathwayt, 6 Sept. 1696).

[48] Above, n. 31.

[49] Marine F² 14, fos. 61ᵛ–62. For Bonrepaus, see Johnsen, p. 89.

les Anglois et autres qui seront pris naviguant sous pavillon du prince d'Orange, pourveu que l'exécution s'en fasse dans les vaisseaux en mer et non dans les ports . . .

Absolutely no evidence of such drastic punishment has come to light; had it occurred, the Whig press must surely have relished it. Whoever made this desperate proposal, the French were careful to stand aside, for three weeks later Middleton was told that the prisoners of Jacobite corsairs, even of those sailing under French commissions, were not to be 'gardez' on French soil but left entirely to James's disposition. That this directive really meant something is certainly implied in a further letter to Middleton of 2 November 1695, in which James is said to have agreed to release prisoners 'retenus dans les prisons flottantes'—not the method used by the French themselves for the custody of prisoners of war.[50] Their release now, at the request of the French government, may argue that Jacobite privateering was foreseen as an encumbrance to the Dijkvelt–Callières peace parleys resumed in the previous June. However that may be, Pontchartrain's letters strongly suggest that James's use of French commissions had not achieved the object of preventing some dire punishments in England. To these we must now turn.

The renewal of James's privateering commissions followed the first of a series of state trials in London, held in accordance with Henry VIII's 'Acte for punysshement of Pyrotes and Robbers of the Sea', which was intended to facilitate convictions for crimes performed at sea by transferring these cases from the admiralty to the common law and a jury: although the admiralty judge was included in the bench and the civilian advocates could prosecute and defend, the procedure in Oyer and Terminer for the Admiralty disregarded the Roman rule of evidence 'testis unus testis nullus'—an advantage not altogether forfeited in January 1696 by the passing of the Trial of Treasons Act when an indictment was for high treason itself and not for piracy, since the Act did not necessarily require two lawful witnesses to the same overt act of the same treason. In the Admiralty Sessions which concern us here, nine privateersmen were indicted for piracy and many more for high treason,

---

[50] Marine F² 14, fos. 107–8 (Pontchartrain to Middleton, 25 Aug. N.S. 1694) and B² 109, fos. 318ᵛ–319 (same to same, 2 Nov. N.S. 1695); cf. ibid. 107, fo. 111.

the majority while the Treason Bills were still being fought.[51] The earlier trials, in February and November–December 1694, and again in December 1695, can therefore properly be featured in the background to the prolonged parliamentary struggle over the later Treason Bills of 1693–5. The piracy charges of February 1694, in particular, aroused public controversy— at a time when common piracy was reviving. Yet to indict for 'High Treason on the High Seas' one of James II's privateers-men, if he could be proved to be a British national, was itself more controversial than indicting a Jacobite plotter or would-be assassin at home, for the accused could colourably argue that they were lawfully commissioned by a government-in-exile or by its ally. They could claim to be treated as prisoners of war, as captured Jacobite soldiers were, especially if they had been with Sarsfield at Limerick and there allowed the honours of war. During the aftermath of the Revolution many British consciences would have been susceptible to the contention of John Golding and others in a petition to the Lords Justices after their conviction in February 1694:

That in Case of any Invasion and Dispossession ensueing thereupon, the Subjects of these Realms are not bound to abide within these Realms, and submit, and become Subjects to the Dispossessor, at the peril of Treason, but may Lawfully still attend their King's fortune, and service, if the[y] chuse so to doe.

That the possession of these Kingdoms obtained through any Invasion does not, either alter the possession of, or Right to the Subject's Allegiance. For that allegiance is a Naturall Relation, and follows the Natural Person of the King, and is not incident or appurtenant to a place, like a Villein to a Mannor . . .[52]

It will be noticed that the petitioners make no claim to be French subjects, although at least two of them had first tried this plea in court,[53] as most of their successors did, usually with better success.

---

[51] The trials were held under Commissions of Oyer and Terminer dated 4 Jan. 1694, 11 Feb. 1695, 25 Sept. 1696; H.C.A. 1/63, fos. 29–31. Their course may be followed in outline through the entries for H.C.A. 1/13–15 in vol. 45 of the *List and Index Society* (1969). For the civilian one-witness rule which gave rise to 28 Hen. VIII, c. 15, cf. Sir W. Holdsworth, *History of English Law*, ix (1926), 203–9, 229–35.   [52] Bodl., MS. Rawl. A. 84, fos. 177ᵛ–178.
[53] Wynne MS. LR. 2 E. 23: notes of the trial at the Marshalsea on 26 Feb. 1693/4 in an unfoliated commonplace book, which I attribute to Owen Wynne admitted to Doctors' Commons on 22 Jan. 1694.

When Golding offered a petition for reading in court before the Commissioners of Oyer and Terminer, which included some of the Privy Council and Admiralty who had already made up their minds, Chief Justice Treby directed the grand jury to reject it—'the one half was impertinent and the other half made against him'. Bills for high treason were found against Golding, the 55-year-old captain (or second captain) of the *Soleil* of St. Malo, John Goold, a Limerick transportee who had joined that privateer for a livelihood, and Thomas Jones, another young survivor from Limerick who had volunteered aboard the *Saint Joseph* of Brest (captain Raymond Géraldin, killed in the course of her capture). Golding and Jones were executed between low and high water mark at 'Redriff' (Rotherhithe) Stairs on 5 March 1694. Goold was discharged from prison on 17 September 1696, along with four other young Irishmen—John Ryan, Richard Chivers, John Sangster, and Constantine Doherty—who had also been sentenced to death, but in their cases for piracy. None of them had anything to do with the *Soleil* or *Saint Joseph*, both of which carried French commissions 'by the permission and consent of King James'. They were caught as members of prize crews on the *Elizabeth* of Plymouth and the *Mary* of Teignmouth, taken by the *Jacques* (Philippe Walsh) and the *Grand Prieur* (Richard Butler), and on the *Happy Return* of Bideford, taken by the *Saint-Aaron* (Jacques Walsh) and the *Providence* (Patrice Lambert). With them had been Darby Collins and Patrick Quidley, who were executed on 5 March 1694 as felons, by a compromise as it were between justice and humanity.[54] What distinguished these six pirates was that they had all belonged to privateers with King James's commission, described by Justice Rookby as 'a void Commission'.[55] By contrast, as Treby, L.C.J., said at Captain Vaughan's trial in November 1696,[56] 'acting by virtue of a commission from the French King will excuse them from being Pirates, tho' not from being Traitors to their own

[54] Wynne MS. LR. 2 E. 23 and H.C.A. 1/52, fos. 147–53, 159, 164, 165ᵛ; MS. Rawl. A. 84, fos. 171–2. Cf. *London Gazette*, nos. 2953, 2955.

[55] Wynne MS. LR. 2 E. 23.

[56] Full text in Hargrave, *State-Trials*, 4th edn., vol. v, cols. 17–39. J. S. Clarke (ed.), *The Life of James the Second* (2 vols., 1816), ii. 527, is technically wrong in saying that Golding was hanged as a pirate, but recognizes that drawing and quartering for high treason was an added punishment in the eyes of the law.

State . . .' From James's point of view, however, the executions of Golding and Jones meant that French commissions afforded no special protection, unless it were the marginal difficulty that high treason could only be preferred against a British subject and that this might be a hard fact to prove. Here, then, could well have been another reason why James resumed his freedom to commission privateers himself.[57]

Collins and Quidley were, in fact, the only Jacobite mariners to be hanged as pirates. It is true that on 12 July 1697 Captain Gerard Bedford and two companions from the *Sainte Marie de Dunkerque* were attainted of piracy, but this was a special case; they had seized a fishing vessel in English territorial waters and their commission had been made out for a different captain. As allegedly British subjects, they were accused of high treason as well. Once again it was decided not to execute the whole group: John Oldfield was selected for the gallows on the ground that 'the butcher who fired the musket was the least deserving of mercy', as the Admiralty Commissioners recommended to the Lords Justices, who seem to have been divided in opinion. By then the war had ended, however, and Oldfield was reprieved 'till his Majesty's returne into England'. King William, reported to have said that 'privateers ought to be hanged' and (by the Jacobites) to have approved Golding's execution, pardoned Oldfield 'absolutely' in 1699 and Bedford in 1701.[58]

The earlier 'pirates' had been captured in October–November 1692, shortly before the first great Commons debate on shipping 'miscarriages', already computed by several speakers at 1,500 ships and £3 million. There was another debate a year later, when Sir Thomas Clarges wondered 'whether we shall save England or Flanders'.[59] Such was the nervous atmosphere in which the first Admiralty Sessions took place. In between these dates, moreover, while Admiralty management came under strong criticism, a drama of high principle disturbed the quiet

[57] The convictions of Golding, Goold, and Jones were also a defeat for Louis XIV, who had promised to reclaim the Irish taken under his flag and later to consider if anything could be done for those taken under James's (Pontchartrain to Melfort, 22 Jan. N.S. 1693, Marine B² 89, fo. 204ᵛ).

[58] *Cal. S.P. Dom. 1697*, pp. 273, 292, 319; H.C.A. 1/53, fos. 30–4; ibid. 1/14, fos. 78, 80, 85, 99–103, 147–8, and 1/15, fo. 29. William's remark is in H.M.C., *Finch MSS.* iii. 191 (Sydney to Nottingham, 3 Aug. 1691); cf. Clarke, ii. 527.

[59] Cobbett, *Parliamentary History*, v. 726–7, 776.

waters of Doctors' Commons. It began with a letter of 20 May 1693 from the Admiralty Commissioners—who had been joined on 15 April by that ferocious Jacobite-hunter Lord Falkland— reminding Dr. William Oldys (Oldish), their advocate-general, that he had not yet replied to their 'Question . . . whether their Majesties' subjects taken serving under the late King James's commission ought not to be prosecuted as pyrats'. Beginning with Sir Thomas Pinfold, the king's advocate-general, all the Crown counsel agreed with Oldys in 'thinking it no ways advisable'. When he was nevertheless ordered to prosecute, Oldys refused. In September, with Pinfold and four other civilians, he appeared before the Secretaries of State and three more Lords of the Council, including Falkland, who lost his temper:

> Pray, Doctor, let us deal more closely with you, for your reasons are such as amount to high treason. Pray what do you think of abdication?
> Dr. Oldys. My Lords, that is an ensnareing and odious question. However it may be, I think of the abdication as you doe. For since it was voted, it binds at least in England. But these gentlemen were in a forreign countrey, and knew nothing of it; and though King James be no king here, yet the colour of authority remaining, and the common acceptation of him as king there, excuses them, as I said before . . .

For adopting this stand, 'Dr. Oldys was removed from his place and Dr. Littleton was put in'.[60]

Littleton had taken the line, in short, that 'King James was now a private person . . . and those that adhere to him are not enemies but rogues . . . no privateers but pirates'. He was supported by that formidable Whig (and later deist) polemicist Dr. Matthew Tindall, who next year attacked his 'Jacobite' colleagues in a 36-page pamphlet of some celebrity.[61] Written in the bullying tone of the left-wing doctrinaire, it makes one essential point, likely to make a strong impression in 1694:

[60] Marsden, ii. 142–8. Cf. two identical manuscript accounts of this episode in Rawl. A. 479 and A. 84, fos. 158–69. There is an attractive account of Oldys in *D.N.B.*, s.v. his son William, the antiquary; the elder Oldys bequeathed his library to Doctors' Commons.

[61] *Essay concerning the laws of nations and the rights of sovereigns . . . With reflections upon the arguments of Sir. T. P. and Dr. Ol.* (1694, two edns.).

There is no way of making a Titular King weary of granting such Commissions, as long as he can find People willing to accept and act by them. Nothing can oblige him, who runs no risque of losing any thing, but may get a considerable Booty by what his Privateers take, as well as disturb and molest his Enemies, to forbear granting such Commissions . . . Therefore Nations have no other way to hinder the disturbing their Commerce, but by using the utmost Rigor against such as accept his Commissions . . .

Nevertheless, Tindall entirely ignores the fact that the Jacobite privateers, as Oldys knew, were subject to the maritime law of France.[62] He prefers the abstract hypothesis that no king could punish the subjects of another on his own soil, and then disposes of any nonsense about the duty of obedience to a government which can no longer provide protection. As for Absolute Obedience, which 'naturally tends to introduce gross Ignorance and Superstition', the promotion of such a doctrine 'is a much greater crime than the encouraging any Rebellion whatever'. This inflated little work ends with a nasty swipe at poor Dr. Newton, who before the Privy Council had desired time to consider: 'Dr. N. said it was against his conscience . . . to have a Hand in Blood. I suppose with this tacit Reserve, except it were in hopes of being Advocate of the Admiralty, whose business it is . . ., to have a Hand in Blood.'

Newton, a protégé of Somers, duly succeeded Littleton as Judge Advocate and went on to a diplomatic career in Italy. Oldys, who henceforth practised as an ordinary advocate, was briefed for the defence of Captain Vaughan and John Murphy, both executed for high treason at the end of 1696. Two of Vaughan's men, Richard Kearney and Charles Macarthy, had been executed a year earlier,[63] but Vaughan had escaped from prison and later there was evidently some difficulty in establishing his nationality. The principal witness to his Galway origin was David Creagh, himself a prisoner in Newgate who turned king's evidence and became the subject of a scandalous ballad;

---

[62] Pontchartrain's letters of 1694–5 (above, pp. 33–4) declined punishment of British prisoners, not of their captors.

[63] Francis Early, also of the *Loyal Clancarty*, was attainted with Lt. Kearney, but pardoned in 1696. Murphy was from a different privateer (above, n. 47) and it is not clear why he was executed, except that he had no friends to appear for him and could get no papers from France: H.C.A. 1/14, fos. 27, 46. Cf. *Cal. S.P. Dom. 1696*, p. 3, and *London Gazette*, no. 3235.

his brother Christopher, a merchant of Watling Street, accused him of blackmail.[64] The court made short work of Oldys's attempt to invoke the evidential rules of the civil law in order to retract Vaughan's unfortunate boast to his captors, out on the Thames flats, that he was an Irishman and 'my intent was to burn the Ships at the Nore'. It was also ruled that the Trial of Treasons Act, in requiring two lawful witnesses to overt acts, did not apply to evidence of nativity. But Oldys had the last though futile word, in recalling the old civilian objection to treating the grand jury as witnesses *ex vicinato* to a crime committed on the high and open seas.

Like Vaughan, nearly all Jacobite privateersmen claimed to be of French birth, even if they had since returned to Ireland and could not speak French, and very few were in fact attainted. The position down to 28 March 1696 was thus summarized by Hedges in advising Shrewsbury against the inclusion in the sea-cartel of a Captain Walsh, lately attainted at an Admiralty Sessions in Ireland:[65]

At the sessions of the admiralty held in February 1693[4] five persons were condemned for treason in the same circumstances as Walsh now is; two were executed, and the other three are remaining in the Marshalsea.[66] At the sessions in November 1694, five were condemned, and these are now in Newgate . . . At the sessions in December last three were condemned, and of these two were executed and the other is in the Marshalsea. This last person was brought in guilty by the jury's mistake, and it was believed would have the king's pardon.

The Judge of Admiralty here refers to the executions of Golding, Jones, Kearney, and Macarthy. Apart from Vaughan, Murphy, and Walsh, no others afterwards suffered the supreme penalty. Of the few condemned, for high treason or piracy or both,

---

[64] Hargrave, v. 31; H.C.A. 1/13, fos. 102–9; *Cal. S.P. Dom. 1696*, pp. 435–6, 453–4, 480.

[65] Ibid., p. 104. Was this Robert Walsh, for whom James II procured a French commission in 1693 and whose ship, the *Soleil* of St. Malo, was taken off Cape Clear in June 1694? He does not appear among the other examinates in H.C.A. 1/52, fos. 185–7, but may have been captured ashore; unhappily, the Irish admiralty records were destroyed in 1920. Walsh was apparently executed: H.M.C., *Buccleuch MSS.* ii (Part i), 319.

[66] This statement conflicts with Wynne MS. LR. 2 E. 23, which accounts for three traitors (of whom Goold was still in custody) and six pirates (of whom two had been executed and four remained in custody). Hedges omits the pirates.

before and after this letter, we have a record of pardon in many cases between September 1696 and May 1701, the last being that of John Noake, son of a former proctor in the Norwich consistory, who had had 'little more to say for himself than that he was a chevalier of fortune' and had been taken as one of Dunbar's prizemasters.[67] Sentenced with him in November 1694 but pardoned in December 1699 were William Jennings of Middlesex, son of the Jacobite exile, and Colonel Daniel Macdonnell of Ulster—easily confused with the Dubliner Daniel Macdonnell, captain of the 4-gun *Fortune* of Dunkirk, who received sentence on the same occasion but no pardon until 1701. These were all in a sense distinguished prisoners. It is more difficult to understand why James Brassell, a simple mariner from Laughlin Cleere's *Princesse*—to which Colonel Macdonnell claimed to have been attached in order to purge himself of a murder—was convicted with these others in November 1694, for he was not the only prisoner who 'spoke both English and French' in a crew of 100, only seven of whom were even tried; his name figures in a list of over seventy against whom no evidence could be found on 15 October previously.[68] Of the whole thirty-one tried on 23 November, twenty-three were acquitted and two delivered by proclamation. A week later, allegedly for want of evidence, the Attorney-General ordered a *Noli prosequi* for the seventeen men of Tully's *Prince de Galles* against whom charges had been brought—out of a crew numbering forty-eight British names. All of the acquitted, who claimed to be French, though of Irish parentage, were on the same day ordered to be detained for exchange as prisoners of war.[69]

Since these men had been caught cruising under French commissions, it would have been necessary but difficult—as we can see from the report of Vaughan's trial—to prove them British subjects. In this respect indictments for high treason were technically less straightforward than those for piracy. In either case the course of justice might be impeded by the absence of witnesses on the side of the captors, who were all in the navy,

---

[67] Wynne MS. LR. 2 E. 23 records the proceedings at the Old Bailey on 23–4 and 30 Nov. 1694. I have found no detailed record of the Sessions in Dec. 1695.

[68] H.C.A. 1/52, fos. 178ᵛ–182; ibid. 1/29, fo. 36, and 1/13, fo. 47.

[69] Ibid., fos. 47–63; Wynne MS. LR. 2 E. 23.

and by the dislike of the common law judges for the written evidence produced in these Admiralty sessions by the civilian advocates.[70] Apart from these technical difficulties, it seems possible that the leniency shown in the Sessions of November 1694 may reflect fears for the fate of Huguenots taken prisoner at Camaret in the previous June: they had just been transferred to the château of Nantes 'sur l'avis que Sa Majesté a eu qu'on avait pendu en Angleterre quelques Irlandois pris sur mer'.[71] It may be significant that the *Noli prosequi* for Tully's men was issued upon order-in-council. However that may be, the government's attitude had hardened by September 1696, when Blathwayt ordered that the cartel should not be extended even to Frenchmen if they were found to be serving on privateers with James's commission; any British were to be prosecuted. At this very moment, nevertheless, the pardons begin: Ryan, Chivers, Sangster, and Doherty—all attainted of piracy—together with Goold of the *Soleil* and Early of the *Loyal Clancarty*.[72] It is of some interest, too, that King William's government in Britain never went so far as a Dutch *Placaet* of February 1696, imposing the death penalty on enemy privateers who should come within the buoys without a protecting fleet, although many of the captured Jacobite privateersmen had compounded their offence by taking prizes 'within the jurisdiction of the Admiralty of England'.[73]

As time went on, it is possible to discern a shift in the attitude of the lawyers themselves. At Vaughan's trial, Justice Holt conceded that Jacobites cruising under the French king's commission became *Gallici subditi* who could wage war on all his enemies except their own countrymen. Hedges, who agreed that no sovereign could commission his subjects to fight one another (much less when divested of his regal power), at least differed from his common law colleagues when he admitted in March 1696 that persons comprehended within the Capitulation of Limerick 'might have some reason to sue for your

---

[70] Cf. Wynne MS. LR. 2 E. 23 for the resistance of Treby and Rookby to the reading of admiralty examinations in the Sessions of Feb. 1694.

[71] Marine B² 100, fo. 263 (Pontchartrain to Middleton, 22 Oct. N.S. 1694).

[72] H.M.C., *Finch MSS.* iv. 453 (Blathwayt to Nottingham, 12 Sept. 1696); H.C.A. 1/13, fo. 121, minutes of Sessions, 17 Sept. 1696.

[73] C. van Bynkershoek, *Quaestionum juris publici libri duo* (ed. J. B. Scott, 2 vols., Oxford, 1930), ii. 99.

Majesty's mercy'[74]—a view that would have spared Golding. In the next century English law was to accept the principle that enemy character attaches to English subjects living on enemy territory, just as William's declaration of war had exempted the French Protestants in England.[75] The problem was sharply and tragically brought to public attention by the Jacobite privateers, and its solution anticipated by the scholarly and courageous Dr. Oldys, whose imaginative understanding preferred to rely on the 'errour' of simple-minded Irish emigrants rather than on the right of a deposed king to wage war— as to which there can never be a single opinion.

[74] *Cal. S.P. Dom. 1696*, p. 104.
[75] Cf. Holdsworth, xii (1938), 99–101, 142–8.

III

Governor Robert Hunter and
the Anglican Church in New York

IN June 1710, Robert Hunter,[1] the newly arrived governor of the province of New York, attended his first Sunday service at Trinity Church in New York City and there, apparently for the first time, met the Reverend William Vesey,[2] rector of the church and leading Anglican minister in the colony. Their greetings were almost certainly very cool. The rector, who had turned out to welcome Hunter's predecessors when they first arrived in the colony, had not bothered to meet Hunter; the governor, whose predecessors had frequently entertained Vesey at dinner, had not yet bothered to invite him to the governor's house. In fact, long before Hunter's arrival the governor and the rector had each expected trouble from the other; now as they met face to face at Trinity, the occasion was not very auspicious.

On first thought, this seems surprising. Both young men were tactful, self-assured, dignified, and personally not given to controversy. More important, they had strong political and religious interests in common. As the leading member of the Anglican clergy, Vesey could be expected to defend the royal governor's authority in the colony. Indeed, of all the organizations in early eighteenth-century America, the one which would have seemed the most natural bulwark of imperial authority was the Church of England.[3] Royal officials, British military officers, merchants with English associates, local politicians with connections in Whitehall—all these people with imperial ties

---

[1] For Hunter, see *D.N.B.* and *Dictionary of American Biography*. All dates in this paper are Old Style.

[2] For Vesey, see *Biographical Sketches of those who attended Harvard College in the Classes 1690–1700*, ed. C. K. Shipton (in J. L. Sibley, cont. C. K. Shipton, *Harvard Graduates*, Cambridge, Mass., 1873–), ix (1933), 173–9.

[3] For a strong presentation of this argument, see S. S. Webb, 'The Strange Career of Francis Nicholson', *W. & M. Qtly*, 3rd ser. xxiii (1966), 513–48, esp. 520, 545.

tended to be Anglican. The period of rapid American expansion in the colonies—the Anglican 'invasion' at the turn of the seventeenth century—coincided exactly with the period of rapid expansion of the institutions of royal control there; the people who opposed the appointment of American bishops tended to be the same people who opposed the appointment of governors with salaries from England. At a time and place where churches were still the most effective political organizations, the Church of England was the institution royal governors turned to for developing their own grass roots' support.

Moreover, of all the royal governors, Hunter would seem the most certain to have received the wholehearted local backing of the Church of England. A devout Anglican, a member of the Society for the Propagation of the Gospel and one who made a point of keeping the Society informed on provincial affairs, a personal acquaintance of Queen Anne, a friend of Dean Swift who urged Swift's appointment as bishop for the American colonies:[4] these were attributes that should have made Hunter one of the most desirable governors from the standpoint of the Anglican Church.

And yet, despite the personal charm of both men and despite the strong reasons encouraging their mutual co-operation, each was profoundly suspicious of the other, virtually from the day of Hunter's appointment. Why was this?

To understand the potential conflict between Hunter and the Anglican clergy, one must understand the troubled background of New York politics, for the Anglican Church had become deeply involved in the Leislerian/anti-Leislerian controversy which had embittered New York politics for nearly two decades. New York's Anglican community had started under James II's governors during the 1680s. In 1689 the last of these, Francis Nicholson, was overthrown in a rebellion led by Jacob Leisler. Most of the Anglican leaders bitterly opposed the rebellion; they openly exulted in Leisler's subsequent execution by British authorities, and for a generation after this the leading Anglicans of New York were also leaders of the anti-Leislerian political faction, so openly so that when a leading anti-Leislerian, Nicholas Bayard, was brought to trial for treason in 1702, Vesey

---

[4] J. D. Fiore, 'Jonathan Swift and the American Episcopate', ibid., 3rd ser. xi (1954), 425–33.

preached publicly in Bayard's behalf every evening during the trial and created so much sympathy for him that the prosecution speeded it up to prevent further sermons.[5]

So the Anglican community in New York City early became identified with anti-Leislerian factionalism through their association with the governors of James II; the identification was reinforced by the fact that in the quarter-century after James's abdication the two governors who sided most openly with the anti-Leislerian faction were Fletcher and Cornbury, the two men most active in the establishment of Trinity Church.[6] In 1693, when Fletcher was governor, the New York Assembly under Fletcher passed an Act providing that the public support of ministers in each of four communities be entrusted to a group of Protestant vestrymen elected by the local freeholders. The Act was ambiguously worded: did the term 'good and sufficient Protestant minister' include Dissenters or was it intended to refer only to Anglicans?[7] The framers of the Act intended it to give public support to Dissenting ministers in places like New York City (indeed, all the towns mentioned in the Act) where Dissenters predominated; Fletcher interpreted it as supplementing his instructions to appoint Anglican ministers to vacant parishes and therefore as allowing him to force the various provincial vestries to support an Anglican minister. For some years there was a stalemate between the Anglican governor and the Dissenter-dominated vestry of New York City. Finally, Fletcher was able to force the vestry to accept an Anglican minister. William Vesey, an Anglican then in England for ordination, was invited to become rector of Trinity Church when he returned to the colony.[8] Vesey never forgot that he owed his appointment to anti-Leislerian favour. Similarly, the lay leaders of Trinity did not forget that they owed the church's

---

[5] Mrs. Martha J. Lamb and Mrs. Burton Harrison, *History of the City of New York* (3 vols., New York and Chicago, 1877–96), i. 457.

[6] See J. R. Reich, *Leisler's Rebellion, a Study of Democracy in New York, 1664–1720* (Chicago, 1953), ch. vii.

[7] The phrase always did refer to an Anglican minister when used in England. D. R. Fox, *Caleb Heathcote, Gentleman Colonist* (New York, 1926), p. 199.

[8] See M. Dix, *A History of the Parish of Trinity Church in the City of New York* (5 vols., New York, 1898–   ), i. 81–96; E. C. Chorley, 'Outline of Two Hundred and Fifty Years of Trinity Parish in the City of New York', *Hist[orical] Mag[azine] of the] Prot[estant] Episc[opal] Ch[urch]*, xvi (1947), 2–95; William Smith, *The History of the Late Province of New York* (2 vols., New York, 1830), i. 128–32.

incorporation to a charter Fletcher granted in 1697, and also that Fletcher had granted Trinity the 'King's Farm', one of several lavish land-grants he bestowed on anti-Leislerian supporters. (The permanent grant was invalidated by Fletcher's Leislerian successor, Lord Bellomont, but reconfirmed in 1705.)

The other strongly anti-Leislerian governor was Lord Cornbury, Bellomont's successor. By an Act of Assembly passed during Bellomont's administration, the governor was prevented from granting Trinity the 'King's Farm' for longer than his own indefinite administration, but he tacitly acquiesced in the church's leasing the land on a long-term basis; moreover, he placed the provincial schools under the church[9] and forced Anglican ministers on communities outside New York City. By the time Cornbury left office the Anglican Church was heavily involved in provincial factionalism.[10]

Hunter's government included New Jersey as well as New York; and, just as many of the Anglican leaders in New York had come to be associated with the anti-Leislerian faction there, the Anglican clergy in New Jersey had also come to be associated with the anti-proprietary faction in that colony. The leader of New Jersey Anglicans, and to some extent Vesey's counterpart there, was John Talbot, rector of the Anglican church at Burlington.[11] Talbot's vestry included nearly all the leading opponents of the Jersey Proprietors in the western part of the colony—Daniel Coxe, Hugh Huddy, Jeremiah Basse, Daniel Leeds: these men, all bitter enemies of both the West Jersey Quakers and the Proprietary party whom Hunter later drew to his support, were pillars of the Burlington church.

[9] Mary L. Booth, *History of the City of New York* (New York, 1866), p. 276.

[10] Edward Vaughan, Minister at Elizabeth, later spoke of 'the freedom I once took in telling Mr. Vesey . . . that it was inconsistent with the Character of a Minister of Peace to foment divisions, to appear in faction and party opposite to Government'. Vaughan to J. Chamberlayne, 8 Nov. 1715, quoted in J. K. Nelson, 'Anglican Missions in America, 1701–1725. A Study of the Society for the Propagation of the Gospel in Foreign Parts' (Ph.D. thesis, Northwestern University, 1962, pp. 281–3).

[11] See E. L. Pennington, *Apostle of New Jersey, John Talbot, 1645–1721* (Philadelphia, 1938), and G. M. Hills, 'John Talbot, the First Bishop in North America', *Pennsylvania Mag. of History and Biography*, iii (1879), 32–55. The Burlington church owed its beginning to Lord Clarendon: G. M. Hills, [*History of*] *the Church in Burlington*[, *New Jersey*] (2nd edn., Trenton, N.J., 1885), pp. 143–4.

Daniel Coxe in particular was the anti-proprietary leader in West Jersey; his colleague from East Jersey was Peter Sonmans, leading member of the Anglican church at Perth Amboy. There the Anglican minister, Thomas Haliday, came under the joint influence of Sonmans and Vesey just about the time of Hunter's arrival. Later Haliday was forced to leave the colony because of a personal fight in which he injured one of the proprietary leaders, but during the period of his ministry he was an active supporter of both Talbot and Vesey.[12]

From Robert Hunter's standpoint the Anglican identification with the anti-Leislerian and anti-proprietary factions was an ominous sign. For Hunter himself was a Whig in English politics, while in the two decades since 1689 the anti-Leislerian and anti-proprietary factions had come to associate themselves with English Tories. Consistently, the anti-Leislerian executives had owed their jobs to Tory patrons. Agents representing anti-Leislerian interests in England found support from Tories; Leislerian leaders like Jacob Leisler, Jr., got help from Whigs in Parliament, and the same arrangement held true in New Jersey. The associations were loose, informal ones, but by the time Hunter was appointed to office, anti-Leislerian and anti-proprietary leaders had long since learned to be distrustful of governors who owed their jobs to Whig support. Local politics on both sides of the Atlantic predisposed Hunter and the Anglican leaders to opposing sides in provincial politics.[13]

Moreover, the Anglican involvement in factional struggles gave the clergy in both colonies experience with the techniques of political pressure. They had mastered the timely political sermon, they knew the political impact of leaving the governors out of their public prayers;[14] they made a point of entertaining prominent parishioners who were also the leading merchants, landowners, and politicians in the province; they called frequent regional meetings of the clergy to petition or address either the governor or authorities at home. These were all effective political weapons. In the Jerseys particularly, the

12 Nelson, 'Anglican Missions', pp. 394–401.

13 See my forthcoming book, *Anglo-American Politics, 1660–1775: Factions and the Diffusion of Power*, ch. iii.

14 See, e.g., Bellomont to the Lords of Trade, 22 July 1699, *Documents Relative to the Colonial History of the State of New York*, ed. E. B. O'Callaghan, cont. B. Fernow (15 vols., Albany, N.Y., 1853–87), iv. 534–5 (cited below as *N.Y. Col. Docs.*).

clergy had taken to holding regular meetings to discuss problems which could include their difficulties with the governors.[15]

They were less sophisticated about the best way to use their
connections in England, but here too they were learning
quickly. In England Vesey had met the Bishop of London. The
bishop was acquainted with some of the cabinet ministers;
moreover, at first through the bishop and later through the
former governors Nicholson and Cornbury and a few well-
connected missionaries, Vesey also had the support of a strong
faction in the S.P.G.[16] Though one must be careful not to over-
emphasize the political power of the S.P.G., it is nevertheless
true that the Board of Trade automatically referred provincial
laws affecting the Church to them for review, their leading
members were also members of the Privy Council, and the
Council as a whole gave serious consideration to the Society's
reports and recommendations on colonial affairs.

The political influence, both English and American, of the
Anglican leaders had been most successfully used against the
Leislerian governor Lord Bellomont, infamous in Anglican eyes
for his cancellation of the grant of the 'King's Farm' to Trinity
Church. Vesey had undertaken a campaign with local politicians and British authorities to unseat Bellomont. In sermon
after sermon he attacked the governor; ostentatiously he omitted
the governor from his prayers and virtually drove him from
attending services at Trinity to worshipping at the Dutch
church. In letter after letter to the Bishop of London he sought
Bellomont's recall, with telling effect: in 1700 Bellomont protested that ''tis said the Bishop of London has writ to . . . Mr.
Vesey who herds it with the angry party, that by Easter he and
his friends will be rid of their grievance'.[17] Had not Bellomont
died shortly after this, there is little doubt that Vesey and his
associates could have obtained the governor's recall.

When Robert Hunter arrived in New York and New Jersey
in 1710, therefore, he found an Anglican leadership already

---

[15] N. R. Burr, *The Anglican Church in New Jersey* (Philadelphia, 1954), pp. 282–5,
discusses the meetings of the clergy between 1702 and 1713.

[16] See Sir E. Midwinter, 'The Society for the Propagation of the Gospel and
the Church in the American Colonies: I, New York', *Hist. Mag. Prot. Episc. Ch.*
iv (1935), 66–115, 281–99.

[17] Bellomont to Secretary Vernon, 6 Dec. 1700, *Cal. S.P. Col., America and West
Indies, 1700*, p. 720.

heavily involved in politics and already masters of the techniques of applying political pressure. For twenty years the anti-proprietary leaders of New Jersey had been working in tandem with the anti-Leislerian faction of New York, and over those two decades the Anglican clergy had been associated with both. The Church structure was by no means a monolithic one: ministers did not always divide along the same partisan lines. When, for example, Governor Cornbury imprisoned the Reverend Thorogood Moore, a proprietary supporter who was briefly taking Talbot's place at Burlington during Talbot's visit to England,[18] Talbot deplored the action but Vesey did not openly oppose it. When Francis Phillips, a Philadelphia minister, was turned out of his pulpit for misconduct, Talbot, whose parishioners had business associations with the Philadelphia supporters of Phillips, supported the dismissal,[19] but so, ironically, did Hunter. Moreover, there were divisions within the Anglican churches themselves, most noticeably in the Amboy church but also in Trinity.

Nevertheless, Anglican leaders in New York and the Jerseys were aware of their common interests and aware of the means by which they could bring pressure on royal governors to give them a privileged position in their colonies far beyond what their numerical strength would warrant. In both colonies the Anglican Church contained a small minority of the inhabitants, but these usually included leading politicians in the colony.[20] In both colonies the Church, despite its minority status, was bitterly critical of governors who felt their political survival depended on co-operation with Dissenters, with Dutch and Puritans in New York, with Quakers and Presbyterians in New Jersey. In their efforts to remove Bellomont the Anglican leaders

[18] Pennington, p. 49; Nelson, 'Anglican Missions', pp. 391–5.

[19] See Phillips's letters to the Sec[retary of the] S[ociety for the] P[ropagation of the] G[ospel], 31 March and 22 May 1715, and to Dr. King, 16 Aug. 1715, in L[ibrary of] C[ongress] Microfilms of American Material in the Archives of the Bishop of London, Rue III, vol. vii. See also Phillips's letter to the Sec., S.P.G., 23 March 1714/15, Talbot to the Bishop of London, 21 Oct. 1715, and Ministers of New Jersey and Pennsylvania to the Bishop of London, 17 March 1714/15, in *Historical Collections Relating to the American Colonial Church*, vol. ii, ed. W. S. Perry (Hartford, Conn., 1871), 90, 93–4, 84–5.

[20] Dissenters outnumbered Anglicans ten to one in New York. Heathcote estimated in 1714 that out of 45,000 inhabitants of New York, no more than 1,200 attended the Anglican church (Fox, p. 228). Burr, pp. 208–11, shows how small a minority of the New Jersey population the Anglicans were.

had enjoyed a heady taste of success, and they were quite prepared to use the same methods with Hunter that they had used
before.

Moreover, Vesey and his supporters were encouraged to
be particularly aggressive in their demands because Hunter's
relations with the British government suffered a serious set-
back at the very time of his arrival in the colony. Hunter,
a Whig in English politics, had been appointed to provincial
office by the ministry headed by Marlborough and Godolphin
(he had fought under Marlborough at Blenheim), but very soon
afterwards Godolphin fell from office and Marlborough from
favour, and were replaced by the Tory ministry of Bolingbroke
and Robert Harley. It was difficult enough for Hunter to have
his patrons out of office, but in addition his arch-enemy, the
former governor Cornbury, still smarting over his removal from
office in 1708, had returned to England determined to use his
powerful Tory connections to discredit Hunter and help his
friend Vesey. Very early, Lewis Morris spoke of Vesey as the
leader of Cornbury's friends in the colony,[21] and Hunter himself complained of Cornbury's influence with the ministry.[22]
Cornbury also had influential friends at the Board of Trade.
Equally important, he was also apparently the leader of a 'high
church' faction within the badly divided S.P.G., a faction
especially powerful in Queen Anne's last years. Hunter, on one
issue, complained to an English friend, 'I need not tell you
what hand a noble peer at the head of a faction of the Society
had in this.'[23] As a powerful member of the S.P.G. and as a
member with claims to first-hand knowledge of New York
affairs, Cornbury headed a number of committees appointed
to consider problems of the Church in the colony. He chaired

[21] Morris to Sec., S.P.G., 20 Feb. 1711/12. *Ecclesiastical Records, State of New York*,
ed. E. T. Corwin (7 vols., Albany, N.Y., 1901–16), iii. 1906–9 (cited below as
Eccles. Recs. N.Y.).

[22] Hunter complained to the Bishop of London, 1 March 1711/12, that Vesey
was sending attacks against him to Nicholson and Cornbury: *N.Y. Col. Docs.*,
vol. v, ed. E. B. O'Callaghan (Albany, N.Y., 1855), 310–12. Hunter later wrote
to the Lords of Trade that his enemies were 'prompted all along from the other
party by a late governor of these Provinces' (28 March 1715), *Documents Relating
to the Colonial History of the State of New Jersey*, ed. W. A. Whitehead, cont. F. W.
Ricord and W. Nelson (10 vols., Newark, N.J., 1880–6), iv. 207 (cited below as
N.J. Col. Docs.). See also *Cal. S.P. Col., America and West Indies, 1711–12*, pp. 172–5,
212–13; ibid., *1712–14*, pp. 154–7, 203–5, 340.

[23] Hunter to William Popple, 14 Nov. 1715, *N.J. Col. Docs.* iv. 223–6.

a committee to study the 'King's Farm'; Vesey referred another committee to Clarendon for a state of the Church.[24] With Cornbury influencing important decisions of the S.P.G., the Society was not likely to back Hunter even though the governor himself was a member.

At the same time as Cornbury was helping Vesey at home, Francis Nicholson, another pillar of the S.P.G.[25] and an early patron of the Anglican church in New York (and the governor overthrown by Leisler's rebellion), was returning to the colonies, warmly backed by the British government as commander of the expedition against Port Royal.[26] Nicholson's real aspiration, well known in New York, was to get Hunter's job away from him; and while his military headquarters were in Boston he made frequent recruiting trips to New York—where he met Vesey and other clergymen—and Vesey in turn travelled to Boston to confer with Nicholson there.

When Robert Hunter began his administration in New York, therefore, the Anglican leaders had a previous record of marked success in New York politics. They had particularly good connections in the S.P.G. and the English ministry—with factions the governor did not support. And they were encouraged to oppose the governor by the presence of a rival candidate for his office— a candidate to whom, as a former governor under James II, they originally owed the establishment of the Anglican Church in the colony. Not surprisingly, the Anglicans were eager to test Hunter's sympathies: they were suspicious of his politics and he was apprehensive of their growing power.

The first test came over the church at Jamaica, New York. This had been erected through public taxation, according to an Act of the Assembly. During Cornbury's administration the S.P.G. had sent over a missionary, William Urquhart, whom Cornbury had installed as the local minister. Urquhart's appointment was accepted grudgingly by the Dissenters, but,

  [24] Vesey to S.P.G., 26 July 1710, S.P.G. Minutes (L.C. transcripts).

  [25] See Ruth M. Winton, 'Governor Francis Nicholson's Relations with the S.P.G., 1701–1727', *Hist. Mag. Prot. Episc. Ch.* xxii (1948), 274–96, and Webb, art. cit., p. 545. Nicholson's association with the Burlington Anglicans is shown clearly in a letter from the rector, and others, of St. Mary's Church to Nicholson (n.d., but 1714), in Hills, *The Church in Burlington*, pp. 118–21.

  [26] One of Hunter's strongest complaints against Nicholson was written in a letter to the Earl of Stair, 18 Oct. 1714, *N.Y. Col. Docs.* v. 453.

just at the time Hunter became governor, Urquhart was replaced by Thomas Poyer[27] and the Dissenters chose the occasion to make an issue of having an Anglican minister imposed upon a predominantly Dissenting community by forcibly taking over both the church and the parsonage. After some violence, the Anglicans regained physical control of the church, but the Dissenters held on to the parsonage, and the town vestry, dominated by Dissenters, refused to pay Poyer's salary.[28] Poyer, urged on by Vesey, took the case to Hunter, demanding that the governor order the vestry to pay his salary. Hunter in turn told Poyer to take the case to court and he, as governor, would pay the costs.

Poyer was reluctant to do this, for several reasons. For one thing he was not at all sure of his ground and hesitated to jeopardize the salaries of other Anglican ministers in the same position by losing a test case.[29] In addition to having genuine doubts about the merits of his case, Poyer doubted his chances of getting an impartial trial before local justices appointed by Hunter (Hunter later admitted regret at these appointments and replaced them),[30] and his salary was so small that New York law forbade appealing for that amount to the higher provincial courts. Moreover, he had well-founded hopes that Hunter would be replaced by a more sympathetic governor, who would use his executive authority either to order payment directly or to permit an appeal to sympathetic judges.

Still urged on by Vesey, who hoped to use the Poyer case to undermine Hunter at home, Poyer appealed to the S.P.G.[31] The Society, with Hunter's own explanation also before them, decided in Poyer's favour and prevailed with the Queen to send Hunter a strongly worded Additional Instruction allowing the clergy to appeal in cases under fifty pounds to the highest

[27] For Poyer, see F. L. Weiss, 'The Colonial Clergy of the Middle Colonies, New York, New Jersey, and Pennsylvania, 1628–1776', *American Antiquarian Society Proceedings*, lxvi (1956), 292.

[28] Dix, pp. 183–4; Smith, i. 170–3; cf. Henry Onderdonk, Jr., *Antiquities of the Parish Church, Jamaica* (Jamaica, 1880), pp. 28–32.

[29] Poyer to Hunter, 17 Jan. 1711/12, *N.Y. Col. Docs.* v. 327.

[30] Heathcote to Sec., S.P.G., 30 Jan. 1711/12, *Eccles. Recs. N.Y.* iii. 1902–3.

[31] Hunter wrote to the S.P.G., Sept. 1711, that 'he fears Mr. Poyer is prevailed on by Mr. Vesey to delay that Matter, that gent Endeavouring what he can to make him [the Governor] uneasy . . .' Minutes of the S.P.G., 11 Nov. 1711, no. 10, S.P.G. Journals, ii (L.C. transcripts).

provincial courts.[32] At the time of Queen Anne's death the court case stood unresolved, but the sending of the Instruction itself was a political set-back for Hunter. It strengthened Vesey's hand, particularly among the clergy.

Poyer's case was the first major issue between Hunter and Vesey; it made clear that the two men's suspicions of each other were justified. Within a few months of Hunter's arrival, in February 1711, Vesey was already circulating a petition against him among the New York clergy and Hunter's close friend Lewis Morris was already complaining of Vesey's political activity.[33] In March 1712, the governor criticized Vesey for 'caballing' with leading assemblymen to obstruct Hunter's salary settlement.[34] On 1 November 1712, and again on 14 March 1713, Hunter wrote to his friend Swift that he had been 'used like a dog' and had 'spent three years of life in such torment and vexation, that nothing in life can make amends for it'.[35] From early in Hunter's administration until Queen Anne's death in 1714, Vesey was the foremost leader of the governor's opposition.

Not only was Poyer's case the earliest issue to set the pattern for trouble between the governor and Vesey; it was also the most important one that Hunter faced, because of the general interest it excited among the New York clergy. Even clergy sympathetic to Hunter felt their own livings jeopardized by a court case involving the 1693 Act, and they joined in a petition on Poyer's behalf in 1712.[36] But there were other important issues between Hunter and the Anglican leaders concerned more narrowly with Trinity Church. Two in particular caused enormous friction: the case of Elias Neau and an attack on Trinity by vandals in 1713. Both were taken up by the S.P.G.;

[32] The Society's representation to the Queen, the Order in Council authorizing ecclesiastical appeals, and the Additional Instruction are in *Eccles. Recs. N.Y.* iii. 1963–4, 1971, 1990. Cf. S.P.G. Minutes, 11 July 1712, nos. 4, 7–10; 4 Sept. 1713, no. 9: S.P.G. Journal, ii (L.C. transcripts).

[33] Morris to Secretary Chamberlayne, 20 Feb. 1711/12, *N.Y. Col. Docs.* v. 318–24.

[34] Hunter to the Bishop of London, 1 March 1711/12, ibid. v. 310–12.

[35] *The Correspondence of Jonathan Swift*, ed. F. E. Ball (6 vols., 1910–14), ii. 10–12, 42.

[36] A strong indication of this is that in an 'Address of the Clergy of New York to Governor Hunter' (n.d., *N.Y. Col. Docs.* v. 325–6), which was generally quite favourable to the governor, the clergy complained of Hunter's handling of Poyer's case.

both were hanging fire in 1714, with the balance of sentiment in the Society going against Hunter.

Elias Neau was a New York merchant, a former Huguenot appointed in 1702 as catechist to the negroes in New York City. After some hesitation at first, Vesey had come to support his work, but in 1712 an uprising of slaves in the city terrified the parishioners of Trinity and Vesey withdrew his support of Neau, despite the fact that Neau was able to show that only one out of several hundred of his pupils participated in the uprising, although two hundred negroes were implicated. Hunter, however, continued to support Neau, and when Vesey refused to allow Neau's negroes to participate in services at Trinity, Hunter got the chaplain of the fort in New York harbour to admit them and personally attended services of their confirmation. Hunter and Neau on the one hand, Vesey on the other sent their complaints to the S.P.G.,[37] but up to 1714 the Society had decided neither to disavow Neau's work and cut off his salary (he was on their pay-roll) nor to endorse his action and urge Vesey to support his work.

Neau's was one issue concerning Trinity Church; the other concerned Hunter's handling of its desecration. In 1713 vandals broke into Trinity Church, destroyed part of the interior, and walked off with valuable plate. Hunter promptly offered a reward for the offenders' capture; he did not, however, call on Vesey or personally express his sympathies,[38] and Vesey made political capital of what he considered the governor's rudeness on the occasion. Properly speaking there was no 'issue' here: Hunter used his executive authority as best he could. But the prolonged and vociferous complaints of Vesey and his friends about the governor's personal behaviour made clear how very bitter the whole struggle had become.

The final major issue between the governor and the clergy concerned New Jersey. Here the Provincial Assembly passed a law permitting Quakers to serve on juries simply by affirming their loyalty to the Government rather than by taking an oath. Talbot protested to the S.P.G. that in communities like his own (Burlington), where Quakers were an overwhelming majority

---

[37] Minutes of the S.P.G., 10 Oct. 1712, nos. 48, 51; Neau to S.P.G., 16 Nov. 1714, 3 Feb. 1715/16; Abstract of Neau's Complaints, 6 Dec. 1715: S.P.G. Journals, iii (L.C. transcripts).   [38] Dix, p. 180.

of the population, they would always dominate juries, and on issues directly involving the Church Anglicans could never obtain a fair hearing. In vitriolic terms he attacked Hunter for not vetoing the Act and urged the Society to bring pressure on the Board of Trade to disallow it. This they did, but the Board finally decided to let the Act pass.[39]

The Poyer case, the negro uprising, the 'King's Farm', the desecration of Trinity Church, and the Quaker Affirmation Act—these were the sources of conflict between Governor Hunter and the Anglican clergy of New York and New Jersey. By 1714, the last year of Queen Anne's reign, it was clear that Vesey and the Anglican Church had Hunter in trouble, both in the colony and in England. Vesey had got an additional instruction to the governor about clerical appeals, he had so far blocked the work of Neau and Hunter in educating negro slaves, and he had succeeded in getting the Society's recommendation for the disallowance of the New Jersey Act allowing Quakers to serve in office without taking an oath. All this he had managed by making the most of the weapons at the clergy's disposal. Vesey and the Anglican ministers had written to their individual friends in the S.P.G. (the Archbishop of York in particular, in addition to the Bishop of London and Lord Cornbury), and through them had put favourable evidence before the Society, had won favourable committee appointments and subsequent recommendations, and had created the image of a persecuted church in danger. Cornbury, the Bishop of London, and the Archbishops of York and Canterbury were also influential in the Privy Council and the Board of Trade, where the governors' instructions were prepared; they also knew Queen Anne. In addition to corresponding with prominent officials, Vesey and his friends had sent petitions signed by a number of clergy; they had, moreover, sent over copies of the Reverend Jacob Henderson's vitriolic pamphlet attack on

---

[39] Pennington, pp. 55–7, and John Talbot, Andrew Sandel, Francis Phillips, and John Humphreys to Nicholson, 11 May 1714, ibid., pp. 129–32. The Society petitioned Queen Anne for repeal of the Act: Nelson, 'Anglican Missions', p. 396, n. 35. The petition from the Churchwardens and Vestry at Burlington to the S.P.G., 25 March 1714, is in Hills, *The Church in Burlington*, pp. 110–13. The Anglicans in Burlington also objected to Hunter allowing a Quaker schoolmaster to teach there in competition with the Anglican teachers. See, e.g., Rowland Ellis to Sec., S.P.G., 20 May 1714, ibid., pp. 114–16.

Hunter in 1712.[40] As a last but very effective resort, they made a series of personal trips to England. Henderson, a missionary at Dover familiar with Church politics in New York, went over in 1713, Vesey in 1715, Daniel Coxe, the lay leader of Talbot's congregation at Burlington, in 1716, and in the following year Talbot himself. From 1712 to 1717 there was thus always in England an articulate opponent of the governor, though this advantage was offset by the fact that by going over in series the clergy and lay leaders could never concentrate their attack, and no one of them had enough influence singly to do Hunter serious harm.

But Hunter was hardly one to suffer clerical opposition without fighting back. One of the most astute politicians in the colony's history, the governor used all his resources to counteract Vesey's influence. In Trinity Church itself, at inter-colonial meetings of the clergy, in the S.P.G., and even with the Queen he opposed Vesey with every resource at his disposal. Far more subtle a politician than Bellomont, who had united the Anglican Church against him by attending the Dutch church, Hunter was careful to give Vesey no opportunity to charge him with hostility to the Anglican Church as a whole. Instead, he sought to win over part of that Church against Vesey. Very early he allied himself with Lewis Morris, the leading Anglican politician who became Hunter's manager in the New York and New Jersey Assemblies and who also, as an active member of the S.P.G., wrote letters to the S.P.G. on Hunter's behalf. Since the governor also early ranged himself on non-religious grounds with the proprietary interest in New Jersey and the Leislerian faction in New York, both of which Morris supported, it could be argued that Hunter's alliance with Morris was an inevitable one—that the Leislerian Morris would have opposed the anti-Leislerian Vesey in any event. But Hunter then won over a far more surprising convert, Caleb Heathcote, Tory politician, originally an anti-Leislerian and along with Morris the other leading S.P.G. member in the colony.[41] Heathcote appeared to

---

[40] Henderson's 'State of the Church of England in New York and New Jersey' (2 June 1712) is in *Eccles. Recs. N.Y.* iii. 1950–1, along with 'Remarks on the Reverend Mr. Henderson's State of the Church of England, etc.', 17 June 1712, ibid. 1951–3.

[41] Talbot had called Heathcote 'the finest Gentleman I have seen in America', and added 'I wish the report were true that he were appointed Governor it would be the best news next to that of the Gospel that ever came over' (Talbot to Sec., S.P.G., 10 Jan. 1707/8, Pennington, p. 117). Heathcote had originally

the S.P.G. a far more impartial observer than Morris; he regularly wrote at great length to the Society about Anglican affairs in the colony. Almost certainly Heathcote did more than any other individual to keep the Society from making even harsher recommendations against Hunter than it did.

Hunter himself did the best he could to see that the S.P.G. got his side of the disputes by writing them constant accounts of New York affairs. Frequently he urged the need for an American bishop; he pressed his friend Dean Swift for the job, and took charge of purchasing a mansion at Burlington for the future prelate.[42] Indeed, on the question of an American bishop, Hunter was on considerably stronger ground than Vesey and he made the most of it. Vesey was hoping to be made Commissary of the Bishop of London, a position that would be redundant if an American bishop were appointed. Hunter personally thought that the sending of an American bishop—particularly Swift—as Vesey's superior would be greatly to his own advantage; like many of his contemporaries, he wanted a bishop in the colonies less because of the administrative functions he would perform than for his potential as arbitrator of disputes within the Church. In Hunter's eyes, Vesey could never have been the effective political opponent that he was if a bishop had been on the spot to keep local disputes in hand.

In other ways Hunter was able to undermine the Anglican Church. In 1712 Talbot and Vesey called a voluntary meeting of the Anglican clergy of New York and New Jersey at Burlington to discuss common problems, and possibly even to circulate a petition against Hunter. But Hunter, acting on his authority as governor, took the occasion to summon a rival meeting in New York a few days earlier, so that only three clergymen were able to attend Henderson and Vesey. The two men protested in outrage to the S.P.G. but could do nothing more.[43] Even closer to home, Hunter was particularly successful

recommended Vesey's appointment to Governor Fletcher (Fox, p. 10). For Heathcote's letters to the Society on Hunter's behalf, see *Eccles. Recs. N.Y.* iii. 1899–1906, and Minutes of the S.P.G., 10 Oct. 1712, nos. 33–5 and June 1714, no. 1: S.P.G. Journals, ii (L.C. transcripts).

[42] Fiore, art. cit.

[43] John Talbot and Thomas Haliday to the Clergy assembled at New York, n.d., Pennington, p. 126; Poyer to S.P.G., 7 March 1712/13, and Clergy of New York and Pa. to same, 30 March 1713, in Minutes of the S.P.G., 4 Sept. 1713, nos. 9, 11: S.P.G. Journals, ii (L.C. transcripts).

in dividing Vesey's own congregation in New York City by rebuilding the chapel in the fort, which had fallen into disuse, and holding public services conducted by the King's chaplain, the Revd. John Sharpe, a friend of the governor. By charging lower rates for pews in the refurbished chapel, Hunter and Sharpe were able to attract many of Vesey's parishioners away from him.[44]

And so from New York all the way to London the quarrels resounded between the governor and his Anglican opponents, Hunter and Vesey each trying to get the other removed from his position, each claiming to be the defender of the Anglican Church against the political machinations of the other. Hunter had played his cards well, but so had Vesey, and down to 1714 Vesey had the upper hand. In that year the change began.

In 1714 Queen Anne died. The significance of the Queen's death for New York was not so much that with the Queen died the movement for an American bishop: if anything, Vesey, not Hunter, probably gained from this. Rather was the Queen's death important for a number of other reasons. First, with the shattering of Anne's Tory ministry and the return of the Whigs to power, Francis Nicholson, Vesey's ally, was put in a temporary eclipse, robbing Vesey of Nicholson's English connections and Nicholson of hopes of the governorship. Moreover, the new Whig ministry briefly brought in Hunter's friend, Joseph Addison, as Secretary of State, and set up a Board of Trade that Hunter could count on to resist pressure from the S.P.G. for disallowance of certain favourable laws or for the drafting of unfavourable instructions. William Popple, Secretary to the Commissioners of Trade, in fact assured Hunter that he had little to fear from either the Bishop of London or the S.P.G.[45] The fact also that a wing of the old Tory party joined the rebellion against the new Hanoverian monarchs in 1715 made it easy to apply the charge of Jacobitism to some of the Anglican colonial leaders with Tory connections, and

[44] See E. B. Greene, 'The Anglican Outlook on the American Colonies in the early Eighteenth Century', *American Hist. Rev.* xx (1914–15), 75.

[45] For Hunter's reassurances, see Popple to Hunter, 16 April 1716, *Eccles. Recs. N.Y.* iii. 2107; Lords of Trade to Hunter, 22 March 1715/16, *N.J. Col. Docs.* iv. 227–8; Minutes of the Board of Trade, 30 Aug. 1717, *Journal of the Commissioners for Trade and Plantations from March 1714/15 to October 1718* (1924), p. 263.

Hunter was quick to make such a charge against Talbot and Vesey.[46]

To some extent these advantages to Hunter were offset by the fact that just before Queen Anne's death Henry Compton, the old Bishop of London, had died, and was succeeded by a new bishop considerably more hostile to Hunter than Compton had been. But with Vesey's political allies in eclipse the new bishop, while personally supporting Vesey as strongly as he could, was hesitant to encourage him to engage in political activity. And the S.P.G. itself, though the membership remained essentially unchanged, seems to have become increasingly reluctant to take action in New York affairs.

Gradually a stalemate set in, and the friction between Hunter and the Anglican leaders began to die down. At first, however, neither side realized the full implications of the English change. In 1715 Vesey went to England to present his case against Hunter to the S.P.G. and the Bishop of London. The Society, after some consideration, decided they could do nothing, since Vesey was not one of their missionaries.[47] Soon after this, however, he was appointed Commissary to the Bishop of London, an appointment which gave him nominal leadership over the other clergy in New York with power to convene meetings of the clergy and supervise clerical discipline.

Vesey thus returned to New York with the bishop's recognition as head of the church there. But there was still trouble ahead, for an illness he had contracted in England had delayed his return home longer than he or the vestry of New York City had expected. Seizing the opportunity to embarrass the new commissary, the vestry refused to pay his back salary, protesting at the length of his absence and demanding to know the reason for his making the journey in the first place. Vesey explained his illness but angrily refused to reveal the reasons for his trip. He claimed that to do so would be to divulge private concerns of the Anglican Church; clearly he did not want to admit to a

46 Pennington, p. 58. See also Talbot to Sec., S.P.G., 1 Oct. 1715, ibid., pp. 137–8; Hunter to Popple, 9 Nov. 1715, *N.J. Col. Docs.* iv. 219–20. Cf. also J. Bass to S.P.G., 6 Oct. 1715; Hunter to S.P.G., 9 April 1715; Minutes of S.P.G., 19 Oct. 1715, no. 5; Talbot to S.P.G., 1 Oct. 1715: S.P.G. Minutes, iii (L.C. transcripts).

47 Minutes of S.P.G., 21 Sept. 1716, no. 2: S.P.G. Journals, iii (L.C. transcripts).

group of the governor's friends that he had gone over to unseat the governor. Hunter, on instructions from the King, ordered the vestry to pay Vesey's salary; the vestry refused for several meetings to bring the subject up. Finally, in August 1716, it gave in and paid Vesey his salary.[48]

The salary controversy was, in a sense, a real turning-point in Hunter's relations with the Anglican Church. For it marked the first occasion of open co-operation between the governor and the commissary. The occasion was not chance: from this time on the open enmity between the two men died down. Each man realized that an impasse had been reached and that there was little worth doing to strengthen his position *vis-à-vis* the other. To Hunter it was clear that he had no chance now—if, indeed, he had ever had—to undermine Vesey with the S.P.G. and the Bishop of London. Despite Hunter's defence of Elias Neau, the Society dismissed him from their pay-roll;[49] despite Hunter's offer to finance Poyer's trial and see that he had a fair one locally, the Society financed Poyer's case itself and asked the Board of Trade to see whether Queen Anne's Additional Instruction to Hunter about ecclesiastical appeals had been renewed by the new monarch.[50] Before this time Hunter had hoped to bring the Bishop of London to his side; now, he spoke bitterly of 'knowing the cause of the Bishop's spleen',[51] and gave up hope of winning the bishop over. Before this time he had also counted on winning a majority in the divided S.P.G. and had written for them his own interpretation of every New York ecclesiastical controversy; now his letters to the Society tapered off.[52] Hunter was in fact so disgusted with the S.P.G. that when, later on, he finally returned to England and two members of the Society called to inquire why he had not paid

[48] W. Berrian, *An Historical Sketch of Trinity Church, New York* (New York, 1847), Appendix E.
[49] Minutes of S.P.G., 7 March 1716/17, nos. 11, 12: S.P.G. Journals, iii (L.C. transcripts).
[50] Poyer to S.P.G., 24 Oct. 1717, S.P.G. Journals, iii (L.C. transcripts); Minutes of S.P.G., 18 March 1714/15, no. 3; 7 April 1715, no. 1; 22 Nov. 1716, 20 Sept. 1717, nos. 9, 36; 18 Oct. 1717, no. 10; 1 May 1719, no. 15; 11 June 1720, no. 8; 17 Feb. 1720/1, no. 6; 15 June 1722, no. 21: S.P.G. Journals, iii and iv (L.C. transcripts).
[51] Hunter to Popple, 9 Nov. 1715, *N.J. Col. Docs.* iv. 219–20.
[52] According to the Society's minutes, Hunter's last letter to them was read on 13 Feb. 1717/18 (no. 14): S.P.G. Journals, iv (L.C. transcripts).

his arrears of dues, they received the reply that Hunter had no intention of paying dues or of ever having anything to do with the Society again.[53]

If Hunter was convinced that particular English religious leaders had made up their minds irrevocably in favour of Vesey, Vesey himself was convinced that Hunter was so strongly in favour with the English political authorities that his own friends could not bring the governor down. To a friend Hunter wrote, 'The Commissary here is the humblest clergyman and warmest Whig all of a sudden.'[54] The Board of Trade allowed Hunter to remove some of Talbot's leading parishioners from the Council of New Jersey; they also allowed him to turn Daniel Coxe, his leading Anglican opponent in New Jersey, out of the New Jersey Assembly, thus creating a majority for the governor there, and when Coxe took his case to England he was welcomed into the S.P.G.[55] (supported, naturally enough, by Cornbury and Nicholson), but got nowhere with the British government. Hunter was now able to settle some long-standing disputes with the New York Assembly and, in fact, gave every appearance of being so strongly entrenched politically that no amount of opposition within the church could bring him down.

Both Hunter and Vesey thus realized that an impasse had been reached in local ecclesiastical affairs; as a result, the second half of Hunter's administration was markedly different from the first. For the remaining five years of Hunter's government there was a superficial peace as both men consciously disregarded opportunities to attack each other. Having met the clergy nearly every year before 1715, Vesey now abruptly stopped arranging such meetings where he might have embarrassed the governor; Hunter appointed Vesey's assistant to be chaplain of the fort and hence minister of the congregation he himself had won away from Vesey. Hunter even returned to Trinity Church himself.[56] Vesey acquiesced in Elias Neau's reinstatement as catechist; Hunter's leading supporter, Chief Justice Lewis Morris, listened favourably to Poyer's case in Jamaica. The constant co-operation and compromise between

[53] Minutes of the S.P.G., 11 June 1720, no. 7.
[54] Hunter to Ambrose Phillips, 29 May 1716, *N.J. Col. Docs.* iv. 254. Hunter wrote in a similar vein to the Lords of Trade, 30 April 1716, ibid. v. 477.
[55] Minutes of S.P.G., 1 Feb. 1716/17, no. 1.
[56] Dix, p. 195.

the governor and the commissary in the second half of Hunter's administration were an astonishing contrast with the continuous friction of the first half.

The Anglican opposition to Governor Hunter was far from being a unique phenomenon in eighteenth-century colonial history: what was unusual, indeed, was the fact that Hunter ultimately did become reconciled with the Anglican leaders. In colony after colony royal governors ran up against the powerful opposition of the Anglican Church, and in colony after colony many of the issues at stake, and the methods used by both sides, were the same. Governors compelled by political exigencies to compromise with strong Dissenting minorities—or even majorities—on questions involving, for example, control of the schools or financial support of the clergy faced Anglican ministers who honestly thought the governors were betraying the national church. In colony after colony, the governor's relations with the commissaries were ill defined because of the governor's ambiguous position as head of the church in the colony. Questions about who, if anyone, had sole authority to convene the clergy remained unsettled throughout the colonial period. Most important, the church, as the single most effective type of organization in early eighteenth-century America, was inevitably drawn into politics by political leaders looking for organizational support, and local politicians opposing royal governors were particularly solicitous for the support of the Church of England. In an age when it was still considered treason to oppose royal government systematically, politicians sought the support of the state church in order to demonstrate that local opposition to imperial governors did not constitute opposition to the Empire itself. Leislerians, anti-Leislerians, and their counterparts in other colonies sought allies in England by appealing against hostile governors to the leaders of the Anglican Church. And so, inevitably, the Church was sucked into political controversy.

From colony to colony the clergy used similar methods in their political appeals. Public prayers, political sermons (especially when the legislature was in session or an important trial was being held), entertainment of prominent vestrymen who were also provincial councillors, convocations of the clergy in order to petition home, letters to the S.P.G. and appeals to the

Bishop of London to block critical appointments, recommend disallowance of local legislation, or obtain royal instructions to the governor to show that he was losing favour at court: these were the weapons Vesey skilfully used and these were the weapons of many of his contemporaries. Local congregations, vestries, the S.P.G., and the Councils of the Bishops of London: these were the typical scenes of conflict between royal governors and their loyal opposition in the Church.

For in colony after colony the early eighteenth century was an age of transition for the church. Not yet at the end of the period of strong church–state ties that characterized the Reformation, not yet arrived at the secular political parties that characterize modern politics, the colonial church was both a descendant of the all-powerful state churches and the ancestor of the modern political party. Nowhere is that transition better illustrated than in Robert Hunter's relations with the church in New York.

IV

Fathers and Heretics in Eighteenth-century Leicester

AROUND St. Martin's, the principal church of Leicester, there stood in the eighteenth century buildings of local importance. To the west, separated from it by a narrow alley, was the magnificent half-timbered hall of the medieval guild of Corpus Christi, at this time used as the town hall. As far as the memory of man would go back, mayor, aldermen, and councilmen with their officers had resorted there to conduct their business. Since 1632 this hall had housed the not undistinguished collection of books which made up the town library, formerly kept in the church.[1] Besides the vicarage, there was also looking on to the churchyard the Wigston's Hospital, a sixteenth-century foundation belonging to the Duchy of Lancaster. This was ruled by two clerics, a master and a confrater.

By the end of the eighteenth century, notwithstanding the regular appointment of a library keeper,[2] the library was in sad disarray. In 1793 Alderman Mansfield's mayoral banquet had drawn so many guests that room had to be made to feed some of them in the library, by removing from their places many books, which lay about for years afterwards in a confused state. In 1802 Richard Weston, a resident given to literary pursuits, had a plan of publishing a historical account of the library, with suggestions for its reform. He was shocked that there had been no benefaction to it since 1743. He complained also that, within seven years of this date,

five [he mentions only four] gentlemen of eminence in the literary way, who lived adjoining to it, published the following volumes:

Thomas Carte, esq. son of the Rev. Samuel Carte, vicar of St Martin's; History of England, 4 vols. fol. 1747

[1] C. J. Billson, *Leicester Memoirs* (Leicester, 1924), p. 54.
[2] *Records of the Borough of Leicester*, vol. v, ed. G. A. Chinnery (Leicester, 1965), 180, 483.

Rev. John Jackson, Master of Wigston's Hospital; Chronology, 3 vols. 4to. 1750

Rev. William Tiffin, Confrater of Wigston's Hospital; a Treatise on Short Hand, 4to, 1751.

John-Gilbert Cooper, esq.; The Life of Socrates; 8vo. Letters concerning Taste; 8vo.

Notwithstanding all these gentlemen lived in or near the Church-yard, not one of their Works were deposited in it; nor, on a strict examination of the donations, and the Catalogue, can I find a single book from any of the Authors, either of the Town or County, though so many have been produced within the last century.[3]

There were other learned men who had lived around the churchyard. In the sixteenth century, that eminent puritan Thomas Sampson had been master of the hospital,[4] and in the seventeenth, William Chillingworth, author of *The Religion of Protestants*.[5] More recently, they were followed by the great Samuel Clarke, rector of St. James, Westminster, master from 1717 to 1729, author of the controversial *Scripture-Doctrine of the Trinity* (1712), from which more than one reading cleric set out on an intellectual journey to Unitarianism. 'I wish you joy of your new Master of Wigstons Hospital', wrote one of the vicar's friends to him on Clarke's appointment; 'As you say, I know no other Objection against him, but his principle concerning the Trinity: & that indeed methinks should have been enough to any person who has true principles of Religion in him.'[6]

Around the churchyard, three points of view were represented in the early years of the century by Thomas Carte, Samuel Carte, and John Jackson.

Thomas Carte Esquire of Weston's list was a non-juring priest, who since 1714 had lived mostly as a layman, but occasionally still officiated as a cleric. A notorious Jacobite, he was probably not a dangerous one. About 1722, for a short time, he served Bishop Atterbury as a secretary, and after 1722, after

---

[3] John Nichols, *History and Antiquities of the County of Leicester*, vol. i (1795), 509 sqq. Weston's bibliographical information is not quite accurate. For J. G. Cooper, see *D.N.B.*

[4] *V.C.H. Leicestershire*, iv (1958), 400–1.   [5] Ibid., p. 402.

[6] Bodl., MS. Carte 244, fo. 115, Montagu Wood to S. Carte, 20 March 1717/18. Wood was rector of St. Michael Royal and St. Martin Vintry in the City of London, and Canon of Wells. All dates in this chapter are given in Old Style, the year, however, beginning on 1 Jan.

Atterbury's exile, he lived abroad, with a price on his head, under an alias. In 1721, before his flight to France, he was in Oxford a good deal, from time to time making excursions to London to visit the Harleian collection.[7] There he may well have met John Ludlam, alderman of Leicester, brother of Sir George, who in 1718 had been chamberlain of London.[8]

Newly come up to Oxford in 1721 was Thomas Secker, later bishop of Oxford and archbishop of Canterbury, and as an older man a pillar of orthodoxy, and a most respectable Whig. He had only recently conformed to the Church of England. Under the patronage of that William Talbot who as bishop of Oxford had preached George I's coronation sermon, he was now proceeding quickly from his Leyden doctorate of medicine to an Oxford degree, as a preliminary to setting his foot on the ladder of church promotions. None the less Secker, in Oxford, was often in Jacobitish company. With Thomas Carte and John Jebb, another non-juring cleric, Sir John St. Aubyn of his college of Exeter,[9] and Dr. King of Cambridge,[10] he 'often drank the Duke of Ormond's Health. but never the Pretender's, nor ever heard them propose it. Yet their meaning seemed intelligible.'[11]

Carte was a learned man who in 1739 avowed to Sir Robert Walpole that his only desire was to lead a studious life, untroubled by worldly excitements. Living mostly abroad, as he wrote, 'I . . . never made a Journey but once a year to see my father, industriously avoiding all other visits to my friends in all other parts of the Kingdom, that I might not give any umbrage to the state.'[12] Quite indifferent to preferment, he placed no reliance on the friendship of mankind. As he told Mr. Buckley, 'when . . . he kept me up 2 nights till 3 o clock in the morning teazing me to accept of the Deanery of Windsor, and the rest of Lord Wiloughby Brooks preferments', 'a man could have no solid or sure foundation of happiness but in his own breast.'[13]

[7] *Diary of Humfrey Wanley, 1715–26*, ed. C. E. and R. C. Wright (2 vols., Bibliographical Society, 1966), i. 100, 117.

[8] Ibid., pp. 100, 456.

[9] M.P. for Cornwall, 1722–44; for his Jacobitism, see *The History of Parliament: The House of Commons 1715–1754*, ed. Romney Sedgwick (2 vols., 1970), ii. 401–2.

[10] John King, Fellow of King's College.

[11] Lambeth MS. 2598, Autobiography of Archbishop Secker, fo. 12. I am grateful for the permission of His Grace the Archbishop of Canterbury to quote from this manuscript, of which I hope soon to publish an edition.

[12] B.M., Add. MS. 34522, fo. 4ᵛ. [13] Ibid., fo. 3.

Carte's conversation of 1739 with Sir Robert was an odd one. He had believed that it was at Sir Robert's instigation that he was sent to Rome to see the Pretender, chiefly to ascertain the Pretender's attitude to the Church of England. He told Sir Robert what he had told the Pretender, that the clergy would be pleased to have episcopal elections made more real by the removal of the threat of *Praemunire*: that the Archbishop of Canterbury should be confined to his proper powers, and not any longer exercise a power of deprivation of other bishops which was derived from the legatine commissions of pre-Reformation archbishops; that the colleges in the universities should be left to the jurisdiction of their own Visitors; that there should be a revival of provincial and diocesan synods; and that there should be restored to the clergy that power of taxing themselves which they had so foolishly surrendered soon after the restoration of King Charles II.[14] All this made an interesting programme of reform, and such no doubt as prelates like Edmund Gibson might in their hearts in some points wish to see. It was hardly practicable when Dr. Codex aroused such opposition, and so soon after he had been dropped as episcopal pilot by Walpole. Carte believed that Walpole had some serious interest in the restoration of the Pretender. In this, he was more gullible than the Pretender was, who for years had warned his friends in England that Walpole might pretend to be a friend, as a device to get information. Walpole indeed in 1739 sounded Carte about what was happening abroad and 'any design that might be formed of invading England with a foreign force'. This service Carte declined.[15] He remained to the end loyal to the Stuart cause. James III was rightly informed that he was honest, 'but very indiscreet'.[16]

During the next ten years Carte was a good deal in England. He was particularly busy not merely writing his *History*, but with collecting subscriptions for it, through a society formed for that purpose. In 1738 he began by a printed appeal to urge

[14] B.M., Add. MS. 34522, fos. 5^v–6^v.
[15] Ibid., fo. 2.
[16] Windsor, Royal Archives, Stuart Papers 151/32, 45, for the reference to Carte, ibid. 238/28. I owe these references to Dame Lucy Sutherland: they are used by gracious permission of Her Majesty the Queen. Dr. G. V. Bennett's forthcoming paper on Walpole's dealings with the Jacobites will put these transactions in perspective.

the necessity for a really scholarly *General History of England* and, apparently unsuccessfully, appealed to the Duke of Newcastle for aid.[17] Not until nearly six years later was the Society for Carte's *History* launched, with the Tory Duke of Beaufort as president. Carte sought help from his college of Brasenose. He begged the support of the Duke of Rutland with Henry Pelham and the Treasury Board in getting access to the public records.[18] In 1744 and 1745 subscribers included Edward Gibbon, Arthur Onslow, and Sir William Calvert,[19] than whom no persons more whiggish could be desired. Horace Walpole decried the City of London for subscribing—'who, from long dictating to the government, are now come to preside over taste and letters'. They 'have given one Carte, a Jacobite parson, fifty pounds a year for seven years, to write the history of England; and four aldermen and six Common Council men are to inspect his materials and the progress of the work. Surveyors of common sewers turned supervisors of literature!'[20]

When the *History* came out, three volumes between 1747 and 1752, and a fourth in 1755 after Carte's death, it was found to be anything but whiggish. It was denounced as altogether too royalist, and for including a defence of the superstitious practice of touching for the king's evil. It was calculated to uphold divine hereditary right, and to bolster up discredited patriarchal theories of political authority. It took a somewhat critical view of the Reformation. Samuel Squire, a Cambridge man of some learning, later chaplain to the future George III as Prince of Wales and in 1761 Bishop of St. David's, denounced it in 1748, warning a young man against its dangerous doctrines, and condemning the too favourable view taken of the ancient Druids as an indirect high church stratagem for promoting the

[17] B.M., Add. MS. 32691, fo. 382, T. Carte to the Duke of Newcastle, 28 Sept. 1738; *Proposal for removing the Impediments of writing an History of England*, 4 March 1736/7, printed circular, in MS. Carte 240, fo. 241.

[18] MS. Carte 175, Minutes of the Society for Promoting Carte's History, fos. 6, 10. The first meeting was 14 Feb. 1744/5.

[19] Ibid., fos. 61–2.

[20] *Yale Edition of Horace Walpole's Correspondence*, ed. W. S. Lewis, xviii (1955), 480, 22 July 1744. The subscribers to the deed of foundation (MS. Carte 175, fo. 105, and mentioned in vol. i of the *History*) included the University of Oxford New College, Brasenose, Magdalen, Lincoln, and Trinity Colleges (not, be it noted, Whig centres like Merton, Christ Church, or Exeter); the City of London, and the Grocers, Goldsmiths, and Vintners.

influence in society and government of episcopally ordained clerics.[21]

The historian's parent, Samuel Carte, essentially a seventeenth-century man, his mind formed in the later years of Charles II, was in the prime of manhood, aged thirty-three, at the time of the Revolution, when, said the Leicester dissenter William Gardiner, 'happily, William [of Orange] brought with him a little common sense, and some Presbyterian sobriety'.[22] A Tory cleric, in a Tory town, Samuel Carte may well have been the Leicester parson who after the Jacobite defeat at Preston spread the tale that a few army officers stationed at Leicester had drunk confusion and destruction to all the clergy of the Church of England. When a local gentleman told him that he should recant or be prosecuted, 'the parson bid [him] do his worst; it was dangerous to meddle with the clergy and would only turn to his own damage in the end. "Don't you know," says he, "what they got that prosecuted Dr Sacheverell?" '[23] Sobriety of the Presbyterian sort was not to Samuel Carte's taste. There was not much difference between the ideas of father and son, except that the elder man accepted George I as king, and the younger, who had accepted Anne as queen, rejected him. Samuel Carte represented the old Caroline divinity and civil ethics. In the later years of William III, in 1694, he had preached and published a sermon, *A Dissuasive from Murmuring, directed against contemners of the Revolution*, but was to find much to murmur about at the Hanover succession, and after it in the behaviour of his neighbour in the churchyard, John Jackson, who was made confrater of Wigston's Hospital in 1719, and master in 1729.

Practically everything about John Jackson, but not quite everything, was calculated to make him obnoxious to the Cartes, father and son, to the Tories of the Corporation of Leicester, to the Tory gentlemen of Leicestershire.

Like the celebrated divine under whom he served as confrater, and whom he was to succeed as master, the *avant-garde*

[21] [S. Squire], *Remarks upon Mr. Carte's Specimen of his General History of England: very proper to be read by all such as are Contributors to that great Work. In a Letter to a Friend* (1748), pp. 12–16.   [22] W. Gardiner, *Music and Friends* (1838), ii. 532.
[23] *The Diary of Dudley Ryder 1715–1716*, ed. W. Matthews (1939), p. 152, 19 Dec. 1715.

philosopher and theologian Samuel Clarke, he was imposed on the local community from outside. Clarke and Jackson represented the new theology, which at this time attracted the young Secker.[24] Clarke, with Isaac Newton and John Locke, was counted by the even more celebrated Benjamin Hoadly as an apostle of modern illumination, dissipating scholasticism, mystery-mongering, and priestcraft.[25] Clarke and Jackson, moreover, arrived at Leicester at a particularly delicate time, Clarke as master in 1718, Jackson as confrater in 1719. Quite apart from quarrels amongst the ruling Whigs, there was still much argument about the views expressed by Hoadly in his sermon before the King in March 1717, aimed at the high church clergy, dangerous to the existing church establishment, destructive of ecclesiastical authority, and subversive of orthodoxy, even of that orthodoxy common to the Church of England and the orthodox dissenters. Hoadly's performances, to men of Carte's mind, suggested designs on the part of Government towards the Church every bit as bad as anything attributed to them in the *English Advices to the freeholders* of England.

Samuel Clarke's book on the Trinity, and rumours of liturgical deviations in his church of St. James, Westminster, made his appointment to the mastership specially alarming. The nomination of Jackson, at Clarke's instance, by Lord Lechmere the Chancellor of the Duchy (a manager of Sacheverell's impeachment) was objectionable also, in that he was forced upon the town, in opposition to a local candidate. The confratership, wrote Clarke to Jackson on 28 May 1719, had been 'much pressed by all the Persons of Quality in that Country, for a Gentleman of the Neighbourhood, nevertheless he has taken a Week's Time to consider, and I incline to think, I shall prevail for you'; and then, several weeks later (2 July 1719), 'I wish you heartily Joy of the Chancellor's Courage in appointing you my Confrater, in opposition to all the Interest in the World.'[26] It was not merely master and confrater at the hospital. It was master and disciple too, with the disciple less temporizing, more vigorously controversial than the master.

[24] Lambeth MS. 2598, fo. 6.
[25] *The Works of Benjamin Hoadly*, ed. J. Hoadly (1773), i, pp. l–liii.
[26] *Memoirs of the Life and Writings of the late Reverend Mr. John Jackson* (1764), pp. 52–4.

There was yet a third ground of annoyance. Samuel Clarke, like most of his predecessors, was generally not resident at the hospital. Jackson, both as confrater and as master, was there all the time. He made the hospital his usual residence, the base for visits to his other preferments or to take the cure at Bath. Alone among the eighteenth-century masters in residing at the hospital, he kept the buildings repaired. In 1751 and 1755 he increased the allowances of his poor.[27]

There was hardly a controversy in which Jackson did not take part. He was numbered among the defenders of Hoadly. He wrote philosophically in defence of free will against moral determinists—this thought by some to be his best work.[28] He attacked Conyers Middleton's contentions that there were no 'ecclesiastical' miracles, and that miracles ended with the Apostles.[29] He contended against deists, upholding amongst other things the supreme miracle of the Resurrection.[30] He rejected Warburton's opinion that there was amongst the Jews in the time of Moses belief neither in life after death nor in rewards and punishments beyond the grave.[31] Of much of this the Cartes, father and son, must have approved.

Jackson offended in his theology of the Trinity, in his doctrinal view of the Church, and in his politics.

Jackson came to Leicester as Clarke's disciple. He remained his disciple to the end. Clarke had argued, and Jackson agreed, that there was no warrant in Scripture for all the doctrinal language used in the Nicene and Athanasian creeds, and certainly not for that language as commonly understood.[32] The various Acts of Parliament governing the holding of office by the clergy, which called for subscription to the Prayer Book and Thirty-nine Articles, did not extend to offices like the mastership and confratership of the hospital, which consequently became the more attractive to Jackson as he became in conscience

---

[27] *V.C.H. Leics.* iv. 403.

[28] *A Defense of Human Liberty, in Answer to the Principal Arguments which have been alledged against it* (1725).

[29] *Remarks on Dr. Middleton's Free Enquiry* (2nd edn., 1749).

[30] Amongst others, *An Address to Deists* (1744).

[31] *The Belief of a Future State Proved to be a Fundamental Article of the Religion of the Hebrews* (1745).

[32] R. N. Stromberg, *Religious Liberalism in Eighteenth-Century England* (Oxford, 1954), ch. iv, 'Arians and Socinians', succinctly sets out the issue.

increasingly unable to profess the Athanasian creed. As the controversy developed, the arguments turned more and more upon this formulary. For Clarke and Jackson its language was unscriptural. It involved metaphysical terms which were generally misunderstood.

To Jackson the chief defender of the Athanasian creed, Daniel Waterland, the learned Chancellor of the cathedral at York, Master of Magdalene College, Cambridge, and Archdeacon of Middlesex as well, was a heretic. Jackson's most serious work of ecclesiastical scholarship was the *Novatiani Presbyteri Romani Opera*, published first in 1728.[33] Novatian's peculiar and rigorous views about ecclesiastical discipline did not so much interest him as the clarity with which his author's work on the Trinity emphasized the subordination of the Son to the Father, in contrast with the tritheism (as he saw it) which Waterland presented as orthodoxy.[34] Thus this third-century Roman schismatic provided ammunition for those in the eighteenth-century Church of England who urged that the Christology of the anti-Nicene Church was not 'Athanasian'. Men of this school not unnaturally found the *Quicunque vult* to be a late and unprimitive document. To rebut precisely these contentions, Waterland set out to show the biblical correctness and practical value of the Athanasian formularies, as he understood them, and above all to demonstrate their antiquity.[35]

Waterland's *Critical History of the Athanasian Creed* was first published in 1724. It is a work of the most elegant perspicuity of argument. Unlike anything else in this or any other of these controversies, it was succinct, concise, and not too long. Waterland argued for a date about A.D. 429 or 430 for the origin of the Athanasian creed, and suggested that it was Gaulish in provenance, probably the work of St. Hilary of Arles.[36] Waterland also vindicated its use in the Church of England as a bulwark against Arianism and the like, against the teachings of such as Clarke and Jackson. He was able to say that 'the wiser and more moderate Part of the *Dissenting Ministers* seem very

[33] Jackson's edition was esteemed by Harnack the best available to him.
[34] Cf. J. Jackson. *A Narrative of the Case of the Reverend Mr. Jackson Being refus'd the Sacrament of the Lord's Supper at Bath, by Dr. Coney Minister of Bath* (1736), pp. 4–6.
[35] D. Waterland, *The Importance of the Doctrine of the Holy Trinity Asserted, in Reply to some late Pamphlets* (1734), ch. ii.
[36] *A Critical History of the Athanasian Creed* (Cambridge, 1724), pp. 99–115, 117–23.

well reconciled to the *Damnatory* Clauses, *modestly expounded*'.[37] Waterland's book was greatly admired by Gabriel Newton, an opulent alderman of Leicester, who in founding charity schools cited it in support of his condition that no parish should benefit from his benevolence where the *Quicunque* was not recited as the rubric ordered.[38]

On the theological plane, a modern reader may well find Jackson in his way no less metaphysical than the subtle early Doctors of the Church whom he condemned. He also may suspect that, in different ways, he and Waterland were both right. Jackson often caught the biblical emphasis, and yet the later formulations (as Waterland put it) were necessary, 'in [their] whole design and end', 'to preserve the *Rule of Faith*, as contain'd in the holy *Scriptures*'.[39]

With a flourish, Jackson set out to discredit his antagonist. Four years before Waterland died, he produced in 1736 *Memoirs of the Life and Writings of Dr. Waterland, Being a Summary View of the Trinitarian Controversy For Twenty Years, between the Doctor and a Clergyman in the Country . . . by a Clergyman.* Waterland's biographer denounced this work as 'a tissue of the coarsest railing and invective'.[40] In a thoroughly Hoadleian fashion, Jackson, from the beginning, posed as the lover of freedom, anxious to rid the consciences of men from the burden of unwarrantable subscriptions founded only in human authority. In a very Protestant atmosphere, amongst a people who still harboured fears of popish designs against their liberties and religion, it was a useful if unfair device to present Waterland as a quasi-popish inquisitorial hierarch, who was attacking Christian liberty and private judgement:

reviving and claiming the Popish Authority of imposing mere humane Interpretations of Scripture, as fundamental Doctrines of Religion and Articles of Faith; . . . and also with an amazing Arrogance calling the Impiety of *Tritheism* and *Cerinthianism*, which are his profess'd Notion, *the Doctrine of the Church*; just as *Papists* call *Transubstantiation* and *Saint-Worship*, and other abominable Impieties, the Doctrine of Scripture . . . . there are Faggots ready, and

---

[37] Waterland, *Critical History*, p. 156.
[38] R. W. Greaves, *The Corporation of Leicester 1689–1836* (2nd edn., Leicester, 1970), p. 96.
[39] Waterland, *Critical History*, pp. 154–5.
[40] *The Works of . . . Daniel Waterland*, ed. W. van Mildert, i (1843), 3.

he has some *small Hopes* of the *Convocation's* being permitted by the Civil Power to sit and kindle them. . . . In the mean Time it wou'd but have been consistent for him to have cited the Country Clergyman before the Consistorial Court of the *Vatican*, or the holy Court of *Inquisition* in *Spain*, or *Portugal*, to answer for his *Scripture-Doctrine* and *Primitive Christianity*, against the *Dr*'s authoriz'd Interpretation . . . in such a Manner, as must make any Church cease to be *Christian*, that can be suppos'd to espouse it.[41]

This is perfectly Hoadleian, in content and in manner. To Hoadly, authority, especially spiritual authority backed by secular sanctions, was a root of all evil. Authority had killed Socrates, delivered Christ to crucifixion, loaded Christianity with medieval fopperies and superstitions, fought the reformation, obstructed 'the Beginnings of this *Church* of *England* itself: and which alone now contests with it the *Foundation* upon which it stands'.[42] That Foundation for Hoadly was Scripture alone, interpreted by private judgement.

Although at times John Jackson seemed to be quieter, and less troublesome to the vicar and his allies on the Corporation of Leicester,[43] the quiet was precarious. In 1721, and again in 1730, the orthodox of Leicester began proceedings against the local heresiarch.

Under a bequest of the Earl of Huntingdon, the great Elizabethan puritan and President of the Council of the North, who among his lesser offices served for a time as Lord Lieutenant of Leicestershire, a lecture was endowed, to be preached by the confrater of Wigston's Hospital on Sundays, and on Wednesdays and Fridays, in St. Martin's church. By an understanding with the parish and the corporation, the lecture was by convention given normally only on Sundays, usually in the afternoon. By the Act of Uniformity of 1662, all lecturers had before lecturing to read prayers, according to the authorized liturgy, and publicly and openly to declare their approval of everything in the Prayer Book; and this, not only at the first time of lecturing, but before the first lecture of every month.[44] This monthly assenting was bound to be disliked by Jackson, even if his master Clarke had

[41] [J. Jackson], *Memoirs of the Life and Writings of Dr. Waterland . . . By a Clergyman* (1736), pp. 100–2.　　[42] Hoadly, *Works*, ii. 571–2.
[43] MS. Carte 239, fo. 465, Wood to Carte, 8 Oct. 1720; fo. 484, 5 Nov. 1724.
[44] 14 Charles II, c. 4, 19.

done it and Clarke's *Scripture-Doctrine* seemed to suggest ways of equivocating subscription.[45] Jackson and others 'of his *Eusebian* Opinions, might as innocently sign *Athanasian* Articles, without being *Athanasians*; as Dr. *Waterland*, and the Church, without being *Calvinists*, do sign Calvinist Articles'.[46]

Edmund Gibson, Bishop of Lincoln, to whose court, and that of his archdeacon, Carte and his friends were taking their cause, had to walk circumspectly. The bishop probably wished a plague on both their houses. He shared the opinion of those whom he designated as Jackson's best friends: 'that he ought to content himself with declaring his sentiments concerning the points under dispute, in print, and not to trouble such a mix'd Congregation with any thing but plain practical doctrin; and so I verily believe they have told him.'[47] Gossip retailed might interest him, even inform him, but he had to observe legality. Carte reported that behind closed doors, not publicly and openly but in the hospital chapel, Jackson after service had closed the book and said, 'I here declare my assent & consent to these prayers & all contained in this book'—and this on Whitsunday, when he had unlawfully omitted both the Athanasian creed and the collect of the day.[48]

If Carte carried rumours to the bishop against Jackson, Jackson carried to the bishop rumours against Carte. Consequently the bishop inquired of Carte whether 'the person who is employ'd by you to read Prayers in the Church, has any singularities in his manner of reading the Prayers for the Royal Family? and, whether, when he Preaches, he prays for the King and Royal Family?'[49] Jackson, an experienced fighter, carried the war into the enemies' camp. In a tart letter he complained of the ill behaviour of Carte's daughter in church, grimacing and grinning behind the pulpit as he preached.[50] He demanded of Carte that he subscribe and declare every first Sunday. After all, Carte was quite certainly a lecturer within the meaning of the Act,[51] whereas Jackson had been advised he was not.

[45] MS. Carte 239, fo. 471, Wood to Carte, 3 June 1721.
[46] *Memoirs of . . . Jackson*, p. 70.
[47] MS. Carte 242, fo. 130, Edmund Gibson to Samuel Carte, 27 Aug. 1720.
[48] Ibid., fos. 135, 135ᵛ, Carte, draft to Gibson, 15 June 1720.
[49] Ibid., fos. 139–40, Gibson to Carte, 11 March 1720/1.
[50] Ibid., fo. 142, Jackson to Carte, 14 March 1720/1.
[51] Ibid., fo. 154, Jackson to Carte, 3 July 1721.

Jackson succeeded in persuading the bishop, and the bishop affected to believe that Carte also was persuaded, that 'Mr Jackson is ready to *subscribe* and *declare* on any occasion that he likes; and that if he decline reading Prayers (by going out of Town, &c,) it is not from any Scruple he has, but because he cares not to be *forc'd* to it'.[52] In the end, Gibson suggested that the two men should take turns in reading prayers in St. Martin's every first Sunday afternoon. To this they agreed.[53]

In 1729 Jackson was promoted by the Duke of Rutland, Chancellor of the Duchy of Lancaster, to succeed his old teacher Clarke as master of Wigston's Hospital. The new confrater, on whom the duties of lecturer would now fall, was Philip Hacket, already known in the town and no cause of uneasiness to the vicar. Nevertheless, Carte extracted from him a promise never to make the master his deputy as lecturer. Jackson, on the other hand, as master, claimed to control the preaching activities in St. Martin's of his confrater. He himself made an attempt to preach, but as he approached the pulpit its stair was filled with boys and he was told that somebody else was expecting to give the sermon.[54] He demanded in writing of Carte that he should hand over to him as master of the hospital the complete disposition of the Sunday afternoon lecture or sermon, to which Carte answered that his pulpit should be open to Mr. Hacket or any of his friends except Jackson, Whiston, and Woolston. As this answer was unsatisfactory, the master kept the confrater away from church and held a rival service at the hospital, ringing its chapel bell at the same time as the bells of the parish church. His service was attended by the poor of the hospital and some seven or eight of Carte's other parishioners. The public congregation waited in the church, while the clerk called out 'Mr. Philip Hackett, come & do your duty'.[55]

Carte busied himself in drafting letters laying his troubles before Gibson's successor at Lincoln, Bishop Reynolds. The churchwardens drew up a great petition to the Duke of Rutland

---

[52] Ibid., fo. 151, Gibson to Carte, 15 June 1721.

[53] Ibid., fos. 161, 161ᵛ, Gibson to Carte, 17 Nov. 1721. Gibson's concern was to avoid the scandal of proceedings in his courts being stopped by writ of prohibition, and a hearing, though a fair one, before temporal judges: this was the argument he used to Carte.

[54] *Memoirs of . . . Jackson*, pp. 101–2.   [55] MS. Carte 117, fos. 446–7, 448.

as Chancellor of the Duchy. They not only expatiated on Jackson's present unheard-of demand, but enlarged upon his bad conduct when preaching as confrater, in scandalizing the congregation with his heterodoxies.[56] The first signatory as churchwarden, perhaps the manager of the campaign, was that alderman of Leicester, Gabriel Newton, who had learned from Waterland's *History* that the Athanasian creed was 'the compleatest body of divinity ever composed since the time of the apostles, and a full answer to all heretical objections to the doctrines and tenets of the Church of England'.[57]

There seems to have been, from the silence of the local chroniclers, no more public confrontation after this. As early as 1722 Jackson's attitude to subscription had hardened. He was already almost resolved never to subscribe the Thirty-nine Articles again, urged by his friend William Whiston to avoid '*popish Equivocation and mental Reservation*', pressed by him to consider that 'Integrity is vastly preferable to Orthodoxy', and exhorted, in capital letters, to 'BE HONEST'. In 1738 he declined a prebend of Salisbury because the bishop, Hoadly of all people, insisted on subscription. The bishop maintained that all others had subscribed, though he would not say that the law required it.[58]

Among the papers contributed to *The Old Whig, or Consistent Protestant* were two of Jackson's minor publications, two essays, both dealing with religious liberty and subscription.[59] Inevitably, in the circumstances of the time, these religious differences had strong political flavour. In Leicester Jackson represented Hanoverianism and Whitehall, to gentlemen of town and countryside who liked neither. The theological opposition he met he put down to 'a long resentment of some Jacobites' against him.[60] The Tories of Leicester cannot have been pleased when Jackson went to the camp of Colonel Churchill's regiment of dragoons there in 1723 to preach on the duty of subjects to their governors. In his discourse he emphasized, after the manner of Locke, that under the providential ordering of

[56] MS. Carte 117, fo. 457. [57] *V.C.H. Leics.* iv. 333–4.
[58] *Memoirs of . . . Jackson*, pp. 74–5, 76–7.
[59] Ibid., pp. 198–9; *The Old Whig*, no. 33 (23 Oct. 1735), no. 39 (4 Dec. 1735).
[60] *Memoirs of . . . Jackson*, p. 65.

Almighty God 'Civil Power is *originally* founded in the Agreement and Consent of the People'. He praised King George I as the best of monarchs, and the situation of Church and State in England as the happiest in the world. In language which literally echoed Hoadly, the language of the party formula, he exhorted the troops before him: 'Let us lay aside all Prejudice, Party and Faction; exert the Spirit of our *British* Ancestors, and like *Christians*, like *Protestants*, like *Englishmen*, unite our Hearts and Hands to maintain and preserve those Laws on which our *Liberty* depends, and by which our *Church*, which was reform'd at the Expence of so much Blood, is establish'd.'[61]

Jackson's political theory and practice were alike in the fullest sense Whig. He was a Whig in church as well as state. In 1718, in one of the earliest defences of Hoadly's Bangorian positions, in an essay on *The Grounds of Civil and Ecclesiastical Government*, a volume in which he had the courage to take on the redoubtable William Law, he showed himself very much a consistent Protestant. He made a bow in the direction of religious rights and spiritual powers as intrinsically independent of the secular power, but made their exercise entirely subordinate to lay control.[62] Bishops and ministerial succession, even if originally apostolic, were in the modern age in his view matters of the merest expediency.[63] This defence of Hoadly won for Jackson in 1722 a prebend, not requiring subscription, in the gift of a Hampshire gentleman of Whig views and dissenting connections.[64]

In Leicester he was one of the Whig watchdogs, used by Government to keep an eye on suspiciously Tory areas and institutions. When in 1738 very curious treasonable papers were found posted about the town, Jackson rushed post-haste to London to inform the Secretary of State, the Duke of Newcastle, of the dangerously Jacobitical inclinations of the Corporation of Leicester. The mayor had not too much difficulty in disposing of these accusations.[65]

Carte died in 1740, Jackson in 1763. They were followed inevitably by rather different sorts of men, with somewhat

[61] *The Duty of Subjects towards their Governors* (1723), pp. 10, 27–8.
[62] J. Jackson, *The Grounds of Civil and Ecclesiastical Government briefly consider'd* (1718), p. 19.
[63] Ibid., pp. 20, 28.   [64] *Memoirs of . . . Jackson*, p. 86.
[65] *V.C.H. Leics.* iv. 125–6.

different preoccupations. In the second half of the century there were new issues to divide and agitate, in both religion and politics: of revolution, or at least radicalism, influenced by events abroad; and of evangelical enthusiasm, Calvinist and Arminian, among Christian teachers and disciples. Yet the questions which had so stirred these two men remained important in the political and religious life of nineteenth-century England, though in vastly changed circumstances. In the time of the Cartes and Jackson, they gave a certain substance to the idea of party, which was more potent locally than it could be, at that time, in Westminster and Whitehall.

V

English Commercial Negotiations with Austria, 1737–1752

THE diplomatic and financial aspects of English relations with Austria during the War of the Austrian Succession have been studied in some detail. This paper examines a further aspect which has been largely overlooked, the negotiations between 1737 and 1752 for treaties of commerce between the two powers.[1] Two areas, the Austrian Netherlands and the Austrian Hereditary Lands, were affected.[2] Although neither negotiation was successful, their history shows how such matters were handled, and illustrates both English and Austrian political and economic structures and attitudes at this time. It also provides further documentation of the gradual attrition of Anglo-Austrian friendship (an attrition largely due to extravagant expectations by each power of what it could get from the other), which pointed the way to the diplomatic revolution of 1756.

The immediate origin of the negotiations about the Austrian Netherlands which opened in 1737 was article 5 of the Treaty of Vienna of 1731.[3] This had revoked the Imperial Octroi in favour of the Ostend Company, established in 1722, and at the

[1] The major source for this paper is the series S[tate] P[apers] 80 Germany (Empire) in the Public Record Office. The volume numbers for the years 1739 to 1752 inclusive are S.P. 80/133–190. These volumes are not foliated. To save space I have grouped references, omitted them when the exact date of a dispatch is given in the text, and refrained from citing individual volume numbers. Dates given are New Style except where stated as O.S. (for Old Style). In both cases the year is treated as beginning on 1 Jan.

[2] England is used here to denote Great Britain, Holland to denote the United Provinces, and Austria to denote the Habsburg Monarchy. 'The Hereditary Lands' of the Monarchy usually meant its German territories, but sometimes included Hungary.

[3] The whole of this section is based on a report by Colonel Martin Bladen, enclosed in Lord Harrington's dispatch to Thomas Robinson of 31 Aug. O.S. 1739, and headed 'A short Recapitulation of the Matters which gave rise to the Conferences at Antwerp, and of the several Points discussed there, in the Years 1737, 1738 & 1739, with some Observations upon them'.

same time stipulated that within two months delegates from England, Holland, and Austria should meet, both to settle the plenary execution of the Barrier Treaty of 1715, and to make a new treaty about commerce, including the level of duties in the Austrian Netherlands. These were deliberately restricted subjects. The Polish Succession War then supervened, and representatives of the three powers only met, at the Town Hall in Antwerp, on 27 August 1737. Procedural difficulties caused further delays until December. More seriously, it soon became clear that the Austrians, while evading the Barrier issue, intended to use the conferences to renegotiate the entire structure of duties on goods traded between the three countries. On 31 May 1738 they presented a paper complaining that England charged the Flemings 50 per cent *ad valorem* on linens and other goods, while English merchants exporting to the Austrian Netherlands only paid 5½ per cent. This was contrary to the treaties of 1604 and 1630. On 2 September, without waiting for a reply, the Austrians completed their opening gambit by tabling the Preliminary Articles of a commercial treaty. This suggested the Anglo-Spanish treaty of 1630 as a basis for negotiations with England, and the treaties of Münster and The Hague of 1648 and 1650 for negotiations with the Dutch. It proposed mutual freedom of trade and navigation by land and sea between the three countries. As between England and Flanders there should be reciprocity, that is equality, of duties. The Flemings and Dutch should charge each other no more than their own subjects.

This initiative appears to have caught the English and Dutch off balance. They did not reply to it until December; and it was not until February 1739 that an English response appeared to the Austrian paper of the previous May, which had been referred to the Board of Trade and the Commissioners of Customs. The answer said that the treaties of 1604 and 1630 were incompatible with the Treaty of Münster, and had been superseded by that of 1667. After a ritual reminder that English import taxes were not really within the scope of the conferences, it argued that the Austrians had in any case mistakenly included the Two-Thirds subsidy in the amount payable, and by understating the price at which Austrian Netherlands linens sold in England, overstated the rate of duty. Further, these linens, if re-exported, were entitled to a drawback which reduced the tax, even on the Austrian figures, to less than 7 per cent. If the Flemings sent finer (and hence more expensive) linens to England they would pay proportionately less duty; the customs valuation was originally for coarse ones only, and had not been changed. If they did send finer linens, however, these would inevitably compete with those from Silesia.

Further Austrian replies merely restated the position taken. Colonel Martin Bladen, a commissioner of the Board of Trade, reflecting on the negotiations to this point, admitted that the Austrian Netherlands merchants paid far higher duties in England than English merchants did in the Austrian Netherlands. Moreover, he estimated the balance of trade between the two countries to be at least £160,000 a year in England's favour. But he foresaw great obstacles to making any concessions on the tariff. The English duties were appropriated to the service of the public debts. The Dutch paid the same rate in England as the Flemings, yet admitted English woollens at half the Flemish one. The domestic linens lobby in England, Ireland, and Scotland would oppose any reduction of duty on foreign linens. The only possible remedies were the freeing of Flanders tapestry, some relief on stuffs imported from the Austrian Netherlands for carpet manufacture, and an increase in the duty on German linens. The last, however, would inevitably hit Silesia: 'it will deserve mature Consideration . . . whether his Imperial Majesty, would not lose more by such an Alteration in Silesia, than he would gain by it in Flanders.'

The incompatibility of the Austrian and Anglo-Dutch negotiating positions at this stage is clear. The Austrians wished, by reducing taxes, to expand trade. The English and Dutch wished to retain the Austrian Netherlands as an economic colony, partly defended by Dutch garrisons paid for by Austria, the position reached in the Barrier Treaty of 1715. The Antwerp conferences therefore stagnated. Some echoes of the issues raised in them were heard at Vienna, where negotiations about trade with England began in the early summer of 1739. The English view was that these negotiations were quite distinct from those at Antwerp. Their scope, Secretary of State Lord Harrington informed the English ambassador Thomas Robinson on 8 May O.S. 1739, was not to extend to the trade of the Austrian

Netherlands. As late as 23 February 1743 Robinson reported to Carteret that he had not raised the latter's suggestion that Ostend might be made a free port, 'as the President of the Council of Flanders, Count Tarouca was for bringing in the Low Countries as a joint Object with the Rest of the Hereditary Countries, in our Commercial Negotiation'.

But the questions were connected, even if England insisted they were not, and this soon became clear at Vienna. On 17 June 1739, for example, James Porter, Harrington's special trade envoy, whose mission is discussed below, reported that Count Philip Kinsky, the powerful Chancellor of Bohemia, had told him how the Flemings pressed, in vain, for admission of their finer cloths to the Austrian market. On 6 February 1740, in conference with the Austrian commissioners for an English trade to Trieste, Robinson took care to point out that Silesia would be ruined if the Flemings' 'extraordinary Demands of Reciprocity [of duties with England] were met'. Kinsky accordingly requested a paper on Flanders and Silesia linens 'by which he may convince the Emperor of the clashing Interests of his several Provinces'. Schwandner, another of the commissioners, pointed out that the Flemings themselves were likely to be ruined if English woollens were admitted preferentially to the Austrian market as was proposed, 'to which Count P. Kinsky answered in the German Language, what do they do for us? and what is it the English do not for us?'[4] Porter claimed that no cloth from the Austrian Netherlands sold in Austria: it came from Liège and Aix. He reported nevertheless on 1 June 1740 that the Council of Flanders had sent to Vienna a memorial in Spanish, in which 'they humbly hoped they would have an equal Admission with any one else, for their Cloths and Stuffs in His Imperial Majesty's hereditary Dominions'.

Austria was in any case more than a little inclined to regard the Netherlands as a liability, not an asset. This was partly because of Anglo-Dutch unwillingness to permit economic expansion there. Count Philip Kinsky told Porter in June 1739

---

4 Robinson and Porter to Harrington, 10 Feb. 1740. In the appendix to Porter's dispatch of 31 March 1740 it is explained that the English duty on Silesia linens was originally for coarse ones only and hence much lower than that on Netherlands linens. The Silesian producers had subsequently developed finer linens, which were taxed at the old rate; and thus achieved an export breakthrough in the English market.

that 'we english were for having all advantages, and giving none, that in every tariff contested, we were for bringing everything to ourselves, and when they wanted a trade in the Netherlands, we were immediately for destroying it'. In March 1740 Robinson reported *Staatssekretär* Bartenstein's view that

he [Bartenstein] had drawn upon himself Enemies enough by abolishing the Ostend Company without having in any manner participated of the Price of that Cession by any ease whatever with respect to the Tarif, it was, he knew, in the Power of the Dutch to give those Countrys some Ease, he disapproved the chicaneing [*sic*] principles upon which the Flemish Comissaries had gone hitherto.

Similarly, a few days later Count Sinzendorf, the Austrian Chancellor, expressed to Robinson the opinion that, if the Ostend Company had been allowed even a limited trade, the Flemings would have borne the inequalities of the present tariff more easily.

But Austrian reservations about the Netherlands were also due to doubts of their strategic viability. Kinsky, pressed by the tactless Porter in one of their early interviews in June 1739, became warm and ran

into a series of politicians flights, recriminating from the treaty of Utrecht, which indeed he said had been so favourable to his Imperial Majesty, to leave Spain to the house of Bourbon, & the Netherlands to that of Austria; a noble exchange! to entail a burthen on us we scarce know what to do with, that does not bring us in one farthing, not that, said he, expressing himself by blowing on his hand, and which we would be better without and poor Silesia and Bohemia must bear all.

In June 1740 Bartenstein assured Robinson that to maintain the Austrian garrisons in Flanders on the scale required by the Barrier Treaty (as England was demanding) would cost over 400,000 florins a year, 'beyond what the low Countrys could, in the present exhausted Condition, afford, & that was too great a Sum for the Emperor to drain out of his other States for the preservation of Flanders, so that Something must be done at Antwerp'.[5] But the Antwerp conferences, evidently

[5] Porter to Harrington, 4 July 1739, about an interview with Kinsky on 30 June; Robinson to Harrington, 2 and 16 March 1740; same to same, 29 June 1740.

overtaken by the swift development of events from the death of Charles VI in October 1740, appear to have broken up without achieving any result. The subsequent campaigns in the Low Countries in the years 1744–5, culminating in the French occupation of Brussels in 1746, gave the situation a new twist. For the French sharply increased the level of import duties in the occupied territories. The Austrian authorities retained these duties when the war ended, and also declined to resume payment to Holland of the interrupted Barrier subsidy. When the question of a commercial treaty reappeared in 1749, therefore, it retained the mixture of economics and politics characteristic of the earlier period. Now, however, it was the Austrians who were content, behind a smoke-screen of good intentions, with the *status quo*, and the English and Dutch who were trying, in vain as it proved, to change it.

The questions of the Barrier subsidy and the new higher duties were locked together. Thus, on 28 July O.S. 1749, the Duke of Newcastle, now Secretary of State, instructed Robert Keith, the new English ambassador in Vienna, to support three Dutch claims. These were the continuance of the annual Barrier subsidy of 1,200,000 florins; payment of arrears due on it before the French occupied the Barrier towns; and relief from the heavy duties levied on Dutch imports to the Austrian Netherlands, contrary to the Treaty of 1715. On 24 December Keith reported a reasonable reception, but argued that the subsidy must be reduced and that reciprocal commercial grievances must be adjusted, not just those of one side. Two years later the position was unchanged. Keith reported to Newcastle in January 1752 that he had again complained, this time to Count Uhlfeld, the President of the Conference, about the continuation of the heavy Netherlands duties on woollens. Their removal would gratify the Maritime Powers at a time when 'all Parties were now agreed, immediately to set about making a proper Treaty of Commerce'. Uhlfeld, though he had promised to report this to Maria Theresia, had observed that the whole of the treaty 'soon to be set on Foot, for putting a final End to all Dispute about the Commerce & ca. of the Low Countries' should logically precede part of it. An Austrian memorial soon followed. It stated that Austria had paid the Barrier subsidy up to the date of the French occupation, but that on the part of the Maritime Powers there had been a chain of neglect and non-performance of obligations. Hence the Austrian Netherlands issue must be looked at as a whole: the commercial question could not be isolated. Newcastle predictably retorted that until the illegal high duties were withdrawn, and the Barrier subsidy paid to the Dutch, no treaty of commerce could be negotiated. In a marginal note he brought in the 'immense Sums' which England and Holland had lately spent 'for the Defence of the House of Austria' as an additional reason for compliance. In February his instructions for Lord Hyndford, who was to be sent to Vienna to plead for an immediate election of Archduke Joseph as King of the Romans, included obtaining justice 'with regard to the Duties, and the Payment of the Subsidy' for the Austrian Netherlands. The commissioners on both sides should start business forthwith. On its part, England was prepared to agree to a reasonable treaty of commerce.

Meanwhile, Keith had reported to Joseph Yorke at The Hague that Uhlfeld and Bartenstein appeared to want a speedy conclusion to the Netherlands negotiation, and had declared that the higher duties were imposed by the Brussels government without their knowledge. Yorke had previously told Keith that the French party at The Hague was promoting the view that France treated the United Provinces better than Austria; and that a party in the United Provinces wanted to withdraw the Dutch garrison in the Barrier fortresses as an unnecessary expense. In March 1752 Newcastle, observing that Count Botta, the Austrian minister in Brussels, was not summoning the commissaries of the three powers to meet, ruefully asked why he should, as Austria already had the higher duties and was not paying the Barrier subsidy.[6] A few days earlier, Keith had discussed the whole question with the Emperor and Empress, Uhlfeld, Bartenstein, and other members of the State Conference. The substance of the Austrian position was that they could not afford to pay the Barrier subsidy unless they reduced the Austrian garrison; and they could not afford to transfer funds from Vienna to Brussels any more than they 'proposed to bring one farthing hither out of the Netherlands'.

[6] Keith to Newcastle, 5 and 15 Jan. 1752; Newcastle to Keith, 21 Jan. O.S. 1752; Newcastle's Secret Instructions for Hyndford, 21 Feb. O.S. 1752; Keith to Yorke, 19 Feb. 1752; Newcastle to Keith, 10 March O.S. 1752.

Keith brusquely stated that he found this hard to believe, and concluded

by saying, that I was astonished to see them treat this Matter so lightly, and that they seemed to consider it, as if the whole Dispute lay about a little more or less advantage to be got in the Commerce of the Netherlands; whereas to me this Negotiation appeared to be one of the most serious and most important, that ever I had been concerned in, as I thought the Preservation of the Republick of Holland, at least the keeping it in our Interest, depended, in a great Measure, upon the Event of it . . .

If the Dutch allied with France 'or even embrace a Neutrality', then

not only the Low Countries would be lost to the Empress Queen, but our whole System would fall to the Ground at once; for the moment that Holland left us, the Alliance between England and the House of Austria might be considered as at an End; that Holland was the link that connected us with our Allies in the Continent . . .

The Austrians were evidently unimpressed by this huffing and puffing. Their rejoinder, while allowing that tariff grievances should be the first item on the conference agenda for the Netherlands, refused to take these separately, and refused to resume the Barrier subsidy. As Maria Theresia, pregnant as usual, told Lord Hyndford on the latter's arrival in Vienna in April,

it was the fault of the Maritime Powers, that matters had not been settled in that Countery many years agoe, That the Dutch had made great profits by pouring in vast quantities of goods, to the great detriment of her own Subjects, That Holland was not in a condition to fulfill their part of the Treaty, haveing hardly Twenty Eight thousand men to guard their own Countery, and the Barrier towns . . .

A few days later Bartenstein, who according to Hyndford 'governs everything here', was proposing to Keith 10,000 Austrian troops, paid by Austria, in Dutch service as a substitute for the Barrier subsidy. Newcastle's response was to restate the claim for the unobtainable: 12,000 Dutch troops in the Barrier fortresses, an Austrian garrison of 18,000 troops, and full payment of the subsidy. Given this English inflexibility, it is not surprising that the commercial negotiations seem to have evaporated. On 7 October 1752 Keith informed Newcastle that Prince Charles of Lorraine, the new Governor of the Netherlands, had received secret instructions to settle the whole Barrier issue; but nothing further is heard of this.[7]

The Netherlands negotiations of the late 1730s and early 1750s were talks about talks, without obvious chance of success, and were further complicated by involving Holland. The negotiations between 1739 and 1745 about Anglo-Austrian trade through Trieste were, at least on paper, much more promising; in 1743 they reached the stage of a complete draft treaty, whose objects were nothing less than the transformation of the Austrian economy on the one hand and the repayment of the English National Debt from the profits of Austrian trade on the other. The initial step here was taken on 12 March 1739, when the Chancellor of Bohemia, Count Philip Kinsky, delivered to Thomas Robinson, the English ambassador in Vienna, a paper suggesting the dispatch of an envoy to discuss mutual trading difficulties. This was clearly a response to a petition to Parliament in the previous year, from merchants representing the growing native linens lobby, for a removal of the customs drawback on German linens. Lord Harrington, perhaps flattered by Kinsky's description of the English nation as 'si éclairée, principalement dans le Commerce', sent a London merchant, James Porter, then aged 29, to conduct unofficial talks. He arrived in Vienna on 9 June 1739.[8]

What was the economic and political background of the ensuing negotiations? Porter was sent to Vienna as 'a Person thoroughly versed in the affairs of our Trade with the Emperor's Dominions . . . a very eminent Trader in that Way, one that has

[7] Keith to Newcastle, 11 March 1752; Hyndford and Keith to same, 12 April 1752. J. Laenen, *Le Ministère de Botta-Adorno dans les Pays-Bas autrichiens . . . 1749–1753* (Antwerp, 1901), ch. ii, states that the conferences opened officially on 4 May 1752 and adjourned indefinitely from December.

[8] The 1738 petition was blocked by ministers acting in response to pressure from Baron Wasner, the Austrian ambassador: Harrington to Robinson and Porter, 16 Nov. 1739. Its significance is explained below.

James Porter (1710–86), born La Roche and evidently of Huguenot extraction, assumed the name of an uncle by marriage, who brought him up as a merchant. He was Ambassador to Constantinople Sept. 1746 to May 1762 and Minister at Brussels 1763–5. He was knighted in 1763 (*D.N.B.* and references there).

been before in those Parts, and is perfectly skilled in all Particulars concerning our Commerce with Them'. He appears to have known or come to know many Viennese merchants, so that his information about the Austrian economy and English trade to Austria partly derived from them and not merely from Austrian officials.[9] The picture which he gives is fairly detailed and of considerable interest.

One of the earliest points brought out in his reports is the central importance to Austria of the linen export trade. In August 1739 he described how Count Kinsky had had a balance drawn from the custom-house books of Bohemian exports and imports. Bohemia here must be taken as including Silesia, the principal centre of Austrian linen production. These books were 'kept with great exactness, as their dutys are levied with great rigour and strictness'. They showed that linens exported had stood at over two million florins a year, for the last four years in succession. Since it was permitted to declare them at one-third of their value, this indicated a true annual figure of about seven million florins (*c.* £823,000). A further half million florins-worth of linen yarn was exported. According to Porter, the greater part of the linens, and much of the yarn, were taken by England. He had previously estimated that three-quarters of all coarse linens re-exported from England came from Silesia, a fact not apparent in the printed customs statistics. From Hamburg (the export port) to England only one English ship was engaged in the trade, but on re-export to the West Indies the shipping had to be English. This indicates that the re-exported Silesia linens went to the same markets, the West Indies and the Americas, as Irish and Scottish linens, exports of which were valued at nearly £80,000 in 1739.[10] It was this trade which was jeopardized by English threats to remove the drawback. For example, on broad Silesia brown linens the import duty was

[9] Harrington to Robinson, 6 April O.S. 1739. Cf. Robinson and Porter to Carteret, 2 Feb. 1743, 'I have not only gone on the Evidence of the Custom House Books, but also on that of the most considerable Traders, which last is to be esteemed the most authentick . . .'

[10] Porter to Harrington, 12 Aug. 1739. In the English Customs books Silesia linens were included with those from Germany: Bladen to Weston, 14 Sept. O.S. 1739. For exports of British linens see E. B. Schumpeter, *English Overseas Trade Statistics 1697–1808* (Oxford, 1960), Tables X, XXXIV. This work does not give figures for re-exports of linens. Exports of British linens were increasing rapidly, and doubled by 1749.

£1. 15*s*. 11*d*., the drawback on re-export £1. 8*s*. 8*d*. On narrow linens the duty was £1. 8*s*. 9*d*., and the drawback £1. 2*s*. 11*d*., and so on.[11] The removal of the drawback would obviously have crippled the trade. The relevance in this situation of a trade with England through Trieste, on the other hand, as was proposed, is less apparent. In December 1739 Kinsky was said to be seeking some port other than Trieste, which was too remote, for Bohemia and Silesia linens, especially since 'the People of Lausenitz in Lusatia had carried away much of their Trade, and even reduced it to a low Ebb . . .' The attempt, which was implausible, lost its urgency with Frederick II's capture of Silesia in December 1740 and Austria's abandonment of it for the time being after 1745.

Besides linens, other Austrian produce which it was felt might be exported to England included antimony, arsenic, brass, calamine, copper, glass, iron and steel, linseed oil, olive oil, potash, quicksilver, salt, timber, and wax. Wine was also important. Austrian and Hungarian wines paid £6 a tun more duty than those of Spain and Portugal. Porter proposed equalization and thought it possible that

the Buda and other Hungarian Wines, may in time mitigate the Monstrous Ballance that is against us in French Wines, as there are qualities near approaching, and by that means prevent the horrid Luxury our People have fallen into, in paying such exorbitant Prices for the growth of France.

Count Kinsky in 1740 was discovering Austrian and Hungarian wines which allegedly equalled or bettered French ones; especially since the Hungarians had taken lessons from imported Burgundian experts.[12] In general, Porter's information about these other items of Austrian trade is, significantly, thin. When he came to the potential market for English exports, on the other hand, he did his best, in obedience to his instructions, to be precise and quantitative. His estimates for a range of colonial and other goods are shown in Table 1.

[11] The figures for drawback are taken from extracts from the English Book of Rates in Robinson and Porter to Carteret, 27 Dec. 1743.

[12] Porter and Robinson to Harrington, 31 March 1740, reporting a conversation with Kinsky on 17 Dec. 1739; Porter's report enclosed in Robinson to Weston, 8 Aug. 1739; Porter to Harrington, 31 March 1740; Robinson and Porter to Carteret, 2 Feb. 1743.

TABLE I. *James Porter's estimates of Austrian consumption*

Produce	Estimated annual consumption in Hereditary Lands (including Hungary)		Principal supplier	Present English share of market
Fish	1,500 tons		Internal; but stockfish from Hamburg	None
Pepper	£30,000–40,000 £60,000	1739 est. 1743 ,,	France via Hamburg	None
Rice	£12,000		Italy	None
Silks	£120,000–150,000		France	None
Sugar	£180,000–240,000		France via Hamburg	Slight
Tobacco	£120,000		Hungary and Turkey	None
Tea	£10,000		Holland	None

Source: Porter's reports of 8 Aug. 1739 and 2 Feb. 1743.

These figures, whatever reservations may have been felt about their accuracy, indicated a substantial Austrian market in which France figured prominently and England little if at all. This was especially worrying since English producers of sugar and tobacco, in particular, were in straits. 'Within these five or six years', Porter commented,

we have wholly lost the Exports of our Sugars . . . And this loss has been evidently owing to the vast increase of French Sugars, and the great quantities shipped for Hambro, from whence these Countries are principally supplied, this will be a Means of our recovering our Exports, and preventing the French not only from exporting, but even making so much Sugar in their Colonies, which for some years has been a Golden Mine for them.

Colonel Martin Bladen, commenting on this, stated that the sugar colonies needed strengthening, especially Jamaica, where large areas of cultivable land were not yet settled. And with regard to tobacco, 'The gaining of a New Market for our Tobacco, would encourage the Colonys of Virginia and Maryland to go on more chearfully in the produce of that Staple; which is at present reduced to so low an Ebb, that the poor Planters are almost undone.'[13]

---

[13] Porter's report of 8 Aug. 1739; Bladen to Weston, 14 Sept. O.S. 1739.

Planters of sugar and tobacco might wilt, and their wilting was cause for concern. Still more serious, however, was the state of the great English woollen textile industry, the backbone of the export trade and a principal employer of labour. Its export performance in recent years had been disappointing.[14] And one cause of this, according to Porter, was the effective loss of the Austrian market since the 1720s. His estimates of the situation are grouped in Table 2. The Austrian tariff included

TABLE 2. *James Porter's estimate of sales of English woollens to Austria, including Hungary*

	Pre-1722	Present (*c.* 1740)	Austrian import duty (where stated)
Woollens*	1,000,000 florins (*c.* £118,000)	£2,000	29⅛%
Fine cloths	£15,000–16,000	£5,000–6,000	29⅛%
Superfine cloths	£18,000	?£5,000	29⅛%
Middling cloths	£25,000	None	29⅛%
Stuffs†	£200,000–300,000	None	28⅓%

Source: Robinson and Porter's report of 2 Feb. 1743.

* This category apparently included those in the next three.
† Cloths without nap made of wool only or a mixture of wool and other fibres.

in Robinson and Porter's report to Carteret of 27 December 1743 shows duties ranging from nearly 30 per cent on English cloths, as above, through 20 per cent to 30 per cent on stockings to 12 per cent on Nuremberg ware and 10 per cent on sugar. Textiles were thus particularly severely taxed. Porter's figures suggest the loss of a market equivalent in the early 1720s to rather more than half of total English exports to the American colonies (£436,000 p.a. 1721–5) or Ireland (£471,000), and a third or so more than exports to Flanders (£200,000) or Turkey (£204,000). Total exports of English woollens in 1720 were nearly £3,500,000.[15] Of this, the Austrian market, taking

[14] The export valuation of woollens was £4,053,000 in 1715, £3,840,000 in 1730, £3,827,000 in 1740; see Schumpeter, Table XII.
[15] Figures from Schumpeter, Tables V and XII. The Austrian tariffs shown were for 1726 for Austria, 1731 for Moravia, 1737 for Bohemia, 1739 for Silesia. The rates in each were similar but not identical.

Porter's upper estimates, would have formed about 10 per cent. This was an outlet well worth regaining.

The explanation for England's loss of ground was partly, according to Porter, the influx of French silks, which were 'of an incredible consumption & scarce to be calculated', partly the competition of the woollen manufacturers of Verviers, Leyden, and Liège, so that generally in Germany 'the article of our fine Cloth is greatly fell, and great quantities of others wore, as they are cheaper by 25 per Cent . . .' More fundamentally, Austrian economic policy was to blame. Until the 1720s, he stated, English woollens were 'the general wear of the Country', and the great support of the fairs at Graz, Krems, Linz, and Vienna. One Vienna house alone imported from London and Exeter £20,000–£30,000 of woollens annually. High protective duties imposed by Austria in 1722–6, however, had squeezed these exports out. This tariff was coupled with a monopoly of cloth manufacture in the Austrias, conceded to the Oriental Company founded in 1719 (when Trieste and Fiume were created free ports) for its factory at Linz; and a monopoly of cotton manufacture for its factory at Schwechat near Vienna. Neither flourished. Porter visited the Linz factory on his way to Vienna, and described it as much decayed. Its foreman, a Swiss, was on the point of leaving. It was only kept up by its owners bribing (unnamed) authority, and it only catered for one-eighth of internal demand. The Schwechat factory was computed in 1743 to produce 24,000 pieces of cloth a year; this, too, was allegedly insufficient to satisfy internal demand.[16] The balance of woollens supply, Porter told Kinsky, was partly made up by smuggling Saxon cloth, hence the Saxons 'constantly reap a benefit, which on that, & many other accounts, would be more natural in our hands'. Porter conceded, however, that there was an indigenous coarse woollens industry, which he located in 1739 in Silesia and Moravia, and in 1743 in Bohemia and Moravia. Its products were 'but bad & ill dressed, tho' of sufficient use for their Army and common consumption'. The resolute Austrian defence of it against

---

[16] Porter's report of 8 Aug. 1739; Robinson and Porter to Carteret, 2 Feb. 1743. For the Oriental Company, cf. F. M. Mayer, *Die Anfänge des Handels und der Industrie in Oesterreich* (Innsbruck, 1882), and V. Hofmann, 'Beiträge zur neueren österreichischen Wirtschaftsgeschichte', Parts I and II, *Archiv für österreichische Geschichte*, cviii (1920), 345; cx (1926), 415.

English attempts to lower the protective duty suggests that it was in fact much more important than Porter realized.[17]

Something must lastly be said about the position of Hungary. In their report of December 1743 Robinson and Porter described this kingdom as

of such vast consequence as to its Trade, and of so great an extent as to its consumption, not having one single manufacture, nor being by its Government & Constitution in a condition to have any, that we humbly apprehend we should have nothing so much at heart as to cultivate and improve it.

Austrian policy towards Hungary had traditionally been 'to cramp & restrain that whole Kingdom in Commerce, so that it should neither have Imports or Exports but singly through the Austrias' and through Vienna at that, after Austrian import duty had been levied, about which the Hungarian Diet had constantly complained. The Hungarian response, particularly since Austria had raised the duties on foreign manufactures in 1725, had been to resort to Poland and Saxony for imports, despite the detour this involved. Earlier in 1743 Robinson and Porter estimated that the Hungarians spent £150,000 to £200,000 annually in Saxony alone, much of it on goods from Hamburg and France. The Hungarian market opened up for England by the draft commercial treaty of 1743 therefore seemed exciting. 'The great & main change of all', commented its two authors, 'is the new acquisition of a vast Kingdom unknown before, for by the Arts of the Austrians & their total precluding [*sic*] that Kingdom it lay almost as much hidden & lost, as if it had not existed . . .'[18]

The scope and rhythm of the commercial negotiations conducted against this general economic background were necessarily affected by the peculiar cast of Austrian politics and administration. The dispatches throw much light on the nature of the difficulties which Porter and Robinson faced here. Porter had arrived in Vienna at a time when the whole machinery of Habsburg government was close to paralysis. He later described

[17] Porter to Harrington, 4 July 1739; Robinson and Porter to Carteret, 2 Feb. 1743. Cf. H. Freudenberger, 'The Woolen-Goods Industry of the Habsburg Monarchy in the Eighteenth Century', *Journal of Economic History*, xx (1960), 383.

[18] Robinson and Porter to Carteret, 2 Feb. and 27 Dec. 1743.

to Carteret the scene of Charles VI's last years in the following terms:

> . . . the last years of that Princes reign, might have been call'd, a mere state of anarchy . . . Each Chancellor, of each Kingdom, each Council of Province, to show their attachment to the states of their country, and to strengthen their own revenues, or those of their famillys . . . endeavoured assiduously, to conceal the riches, & power of their countrys, in order to lessen their imposts . . .

Hence the Emperor never knew his real power or resources, and his enemies concluded that the empire must break up when he died. The absence in the period before this of the firm central direction which might have averted these perils was a commonplace of court gossip. 'I have been told farther', Robinson wrote to Harrington in April 1740,

> that upon some warm Contests between the many Ministers, and Tribunals concerned in the Military and Civil Oeconomy, the Emperor's constant Answer has been, agree amongst yourselves, whereas their Representations are, that his Imperial Majesty would be pleased to chuse one himself, out of so many Projects.

In the same dispatch he described how Sinzendorf, the Austrian Chancellor, had, not for the first time, bewailed 'the Loss of the late Prince Eugene'. Robinson agreed 'that the late Prince of Savoy's yes or no, whether well or ill founded, had, as I remembered, such a Weight, as beat down all Opposition . . .'

In these circumstances, the committee-ridden nature of Habsburg government and decision-taking was reinforced. As Robinson commented after a warning on the subject from old Count Starhemberg in February 1740, 'It is to be more observ'd here than in any other place, that 'till Things become the Act of the whole Counsel, whatever is related as falling from this or that Minister is more to be regarded as the effect of ye particular Tempers of Each than as the Pulse of the whole Court.' The economic and political attitudes of ministers and of the councils they presided over were to be an important variable in the commercial negotiations. Count Philip Kinsky's principal concern in their early stages was the linen export trade of Silesia. According to Robinson, however, 'to do every Body Justice, it was from Monsieur Bartenstein that the Thought came originally, of such an extensive commerce'. Bartenstein,

Porter was later told, had fixed on Count Kinsky 'as his chief Friend and Support amongst the great nobility, so generally the Cause of the One became That of the Other, and things seldom failed in their hands'. Count Harrach, in an earlier conversation, had put the emphasis differently, hinting that 'Count Kinsky without Mr. Bartenstein was nobody'.[19]

It is thus significant that Bartenstein's brother-in-law, *Hofrath* Karl Holler von Doblhoff, was appointed, together with Kinsky, as one of the three Austrian commissioners for the trade negotiations with England. The choice of the third commissioner, Joachim Georg Schwandner, was equally significant. Schwandner was a Councillor of the Bank Deputation, and a close adviser of its President, the aged Count Gundakar Starhemberg, who 'has had upwards of forty years, the supreme Direction of the whole in Money Matters'. The count, by then aged 75, occasionally showed the vigour other ministers lacked. He would 'exert himself now and then for a Moment, and then flags, as being contented with having spoken his Mind, and barely satisfied his Conscience'. He was thought to be averse to Kinsky's and Bartenstein's proposals for financial innovation, and possibly as hostile, for similar reasons, to the commercial proposals. Schwandner, who was a Customs expert and had particular influence on Starhemberg, was certainly suspicious of Kinsky's motives. He told Porter in April 1740 that Kinsky only wanted to exclude Flemish cloth from the Hereditary Lands in order 'to erect new Fabricks of his own of that kind of cloth in Bohemia', and that as regards Kinsky's proposals for trade with England, 'tho' he Schwantner was not absolutely the man who could prevent it, this view should not succeed nor his Plan would not meet either with the Emperor's or the Ministers of the Conference's Approbation . . .' It was presumably for these reasons that Kinsky told Porter in July that if only Bohemia, Moravia, and Silesia were concerned, there would be no difficulty in agreeing to the English proposals, 'but as the Austrias was a principal Point they brought strong opposition on him which however he doubted not now to get

---

[19] Porter to Carteret, 17 May 1742; Robinson to Harrington, 30 April 1740; same to same, 2 March 1740, 7 Oct. 1739; Porter to Harrington, 6 July 1740, reporting the opinions of Kannegiesser, 'Referendary of Bohemia and Silesia'; Robinson to Harrington, 3 Feb. 1740. For Kannegiesser, see below, n. 26.

quite over . . .' Maria Theresia's accession brought a new force
to bear on the negotiation. 'The queen was quite for' the treaty,
Porter reported in August 1742; in February of the following
year she was stated to be 'passionately bent upon this Commercial affair', and in December 'to have laboured this matter
indefatigably'. Significantly, however, she had laboured it
against 'the Austrian councils', and Schwandner appears to
have been reserved or hostile to the end.[20]

The course of the commercial negotiations fell into three sub-
stages. First, up to the Emperor Charles VI's death in October
1740; second, from then until March 1742, when Porter was
ordered to return to England; and last, from Porter's return to
Vienna, in August 1742, until 1745. On his arrival in Vienna
Porter brushed aside Kinsky's invitation to talk about a mutual
trade through Trieste with Baron Rheigersfeld, 'Imperial
Assessor' there, and demanded someone more senior. On 27
June 1739 he was therefore presented to Count Starhemberg,
presumably as the senior economic minister; the old count
simply said it was a matter which concerned Bohemia, and
referred him back to Kinsky. In a further long interview with
the latter on 30 June Porter insisted, over his protests, on the
readmission of English coarse and middling cloth to the Austrian
market. In his dispatch home on this occasion he observed that
Kinsky fluctuated in his views and was not on top of his subject.
However, it had now been arranged that the negotiation would
proceed between Porter on the one side and Kinsky, Bartenstein's brother-in-law Doblhoff, and Count Starhemberg's
official Schwandner on the other.

After an interval, in which Robinson introduced Porter to
Bartenstein, who said that 'if any delay was occasion'd it was
only for want of a proper person, in the Chancery of Bohemia
. . . the old director of these affairs being dead', and a further
talk with Baron Rheigersfeld, Porter met the Austrian

    [20] Robinson to Harrington, 20 Jan. and 9 March 1740; Porter to Harrington,
29 April and 6 July 1740; same to Carteret, 22 Aug. 1742; Robinson to Carteret,
1 Feb. 1743; Robinson and Porter to Carteret, 27 Dec. 1743. Count Gundakar
Starhemberg (1663–1745) was no longer President of the Hofkammer, but retained a powerful position as a member of the Finance Conference and head of
the Bank Deputation. Doblhoff, who was a *Hofrath* in the Austrian Chancellery,
and Schwandner usually figure in the dispatches as 'Doublehoven' and 'Swantner'.

commissioners again on 16 July, when they admitted the defects of their existing system and asked him for a paper on a mutual trade. As Porter patronizingly remarked to Harrington, 'I find they must principally depend on us, to put them in the right way, & even to form some consistent plan for them.' This 'consistent plan' took the shape of a long report which Porter sent to Harrington's secretary, Edward Weston, on 8 August 1739. It described the potential market for English produce and argued that if England were given 'an exclusive Trade to Trieste, on which the supposition is founded, and as being the only point they propose', a 'prodigious real profit' could be expected for English woollens. In return, Austrian goods shipped from Trieste might be spared the 1 per cent special duty charged on English ships coming from the Mediterranean.[21]

Later in August 1739 the Austrian commissioners, joined on this occasion by 'the new referendary Baron Rhigersfeldt', declared willingness to lower the duty on English woollens, even if this harmed their own. But reciprocal concessions from England must be examined first. In December, Kinsky was declaring that an exclusive trade for England, or a tariff preference, were all one to him: 'he could not but confess their great ignorance in Trade, and how unable they were to go on of themselves, therefore they must intreat our assistance.' He suggested that English merchants should establish houses in Breslau, Prague, Trieste, and Vienna, and hence 'enable the Hereditary Countries to reap the advantages proposed; for in truth he had little relyance on the People of these several Countries'. It soon became clear, however, that the Austrian concession on woollens was more apparent than real. In January 1740 Kinsky, undoubtedly under pressure from his colleagues, proposed the formal exclusion from the Austrian market of English cloths selling at ten shillings and under.[22] In June Schwandner

[21] Porter to Harrington, 17 June, 4 and 22 July 1739. The 1 per cent duty was first levied by 13 & 14 Charles II, c. 11 (1662). It did not apply to ships with a specified level of armaments and was intended as an incentive to arm against the Barbary pirates. Porter's report of 8 Aug. 1739 was fictitiously addressed 'James Nelson' and written on especially thin paper to deceive the Austrian postal authorities.

[22] Porter to Harrington, 26 Aug. 1739; Porter and Robinson to Harrington, 31 March 1740, reporting a conference with Kinsky on 17 Dec. 1739; Robinson to Harrington, 16 Jan. 1740.

repeated this: the Oriental Company's monopoly of exporting cottons had just been ended, which would enable England to expand its sale of fine cloths to Austria; but England must not be permitted to send its coarse woollens there.[23] In his dispatch of 8 October 1740, written just before Charles VI's death, Porter stated that Schwandner, 'on whom, even Count Kinsky told me, the whole depends', was still harping on this theme. In April Schwandner had told Porter he considered an 'open free & undistinguished Trade was the most beneficial'. No wonder Robinson was already doubting the success of the entire negotiation.

Meanwhile, the English officials' plans had been submitted to expert opinion at home. In September 1739 Colonel Martin Bladen wrote to Weston enclosing a Mr. Gore's comments on the proposals together with his own. Gore's remarks were largely favourable, though he feared Dutch umbrage if an exclusive trade were sought, and emphasized the necessity to stop ships being sent from Trieste to the East Indies. Bladen wished to promote the export to Austria of English cottons, fish ('not an Article in Trade of greater importance to England'), hardwares ('now become one of the Principal Manufactures of Great Britain'), rice, and tobacco. He too, however, doubted whether an exclusive trade, which would arouse Dutch animosity, was feasible. He favoured a preference similar to that conceded by Austria to the Turks at the Treaty of Passarowitz in 1718. Under this, he explained, Greek traders had dominated the whole trade of Sicily. In November 1739 Harrington collated these opinions, and perhaps some others, and sent them to Robinson and Porter. These 'Observations upon Mr. Porter's Memorial' underlined the importance of export of English woollens, coffee, tea, cottons, fish, sugar, and tobacco. The Austrians, it was declared, had 'found, by experience, that all their Schemes for erecting Woollen Manufactures in opposition to our's, have not only proved abortive, but likewise detrimental to their own Interest'. The readmission of English 'middling & coarser cloths' should therefore be the principal

[23] Porter to Harrington, 1 June 1740. Cf. Robinson to Harrington, 11 May 1740: the Oriental Company's monopoly of exporting cottons would be ended from 31 Dec. 1740 and this was the only profitable branch of its trade. (The correct date for the expiry of the company's fifteen-year cottons monopoly was in fact 8 Jan. 1741, as Hofmann shows; see above, n. 16.)

object of the negotiations, and these cloths 'would soon put an End to Those lately erected in the Hereditary Dominions'. For these and the other items Porter should send estimates of probable English sales. A tariff preference rather than an exclusive trade should be aimed at, and this would require careful study of appropriate levels of duty. As to Austrian imports, it was agreed that the linens position might stay as it was and some reduction be made in the duty on potash, wine, and wax; iron and timber could be put on an equal, though not a preferred, footing.

This may not seem very much. But the general English line appears to have been that it was Austria, not England, which was on to a good thing. For example, when Count Starhemberg observed to Robinson in February 1740 'that had the Emperor been helpt, even with a little Money, during the last war with France, he might perhaps have prevented the extreme Necessities he was under at present', Robinson grandiloquently replied that

whatever Hurt this Court might have suffered by their late losses, and the Diminution of their Revenues, They would, I could assure him, find themselves bettered an hundred fold, by the Advantages we were offering to the Emperor, in the Point of Trade, and by Our adopting, if I might be allowed the Expression, these Hereditary Countrys instead of Spain . . .

This vague but splendid bait was no doubt intended to make a direct appeal to Starhemberg's master, briefly King of Spain, 'whose idol was trade' and who 'had made it almost his only study to introduce Commerce in these Countries'.[24]

By 20 October 1740, when Charles VI died and the subsequent uncertainty about Austria's future made it 'doubtful . . . what this People may, in their present circumstances, dare to give to England, & what England will care to take from them', the commercial negotiations had thus assumed more or less fixed general characteristics. The English wanted to get their woollens, particularly their middling and coarser woollens, back into the Austrian market on preferred terms. They were

[24] Porter to Harrington; Robinson to same: both 29 April 1740; Bladen to Weston, 14 Sept. 1739; Harrington to Porter, 16 Nov. O.S. 1739; Robinson to Harrington, 24 Feb. and 5 March 1740; Porter's 'Answer to the Report of the Lords of Trade', 27 Dec. 1743. Mr. Gore was probably the merchant John Gore.

prepared to make tariff concessions on some Austrian products, and to retain the drawback on Austrian linens, but not to reduce the duty on them, which helped to service the national debt. The Austrians wanted to trade with England in order to make Trieste flourish as a port, and to get themselves out of 'their own dull inactive State'. They regarded the privileges of the Linz woollens and Schwechat cottons factories belonging to the Oriental Company as negotiable, but not the native coarse woollens industry (with some waverings). Part of the difficulty of customs concessions was that, for Austria too, duties were settled to service government debts. In any case, some councillors opposed the development of Trieste, claiming that the Emperor had already wasted five million florins by trading projects.[25]

The second phase of the negotiations lasted from the Emperor's death until March 1742. During this confused and tense period for Austria, the English officials understandably made no progress. The commercial barometer at this stage was changeable. In November 1740 there were rumours of special concessions to Hungarian trade. In 1741 there were alarms about a possible Austrian free-trade treaty with Saxony to entice her into alliance. Admission of Saxon cloths on this footing would have ruined the chances for English ones, and it was therefore fortunate that in the end Saxony joined the coalition against Austria. Porter now had little to do. In July 1741 he informed Harrington that 'the unfortunate circumstances attending this Court, naturally stagnated our proceeding'. Meanwhile, Robinson and Lord Hyndford were engaged throughout the summer in their complex attempts to persuade Frederick II to renounce Silesia, into which he had marched on 16 December 1740, an object only force would have achieved. Despite their offering, with Maria Theresia's consent, first Gelderland and Limburg in the Austrian Netherlands, and then the entire northern half of Silesia to buy him off, he would make no concession. On 9 October 1741 the Convention of Klein Schnellendorf yielded the greater part of Silesia in return for Frederick's neutrality. This cut off the most flourishing sector of Austrian linen production, and thus wrecked the

[25] Robinson and Porter to Harrington, 30 Nov. 1740; Porter to Harrington, 31 March 1740.

assumptions on which the commercial negotiations had so far been based. On 28 March 1742 Porter acknowledged the new Secretary of State Lord Carteret's orders to return to England.

The next, and as it turned out final, phase of the negotiations began in August 1742, when Porter, on instructions from Carteret, returned to Vienna to reopen discussions there. Anglo-Austrian relations were by this stage at a low ebb: the Treaty of Breslau, concluded through Hyndford, had just confirmed formally Prussian possession of Silesia. Porter none the less found the Queen 'glad of the opportunity to come to a more strict union, with the English nation', and reported that Count Uhlfeld had stated to him that 'not only the queen was quite for it, but they the ministers unanimous to bring it to a conclusion, that tho' they were sensible the greatest advantage would necessarily accrue to us, yet whatever they might reap by it was clear proffit to themselves'. The negotiating paper which he gave Uhlfeld at this interview fully confirmed, by its emphasis on Austrian concessions, that it was England which would have the balance of advantages. By the end of November, when Porter informed Carteret that only the return of Kannegiesser, 'Referendary of Bohemia', delayed the reduction of the proposals 'to such a consistency as might be proper to be laid before the King', this was clearer still. The Austrians had modified their former intransigence on coarse cloths by agreeing to halve the customs duty on all imported English cloths, silks, and rice, and to ban all French silks. They were sticky only about tobacco and cottons. The discussions evidently continued through the winter, for on 2 February 1743 Porter and Robinson were able to send Carteret a mammoth dispatch comprising the heads of a treaty accompanied by a detailed commentary, which included calculations of the cost of English exports to Austria on the old footing and the proposed new one. In a covering letter, Robinson commented that one year of the new trade would repay England's Austrian subsidies of the last two years, 'a thought extensible to the possibility of drawing out of these Hereditary Countries, the discharge of the whole National Debt in a given time', and added that he might 'in some measure attribute to myself the first discovery of this new Peru to my Country'. He correctly pointed out, however, that political considerations, in this case Austrian hopes in Bavaria and Italy, would continue to affect the success of the negotiations.[26]

The structure of the proposed treaty was familiar: modest English concessions, substantial Austrian ones. After a flourish about the need for union between the two countries, which only commerce could procure, England promised the existing customs duty and drawback on Austrian linens imported (now presumably a minor item); a drawback and a halving of the existing duty on Austrian antimony, arsenic, olive oil, quicksilver, steel, and wax; the lowest existing duty on Austrian wood and iron, and remission of all duties on potash. Austrian and Hungarian wine and brandy would pay the same rates as Spanish. The Aliens Duty (the higher customs rate paid by foreign importers) and the 1 per cent Mediterranean levy would be remitted on Austrian goods entering English ports from Trieste. So far as English goods imported to Austria were concerned, the duty on woollens was to be reduced still further, by two-thirds, from 90 to 30 kreuzer an Austrian ell. The duties on silks were to be halved, those on mixed silks and woollens reduced to a quarter. Duties on fish and pepper were also to be halved, and small concessions were to be made on sugar and tea. Tobacco, whose revenue was farmed in Austria, was, however, to be retained at its existing rate. On top of all this, imports of French oil, silks, and wine were prohibited. It was proposed that the treaty should initially be for twenty-five years.[27]

Besides conveying a series of estimates of probable English sales if these arrangements came into force, Porter tried to assess their effect on freight costs. His calculations for certain items of woollens are grouped, in recast form, in Table 3. For these goods, the difference in freight and insurance charges between the Hamburg and Trieste routes was unimportant.

---

[26] Porter to Carteret, 22 Aug. 1742, enclosing copy of paper given to Count Uhlfeld; same to same, 22 Nov. 1742; Robinson to same, 1 Feb. 1743. Hermann Kannegiesser (whose name has several extraordinary spellings in the dispatches) was a *Hofrath* in the Bohemian Chancellery.

[27] Robinson and Porter to Carteret, 2 Feb. 1743. Imports of French oils, silks, and wine were prohibited in the Austrias from 31 Jan. 1743, and in Bohemia from 15 Feb. 1743: Robinson and Porter to Carteret, 27 Dec. 1743. The Act 15 George II, c. 29, imposing an additional duty from 1 Aug. 1742 on foreign cambrics, to finance an export bounty on British linens, is not referred to in the correspondence.

TABLE 3. *Probable freight costs of English exports to Vienna under proposed 1743 duties*

Costs*	18 pieces of Yorkshire cloth sent to		41 pieces of Camlets sent to		51 pieces of druggets sent to	
	Hamburg	Trieste	Hamburg	Trieste	Hamburg	Trieste
Initial cost in England	1,142.16	1,142.16	1,394.00	1,394.00	1,326.00	1,326.00
Sea freight	22.54	23.00	12.54	21.26	16.00	31.30
Sea insurance	14.16	34.16	17.00	42.00	17.00	40.00
Land freight	94.52	35.15	42.11	13.45	64.16	23.45
Total freight and insurance	132.02	92.31	72.05	77.11	97.14	95.15
Duty at Vienna (old rates for Hamburg, proposed new rate for Trieste)	1,479.00	493.00	325.05	116.10	338.00	130.30
Total costs (other than initial)	1,611.02	585.31	397.10	193.21	485.14	225.45

Source: Robinson and Porter to Carteret, 2 Feb. 1743, 'Calculations' 1 to 3.
* All amounts in Austrian florins and kreuzer. 60 kreuzer = 1 florin; 8½ florins = £1.

Cheaper land-carriage from Trieste to Vienna than transport from Hamburg to Vienna, via Nuremberg and Ratisbon, was offset by higher insurance (3 per cent to Trieste against $1\frac{1}{4}$ per cent to Hamburg) and sea freight. The crucial difference in the final sale price was made by the proposed lower duty at Trieste. If everyone else had to pay the former duties (as was intended), English merchants would have an import monopoly in the Austrian market in all but name.

Not surprisingly, the Board of Trade had little criticism to make, and on 1 April O.S. 1743 Carteret instructed Robinson and Porter to conclude a treaty in time to be laid before Parliament in the winter.[28] Punctually, they remitted a draft treaty in 43 articles on 27 December 1743, whose object was 'to endeavour to redress all those grievances which the Commerce of these Countries has laboured under for many Centuries'. It incorporated the reductions in Austrian duties already discussed, and in one or two cases (ribbons, sugar) extended them. It had not proved possible to secure one tariff alone, but those for each province were stated to be similar. A number of other points were either introduced or clarified. The Hereditary Lands were defined as the whole Habsburg Lands except Italy

[28] For this section see Carteret to Robinson, 1 April O.S. 1743, enclosing a report of the Board of Trade dated 30 March 1743; Robinson and Porter to Harrington, 21 Nov. 1744; 28 Dec. 1744, enclosing a paper by Sir John 'Bernard'; 12 May and 22 Sept. 1745; Robinson to same, 22 Sept. 1745. By this stage the Board of Trade had added a half-duty on glass and a 'Portuguese' rate on wines to its concessions to Austria: Bladen's report in Harrington to Robinson, 28 Dec. 1744.

and the Netherlands. The ports affected by the treaty were to be Trieste, Fiume, Buccari, and Porto Re. English merchants were to pay Austrian duty once and for all at Trieste. No further state or private transit and other tolls were to be charged. English goods, including cottons at half rates, might be imported into Hungary from Trieste and Fiume by the rivers Sava and Drava, and not through Vienna only as the Austrians had at first insisted. Austrian and Hungarian goods might be sent out through Trieste without paying transit taxes or provincial export taxes. English factors might establish themselves anywhere in Hungary and the Hereditary Lands, with defined privileges, 'a practice unknown in them before, as every one qualified for Trade, must have the freedom of their Towns, which is a most difficult, & almost impossible Point to obtain for Protestants'. Similar provision was made for Austrian factors in England. Freedom was conceded to English merchants to set up sugar refineries at Trieste and Fiume. Appeals by English litigants from a council of commerce to be set up at Trieste were to be to 'the President and Council of Commerce to be established at Vienna'. A series of other provisions covered mutual appointment of consuls, exemption from Austrian military service and quartering, freedom to choose professional advisers, rights of succession, freedom to trade with the Turks, and so on. It is not difficult to infer from their general tenor that the English negotiators considered English merchants would be operating in a potentially hostile environment, a nice comment on the alliance between the two powers.

This marked the peak of the commercial negotiations. As the year 1744 progressed, politics once more began to overshadow economics. Prussia came back into the war in August, and renewed tension developed between Austria, suspicious of English collusion with France in the Netherlands, and England, fearful of being dragged further into Austria's duel with Frederick II. In November 1744 Porter and Robinson reported to Carteret, now Lord Granville, that it was nearly a year since there had been anything to say about the trade negotiations. A cautious memoir by Sir John Barnard in December 1744, and a further undated dispatch by Porter early in 1745, simply covered old ground. In May 1745 Robinson and Porter stated that they had recently gone through the entire draft treaty with the

Austrian commissaries 'in a most amicable Manner', but that then at the last moment the Austrians had produced a stiffer-than-ever list of demands, complaining (how correctly) 'that we have so little to give them in Return'. In September, Maria Theresia was still believed to be in favour of concluding an agreement, but Schwandner was pessimistic about the draft treaty's repercussions on Austrian revenues and domestic trade; he feared that admission of resident English merchants would ruin the burghers and shopkeepers of Vienna. Meanwhile, England, as in 1741, was exerting diplomatic pressure on Austria to buy off Frederick II by confirming his possession of Silesia. This was achieved in the Treaty of Dresden in December. The ensuing virtual collapse of Anglo-Austrian relations made substantial Austrian commercial concessions to England, complacently described by Robinson as late as September 1745 as 'a grateful Return for what has been already done for the House of Austria', improbable. The negotiations adjourned to the Greek Kalends. In 1746 Porter was sent to Constantinople as English ambassador.

What general conclusions can be drawn from the history of this dual episode in Anglo-Austrian relations? So far as the Austrian Netherlands were concerned, England wished throughout to maintain the existing economic and strategic *status quo*, and was not prepared to pay by concessions there for Austrian concessions on the proposed trade through Trieste. In this she was partly influenced by the need to placate Holland, whose hostility to the economic pretensions of her southern neighbour was well known. But England had more than sufficient reasons of her own for her unyielding attitude. Strategically, defence of the Austrian Netherlands by the system of 1715 (an Austrian garrison, with Dutch garrisons in selected fortresses) still appeared the best to Newcastle in 1752, even after Marshal Saxe's campaigns had demonstrated its vulnerability and, in doing so, justified Austrian reluctance to restore it. Economically, England wanted to retain her pre-1746 tariff advantages, and the favourable trade balance with the Netherlands which was thought to depend on them. She treated Flemish pretensions to lower duties in England, or to direct entry into the East Indian trade, with glacial dismay.

A similar range of attitudes was displayed in the negotiations about trade through Trieste. The tone of English policy throughout was selfish and acquisitive. Trade with Austria was to be as much as possible in England's interests, and as little as possible in anyone else's. Although fears of hostile Dutch, and to a lesser extent Venetian, reactions led England to modify initial Austrian attempts to concede a trade monopoly, the preference negotiated for instead was intended to have much the same effect. In particular, the hold of France on the Austrian market was to be broken, with multiple consequences for French trade in sugar and silks. Again, it was hoped that preferences for Austrian wine would injure the French grower. Similar results were intended for Saxony, whose export of woollens to Austria in the 1730s seems to have been regarded by Porter as a moral affront.

The picture given in the sources of English colonial production, especially in sugar and tobacco, is gloomy. It was hoped that trade with Austria would at least stimulate sugar. Domestically, Birmingham and Manchester are depicted as flourishing, but the great woollens manufacture, with its multiple productrange, was obviously thought to have suffered badly in its exports to Europe since the turn of the century. The trade to Austria was intended as a cure for this. The English negotiators entertained especial hopes for woollens and cottons in Hungary and Turkey. In the process, it was casually assumed, Austrian production of woollens would be polished off. The general pattern of trade envisaged was a colonial one. English textile and metal manufactures, and re-exports of colonial produce, would be exchanged for Austrian drugs, oil, iron, quicksilver, potash, and timber. Austrian glass, brandy, and wine were rather reluctantly added to this list. Austria, in short, would become a kind of European America. It seems, however, to have been expected that Austrian imports from England would greatly exceed those of England from Austria. England would 'adopt' Austria instead of Spain; and the resultant inflow of bullion would help to pay off the English National Debt. It was not accidental that Robinson compared Austria to an English Peru. These attitudes amply justified Kinsky's complaints in 1739 that the English wanted 'to concentrate all manufactures in themselves', and 'were for having all advantages, and giving none'. The lack of sophistication in the English approach is obvious. Austria's need under a bilateral trading system for expanding income, derived from English purchases of Austrian produce, if it was to buy expanded English exports, was largely ignored. The probable effects on Austrian policy of a lengthy adverse balance of trade with England, made good by a drain of Austrian metallic reserves, were apparently not even contemplated. The fear of imports, the almost superstitious worship of exports, are clearly demonstrated. This evidence suggests that in the diplomatic and mercantile circles involved in these negotiations trade was still thought of as very much a system of grab. If these basically seventeenth-century attitudes were typical, and there is much other evidence that they were, they help to explain Chatham's appeal for his generation.

English policy towards a new trade with Austria was largely determined at a technical level by James Porter and Thomas Robinson. The comments by the mercantile experts Barnard, Bladen, and Gore, and by the Board of Trade, seem to have been of only marginal utility. It is difficult to resist the impression that Harrington and Carteret were ignorant of trade, and content to accept the (often exaggerated) views of their advisers, though well aware of the political relevance of trade concessions. Porter's performance was able, but at a high level of optimism; and he showed throughout the negotiations the genial contempt for foreign abilities sometimes characteristic of Englishmen of foreign extraction. His statistical approach to the problems involved was common form for his period, and where his figures can be verified they appear to be of the right order of magnitude. Particularly in his forecasts of English sales in Austria, however, he made assumptions about Austrian attitudes which were hardly plausible. In general, English policy-formulation in this field must be regarded as amateur, in the sense of relying too much on single opinions, unverified data, and naïve assumptions about the political behaviour of foreigners. It may, however, be argued that it was no more so than English foreign policy as a whole at this time.

Austrian methods and attitudes are indicated less clearly in the sources, but several conclusions are suggested which other evidence confirms. The decisive importance in Habsburg government of one voice overriding the paralysing internal

I

quarrels of the provinces and departments of government was demonstrated positively, according to the English officials, by the vigour first of Prince Eugene and later of Maria Theresia, and negatively by the supineness of Charles VI in his last years of life. It is of some significance, however, that the project for a special commercial relationship with England began under Charles VI, a reformer *manqué* in many spheres, 'whose idol was trade'. The interests of the Habsburg provinces conflicted with each other, and each province pursued its own, where necessary at the expense of those of the rest. This was brought out during the commercial negotiations in Bohemia–Silesia's attitude to the Austrias, in the latter's attitude to the other German Hereditary Lands and to Hungary, and in the attitude of the Hereditary Lands as a whole to the commercial pretensions of the Austrian Netherlands. These conflicts were exemplified by thinly veiled hostility between Count Philip Kinsky and the aged Count Gundakar Starhemberg. The importance of subordinates from outside the ruling families is hinted at by the part played in the negotiations by Bartenstein, Doblhoff, Kannegiesser, Rheigersfeld, and Schwandner. All this largely tallies with, for example, the statements in Maria Theresia's *Political Testaments* of 1750–1 and 1755–6.[29]

The timing of the negotiations about a trade through Trieste was decided by a mixture of economic and political causes. Thus the slowness of the initial phase of talks, in 1739–40, was partly due to internal quarrels about the relative interests of Bohemia–Silesia and the Austrias, but also both to Austrian hopes of squeezing concessions from England in Antwerp, and to understandable fears about being sucked into an English alliance-system directed against France. The renewed vigour of the negotiations in 1743 can be ascribed to the wish of two very different personalities, with very different motives, Lord Carteret and Maria Theresia, to push them to a successful conclusion. The stagnation of the whole affair in 1744 and its abandonment after 1745 were partly due to Austrian doubts about the value of England's concessions, but were also clearly connected with the foundering of Anglo-Austrian plans for an effective attack on France and Prussia, ending with Austria's

[29] Most recently reprinted in F. Walter (ed.), *Maria Theresia, Briefe und Aktenstücke in Auswahl* (Darmstadt, 1968), pp. 63–97, 108–30.

reluctant recognition, under English pressure, of Prussia's title to Silesia.

Why were the negotiations not revived? The remaining years of the War of Austrian Succession served only to underline the divergence of English and Austrian interests and the unsatisfactory nature, so far as Austria was concerned, of alliance with the Maritime Powers. The making of the peace of Aix-la-Chapelle recalled for Austria the English 'betrayals' of 1713 and 1733. And not long after it the shadow of a new and larger conflict began to stretch across Europe. In February 1752 Count Uhlfeld reported to Keith that the French ambassador, de Hautefort, had told him that

the Affairs in dispute between Great Britain, & France, in the West Indies . . . were of such a Nature, as might, one Day, or other, Occasion a New War between the two Nations; insinuating at the same time, as if England was seeking for a Pretence for a Rupture . . . He said, he was afraid That England, as usual, might draw Her Allies into a Quarrel; and he expressed his Fears of this Court's [i.e. Vienna] being brought to take Part, in the War, if it should break out.[30]

By this date, Count Kaunitz, accurately foreseeing this possibility and also the growing neutralism of Holland, was already pushing towards his dazzling goal of a recovery of Silesia through a French alliance purchased by cession to France of the Austrian Netherlands. In these circumstances, Austrian concessions to England and Holland over the Netherlands tariff and the Barrier subsidy would have been pointless, and the conclusion of a treaty giving England virtual monopoly of import to the Hereditary Lands an act of political suicide.

Considerations of economic policy and political power strongly reinforced this incipient change of direction. The whole tenor of the commercial negotiations of 1737–52 had been, so far as England was concerned, that the Austrian Netherlands and the Austrian Hereditary Lands should either remain or become colonial dependencies of England, existing primarily for the benefit of English merchants and manufacturers. Austrian policy from the mid-1740s pointed away from such dependency towards a programme of economic autarchy. The establishment of a Directory of Commerce in 1749 was the first step

[30] Keith to Newcastle, 12 Feb. 1752.

towards the systematic building up of Austrian industry behind high tariff walls and under close state supervision: a return, on a larger scale, to the policies of Charles VI. At the same time, trade through Trieste began to expand with active government support. In 1750 a new Company of Trieste and Fiume was established with Austrian Netherlands finance to take over and expand the role of the defunct Oriental Company, and in 1752–3 discussions began about a preferred commerce for Belgian merchants to Trieste. These plans, which foreshadowed the economic integration of the entire Habsburg Lands, were to raise many of the same problems as the earlier and similar discussions with England. So far as Hungary was concerned, the reign of Maria Theresia showed a pattern of considerable expansion of trade based on exchange of Austrian manufactures for Hungarian agricultural produce: a 'natural' version of the relationship Porter had wished to capture for England.

Meanwhile, Count Haugwitz's administrative reforms aimed to increase and rationalize direct taxation in Austria, break the political pretensions of the provinces, and set up a new structure of central and provincial government. From the early 1750s, the first regular census of the whole Austrian population was set on foot to provide another essential tool for fiscal and military planning. In the Netherlands, under the guidance of the former French official Dupuy, similar policies were followed in some fields, among them those of statistics of revenue, population, and industry.[31] In 1765 James Porter, by then knighted and British minister in Brussels, reporting to London on the state of the Belgian economy, sadly described how a high tariff policy had been followed there since January 1749 for the benefit of native industries and to the detriment of English exports. He clearly thought that this was a great mistake, much as he had regarded Charles VI's attempts to develop the Austrian textile industry nearly thirty years before.[32] In short, the paths of Austria and England had diverged. They were only to come together again in the very different circumstances of the closing years of the eighteenth century.

[31] P. Moreaux, *Les Préoccupations statistiques du gouvernement des Pays-Bas autrichiens* (Brussels, 1971). I hope to discuss some of the other aspects referred to in a study under preparation on finance and commerce under Maria Theresia.
[32] P.R.O., C.O. 388/95, dated 10 Feb. 1765.

VI

George II Reconsidered

To attempt a reconsideration of George II may well be to tilt at windmills. Few monarchs who have ruled any major nation for more than thirty years have attracted less comment from historians. It is general knowledge that, because of his love of Hanover and his tendency to promote its interests in the conduct of foreign policy and war, he enjoyed relatively little popularity among his British subjects; that he was utterly devoted to, though at times singularly inconsiderate of, his intelligent and politically articulate wife, Queen Caroline; that he had a deep and abiding hatred of his 'half-witted coxcomb' of a son, Frederick, Prince of Wales; that his patronage of Handel was untypical of one whose ignorance of the arts was summed up in his guttural distaste for 'boetry and bainting'; that he was the last British monarch to lead an army in the field, his physical courage—unlike his political courage—never being called in question; and that his passion for things military and his admiration of prowess in battle were wittily expressed in his hope that, if James Wolfe were mad, he should bite some of his fellow generals. But otherwise the second of the Hanoverians remains for the most part a somewhat shadowy and little-considered nonentity. It is difficult, if not impossible, to revise opinions and interpretations that have rarely been clearly and precisely formulated.

Yet it is probably fair to argue that most historians have tended to assume—if not state explicitly—that George II was an ineffectual king, and that during his reign a decline in monarchical power that had begun under his father became ever more marked. His only biographer significantly entitled his work *A King in Toils* and prefaced it with these words:

It was a cardinal principle in the Whig conception of government that the king should be reduced to the position of a cipher in politics; and every royal excursion into the political arena, whether

legitimate or otherwise, was regarded as an impudent interference
with the privileges of the party politicians. Thus the king was sub-
jected to all sorts of indignities at the hands of those whom he had
chosen to direct the affairs of his kingdom.[1]

Ian Christie felt years ago that George II 'emerges for us from
his portraits and from contemporary accounts as a pompous,
dapper little man, irritable and inclined to fly into fits of temper, energetic and yet somehow ineffectual'.[2] D. Lindsay Keir
conceded that in the eighteenth century 'successive Kings
occupied identical constitutional positions, employing their
powers differently only to the extent that their personal qualities and political aims varied';[3] yet he also claimed that from
the fall of Walpole to the death of George II 'the King's ability
to form and maintain ministries was steadily on the decline'.[4]
Even two of the most distinguished of eighteenth-century
specialists did not wholly break with this tradition. Richard
Pares admitted that 'there is no great reason to think that
George II willingly or deliberately accepted any constitutional
limitations which his grandson tried to flout',[5] yet he had little
doubt that George II was in some sense a failure as a king:

> It was weakness, and weakness alone [he wrote], that prevented
> this active and businesslike king from exercising the influence which
> the constitution would have allowed him, outside the departments,
> such as the army and the Bedchamber, which the politicians did
> not mind leaving to him. Had his strong-minded wife lived, the
> royal power might have been exerted more effectively. . . . But
> without his queen or Walpole near him, George II did not know
> how to deal with the politicians. He suffered public defeat, three
> times, in his attempts to use the most important of the surviving
> prerogatives, that of choosing his own ministers, and the leadership
> which he should have exercised passed to the Pelham family, indeed
> to the political class as a whole.[6]

Thus 'George III grew up to deal with a generation of politicians who, having had the run of the place for twenty years,
had almost ceased to take account of anybody's opinion but

---

[1] J. D. Griffith Davies, *A King in Toils* (1938), p. vi.
[2] 'The Personality of George II', *History Today*, vi (1956), 516.
[3] *The Constitutional History of Modern Britain, 1485–1937* (1938), p. 317.
[4] Ibid., p. 333.
[5] *King George III and the Politicians* (Oxford, 1953), p. 61.
[6] Ibid., pp. 63–4.

their own';[7] and 'in the last resort . . . Newcastle governed George II and George III governed North'.[8] Even Sir Lewis Namier sounded surprisingly whiggish when he wrote thus of the early Hanoverians:

Under the first two kings of the Hanoverian dynasty certain forms and even principles of Cabinet government seemed to have been established. The Government was based on a party majority in the House of Commons, the King had to accept the leaders or makers of that majority, and had to act, and even think, through them—they were already conscious of knowing the King's (constitutional) mind better than he knew it himself.[9]

Of course, Namier was here dealing with appearances rather than realities, and he was quick to add that the politicians of George II's reign, 'while at times expounding what would seem the full doctrine of responsible Parliamentary government, had no conception of a party-government unconnected with the King, and hence of a constitutional Parliamentary Opposition'.[10] Yet the implication remains, even if stated with greater sophistication, that George II was dominated by the political magnates of his time, and played little part in the formulation of policy or in the determination of his ministries. Was this really so?

Let it be conceded at the outset that George II, with his ill temper and blustering outbursts, provided apparently convincing support for those who subsequently claimed that he had been ineffectual. After reluctantly accepting the Broad-Bottom administration in 1744 he bitterly rejected Hardwicke's accusation that he was openly showing disapproval of his own work by barking out: '*My work!* I was forc'd: I was threatened';[11] and went on to add, even if with a smile, 'Ministers are the Kings in this Country.'[12] When lamenting the imminence of his return from Hanover in the autumn of 1755 he protested: 'There are Kings enough in England. I am nothing there. I am old and want rest, and should only go to be plagued and

[7] Ibid., p. 64.   [8] Ibid., p. 183.
[9] *England in the Age of the American Revolution* (2nd edn., 1961), p. 45.
[10] Ibid., p. 51.
[11] P. C. Yorke, *The Life and Correspondence of Philip Yorke, Earl of Hardwicke* (3 vols., Cambridge, 1913), i. 382.
[12] Ibid. i. 383.

teased there about that d——d House of Commons.'[13] Con-
fronted against his inclination by the Pitt–Devonshire ministry
of 1756–7, he appealed to Newcastle to rescue him, angrily
asserting that he 'did not look upon himself as King whilst
he was in the hands of these scoundrels';[14] yet within days he
was snorting, 'I shall see which is King of this Country, the
Duke of Newcastle or myself.'[15] All these and many other similar
protests might suggest that George II was indeed 'a king in
toils'. Yet although George III, especially when faced with the
demands of Rockingham and Charles James Fox, spoke in
similarly vigorous terms, and was driven to desperation and
to thoughts of abdication by the politicians of his day, it would
be a brave historian who claimed that his outbursts of irritability
signified a decline of monarchical power between 1760 and
1784. Indeed, this brings us to the core of the problem. The
real clue to the popular view of George II lies in the always
implied contrast between his reign and that of his successor.

To some extent this contrast is understandable. Sir John
Fortescue's six large volumes of George III's correspondence,
with the five subsequently edited by Arthur Aspinall, provide
ample evidence of that monarch's passionate interest and active
participation in all aspects of the political life of his time. If
George II's political writings were ever published, they would
fill no more than a leaflet, and would consist largely of scribbled
abuse or approval at the bottom of ministerial memoranda
submitted to him. But it would be foolhardy to assume that,
because George II hated writing, he was politically inactive.
Unfortunately his constant activity, through no fault of his
own, has long been viewed through a haze of historiographical
mist. Since the accession of his grandson in 1760, historians
have intermittently debated at great length the significance of
that accession. Those of the Whig school believe that in some
sense George III departed from the constitutional practice of
his grandfather; that, whether or not he read Bolingbroke or
was repeatedly exhorted by his mother to 'be a King', he
sought—with the aid of a judicious amalgam of 'King's Friends'
and reinvigorated Tories—to reassert the lost power of the
Crown, and by so doing threatened liberty in both England and
America. There are of course many subtle refinements of Burke's

---

[13] Yorke, *Hardwicke*, ii. 284 n.   [14] Ibid. 365.   [15] Ibid. 388.

original Whig view, and space will not permit consideration of recent exponents so apparently persuasive as Sir Herbert Butterfield and W. R. Fryer.[16] But all Whig versions of George III's reign rest on the assumption, explicit or implicit, that George II behaved in the last analysis as a good, sound, constitutional monarch, bowing to the will of a parliamentary majority in the House of Commons and accepting the advice of his ministers, however reluctantly, in a manner that would have done credit to Queen Victoria. On the other side we have the views of the so-called 'Tory critics', who reject the Whig charge of unconstitutionality levelled against George III. Instead, they see him as merely and justifiably trying to reverse an unconstitutional cornering of power by the most prominent Whig magnates of the previous reign, who, by their machinations, had reduced George II to the position of a veritable 'Doge of Venice'. Their arguments might seem plausible in that they derive in part from opinions openly asserted in the reign of George II, most notably by adherents of Leicester House. Successive Princes of Wales, in justifying their opposition to the reigning monarch, felt obliged to counteract charges of unconstitutional behaviour by asserting that they were opposing neither the King nor his Government, but a rascally oligarchy of ministers who had gained control over the King and were forcing him to accept bad advice. The ideas most cogently expressed in modern times by 'Tory historians' like Pares and Namier were imbibed in crude form by the future George III during his adolescence at Leicester House, and stated with blunt simplicity by that prince of place-hunters, George Bubb Dodington, when he wrote to Lord Bute on 26 November 1760:

During the two last reigns a set of undertakers have farmed the power of the Crown at a price certain under colour of making themselves responsible for the whole, have taken the sole direction of the Royal interest and influence into their own hands and applied it to their own creatures without consulting the Crown or leaving any room for the Royal nomination or direction.[17]

[16] See esp. Sir H. Butterfield, *George III and the Historians* (1957) and W. R. Fryer, 'King George III: his Political Character and Conduct, 1760–1784. A New Whig Interpretation', *Renaissance and Modern Studies*, vi (1962), 68–101.

[17] Quoted in *The Political Journal of George Bubb Dodington*, ed. J. Carswell and L. A. Dralle (Oxford, 1965), p. 402.

Certainly the young King believed this cant when he ascended the throne. As a result he thought that all he need do, as soon as was convenient, was to oust the leading ministers of his grandfather's reign, elevate his dearest friend, Lord Bute, to the headship of the Treasury, abolish corruption, and everyone would live happily ever after. Parties and factions would be eliminated, and all would join enthusiastically in the new reign of virtue. What the pathetically naïve young King failed to realize was that the existing Pitt–Newcastle ministry was in fact his ideal—no oligarchical cabal, but an all-embracing coalition conducting a successful war with the whole-hearted support of Parliament and the nation. Instead of welcoming his inheritance, he persisted with his original intentions, and in so doing acted as midwife to the future Rockingham Whigs and stirred up forces that were to pose greater problems for the monarchy than his grandfather had ever had to face. His original misconceptions about Whig cornering of power in the first half of the century had led him into grave *political* error. When Tory historians accepted the same Leicester House fiction at its face value, it led them into grave *historical* error. One can explain George III's ideas and motives without necessarily accepting the truth of the assumptions on which they were based.

It is an accident of historiography that the accession of George III has been allocated a pivotal importance in the politics of the eighteenth century, though it would be foolish to deny that the 1750s and 1760s witnessed a gradual but significant change in political circumstances. But what is of crucial significance to the study of the reign of George II is that he has been forced into a preconceived mould in order to support two opposing and equally erroneous theories about the reign of his more celebrated grandson. Both Whig and Tory schools must of necessity portray George II as an ineffectual monarch; whether the limitations upon him were virtuously self-imposed or villainously enforced by Whig magnates matters little. Thus the second of the Hanoverians has scarcely ever been studied in his own right, and until this historiographical mist has been dissipated it is difficult to get him clearly in focus. None the less, the contrast between him and his grandson is manifestly less striking than is usually suggested, and there are many obvious parallels between their two reigns. George III may have succeeded in establishing political stability under both North and the younger Pitt, but George II had achieved the same under Walpole and Henry Pelham. George II may have been unable to retain in power his favourite, Carteret, but George III was no more successful in retaining Bute in 1763 or Shelburne in 1783; and George III's exclusion of Fox from office for more than a few years finds its counterpart in George II's exclusion of Pitt from more than minor posts for most of his reign. If George III's most striking success was the defeat of the Fox–North coalition in 1783–4, George II had dismissed the Pitt–Devonshire coalition in 1757; and if Pitt had to be accepted back within a few months, it was only on condition that he served with Newcastle and other ministers whom he had previously denounced and with whom he had vehemently refused to associate. When it came to ministerial appointments both monarchs had their ups and downs. If George II had at one time or another to accept the elder Pitt or bow temporarily to the Pelhams, George III more than once had Charles James Fox thrust upon him and had to bow to King Rockingham; and if George II could not retain in Walpole a minister who was mismanaging a major war, George III was no more successful in preventing the fall of North. True, the American war had been virtually lost before North was forced out. But it was Parliamentary distrust of an apparently disloyal opposition, rather than the favour of the King, that explained the relative longevity of North's ministry.

If one turns from the sphere of central ministerial appointments to broader issues of patronage and policy, the same parallels are evident. Because George III was forced to take a very active part during the war years of North's ministry, he acquired the reputation for being primarily responsible for the determination of policy; and because of the notoriety which Burke attributed to the 'King's Friends', the monarch was assumed to have reasserted royal control over patronage and enlarged its extent. As far as patronage is concerned, it has been convincingly shown[18] that it diminished rather than increased during the first twenty years of George III's reign,

[18] I. R. Christie, 'Economical Reform and "The Influence of the Crown", 1780', *Cambridge Historical Journal*, xii (1956), 144–54.

though Dunning and his supporters on 6 April 1780 certainly believed otherwise; nor is it evident that George III interfered any more, or for that matter any less, than had George II. Namier was merely following Horace Walpole when, speaking of the 1760s and early 1770s, he remarked that George III, having appointed his ministers, seldom interfered with them until the time came to contemplate their dismissal.[19] The 'King's Friends' were anyway no creation of George III's but, as a combination of the Court and Treasury party and what one might call Court independents (i.e. independents who, *ceteris paribus*, were inclined to support the ministry of the day), had existed since the seventeenth century. That their primary loyalty was to the Crown had been concealed under the early Hanoverians solely because that loyalty could, during the long ministries of Walpole and Pelham, go conveniently hand in hand with allegiance to the Old Corps of Whigs. George III's bewilderingly rapid changes of ministry in the 1760s merely forced the 'King's Friends' to show their true colours, but they did not do so at the specific behest of the monarch. As for George II, he naturally insisted on being consulted on all matters of patronage, though unless he was temporarily at odds with his ministers compromise was usually possible when differences of opinion arose. Certainly he was even more jealous of army and Court appointments than his grandson. Old Horace Walpole wrote to Robert Trevor on 22 February 1740:

> Sir Robert Walpole has very little to doe in the military promotions. He recommends friends and relations of members of Parliament to be ensigns and cornets, but His Majesty himself keeps an exact account of all the officers, knows their characters and long services, and generally nominates at his own time the colonels to the vacant regiments. He frequently mentions these promotions to my brother who, when he lets fall a word or two in favour of some officer, is told (that is between you and me) that he does not understand anything of military matters, and by this means he has often the ill-will of disappointments, which were not in his power to prevent.[20]

Henry Pelham was similarly forced to confess to Lord Marchmont in 1748 that he and Newcastle 'did not meddle in the

---

[19] *Crossroads of Power* (1962), p. 215.
[20] B.M., Add. MS. 9176, fo. 34.

army, the King and the Duke [of Cumberland] ordering that themselves'.[21] As for court officials, Edward and William Finch (Groom of the Bedchamber and Vice-Chamberlain respectively) were protected from dismissal not only in 1744 but even in 1746, despite the fact that they were close associates of Carteret and after 1744 acted as intermediaries between the King and his 'minister behind the curtain'; and when Newcastle tried to interfere in Bedchamber appointments in 1755 he was bluntly told by the King that he should confine his attention to the Treasury, and that there was no such thing as first minister in England. Nor did Hardwicke's attempts to defend his friend produce anything but the brusque retort: 'The Duke of Newcastle meddles in things he has nothing to do with. He would dispose of my Bedchamber, which is a personal service about myself, and I won't suffer anybody to meddle in.'[22]

It was not only in the areas of the army and the Court that George II wielded a significant, and often decisive, influence. He was particularly sensitive about the conferment of peerages. When in 1757 Hardwicke suggested that Henry Bilson Legge be made a peer and First Lord of the Admiralty, the King retorted peremptorily that he was determined not to do two great things for one man at the same time,[23] and he was equally adamant at the subsequent suggestion that Lord Chief Justice Willes should be given both a peerage and the woolsack.[24] Even so brilliant a lawyer and so staunch a government supporter as Lord Mansfield had only with the greatest difficulty achieved a peerage on his appointment as Lord Chief Justice of the King's Bench in 1756.[25] When it came to vacancies in the Order of the Garter, George II was equally determined that his own wishes should be respected. Despite almost indecent pressure from Pitt and Newcastle in 1759, the King at first steadfastly refused to confer the Garter on Lord Temple, and was persuaded finally to yield to the request only after Temple had resigned and made a formal apology to the King for his earlier offensive conduct.[26] On the other hand a similar honour had been conferred on the King's favourite, Lord Waldegrave,

[21] *A Selection from the Papers of the Earl of Marchmont*, ed. G. H. Rose (3 vols., 1831), i. 271.   [22] Yorke, *Hardwicke*, ii. 224–5.
[23] Ibid. 403.   [24] Ibid. 408.
[25] Ibid. 302.   [26] Ibid. iii. 57 sqq.

without consulting any of the ministers whom Waldegrave in 1757 had been entrusted by the King with attempting to supplant.[27]

In ecclesiastical matters also, George II had ideas of his own, and Newcastle in his capacity as 'ecclesiastical minister' was far from undisputed master of episcopal appointments. In 1750 the King insisted on the translation of Joseph Butler from Bristol to Durham; in 1752 he caused Newcastle many uneasy hours before finally aggreeing to accept Richard Trevor as Butler's successor; in 1754 all that he was prepared to grant Dean Asburnham, after many years of unsuccessful supplication by Newcastle, was the bishopric of Chichester; and while the old Duke was fleetingly out of office during the brief Pitt–Devonshire ministry, the King seized the opportunity of Archbishop Herring's death to translate Matthew Hutton from York to Canterbury, and achieve two other translations and one nomination.[28] As with appointments, lay and spiritual, so with parliamentary elections. Walpole, Pelham, and Newcastle were as First Lords of the Treasury successively responsible for the management of all general elections from 1727 to 1754, but in each case the King insisted on being kept informed of every detail, and his approval was sought for all Government candidates and for the disbursement of all Government money. If he normally accepted the recommendations of his ministers, he did so because they *were* his ministers; and when he occasionally had to employ those in whom he had little confidence, he had no hesitation in opposing their wishes, as when he vetoed the nomination of Pitt's follower, George Hay, for the Admiralty borough of Rochester during the Pitt–Devonshire ministry.[29]

If the King made his influence felt in all aspects of patronage, his role in the formulation of policy was even more important. George III may have made no secret of his views on the two great divisive issues of the 1760s and 1770s, that is, the relations between Britain and her American colonies, and the incipient radicalism that found a temporary focal point in the multifarious activities of that endearing demagogue, John Wilkes.

[27] James, Earl Waldegrave, *Memoirs from 1754 to 1758* (1821), pp. 135–6.
[28] Norman Sykes, *Church and State in England in the Eighteenth Century* (Cambridge, 1934), pp. 39–40.
[29] Namier, *England in the Age of the American Revolution*, p. 112.

But George II was no less active and forthright over the single divisive issue of his reign—the role of Hanover in the foreign policy of Britain. Here the action of the King was more often than not decisive and frequently detrimental to British interests. Walpole's attempt in 1740 to detach Frederick of Prussia from France by offering concessions in Jülich and Berg foundered above all on George II's insistence that equal concessions be gained for Hanover. The following year the King concluded, with the connivance of Lord Harrington who had accompanied him abroad, but to the consternation of all the ministers at home, a treaty for the neutrality of Hanover, thereby gravely endangering the allied war effort and the parliamentary position of his government. Years later, between 1750 and 1752, George II began by encouraging Newcastle in his dubious project of subsidizing the German electors to obtain the election of Maria Theresia's son, the Archduke Joseph, as King of the Romans; but in the end he undermined Newcastle's position by negotiating separately as Elector of Hanover, privately encouraged the already unenthusiastic Empress to withdraw from the transaction, and snubbed the Duke by casually remarking: 'You have this thing much at heart. I have it not so much.'[30] In the early stages of the Seven Years War, George II displayed his Hanoverian partialities for the last time. While the British Parliament was raising money to defend the Electorate, the King and his Hanoverian ministers were secretly negotiating, without the knowledge of the British Cabinet, for a treaty that would extricate Hanover from the war. Fortunately, the Convention of Klosterzeven, negotiated after defeat at Hastenbeck by a panic-stricken Duke of Cumberland, left Hanover at the mercy of the French without any of the advantages that George II had hoped to gain. He therefore denounced the son in whom he had placed so much trust and affection, repudiated the Convention, and at last threw himself and his Electorate whole-heartedly behind the war.

It was, however, during the middle stage of the War of the Austrian Succession that George II's influence on policy had been most emphatic and pernicious. When his grandson actively intervened in the War of American Independence, he at least had the excuse that he was 'fighting the battle of the legislature',

[30] Yorke, *Hardwicke*, ii. 5.

his activities were necessitated by North's dilatory conduct, and his sole aim was British victory. George II had no such excuse in the 1740s; his interests were almost exclusively Hanoverian, and their effect was for several years to thwart the combined efforts of Britain and her allies. Between 1742 and 1746 George II, encouraged for his own political ends by Carteret, continuously defied the great majority of his ministers. He alone was responsible for the continued inactivity of the British army on the Continent in 1742–3, and again after the battle of Dettingen. It was not permitted to cross the Rhine and enter Germany, for the simple reason that Frederick of Prussia had sardonically conveyed to the British monarch that if he felt tempted to contemplate such a step he should remember that at the moment his Hanoverian dominions were pretty much exposed. The King was wholly unprepared to risk any attack on his beloved Electorate, and the army—to the great chagrin of the British ministers—was prevented from seeking out the enemy. Newcastle put the position in a nutshell when he wrote to Hardwicke on 24 October 1743:

> During the whole winter, I never ceased pressing Lord Carteret to determine to send an army into Germany, knowing well that nothing could be done anywhere else; and that the not doing it must be ascribed to Electoral considerations only. All I could say had no effect; and I never could get him once to be clear that they should go. He dealt in excuse that it was time enough to determine. I soon found out his meaning; and indeed he once owned to me, that if the King of Prussia should once put his threats into execution, what would be the consequence of it? or to that effect, which was a key to the whole proceedings; and to his irresolution and apprehensions of the consequences, that the sending of our army to Germany might have, with regard to the Electorate of Hanover, I attribute great part of the misfortunes which have since happened.[31]

Nor was there much improvement after Dettingen, when again the King for long fought a delaying action, the effects of which were accentuated by another of his prejudices. The Dutch, as usual, were proving singularly lethargic in supplying their promised quotas of men and money, and the British ministers constantly urged firm representations to make them fulfil their

[31] Add. MS. 32701, fos. 198–200.

treaty obligations. But George II, again supported by Carteret, obstinately refused to bring adequate pressure to bear—solely because he feared that, in return, the Dutch would insist upon Hanover entering the war as a principal, instead of merely providing mercenary troops. In the end the Pelhams chose the Dutch issue on which to make a stand against Carteret, whom they succeeded in forcing out of office at the end of 1744; but by then the King for two years had virtually dictated a sterile war policy—a strange achievement for a monarch usually regarded as powerless. When the King was abroad in Hanover with one of his Secretaries of State, the ministers at home were in constant fear that policy would be determined behind their backs; when he was at home, and especially when opinion in the Cabinet was divided (as it was during a significant part of the two major wars of his reign), it required considerable persistence and strength of character to impose views upon him. Minutes of Cabinet meetings give us little evidence of royal power because they tended to reflect the first digestion of affairs by the principal ministers, but the political correspondence of the times offers ample evidence of furious activity in the royal Closet, the more intimate atmosphere of which gave the King opportunity to exert a greater influence on policy than he would have been able to exercise at the more formal and larger meetings of the Cabinet. When Newcastle had Carteret as his Closet-companion in 1744 he lamented mournfully to brother Henry: 'No man can bear long, what I go through every day, in our joint audiences in the Closet';[32] and to Hardwicke, 'every day produces some new disagreeable incident in the Closet.'[33] A year later he was protesting to Richmond at the language the King was using: '*Incapacity* to my brother, spectator of other people's policy and measures, and yesterday pitiful fellows.'[34] Of course, George II, despite heated rebukes and denunciations, frequently yielded to ministerial advice, but there is little reason to doubt the truth of Hardwicke's remark, when he was trying to quell disharmony at the Regency Board during the King's absence in Hanover in 1740: 'It is my firm opinion that, more especially whilst the King is abroad (*who when here was a kind of centre of unity, at least his final opinion*

[32] Add. MS. 32703, fo. 281.   [33] Add. MS. 35408, fo. 42.
[34] H.M.C., *Report I*, p. 115.

concluded everybody else), the utmost endeavours should be used to preserve harmony and good agreement.'[35]

Enough has been said of the participation of George II in the spheres of appointments and policy to suggest that the contrast between his performance and that of George III is not as marked as might at first sight appear. Particularly is this so when one takes into consideration the differing circumstances of the two reigns which, initially at least, allowed George III much more political elbow-room than his grandfather had ever felt able to afford. George II had been brought up to believe that all Tories harboured Jacobite sympathies and must therefore be proscribed from office. Occasionally, as with the temporary employment of Sir John Philips and Sir John Hinde Cotton in 1744–5, or with the concessions concurrently granted the Tories over membership of Commissions of the Peace, he might make a partial exception; and of course, former Tories who thirsted for office could and did easily qualify by joining the Whig fold and supporting the administration of the day. But, by and large, all but the final three years of George II's reign witnessed between 100 and 150 Tories firmly entrenched on the Opposition back benches. George III had no such permanent body of members with which to contend. Jacobitism was finally acknowledged as a spent force, a new generation of Tories had become weary of the game of perpetual opposition and had come round to support of Pitt's supposedly 'country' war policy after 1757, and at the opening of the new reign Tories re-appeared at court, became eligible for office, and rapidly disintegrated as an identifiable group. George II had also been politically limited for many years—specifically from 1737 to 1742, from 1747 to 1751, and from 1755 to 1756—by the vigorous opposition of successive Princes of Wales, which contributed not a little to the fall of Walpole in 1742 and of Newcastle in 1756; and his freedom of action was at other times confined by his extreme reluctance ever to employ anyone who had been associated politically with either Frederick or the young Prince George. George III, until the 1780s, suffered no comparable embarrassment, and such opposition as he had to face had no convenient social and political centre in Leicester House. Finally, George II rapidly became convinced that any ministry,

[35] Yorke, *Hardwicke*, i. 239. My italics.

to be viable, must enjoy the support of that large, amorphous mass of members known as the Old Corps of Whigs, who acted together for two generations under Walpole and Pelham. His grandson had no such conviction, and such solidarity as the Old Corps had possessed had anyway largely vanished by the time of his accession. The failure to provide them with a competent leader in the Commons after Pelham's death in 1754 had begun their disintegration, and the abnormally broad base of the Pitt–Newcastle coalition prevented them from regaining any significant sense of separate identity. No Tories, no Leicester House, no Old Corps. George III was indeed dealing with a different political world than that which his grandfather had regarded as the normal order of things. Politics had become atomized, parties in any meaningful sense had virtually ceased to exist. The new King could enjoy a degree of political freedom that no monarch since William III had known, yet he threw away all his advantages by his calf-like devotion to Bute and by his petty and spiteful treatment of the old royal servants of his grandfather's reign—petty and spiteful, but far from sinister or unconstitutional. George II, only slightly less devoted to Sir Spencer Compton, would have done the same in 1727 had not Queen Caroline been there to point out the political folly of such a move, and had not the King been basically shrewd enough to grasp the difference between a shadow Court at Leicester House and the real Court at St. James's. His grandson, in many ways a less perceptive monarch, lost the initiative and in the end only just managed to hold his own against the politicians whom he drove to new heights of factious rivalry by his early political ineptitude.

It must of course be recognized that George II, to the extent that the above limitations were self-imposed, denied himself considerable freedom of action that he might otherwise have enjoyed. In this sense he gave some superficial credence to the view that he was 'a King in toils'. Yet it is easy to underestimate the degree of authority he exercised within his admittedly restricted terms of reference, and by no means obvious that his grandson was more effective in imposing his wishes upon the politicians of his reign. The case for the weakness of George II rests essentially on his four famous defeats. In 1742 he was forced to part with Walpole, in 1744 with Carteret; thus within two years he had lost two ministers in whom he still had every confidence. In 1746 he failed to form an alternative ministry around Carteret and Bath, and found himself accepting the Pelhams back on their own terms. Finally, in 1756 and again in 1757, he had the elder Pitt thrust upon him. *Prima facie,* this seems indeed a dismal record but, as has already been argued, George III fared little better. He had to part with North and with Bute, though he had enough sense not to try to restore the latter as his grandfather had tried to restore Carteret. He also had to accept Rockingham in 1782, the Fox–North coalition in 1783, and Fox again in 1806. In fact the one real contrast between the two reigns was that George II failed to oust the Pelhams in 1746, whereas George III succeeded in demolishing the Fox–North coalition in 1783–4. These two crises indeed throw into bold relief the paradoxes and uncertainties of the eighteenth-century constitution, which continued to recognize a royal executive that could, in the last analysis, be rendered ineffectual if the politicians of the day could combine sufficiently to command the House of Commons and impose their wishes on the monarch. But if, in the course of the intermittent battle between King and politicians, either adopted an attitude unacceptable to the majority of a Commons that was still basically independent, political defeat would be certain. In 1783 the coalition pushed its luck too far, and George III was able to benefit from the inevitable reaction. In 1746 it was George II who misjudged the situation, and it was he who had to pay the penalty. Indeed, since the fall of Walpole he had been flirting with political disaster in trying to confine his confidence to Carteret and Bath, the two most notoriously unpopular politicians of the age. The Old Corps detested them because they had been largely responsible for Walpole's fall; the Opposition detested them because they had then immediately forced their way into office with a handful of their own personal followers and treated their erstwhile colleagues with disdain; and they were condemned on all sides because of their known encouragement of the King's Hanoverian predilections. George II might well have been able in 1746 to form a ministry exclusive of the Pelhams, had he not insisted on Carteret and Bath as the only alternatives. But if he could not have them, he preferred the Pelhams as second-best, and soon came to accept them as enthusiastically as he had earlier accepted Walpole and Carteret. As in 1742, so in 1746; the Commons might directly or indirectly impose a veto on particular ministers, but they did not dictate whom the King *should* employ. If George II chose to limit his options, that was his privilege.

The fiasco of 1746 has indeed been widely misinterpreted. It is frequently portrayed as a joint resignation by an oligarchical cabal of ministers, who took advantage of the Jacobite rebellion to force George II to admit Pitt to office. Were this true we might well regard that monarch as a helpless victim of scheming politicians, but there is no vestige of truth in it. Pitt was not the issue, for he had abandoned his claims to office before the crisis broke; the chief ministers, with infinite patience, waited till the Jacobite danger was over before making strong representations to the King, and it was anyway he, not they, who took the initiative by announcing his intention of replacing them; and although over forty individuals subsequently resigned their offices, only Pelham, Newcastle, Hardwicke, and Harrington did so as a result of prior consultation. The cogent reasons that persuaded them to do so also prompted a large number of other office-holders to follow their example. Ever since 1744, George II had continuously flouted the advice of his ministers and followed that of Carteret 'behind the curtain'. Those ministers were thus held responsible for a policy in the formulation of which they had virtually no part, and in particular for an unsuccessful war policy and an early refusal to treat the Jacobite invasion as a matter worthy of serious attention. As early as February 1745, Newcastle was mournfully lamenting to Chesterfield:

You are certainly in the right, that many things to and from foreign courts are conveyed through . . . channels unknown to us. And most of the material foreign ministers are as much attach'd to a certain person [Carteret], and act as much in concert with him as formerly; and what is worse, I am afraid, this is not only known but approved and done in concert with somebody else [George II]. The time will come, and that soon, when all that must be explained. The King's servants must be his ministers, exclusive of all others; or they cannot remain his servants.[36]

[36] Add. MS. 32804, fos. 231–2.

But there was no improvement, and in May Newcastle reported to Cumberland:

We thought it our duty not to distress His Majesty's affairs, just upon his going abroad, or obstruct and delay his journey; but have, my Lord Chancellor, my brother, and myself, represented in the most dutiful manner the impossibility of *our* opening another session of Parliament, if His Majesty at his return should not have a more favourable opinion of us, and our endeavour for his service, than he has at present.[37]

Even the Jacobite rebellion brought no reprieve, and in September Newcastle was still complaining to Chesterfield:

Sanguine councils and sanguine councillors, behind the curtain, have got entire possession of our hearts and minds; and, in one word, nothing but a rebellion in the heart of the kingdom would or should hinder us from retiring from the most disagreeable and perhaps the most dangerous situation that ever ministers were in.[38]

Of course, Newcastle was a neurotic, and his rather pathetic utterances may seem suspect. But Henry Pelham, the most level-headed and responsible of statesmen, spoke with the same voice. In September he wrote to Devonshire:

Everything at C——t continues as you left it, I have seen the K—g twice, his behaviour is not at all mended. I heartily wish this rebellion was put an end to, for then I should personally at least be under no difficultys. As things are, I don't know what to do, but I am determined on no account to answer for the sessions, unless I previously know what is to be done, and that we are to be supported in what we do. I see no prospect of this. It looks to be rather as if some desperate stroke would be taken.[39]

A few days later, Pelham confided further to Devonshire:

The conduct of a certain person is worse then ever. To speak of personal treatment is idle at this time, but we are not permitted either to give our advice or to act in consequence of any advice that is given. . . . It will be incumbent upon us all, and especially upon myself, to let the King know that the meeting of the Parliament is called so early only to put this nation in a proper state of defence, to pass such laws as are necessary for the preservation of his govern-

[37] Add. MS. 32704, fo. 194.
[38] Add. MS. 32705, fos. 201–3.
[39] Chatsworth, Devonshire MSS.

ment, when there is an actual rebellion in the kingdom. But that we do not engage to carry through the business of the sessions with regard to foreign affairs upon the plan which he has been advised to by other people.[40]

In February 1746 came the 'desperate stroke'; George II commissioned Bath to form a ministry. Who can blame the Pelhams for then deciding to hand in their resignations or, when asked to return, for stipulating that they, and not Carteret and Bath, should have the confidence of the King? And who can accuse them of acting as an oligarchical cabal who held the King in thrall?

Many of George II's difficulties were, then, self-imposed. Others arose out of the political and constitutional conditions of the eighteenth century as a whole, and applied to the reign of George III no less than to that of his grandfather. If any monarch of that era were to enjoy a prolonged period of political stability he had to satisfy two basic conditions. First, he must have a Commoner at the head of his ministry—a man who could act as a link between the two chief sources of political power, the Closet and the Commons. Walpole was the first minister to occupy this position and to grasp in his own hands the three aspects of the eighteenth-century primacy—the confidence of the King, the leadership of the Commons, and the headship of the Treasury. On his fall, Lord Hervey was quick to advise George II that he must find a successor. In July 1742 he wrote:

It is . . . necessary . . . to the safe and quiet conduct of Your Majesty's affairs that you should unite in the same person the favour of your closet and the power of it. At present, the favour is all bestowed on Lord Carteret, and all the power exercised by Mr. Pulteney. This cannot last; favour and power must go on together, or neither can go on long.[41]

Yet it was not until after February 1746 that Henry Pelham was finally to gain the royal confidence and provide George II with his second long spell of political stability. When Pelham died in 1754, neither Newcastle nor Hardwicke was eager to knuckle down to such dominant characters as Henry Fox or

[40] Ibid.
[41] *Some Materials towards Memoirs of the Reign of George II*, ed. Romney Sedgwick (3 vols., 1931), iii. 952.

the elder Pitt, and the King was persuaded that Newcastle could control the Commons from the House of Lords. But the experiment was a dismal failure, and when the Pitt–Newcastle coalition finally ended the resulting chronic instability, Hardwicke felt obliged to warn Newcastle that he could not hope to rival Pitt in the Lower House. In October 1757 he wrote:

> It cannot be disguised that the avowal and appearance of the same sole power in your Grace in the House of Commons is not to be expected. All sorts of persons there have concurred in battering down that notion, and the precedents of my Lord Godolphin's and my Lord Sunderland's time have been over-ruled by the long habits of seeing Sir Robert Walpole and Mr. Pelham there, which go as far back as the memory of most people now sitting there, or indeed now in business, reaches.[42]

Only during the long ministries of North and the younger Pitt was George III to enjoy the stability that Walpole and Pelham had afforded his grandfather.

The second necessary prerequisite for political tranquillity was the maintenance of friendly relations between St. James's and Leicester House. Had Frederick not been temporarily reconciled to his father between 1742 and 1746, the political confusion of those years would have been even worse, and Henry Pelham was well aware of the threat to his power that Frederick was beginning to mount when death cut short his activities in 1751. When the young Prince George reverted to opposition in 1755, it was yet another blow to Newcastle's ill-fated ministry, and Hardwicke again neatly summed up the situation when he wrote to Newcastle in April 1757:

> I am inclined to think that the right and honest way will be to take some proper method of informing the King that no solid plan of administration can be made for him by anybody, that will give him ease and comfort for the remainder of his days,—ease at home or procure peace abroad, but such a one as may, if possible, unite the whole Royal Family and bring *the succession* to support and give quiet to *the possession*. Everything else will be perpetual contest.[43]

When the King was old and ailing, the reversionary interest was at its height and, as the regency crisis of 1788 was subsequently to show, George III was no more able than George II to ignore its divisive force.

[42] Yorke, *Hardwicke*, iii. 38–9.   [43] Ibid. ii. 392.

What then is a revised verdict on George II? Partly because of certain self-imposed limitations, and partly because of the particular political circumstances of his reign, his room for political manœuvre was considerably less than that which his grandson enjoyed—at least during the 1760s and 1770s. Otherwise the position of the two monarchs was remarkably similar, as were their political successes and failures. Within the context of eighteenth-century conventions George II managed to get his own way more often than has generally been recognized. Frequently, and often with impunity, he ignored or overrode the advice of his ministers; his was the dominant voice in the conduct of war and diplomacy; and he kept a close eye on all aspects of patronage, especially those in which his interest was most engaged. There was indeed a decline in monarchical power under the Hanoverians; it came, not in the reign of George II, but in the latter part of that of his grandson. The reasons were varied. Increasing pressure of business during the long wars against France made it difficult for the King to keep control of detail; large-scale measures of economical reform steadily diminished the influence of the Crown; the growth of extra-parliamentary agitation and the rising power of the press began to forge a more articulate public opinion; and the ideological impact of the French Revolution, together with the socio-economic changes wrought by ever-increasing industrialization, led to the emergence of party in a more clear-cut sense than had hitherto existed—and party was to be the final solvent of the last vital royal prerogative of choosing and dismissing ministers. But in the reign of George II all this lay far in the future. Meanwhile, George II, as his grandson was to do after him, struggled against the politicians to the best of his not inconsiderable ability, and held his own as well as was possible for any monarch who had to cope with the realities of a period of mixed government. Few of those politicians had more experience of, or were more expert at, managing George II than Walpole and Hardwicke. The former was quick to advise Henry Pelham how to overcome his difficulties in 1743. On 20 October he wrote:

The King must, with tenderness and management, be shewn what he may with reason depend upon, and what he will be deceived and lost if he places any confidence and reliance in. . . .

This leads me to the most delicate part of the whole; I mean your behaviour, and your manner of treating this subject with him. It is a great misfortune that you have not time; for time and address have often carried things, that met at first onset, with great reluctance. . . . Address and management are the weapons you must fight and defend with; plain truths will not be relished at first, in opposition to prejudices, conceived and infused in favour of his own partialities; and you must dress up all you offer, with the appearance of no other view or tendency, but to promote his service in his own way, to the utmost of your power. And the more you can make anything appear to be his own, and agreeable to his declarations and orders, given to you before he went, the better you will be heard.[44]

Hardwicke was more laconic but equally penetrating when he commented to Pitt on 2 April 1754:

It would be superfluous and vain in me to say to you, what you know so much better than I, that there are certain things which ministers cannot do directly; and that, in political arrangements, prudence often dictates to submit to the *minus malum* and to leave it to time and incidents, and perhaps to ill judging opposers, to help forward the rest.[45]

These are scarcely the words of politicians who dictated to their sovereign and who 'had almost ceased to take account of anybody's opinion but their own'.

---

[44] William Coxe, *Memoirs of the Administration of the Right Honourable Henry Pelham* (2 vols., 1829), i. 104–5.
[45] Yorke, *Hardwicke*, ii. 212.

VII

The Rockingham Whigs and America, 1767–1773

THE notion that the opponents of George III were also the proponents of American liberty is one of the more enduring articles of faith promulgated by the Whig historians of the nineteenth century in their portrayal of the eighteenth. Though the surrounding mythology lies largely in ruins, this element remains to a considerable extent intact, and while the traditional view that the King himself was the chief author of colonial misfortunes has been generally abandoned, the idea that 'Whiggism' in America had much in common with that in England lingers on It is true that the Rockingham Whigs, the party of Burke and Fox, supported or appeared to support the colonial cause at two critical periods; they were responsible for repealing Grenville's Stamp Act when in office in 1766, and they played the major part in the parliamentary opposition to the war against the colonies in the 1770s. However, there are circumstances which considerably reduce the value of these facts.

In the first place, Rockingham and his colleagues had initially shown no disposition to champion the American opposition to the Stamp Act; indeed, all the evidence of the early months of their administration suggests that under the leadership of the Duke of Cumberland they had every intention of taking an extremely authoritarian and conservative view of the colonial problem. Even when after Cumberland's death they repealed the Stamp Act, they did so primarily to appease the mercantile and manufacturing community and only after passing a Declaratory Act which explicitly rejected the constitutional claims of the colonists. Their opposition a decade later to the American War of Independence must also be qualified. After all, opposition to the North Administration's measures before and during the war was not necessarily synonymous with support for the American standpoint. Even the ultimate readiness of Rockingham and his friends to cast off the colonies and concede independence can hardly be said to have stemmed from a basic conviction of the soundness of the colonial cause; there were too many complicating factors, domestic, diplomatic, and strategic, by the late 1770s for the issue to remain in their eyes a straightforward one of imperial authority versus American liberties.

This is not necessarily to argue that the Rockinghams were in no sense liberals in the American context; it is worth remembering, however, that their more obvious contributions, the repeal of the Stamp Act in 1766 and opposition to war in the 1770s, are not entirely satisfactory as evidence of their good intentions towards colonial aspirations. In some ways the intervening, rather less hectic period between the repeal of the Stamp Act and the Boston Tea Party provides a fairer test of 'Old Whig' principles. In those years the economic pressures, despite the colonial non-importation campaign, were by no means what they had been in 1766, and war with its attendant flood of new problems was still a long way off. The Rockinghams were of course in opposition, but the American issue was not so overwhelmingly the foremost one of the day as to force them into artificial or ill-considered positions. On the other hand, there was ample opportunity for them to assert their basic views of the imperial problem, particularly in the disputes engendered by Charles Townshend's duties of 1767. Townshend's Act, a deliberate attempt to tax America through its commerce, logically raised the fundamental issue of British sovereignty, and American friends of the Rockinghams pressed them to treat it as they had treated the Stamp Act. Thus James De Lancey of New York assured Rockingham, 'I flatter myself with hopes that the repealers of the Stamp Act will again befriend the colonies.'[1] Some of Rockingham's closest allies in England were similarly concerned. In December 1768, for instance, when Lord Hillsborough, the new Secretary of State for the Colonies, seemed intent on carrying the question of the Townshend duties to a firm conclusion, the Duke of Richmond remarked to Rocking-

[1] Sheffield City Library, Wentworth Woodhouse Muniments, Rockingham Papers (hereafter cited as WWM.R), 1–1156, 4 Feb. 1769. I am indebted to Earl Fitzwilliam and his trustees for permission to quote from these manuscripts.

ham: 'We shall have Lord Hillsborough's proposals relative to America, and as we know his system to be the reverse of ours, I do hope we shall assert our old opinions and divide upon it.'[2] The old Duke of Newcastle also felt that the Rockinghams' record on the Stamp Act left them no room for hesitation:

I hope [he wrote to Rockingham on 12 September 1768], our friends will adhere to the principles, that they acted upon, when we repealed the Stamp Act. It is the same question; and my Lord Hillsborough's view plainly is, to set up, and support the contrary doctrine. There, I hope we shall disappoint him; for, I think, when it comes to that, the Parliament will never join in a measure, that must totally destroy all connection with the colonies; and is directly contrary to their proceedings in the repeal of the Stamp Act; and the principles upon which that repeal was founded.[3]

Newcastle, of course, held views on the repeal of the Stamp Act which were not precisely those of his colleagues, but the moral is sufficiently clear. If the Rockinghams were in any significant sense friends of America, they had ample opportunity to demonstrate their sentiments in the years following their departure from office in 1766.

In fact their record during this period was not, from the American point of view, a very satisfactory one. Colonial hostility to the Townshend duties was determined and widespread practically from their inception, partly because they were patently intended to be revenue taxes rather than regulating duties,[4] partly because their proceeds were to be used to finance the expenses of royal government in America and thus free it from the control of the provincial assemblies, and partly because they incidentally involved the establishment of a new and rigorous Customs system at Boston. Yet Rockingham and his friends do not appear to have been alarmed by this provocative measure. In the original debates on Townshend's proposals in the Commons in 1767 they made no attempt to amend or defeat them, apart from an insignificant sally on a

[2] WWM.R 1–1129, 12 Dec. 1768.
[3] WWM.R 1–1096.
[4] The duties were laid not on foreign goods but on imperial products—glass, paper, lead, and paint manufactured in Britain and tea handled by the East India Company. It could not be claimed, therefore, that they were in the economic interest of the empire.

point of detail.[5] Still more surprisingly, even when the colonists had made plain their unreserved opposition to the new taxes, this negative attitude did not change dramatically. Though Burke felt able by 1769 to declare in public that 'Absurdity itself never did concert such a plan of taxation'[6] as the one proposed in 1767, he did so at a time when most other politicians, including the ministers themselves, were equally contemptuous of Townshend's scheme. On the really important question of whether the demand of the colonists for repeal of the duties should be conceded, Burke and his colleagues were decidedly evasive. Thus when Dennys De Berdt, the Massachusetts Bay agent, asked their support for a petition for repeal in February 1769, they declined to become involved.[7] Two months later, when Thomas Pownall raised the matter in the Commons, 'The two Mr. Burkes spoke upon the subject, in a very general manner, but without giving any direct opinion whether they ought or ought not now to repeal'; and Rockingham himself afterwards boasted that 'No actual Motion was made for the repeal and indeed I tryed all I could and perhaps was very instrumental in preventing its being moved'.[8] Not surprisingly, it seemed to one American agent that the Rockingham party did 'not seem through the sessions really to have wished the repeal of the act, but rather that it should remain to embarrass the present Ministers, and as a means of their destruction, to whom they hope to succeed'.[9] Only in 1770, when the North Administration

---

[5] See P. D. G. Thomas, 'Charles Townshend and American Taxation in 1767', *E.H.R.* lxxxiii (1968), 50, and for a somewhat unconvincing reply, D. Watson, 'The Rockingham Whigs and the Townshend Duties', ibid. lxxxiv (1969), 561–5. Though Burke later claimed that he had publicly declared his opposition to Townshend's scheme from the beginning, there appears to be no contemporary confirmation of his having done so. The only indication of any opposition at all by the Rockinghams is Frederick Montagu's remark that 'I understand Dowdeswell and Sir W. Baker mean to attack the American duties on glass propos'd by the Chancellor of the Exchequer' (B.M., Add. MS. 32982 (Newcastle Papers), fo. 317, Montagu to Newcastle, 12 June 1767).

[6] B.M., Egerton MS. 219, fo. 298, Sir Henry Cavendish's Debates, 19 April 1769.

[7] 'Letters of Dennys De Berdt', ed. A. Matthews, *Publications of the Colonial Society of Massachusetts*, xiii (1910–11), 355–6.

[8] *Collections of the Massachusetts Historical Society*, 5th ser. ix. 337, W. S. Johnson to Gov. Pitkin, 26 April 1769; WWM.R 1–1186, Rockingham to J. Harrison, 19 May 1769.

[9] *Coll. Mass. Hist. Soc.*, 5th ser. ix. 338, W. S. Johnson to Gov. Pitkin, 26 April 1769.

itself partially revoked the Townshend legislation, did the Rockinghams adopt a less equivocal stance.

This record is not improved by an examination of the other issues which affected the American colonies in these years. The petition for drastic reforms in imperial commerce, which was received from the New York merchants in January 1767, was actually quashed as the result of consultation between the ministerial and Opposition leaders. 'I understand', Rockingham reported to Newcastle, 'that Administration mean to have it *lie upon* the table and to which we shall assent. Charles Townshend, Conway, Dowdeswell and Burck talked about it yesterday and agreed much in opinion.'[10] Moreover, when Townshend outlined the Government's plans for dealing with the recalcitrant New York assembly in its campaign against the American Mutiny Act, 'Dowdeswell spoke against the whole as insufficience' and advised the adoption of a scheme which would actually have been more repressive than the court's,[11] while Sir George Savile, one of Rockingham's oldest and most influential friends, 'thought strong measures were necessary as we were only carrying on acts of parliament against acts of assembly and making paper war'.[12] In fact, when the Rockingham party did oppose the Administration's American policy in this period, it was apt to be on relatively safe topics like the threatened application of the treason statute of 35 Henry VIII to the thirteen colonies. Even when they launched a full-scale assault, as in May 1770 in the aftermath of the Boston massacre, the result was a set of resolutions, penned by Burke and proposed in both Houses, which Horace Walpole not unreasonably described as 'strangely refined and obscure'[13] and which revealed no major principle or policy.

The refinement and obscurity noted by Walpole were indeed only too characteristic of the pronouncements of the Rockinghams, who in their declarations showed no more desire to adopt the colonial standpoint than in their actions. In the negotiations between Rockingham, Grenville, and Bedford in the summer of 1767, the American issue raised tempers on

[10] Add. MS. 32980, fo. 109, 16 Feb. 1767.
[11] Add. MS. 32981, fo. 377, J. West to Newcastle, 13 May 1767.
[12] Ibid., fo. 378.
[13] Horace Walpole's *Memoirs of the Reign of King George the Third*, ed. G. F. R. Barker (4 vols., 1894), iv. 99.

all sides, but not for the obvious reason. Rockingham's fury apparently proceeded less from reluctance to accede to Grenville's doctrines than from indignation that any kind of statement was necessary:

> I own I felt warm [he informed Hardwicke], and expressed my surprise that we should be called upon for a declaration of our creed on the subject of North America; that nothing in our conduct could give ground for a suspicion that we did not, and had not always meant that this country should maintain its sovereignty.[14]

Nor did the Rockinghams rush to state their view of the colonial problem later on. Where Grenville was inclined to raise the American issue on the slightest pretext—as William Strahan the printer observed, 'In all his Speeches he never fails to bring in North America'[15]—Rockingham and his friends seem positively to have evaded it. Only if called upon to defend their own work, the repeal of the Stamp Act, would they readily resort to comment, and then in such a way as to give little satisfaction to the colonists. Thus Charles Garth, the South Carolina and Maryland agent, noted of one occasion in the Commons in November 1768 that 'The Propriety of the Repeal of the Stamp Act was Attack'd, but Mr. Burke in a very able Speech, supported that Measure, tho' he chose to confine himself to the Ground of commercial Interests'.[16] Indeed it is quite clear that Burke and his friends did not regard their conduct in relation to America as a matter of central interest or importance. In the *Thoughts on the Cause of the Present Discontents*, in which they set out to present the public with what they described as 'a fair state of our principles',[17] there is nothing on Anglo-American relations, and when Rockingham addressed himself

---

14 *Memoirs of the Marquis of Rockingham and his Contemporaries*, ed. Lord Albermarle (2 vols., 1852), ii. 51, 2 July 1767; cf. J. Brooke, *The Chatham Administration, 1766–68* (1956), pp. 205–8. The negotiations eventually broke down as the result of disagreement not over the American issue but rather over the disposal of places in the projected administration.

15 'Correspondence between William Strahan and David Hall', *Pennsylvania Mag.* x (1886), 330, 13 Feb. 1768.

16 'Garth Correspondence', ed. J. W. Barnwell, *South Carolina Historical and Genealogical Mag.* xxx (1929), 231, Garth to Committee of Correspondence, 10 Nov. 1768.

17 Nottingham University Library, Portland MSS., PwF 9023, Rockingham to Portland, 5 Dec. 1769. I am indebted to the Duke of Portland and the University of Nottingham for permission to quote from these manuscripts.

to the task of defining 'the fundamental principles' of his party
in terms of 'two material points', they turned out to consist
merely of permanent opposition to two personal political
enemies, Bute and Grenville.[18] Against this background it is
not surprising that some Americans entertained doubts of the
sincerity of the Rockinghams when they declared their friendship to the colonies. Dennys De Berdt, who as well as being the
Massachusetts agent was also a prominent London merchant
and a friend of the Rockinghams, constantly assured his employers that Rockingham and his associates were 'steady
friends' and 'much in your favor'.[19] To others this was not
obvious. William Samuel Johnson, who came to England as
Connecticut agent after the repeal of the Stamp Act, with few
preconceptions about British politicians, judged them on their
performance in the late 1760s, and found them wanting.
'Opposition [would not] take up our cause with spirit; at least,
if they do, I fear it will be only so far as may serve the purposes
of pure opposition, not upon the great principles upon which
we stand, and if so, what they will do will lose much of its
weight.'[20] It is difficult to contest this judgement. De Berdt's
contrary claim, that 'the Whigs, or friends to liberty are also
friends to America',[21] is not one which can readily be substan-
tiated by their conduct in the years after 1766.

   The Rockinghams themselves attempted to explain their
inadequacies by stressing the difficult circumstances in which
they found themselves. When urged by the American agents
to take action they were inclined to reply that 'the present was
not a favourable opportunity', or that the proposed measures
'would not be attended with the least chance of success'.[22]
These were not very satisfactory arguments, nor was that which
Burke produced when taxed with his lack of constructive suggestions; it was for the ministers, he insisted, to make the
suggestions—'Parliament can't govern the detail of America.
God send, it may fall into the hands of those, who can govern.'[23]
On a different tack, it can be pointed out that in their reluctance

[18] Ibid. 8991, Rockingham to Portland, 17 Sept. 1767.
[19] 'Letters of De Berdt', p. 350, De Berdt to S. Cushing, 2 Jan. 1769.
[20] *Coll. Mass. Hist. Soc.*, 5th ser. ix. 406, Johnson to Pitkin, 3 Feb. 1770.
[21] 'Letters of De Berdt', p. 358, De Berdt to R. Cary, 2 Feb. 1769.
[22] Ibid., p. 356; WWM.R 1–1186, Rockingham to Harrison, 19 May 1769.
[23] Egerton MS. 222, fo. 24, Debate of 26 April 1770.

to give the colonists firm backing Burke and his friends were in very good company. Chatham, widely regarded on both sides of the Atlantic as the champion of colonial rights, grew noticeably less enthusiastic in this respect during the years after the repeal of the Stamp Act; moreover, the merchants and manufacturers, who had done so much to bring about repeal in 1766, were notoriously indifferent to the urgings of their transatlantic colleagues in relation to the Townshend duties. Indeed opinion in general, both in and out of Parliament, was not well disposed towards the colonies in these years. As Thomas Townshend junior pointed out in the Commons in February 1769, the revenue duties of 1767 had passed because there was widespread support for them: 'It was not the opinion of one man, but of numbers; it had persuaded the nation, that it was absolutely necessary to do something.'[24] Such arguments, if they are accepted at all, do not, however, carry much weight; at best, from the American standpoint, they tend to explain rather than excuse the backwardness of the 'Old Whigs' in their cause. Marginally more plausible is the belief of some observers that Rockingham's conduct was dictated solely by political necessity, and in particular by the need to avoid alienating George Grenville. In 1767, of course, when the Townshend duties were introduced, Rockingham was on very bad terms with Grenville and would by no means have trimmed his course to suit the man he regarded as one of his worst enemies. On the other hand, in 1769 and 1770, it was obviously important for the so-called united opposition of Grenvilles, Rockinghams, and Chathams to avoid as far as possible the potentially divisive issue of America and concentrate on the questions raised by the Middlesex election. Moreover, when colonial affairs were actually before Parliament some diplomacy was undoubtedly employed. Thus Burke reported to his friend O'Hara that in the Lords' debate of 18 May 1770, Rockingham had spoken 'with great dexterity, so as not to give the least offence to the opposite sentiments of some of the Allies'.[25] Even so, political manœuvring was probably of limited significance; it is a little difficult to believe that in every member of the Rockingham

[24] Egerton MS. 217, fos. 267–8, Debate of 8 Feb. 1769.
[25] *The Correspondence of Edmund Burke*, ii, ed. Lucy S. Sutherland (Cambridge, 1960), 139, 21 May 1770.

party there was a frustrated American radical struggling to get out.

Unfortunately, while it is clear that Rockingham and his friends did little to render great services to America, it is by no means easy to be certain as to the precise nature of their views. If they had proved negative and unhelpful in their comments on the American problem in the years before the partial repeal of the Townshend duties in 1770, they were not less so in the years immediately after. America receded as a major issue, and like other politicians they were preoccupied with a plethora of new questions—the Middlesex election and petitioning movement, the Falkland Islands crisis, the Printers' Case, the Jury Bill, the Royal Marriage Act, the Irish Absentee tax, and East India Company affairs. The crucial decision of these years in American policy, the clause in the East India Tea Export Act of 1773 which exempted Company tea exported to America from all import duties, was apparently neither opposed nor noticed by the Rockinghams. The result was that in 1773 as in 1767 they expressed no objections to a scheme which was instantly interpreted on the other side of the Atlantic as a provocative attack on colonial rights, and one which their own friends in America immediately and correctly informed them would 'cause as much noise as the Stamp Act did'.[26] Moreover, there must be some doubt as to whether they were ever very much united in their sentiments. Newcastle thought that the party was seriously divided on American questions, and Dowdeswell also seems to have feared disagreements among his colleagues.[27] All that can be attempted is a tentative assessment of the views of the four most important members of the party, Rockingham as leader, Savile as his close if independent friend, Dowdeswell as the principal spokesman in the Commons, and Burke as an influential but essentially subordinate adviser, publicist, and man of business.

If anything is clear about the attitudes of these men, it is their extreme disapproval of the activities of the colonists in the years

[26] WWM.R 1–1457, J. De Lancey to Rockingham, 26 Oct. 1773; cf. B. Donoughue, *British Politics and the American Revolution* (1964), p. 24.
[27] WWM.R 1–1096, Newcastle to Rockingham, 12 Sept. 1768; William L. Clements Library, Dowdeswell MSS., Dowdeswell to Rockingham, 10 Jan. 1767. I am indebted to the Clements Library, University of Michigan, for permission to quote from these manuscripts.

after 1766, and their strong conviction that their own action in repealing the Stamp Act had been misconstrued and improperly exploited in America. Typical was the language of Burke who described the colonists as 'wild and absurd', and of Dowdeswell who remarked that they were 'liberty mad, and . . . so fully possessed with enthusiasm upon this subject, that nothing temperate and wise is to be expected from them'.[28] Even more striking were the comments of Sir George Savile, who had had much to do with the decision to repeal the Stamp Act and was by no means insensitive to colonial interests. He wrote to Rockingham after an incident in Boston involving the destruction of 'a fine sailing pleasure Boat' which belonged to his friend Joseph Harrison, the local Customs collector:

> If the boat had been burnt before the repeal of the stamp act, I know not how I should have voted. To be sure it ought to have made no difference; but no body can quite command their resentments. . . . I know I shall grow a little cautious of playing too familiarly with a bear that was given me a pretty little merry good humour'd cub. He's not cross now; but stronger than I am.[29]

To Thomas Moffat, the prominent Rhode Island conservative, he was even more emphatic:

> I think and say, that you are a distempered and delirious people, and therefore deserve much pity and compassion, because you certainly have not known what you were doing. I do not know or think that ever I shall be benefited twenty pounds by all the taxes that will ever be levied in North America, and from the local situation of the chief part of my landed estates,[30] there are but few persons in England that will be more immediately affected by the increase or decay of your trade. But, do you think, because of that consideration, that I shall be at any loss to choose my side, if matters shall be insolently driven up to an extremity by you? And the Americans have supposed that they have fast hold upon us, upon

[28] *Burke Correspondence*, ii. 77, Burke to Rockingham, 9 Sept. 1769; Dowdeswell MSS., Dowdeswell to Rockingham, 14 Aug. 1768.

[29] WWM.R 1–1077, 31 July 1768; cf. the corrupt reading in *Memoirs of the Marquis of Rockingham*, ii. 76. For Harrison's own account of the incident, see D. H. Watson, 'Joseph Harrison and the *Liberty* Incident', *W. & M. Qtly*, 3rd ser. xx (1963), 585–95.

[30] As a prominent Yorkshire landowner, Savile was always particularly attentive to the interests of the West Riding manufacturers, many of whom depended on the American market for their livelihood.

account of their commerce with us, and have piqued themselves upon it, and have boasted that they will go in rags, and be proud of them, rather than purchase the commodities of Great Britain. Lord Pity them! Because there was once a clamour raised here, which we turned to their favour and advantage, do not they think or can they not consider what we can do, if we are heated, driven, or worked into a frame or spirit big with resentment and rage against you? But I say again, that you are mad, or else you conclude that we are debilitated and heart-broken with the burden and expenses of the late war. But tell them, because I tell it to you, that the eighty millions which we then spent has scarcely wounded us through the skin; not a single luxury either lopped off, or re-trenched here; hardly enough of our fulness and fatness purged down, to fit us for hard labour: we are but breathed, if we should come to be earnest with you.[31]

In addition to this general reaction of anger and dismay at the violence of the colonists, there was an element in the attitude of Rockingham and his friends which should not be under-estimated; this was a firm and sincere attachment to the right of the mother country to tax America. Though they had intro-duced the Declaratory Bill in 1766 in part as a political strata-gem, they were none the less convinced of its absolute legal validity and, as the Connecticut agent observed, they 'assert the supremacy of Parliament in almost as strong terms as the Ministerial party'.[32] In 1767 Dowdeswell even felt the need to stress this principle against what he regarded as the unnecess-arily pro-American policy of the Chatham Administration. 'I am desirous', he told Rockingham on 10 January, 'of laying claim to the right in as strong terms as is possible, not only to justify my own opinion of last year but to oppose that of those who are at this time first in power.'[33] This opinion was indeed frequently repeated in the House of Commons; in January 1769, for example, Dowdeswell insisted, 'I never was more in earnest in my life. I for one was always for maintaining the authority of this country by every reasonable effort.'[34] Rocking-ham himself was no less unequivocal on this point. 'The Declaratory Bill', he assured his American friend Harrison,

[31] *Grenville Papers*, ed. W. J. Smith (4 vols., 1852–3), iv. 512.
[32] *Coll. Mass. Hist. Soc.*, 5th ser. ix. 338, Johnson to Pitkin, 26 April 1769.
[33] Dowdeswell MSS.
[34] Egerton MS. 216, fos. 125–6, Debate of 26 Jan. 1769.

'which *we* brought in to fix and ascertain the rights of this country over its colonies—is what I must and ever shall adhere to.'[35]

Equally important is the attitude of the Rockinghams to the question of how and when the right to tax the colonies was to be employed. The traditional view, that they would on no account endorse the laying of taxes in practice, is based largely on Burke's speeches and writings, about which there must be some reservations. In the first place, Burke's major commentaries on imperial relations date from 1774–5, when the conflict between the colonies and the mother country seemed imminent. Though he had stated his central thesis of 'a real distinction between the ideal and the practical right of the constitution'[36] in the debates on the repeal of the Stamp Act in 1766, he had also proved cautious in his comments on American taxation in the years which followed. While clearly moving towards the view that any taxation for revenue purposes from Westminster was impracticable, he seems deliberately to have restrained his thinking in this field until the great speeches of 1774–5. In any case, Dowdeswell was far more representative of and important to the party than Burke. It was he whom Rockingham consulted first and foremost, and it was he who directed the party's activities in the Commons.

Dowdeswell in fact had no doubt that American taxation was both proper and permissible. The celebrated theory of legislation and taxation adopted by Chatham he strongly deprecated. 'The distinction between external and internal taxes', he informed Rockingham, 'has been found frivolous, as indeed I always thought it. And your Lordship knows that I have never been able to distinguish between the right of passing one law and the right of passing another.'[37] Even the Townshend duties did not seem to Dowdeswell particularly unreasonable. As a financial burden they were 'really too insignificant to be an object either to them or to us', and they were after all based partially on proposals first made under the Rockingham ministry, in which Dowdeswell had been

[35] WWM.R 1–1100, 2 Oct. 1768.
[36] 'Parliamentary Diaries of Nathaniel Ryder, 1764–7', ed. P. D. G. Thomas, *Camden Miscellany*, xxiii (R. Hist. Soc., Camden 4th ser. vii, 1969), 273, 3 Feb. 1766.
[37] Dowdeswell MSS., Dowdeswell to Rockingham, 14 Aug. 1768.

Chancellor of the Exchequer.[38] What he found objectionable in the Duties Act of 1767 was not the principle of taxation involved, but rather the provocative form it took: 'Had it been proposed in our time I should have liked the thing well enough, but I would have advised sending it out under some other name, made commerce its first object, and the revenue a secondary object for defraying the expenses of that commission and of the civil governments.'[39] In fact Dowdeswell himself, with his colleagues in the ministry of 1765–6, had been responsible for a tax which did not differ significantly from those levied by Townshend, and which indeed came to be seen in a similar light by the colonists. As Joseph Harrison, perhaps Rockingham's closest American friend, wrote from Boston, 'Even the penny a Gallon Duty on Molasses (which Your Lordship will remember, was admitted by the Americans themselves in 1766, as so proper and easy an Imposition, that no Objection could possibly be made to it) is now found out to be oppressive and illegal.'[40] Dowdeswell also fully appreciated the significance of the molasses duty of 1766 and its reception. The colonists, he pointed out to Rockingham, in their opposition to the Townshend duties

do not appear to make this stand against *these duties* on account of their pressure, but against the general principle of raising *any* revenue in America, and therefore extend their opposition even to a reduced duty on the molasses, meant now to be really collected, and to say the truth for revenue not for commerce, for it is laid general on British as well as French produce.[41]

Dowdeswell and his friends evidently interpreted the resistance of the Americans to the Townshend duties as a frontal assault on the commercial system which united the mother country and one which had no logical stopping-point. There was

[38] Ibid.; R. J. Chaffin, 'The Townshend Duties of 1767', *W. & M. Qtly*, 3rd ser. xxvii (1970), 90, 95.

[39] Dowdeswell MSS., Dowdeswell to Rockingham, 14 Aug. 1768.

[40] D. H. Watson, art. cit. *W. & M. Qtly*, 3rd ser. xx (1963), 588, Harrison to Rockingham, 17 June 1768.

[41] Dowdeswell MSS., 14 Aug. 1768. The old molasses duty of 1733 and Grenville's modified version of it in 1764 had both been intended to discriminate against foreign produce. In 1766 the Rockingham ministry had reduced the duty in response to American demands, but in so doing had incidentally destroyed the element of discrimination.

certainly evidence to sustain such an interpretation. Mercantile communities throughout the colonies made no attempt to conceal the fact that they objected to much more besides the duties in the Act of 1767. Thus one Virginian merchant bluntly informed his English correspondent in November 1769:

I am an Associator in Principle, and shall not import any more necessaries till the hateful Acts are repealed. The Ministry promised to get a Repeal of that imposing the Duties on Glass Paper and Colours; But, tell Them in plain English, That alone wont satisfy America. Madeira Wine and other Things are unconstitutionably taxed. These must be taken off, or We shall hardly thank them for the other.[42]

Rockingham himself stressed the danger in such demands. 'If the affairs in America go on with warmth,' he told Harrison in October 1768, 'I have no doubt but that the restrictions of the Act of Navigation will be considered as a virtual taxation.'[43] With the whole basis of the imperial system as they knew it apparently under attack, it is not surprising that Rockingham and his followers found it difficult to give their support to the agitations of the colonists.

To recognize the fundamental authoritarianism of the Rockinghams in their imperial attitudes is not to depict them as extreme reactionaries. They never adopted Grenville's measures,[44] never committed themselves to a policy of coercion, and were never hysterically anti-American. On the other hand, they were obviously not in any significant sense supporters of the new demands which were emerging in the thirteen colonies in the years after the Seven Years War. If they were

[42] *John Norton and Sons*, ed. F. N. Mason (Richmond, Va., 1937), p. 113, W. Nelson to J. Norton, 18 Nov. 1769. Cf. A. M. Schlesinger, *The Colonial Merchants and the American Revolution, 1763–1776* (New York, 1939), pp. 131–4.

[43] WWM.R 1–1100, 2 Oct. 1768.

[44] This is not, however, true of all Rockingham's supporters. According to Newcastle, Sir William Baker strongly supported Grenville's potentially explosive idea of a Test Act compelling American office-holders to swear an oath subscribing to the Declaratory Act, and Charles Yorke, formerly Attorney-General in the first Rockingham ministry, also expressed his approval of it in the Commons (Add. MS. 32982, fo. 51, Newcastle to Rockingham, 17 May 1767; 'Parliamentary Diaries of Nathaniel Ryder, 1764–7', p. 346, 13 May 1767). Newcastle even claimed that 'Some of our friends' were inclined to favour 'The measure of conquering the colonies, and obliging them to submit' (WWM.R 1–1096, Newcastle to Rockingham, 12 Sept. 1768).

friends to America, their friendship did not allow for a real change in the traditional relationship between the mother country and the colonies. As Burke, in his capacity as New York agent, reiterated to his employers, 'All the true friends to the Colonies, the only *true* friends they have had, or ever can have in England have laid and will lay down the proper subordination of America, as a fundamental, incontrovertible Maxim, in the Government of this Empire.'[45] There is indeed little to distinguish the views of Burke and his friends on the basic questions involved in the American Revolution from those of most other Englishmen. The statement which Lord North made from the Treasury bench in March 1770, for example— 'I am for retaining our right of taxing America, but of giving it every relief that may be consistent with the welfare of the mother country'[46]—could easily have been made by Rockingham, Dowdeswell, or Burke. This perhaps is the most significant fact for the history of Anglo-American relations at this time; even the better-disposed of British politicians were not really prepared to make the kind of concessions which so many Americans were coming to regard as essential for the continuance of the imperial connection. William Samuel Johnson's comment on the politicians and parties whose antics he observed as an American agent—'They have *all* long since agreed that America must be governed and rendered effectually useful and subordinate to this country, though they have differed in the mode'[47]—was as much a comment on the future of the Empire as on the state of politics in England.

Only in one respect did the Rockinghams really differ significantly from their contemporaries on this subject. This concerned not an issue of principle, but rather the possibility of a war to the death against the colonies. As early as 1768 Dowdeswell forecast to Rockingham:

I think we shall be soon trying who shall stand most forward in proposing terms of accommodation to end a struggle by which this

[45] *Burke Correspondence*, ii. 528–9, 6 April 1774.
[46] *Parliamentary History*, xvi. 855, 5 March 1770.
[47] *Coll. Mass. Hist. Soc.*, 5th ser. ix. 366, Johnson to Pitkin, 18 Sept. 1769. For a statement of the view that there was no significant body of opinion in Britain in favour of colonial claims, see J. Shy, 'Thomas Pownall, Henry Ellis, and the Spectrum of Possibilities, 1763–1775', in *Anglo-American Political Relations, 1675–1775*, ed. A. G. Olson and R. M. Brown (New Brunswick, N.J., 1970, pp. 155–86).

country, possesst of everything has everything to lose and nothing to get. For a contest with the colonies, supported as it will be by the enemies of this country, must be destructive to us in the first place.[48]

This sentiment, which served to counterbalance the anger and irritation provoked by the violence of the Americans, did not diminish with the passing years. By January 1774 Rockingham could inform Burke, 'Notwithstanding all that has passed, I can never give my assent to proceeding to actual force against the colonies.'[49] It was a lack of stomach for a real conflict rather than doubt about the principles concerned which to some extent separated the Rockinghams from the other parties of the day. Unlike most of their compatriots, they were not prepared for a fight, and this at least tended to make them softer and perhaps more realistic in their attitudes and reactions when colonial problems came to the fore.

This factor also helps to explain the apparent change of stance on the part of the Rockingham party in the 1770s. Many things occurred in 1774–6 to bring about such a change. The growing strength of the North Administration as well as its increasingly hard line on American affairs, the decline and death of Dowdeswell with the corresponding emergence of Fox and growing predominance of Burke, and above all the War of American Independence itself, all impelled the Rockinghams, if somewhat reluctantly, towards complete rejection of the policy favoured not merely by the Government but by the overwhelming majority of Englishmen. Insistent as they had always been on British sovereignty and American subordination, they preferred to qualify and finally abandon both rather than enforce them by war. In this they were to be for long at complete variance with their contemporaries, as they had never been previously. Moreover, as their attitude became increasingly difficult to distinguish from that of the colonists themselves, their own view of past events changed. The need to demonstrate their consistency, ever a particular shibboleth of the Rockinghams, forced them to represent their earlier conduct in a new light. The repeal of the Stamp Act, which could now safely be seen as a liberal concession to American sentiment and the

[48] Dowdeswell MSS., 14 Aug. 1768.
[49] *Burke Correspondence*, ii. 516, 30 Jan. 1774.

embodiment of an enlightened imperial policy, received more and more emphasis from Burke and his colleagues, while their original view of the Townshend duties was conveniently forgotten. Thus Rockingham, looking back from 1774, described the repeal of the Stamp Act as 'the returning to the old system and we would not leave a pepper corn' and the Townshend duties as a 'revival of taxes . . . an immediate attack', which 'must have shewn the Americans that they were again fallen under harsh task masters'.[50] Still more significantly, the Declaratory Act, which Rockingham and his friends had not hesitated to uphold in earlier years, now came increasingly to be seen as a regrettable necessity imposed by the circumstances of the time, and little more. By 1775 the Duke of Richmond was publicly referring to it 'rather as necessary at the time, than strictly right';[51] and even Burke, who strove to demonstrate his fidelity to 'the system of 1766', subtly altered his interpretation of it.[52] In 1766 he had boasted that 'the constitutional superiority of Great Britain was preserved, by *the act for securing the dependence of the colonies*'; but a decade or so later, under attack from Price and Abingdon and the more radical opponents of the North Administration, he stressed that what was involved was 'a point, after all of mere speculation', and claimed merely that 'the Act as an abstract proposition of law, was wise at the time it was made'.[53] In fairness to Burke it must be said that he never attempted to deny his own belief in Parliamentary supremacy over the colonies. On the other hand, in common with his friends, he was inclined to forget the extent of his party's hostility to colonial demands in the years before the war. 'Charged with being an American',[54] in 1777 it was all too easy to imagine that the same charge could have been made in 1767. 'I conceive', he wrote in his *Letter to the Sheriffs of Bristol*, 'it would be happy for us if they [the Americans] were taught to believe, that there was even [?ever] a formed American

[50] WWM.R 1–2143.

[51] *The Correspondence of Edmund Burke*, iii, ed. G. H. Guttridge (Cambridge, 1961), 102–3, Burke to the Citizens of Bristol, 20 Jan. 1775.

[52] *The Works of Edmund Burke* (Bohn's British Classics, 8 vols., 1854–89), i. 437, 'Speech on American Taxation'.

[53] Ibid. 182, 'Short Account of a Late Short Administration'; *Burke Correspondence*, iii. 254, Burke to R. Champion, 19 March 1776; *Parl. Hist.* xix. 1012, 6 April 1778.

[54] *Burke's Works*, ii. 25, 'Letter to the Sheriffs of Bristol'.

party in England, to whom they could always look for support.'[55] The record of the Rockinghams in the years between the repeal of the Stamp Act and the Boston Tea Party does not suggest that they were truly such a party.[56]

[55] *Burke's Works*, ii. 20.

[56] I wish to acknowledge the kindness of Mr. J. Brooke in reading and commenting on this paper, without committing him in any way to the views expressed in it.

VIII

Joshua Johnson in London, 1771–1775: Credit and Commercial Organization in the British Chesapeake Trade

THOUGH international trade has hardly been neglected by historians, relatively little attention has been given to the independent merchants who carried on at least three-fourths of British overseas trade in the seventeenth and eighteenth centuries. Part of this neglect is traceable to the rarity of surviving firm records that would tell us something about capitalization, credit, and earnings. Particularly mysterious is the fate of the records of houses trading to North America before 1776. These records were preserved for decades after the war to facilitate the collection of pre-war debts; after 1800 they had to be surrendered as evidence of claims to government commissioners paying compensation for uncollected debts. What happened to them afterwards is anyone's guess.

There were, however, a few merchant houses in London which lost less from debts rendered uncollectable by the American Revolution and filed no claims. These were firms which adhered to the American cause, particularly firms with American partners and connections: two well-known examples in the Virginia trade were William Lee and John Norton & Sons. Much of the correspondence of Lee and of the Nortons has survived, but we lack their ledgers and journals and thus know relatively little about their capitalization and internal life. This deficiency is remedied, however, in the records of a similar firm—Wallace, Davidson, & Johnson, of Annapolis (Maryland) and London. Its London partner, Joshua Johnson, like William Lee, went over to France in 1777 and there served commercial and public correspondents in America during the war. Years later, he had difficulty settling accounts with his pre-war

Annapolis partners and commenced an interminable suit in chancery in Maryland, which has left all the pre-war accounts of his London house preserved for posterity in the Maryland Hall of Records.[1] In addition, partly because of the distinction he attained by his daughter's marriage to President John Quincy Adams, a sprinkling of his papers survives in other U.S. repositories.[2]

Joshua Johnson (1742–1802) sprang of an extensive Maryland family. The Johnsons of Maryland were descended from the Johnsons of Great Yarmouth, Norfolk, a family which furnished two Members of Parliament in the seventeenth century. Thomas Johnson I of Great Yarmouth emigrated *c.* 1689 to Maryland, where he was relatively unsuccessful as planter and trader. His only son Thomas II (1702–*c.* 1777) did better as a planter and frequently represented Cecil County in the Lower House of the Assembly, though his principal residence was in Calvert County on the Patuxent, near the mouth of St. Leonard's Creek, in the heart of the Maryland tobacco country. Thomas II had a large and quite successful family, including seven sons. His second son, Thomas III (1732–1819), became a prosperous lawyer in Annapolis, acquired land thereabouts, and was elected to the provincial assembly by Ann Arundel County from 1762; he became a delegate to the Continental Congress, the first Revolutionary governor of Maryland, and a justice of the U.S. Supreme Court. Four of his younger brothers settled in western Maryland, James and Roger being pioneers in the nascent iron industry. Of the seven, only Joshua had a 'foreign' career.[3]

Of the other partners, we know less. The head of the firm was Charles Wallace (1727–1812) of Annapolis, a wealthy landowner and businessman, with broad interests, who seems to

[1] Annapolis (cited below as HR), Private Account Records (cited as p.a.), vols. 1507–33.

[2] e.g. Library of Congress; Maryland Hist. Soc., Baltimore; Mass. Hist. Soc., Boston.

[3] E. S. Delaplaine, *The Life of Thomas Johnson* (New York, 1927), esp. pp. 1–15, 351. After the Revolution, Johnson returned to London, where he was U.S. consul 1785–97. He married Catherine Nuth in London *c.* 1772. His daughter, Louisa Catherine (1775–1852), married John Quincy Adams in London in 1797. Cf. D. Bobbé, *Mr. and Mrs. John Quincy Adams* (New York, 1930), pp. 15–17; Andrew Oliver, *Portraits of John Quincy Adams and his Wife* (Cambridge, Mass., 1970), pp. 22–3.

have devoted only part of his time to it. Johnson's letters treat him as available only for business of a special sort, such as obtaining consignments from important planters. Member of the Lower House and some of its important committees, he became contractor for building the new Maryland State House— a £7,500 project.[4] The third partner, John Davidson (1738–94), was at this time less conspicuous, but distinguished himself as a patriot during the Revolution. He seems to have looked after the firm's day-to-day business in Annapolis, particularly book-keeping. Johnson was to wish Davidson would hire someone else to do the books and spend more time going out collecting debts.[5]

Before 1771, Wallace, Johnson, and Davidson had apparently all been in business separately in Annapolis. The several businesses were merged by a new agreement of partnership that must have been concluded about 1 January 1771. Johnson turned over to the enlarged firm the debts owed his old business and the new premises and residence he was building in the market at Annapolis facing the dock.[6] We do not know the total capital of the new firm, but when Johnson went over to London in 1771 the working capital of the London branch was £3,000,[7] apparently an advance from the Annapolis main house. In addition, the London branch generated £3,842. 15s. 3d. in retained earnings over the next four years and this was carried as its entire capital in a statement of 31 July 1775.[8]

The £3,000 taken by Johnson to London was in bills of exchange drawn by Davidson on Osgood Hanbury & Co. Since the partners did not intend shipping tobacco, they hoped for assistance from the Hanburys, the wealthiest firm in the London

---

[4] E. S. Riley, '*The Ancient City*': *a History of Annapolis, in Maryland, 1649–1887* (Annapolis, 1887), pp. 161, 170, 177; and *Maryland Hist. Mag.* xxviii (1933), 223, 228; xlii (1947), 273; xliv (1949), 89; li (1956), 50–3; R. R. Beirne, *William Buckland, 1734–1775, Architect of Virginia and Maryland* (Baltimore, 1958), pp. 69, 100–1.

[5] Riley, pp. 170, 198; *Maryland Hist. Mag.* xxviii (1933), 207, 209; xl (1945), 224; xlii (1947), 282; l (1955), 271. Both Davidson and Wallace may have been born in Scotland. HR, p.a. 1507 (Johnson's London Letter-book I, 1771–4), to D. [Davidson], 22 June 1772; to W. [Wallace], 2 July 1773.

[6] Cf. HR, p.a. 1507, to W. and D., 4 June, 3 July 1771; to D., 22 July 1771. Johnson had previously dealt with W. Molleson and J. Russell, Davidson with Hanburys, who had a good opinion of him; Wallace had once dealt with Hanburys, but had become estranged from them.   [7] Ibid., to W. and D., 26 July 1771.

[8] HR, p.a. 1514, WD&J [Wallace, Davidson, & Johnson] Journal (1774–5), p. 357.

tobacco trade, founded by John Hanbury in the 1720s and carried on after John's death in 1758 by his son Osgood and cousin Capel; after the latter's death in 1769 the partners consisted of Osgood Hanbury and his cousin John (1751–1801), Capel's son, who were joined in 1774 by Osgood's brother-in-law, John Lloyd (1751–1811). The Hanburys were part of the banking cousinhood of Quakers who were to be so fabulously wealthy in the next century—when Osgood died in 1784, his executors included a Lloyd, a Barclay, and a Gurney.[9] Johnson found the young partners, John Hanbury and John Lloyd, rather ignorant of the trade and Osgood disinclined to push it.[10] After his cousin's death, in fact, Osgood had begun to disengage from tobacco. In 1770, he put £5,000 of his own capital into the bank he founded with his Birmingham brother-in-law, Sampson Lloyd (1728–1807): Hanbury, Taylor, Lloyd, & Bowman, a London ancestor of Lloyds Bank. Within a few years, he and his sons were to confine themselves to banking or venture into brewing, as did his son Sampson Hanbury and counsin John.[11] These moves were of little consolation to Joshua Johnson, who would have preferred introductions to a more enterprising house.

Because of them Johnson chose to entrust his cash to the affiliated bank of Hanbury, Taylor, Lloyd, & Bowman. Almost the only credit service they performed for him was discounting accepted bills of exchange.[12] In the difficult year following the crisis of June 1772, his Annapolis partners sent Johnson letters of credit which, they hoped, would induce Osgood Hanbury to make them a substantial advance—but to little purpose.[13] With Hanburys increasingly suspicious and unco-operative as the new firm's business expanded and impinged on their own,

[9] HR, p.a. 1507, pp. 321–2, to WD&J, 6 April 1774. Cf. A. A. Locke, *The Hanbury Family* (1916). O. Hanbury married Mary Lloyd of Birmingham, sister of Sampson Lloyd, founder of Lloyds Bank.

[10] HR, p.a. 1507, pp. 172–7, 204, 321–2, to WD&J, 28 June, 6 Oct. 1773, 6 April 1774.

[11] Cf. R. S. Sayers, *Lloyds Bank in the History of English Banking* (Oxford, 1957), pp. 10–12.

[12] HR, p.a. 1507, to W. and D., 26 July, 29 Aug. 1771.

[13] Ibid., pp. 172–6, to WD&J, 28, 29, 30 June 1773. Daniel Wolstenholme, Esq., of Maryland, legal representative of Hanbury there, introduced the new firm to Hanbury in 1771 and signed the letter of credit in 1773. O. Hanbury handled official Maryland business in London besides funds for the wealthiest planters.

Johnson found them and their friends less useful. He soon entrusted his banking to Prescott, Grote, & Co.,[14] one of whose partners, Andrew Grote, was a wealthy London merchant sprung of a Dutch family established at Bremen and a big buyer of tobacco for Holland and Germany—a useful friend to a Maryland merchant in London.[15]

With only a limited stock advanced by his Annapolis partners and no access to long-term private loans or bank credit for anything more than discounting sixty-day bills of exchange, Johnson had to confine his London ventures within the limits of ordinary commercial credit. This was consistent with his original intentions on setting out for England in the spring of 1771. Before then, apparently, he and his partners had been general merchants at Annapolis, importing goods which they sold both retail and wholesale. They traded to the West Indies, but did not have ships in the trade to Britain. Instead, they freighted from London on others' ships and reimbursed their London correspondents (Hanbury for Davidson, Russell for Johnson) by returning bills of exchange. (They may occasionally have shipped tobacco on consignment, but there is no reference to this in their correspondence.) In such a trade, they had to be content with the terms offered by the relatively few houses who would ship to them on credit. They could not be sure they were getting the full benefit of credit facilities available at London, or of the associated discounts allowed for prompt payment, or of the bounties paid by the Government on the export of British linens or the drawbacks paid on the export of foreign linens, silks, teas, sugars, etc.

By sending their partner, Joshua Johnson, to London, the new firm of Wallace, Davidson, & Johnson hoped to go behind their previous suppliers and buy on better terms. At first, they intended to continue making remittances only in bills of exchange, so Johnson's mission was entirely that of a buyer,

---

[14] Ibid., pp. 92–4, to WD&J, 17 July 1772; ibid., 1514 (Journal), p. 104.

[15] Grote was brother-in-law of the Virginia–Maryland merchant, Silvanus Grove, whom Johnson described as the only merchant in the trade other than Hanbury who always had cash enough to pay the duties; both of course had banking connections. HR, p.a. 1507, p. 446, to WD&J, 4 Aug. 1774; cf. Jacob M. Price, 'Capital and Credit in the British–Chesapeake Trade, 1750–1775', in V. B. Platt and D. C. Skaggs (ed.), *Of Mother Country and Plantations* (Bowling Green, Ohio, 1971), p. 32; M. L. Clarke, *George Grote* (1962), pp. 1–4.

intended to expand the scope of their limited capital by taking fullest advantage of available commercial credit (commonly twelve months in the export trades). For each commodity shipped, he would find the sellers who offered the most generous and flexible credit. Equally, he would make sure that, when he was in funds (as he was on his arrival), he obtained the full rebate for early payment (commonly computed at 10 per cent p.a.). It would also be his job to study carefully the prices offered by sellers of taxed or subsidized commodities, calculating if it would be more to the firm's interest to buy at the full internal, 'long' price and then go to the trouble and expense of obtaining the bounty or drawback from Customs (a tedious procedure), or if he ought not to buy at the 'short', external price and leave the drawback or bounty to the seller.[16] He would also have time to select all his purchases after personal inspection, while the bigger houses (Russell, in particular) bought unseen on price and credit terms only.[17] With the advantages of bounties, drawbacks, discounts, long credits, and better selection, the partners calculated that they would be able to buy so much more advantageously in London that they could well afford the expense of maintaining Johnson there,[18] even though he had nothing to do but buy for them and do similar limited errands for some Baltimore houses, particularly William Lux & Bowly.

Johnson also had hopes at first of getting behind the London middlemen, besides the export merchants, and buying directly from manufacturers. On arrival in Bristol, in May 1771, he made contact with a large-scale shoe manufacturer, but later found it more feasible to buy shoes in London.[19] He had hopes of a trip to Holland and 'Jarmina', of arranging with someone at Bremen to buy German linens ('oznabrigs') for him, but was detained by illness.[20] He did travel through the Midlands manufacturing districts in the spring of 1772, though he failed to find 'large Warehouses well stocked'. The small putting-out hardware manufacturers visited at Gloucester, Tewkesbury,

[16] HR, p.a. 1507, pp. 55–8, to W. and D., 25 Feb. 1772.
[17] Ibid., to same, 4 Dec. 1771.
[18] Ibid., to same, 3 July 1771.
[19] Ibid., pp. 71, 82–6, to same, 28 April, 26 July, 26 Aug. 1771, 22 June 1772: 'Knight is the first Shoe Warehouse in London.'
[20] Ibid., p. 66, to same, 6 Nov. 1771, 25 March 1772.

Bromsgrove, Birmingham, Coventry, and Woodstock were totally dependent on the big, wholesale ironmongers of Bristol and London and did little marketing by themselves:

> The Agents [putters-out] who reside in those Towns employ the poor Men & their Families for ten or a dozen miles round them (they mostly collect together in small villages, which are generally on Runs of Water for the advantage of getting Provision) they deliver them as much Iron &c as they can work up in a week which is returned on Saturday night when they are paid for their Labour, which is hardly sufficient to find 'em Milk & Bread much more meat. The Agents as soon as they collect a Load send it immediately to their Principal or Correspondent in London Bristol &c. & draw at 50 d/s [days' sight, i.e. 50 days after presentation] for the amount which is generally discounted at the Banks or passes as our Bills with you does; They [the putters-out] are Weekly acquainted with the rise & fall of the Price so that you cant get any allowance of 'em. I have engaged one at Birmingham to deliver me what quantity of Nails we may want at Bristol from time to time as we shall think fit to order them; . . . I assure you that I am convinced one may always do better in London.[21]

Even if one could locate a reliable supplier at Birmingham, Johnson found it impossible to buy ironmongery and cutlery there advantageously except for cash, an increasingly unattractive prospect.[22] Save for a few nail purchases at Birmingham (for which six months' credit was available) and an occasional order to a sailcloth maker at Lichfield (to whom he had been personally recommended), he thereafter made no effort to buy directly in the country.[23]

Even 'in town', Johnson found purchasing conventions quite complicated. Young John Hanbury took him around 'to all his Tradesmen [some of whom were richer than all but a few export merchants] to introduce and recommend me to 'em'.[24] (Hanburys agreed to help, provided that Johnson stayed out of the tobacco trade.)[25] If silks could be bought for fifteen

---

[21] Ibid., p. 71, to same, 17 April 1772.
[22] Ibid., pp. 83–4, 98–101, to same, 22 June, 20 Aug. 1772.
[23] Ibid., p. 39, to same, 2 Dec. 1771; to John Tunstall, 26 Aug. 1771. Johnson was recommended to Tunstall, of Lichfield, by Samuel Gist, merchant of London.
[24] Ibid., to W. and D., 3 July 1771.
[25] Ibid., to D., 22 July 1771.

months' credit, linen, woollens, and ironmongery generally had to be paid for in twelve, chinaware in six, grocery and lead shot in nine. Some comestibles, particularly sugar, had to be paid for in cash or a sixty-day bill or note (as did tobacco), while tea could be most economically purchased for cash at the East India Company's auctions.[26] (Johnson was reluctant to touch tea, except in 1772–3, because of the non-importation 'associations'.)[27] Again and again he had to instruct his partners that differences in credit terms were reflected finely in prices, and that they would do well to borrow (particularly when in Maryland they could get money for as little as $3\frac{1}{2}$ per cent) for the sake of the rebate at 10 per cent on early payment of goods sold at long credit.[28] When not in cash (as in 1773), he had perforce to deal with the largest houses, best able to offer long credits. In such circumstances, of course, he could not expect to be treated as well as in 1771, when he paid cash or settled early.[29]

There were also problems of package and quality, particularly in linens, the major single item in Johnson's purchases. He divided his first Irish linen purchases between Barclays, the great Quaker linen merchants (connected with the Hanburys), and David Harvey, though Harvey would not give more than six months' credit and 'will not breake but only sell in Lotts as put up in Ireland'. One reason was that Harvey, Irish linen merchant of Lawrence Lane, Cheapside, sold his linens on commission for printers in Ireland, while David and John Barclay, linen merchants at 108 Cheapside, traded on their own account, employing agents in Ireland who purchased linens from twenty-five different printers:

[26] HR, p.a. 1507, to W. and D., 26 July, 2 Dec. 1771, 25 Feb., 22 June 1772, 6 Jan., 16 Feb. 1773. Johnson found it difficult to find sugar bakers or grocers with enough sugar on hand to fill his orders and had to deal with 'Piercy, . . . the most Capital House in London'. He also reported that some of his big competitors (e.g. Russell and John Buchanan) were able regularly to get 15 and 18 months' credit from suppliers when 12 months' was normal, but had of course to pass on the costs of that extra credit in the prices of their purchases: to W. and D., 4 Dec. 1771. Cf. ibid., pp. 135–7, to Richard Tilghman Earle & Co., 15 Feb. 1773.

[27] Johnson repeatedly reported the direct and indirect (via Philadelphia) tea shipments of his competitors (Buchanan, Philpot, Russell, etc.), and it was his advice in 1774 which probably led to the burning of the *Peggy Stewart*: ibid., to W. and D., 24 July, 18 Aug. 1771; p. 447, to WD&J, 4 Aug. 1774.

[28] Ibid., pp. 55–8, 83, to W. and D., 25 Feb., 22 June 1772.

[29] Ibid., pp. 165–6, to WD&J, 17 May 1773.

... Barclays who is ... undoubtedly the first House in their Business ... will not open an Account with any one in our Trade but [those introduced by] Hanbury[;] they have 2 or 3 ships that Runs from Philadelphia & New York which they load with Goods likewise ship Large Quantities to the West Indies which is all they do ...

Johnson also divided his first purchase of German 'Oznabrigs between Barclays & Mee & Cº. [Mee Son & Cassau] the latter is a very capital wholesale Hambro House who serve many of the linen drapers to the amount of thousands per Annum[;] they both are importers of it & the only difference respecting the Sale is you may have a single piece of Barclays & not less than 10 pieces of Mee & Cº.'[30] Later, he was to prefer the major house of Nash, Eddowes, & Martin, which received linens from twenty to thirty Irish printers and sold much to the American trade; but his partners were unimpressed with their quality, despite attractive price and credit terms.[31] Silks, fancy cottons, and woollens were even greater problems, because of higher unit costs and worry over whether what was 'fashionable' in London would be recognized as such in Maryland. Johnson thought of trying to buy cloth at the Bristol Fair,[32] but found it more prudent to buy woollens like other things in London. There he favoured the big warehousemen, Mauduit, Wright, & Co., 'the first House in that way', run by the celebrated Dissenters, Jasper (1697–1772) and Israel Mauduit (1708–87). He found them so suspicious and demanding during the credit stringency of 1773, however, that he had to transfer his cloth business elsewhere.[33]

From the first, Johnson expected to ship his partners goods worth £10,000–£12,000 yearly. His shipments in summer 1771 gave such satisfaction that he rather expanded operations in the opening months of 1772, shipping over £16,000 worth

[30] Ibid., to W. and D., 26 July 1771, 22 June 1772. David Barclay (1729–1809), who is to be distinguished from his father of the same name (1682–1769), married Rachel Lloyd, whose sister Mary was the wife of Osgood Hanbury.

[31] Nash, Eddowes, & Martin are described in the directories as 'wholesale linen-drapers' of Cheapside, but supplied Johnson with spices, grocery, wine, olive oil as well as linen. See HR, p.a. 1513 (Journal, 1771–3) and p.a. 1507 (Letter-book I), to W. and D., 24 July 1771, pp. 83, 92–4, and to WD&J, 22 June, 17 July 1772.

[32] HR, p.a. 1507, to W. and D., 17 Sept. 1771.

[33] Ibid., p. 83, to same, 22 June 1772. On the Mauduits, see M. G. Kammen, *A Rope of Sand: the Colonial Agents, British Politics, and the American Revolution* (Ithaca, N.Y., 1968), p. 325 *et passim*.

between December 1771 and July 1772.[34] As he only brought
£3,000 with him, continued operations depended on the
timely arrival of bills of exchange from his partners. He preferred London bills and advised his partners to pay a ½ per cent
premium for them. He did not trust the outports much;
having desired to avoid correspondents there to negotiate these
bills, he discovered he would have to pay a ½ per cent commission for such services if he had no regular correspondents.
Outport bills were also slower to collect: even if payable in
London, a week or two might be lost while they were sent
to the ports of address for acceptance.[35]

The trade had its rhythm. 'Spring goods' were purchased in
November–January and shipped in the New Year to reach
Maryland at latest in February/March. 'Fall goods' were shipped
in June or July to be in Maryland by early September, before
the autumn meeting of the Provincial Court and 'the September
races'. Johnson frequently urged his partners to send their orders
well in advance, to give him a month or two in which to shop
carefully.[36] He could afford to purchase or order goods a month
or more before shipment because the year's customary credit
began, not with the order, but with the date of the invoice—
the time of delivery or shipment.[37] As often as not, however,
his partners were slow in getting their orders to him and he
had to scramble at the end. He was very jealous of his biggest
competitor, the firm of William & Robert Molleson, who always
seemed to get their exports first to Maryland and their tobacco
soonest home.[38]

All in all, the affairs of the London branch of Wallace, Davidson, & Johnson promised well at the beginning of June 1772, on
the eve of the great financial crisis. During the spring Johnson
reported a few striking failures in London and Cadiz, but had
no sense of the extreme misgivings which had developed as
early as April among the Bank directors and other City
grandees.[39] Thus a note of ingenuous amazement runs through

---

[34] In addition, his firm expected to import about £1,500 worth from the West
Indies: HR, p.a. 1507, to W. and D., 26 July 1771, 4 Nov. 1772.
[35] HR, p.a. 1507, to same, 17 Sept. 1771.
[36] Ibid., to same, 6 Nov., 2, 4 Dec. 1771.
[37] Ibid., to same, 17 Sept. 1771.   [38] Ibid., to same, 26 July 1771.
[39] Ibid., to same, 25 March 1772, 6 May 1772. Cf. R. B. Sheridan, 'The British
Credit Crisis of 1772 and the American Colonies', *Journal of Econ. Hist.* xx (1960),

his letters of June–July 1772 as he reports the failure of Neale, James, Fordyce, & Downe; the sudden collapse of other houses first in London, then in Edinburgh; and all too soon failures in the Chesapeake trade itself, starting with Bogle, Bogle, & Scott, a new Scottish house in London. Next year and beyond, he was to report often that yet another house in the Chesapeake trade had called in its creditors. In some cases (e.g. James Russell, one of the biggest houses in the trade), the creditors decided to continue the business on its previous scale, but under the supervision of trustees. In others (like the important Maryland house of John & Gilbert Buchanan), calling in the creditors was the first step to winding up the firm.[40]

The crash of 1772 is generally associated with unwise credit expansion, through the drawing and redrawing of bills between London and Scotland, and with the excessive speculation on the stock market that undid Sir George Colebrooke, Governor of the East India Company, and Fordyce the banker. There were aggravating factors in the Chesapeake trade. High tobacco prices in the late 1760s had greatly increased liquidity in the Chesapeake and stimulated the formation and expansion of autochthonous business firms. These were supplied from London by a new generation of consignment houses who came to specialize in the 'cargo trade': on the receipt of orders, but with no effects in hand, the consignment merchant purchased goods in London on one year's credit for a correspondent in the Chesapeake, on the understanding that the American house would remit either tobacco or bills of exchange before the expiry of credit from the warehousemen, linen-drapers, or other suppliers. This trade assumed a continuing strong demand for European goods in the Chesapeake, a firm bill market between the Bay and London, and a continued buoyancy in tobacco prices. These need not last for ever.[41]

In 1770 Virginia and Maryland produced the first of five successive record-breaking crops. The 1770 crop was shipped

161–86; L. S. Sutherland, 'Sir George Colebrooke's World Corner in Alum, 1771–73', *Econ. Hist.* iii (1936), 237–58; H. Hamilton, 'The Failure of the Ayr Bank, 1772', *Econ. H. R.*, 2nd. ser. viii (1956), 405–17; Jacob M. Price, *France and the Chesapeake* (2 vols., Ann Arbor, Mich., 1972), i. 639–42, 696–700.

[40] HR, p.a. 1507, pp. 83–5, to W. and D., 22 June, 1, 4 July 1772.

[41] Cf. Price, 'Capital and Credit', in Platt and Skaggs (ed.), *Of Mother Country* pp. 34–5, and *France and the Chesapeake*, i. 674–6, 844.

in 1771; by the end of 1771, as warehouses filled in London and Glasgow and word came of another great crop, prices began to sag. By 1772 they were in full retreat.[42] This meant that tobacco shipped to cover debts in Britain, on the basis of optimistic price expectations, in fact proved insufficient. Similarly, bills of exchange drawn on London by consigning tobacco planters and merchants, and thought to be covered by tobacco shipped, proved overdrawn. In the optimistic early months of 1772, most of the new, aggressive houses in the London Chesapeake trade tried to oblige their correspondents in America both by accepting their bills of exchange, even without sufficient effects on hand, and by continuing to ship cargoes ordered, even though the previous year's cargoes had not yet been fully paid for. These over-shipments created a glut in the dry-goods trade in the Chesapeake by the early months of 1772, reducing the velocity of trade and making remittance to Britain even more difficult.[43] Thus, when the crisis of 1772 broke, many of the most active houses in the trade were highly extended.

All this was immediately relevant to Joshua Johnson even though he was outside the tobacco trade and, except for shipments to his own firm in Annapolis, had sent only modest cargoes to his brothers and a few close friends like William Lux & Bowly of Baltimore.[44] In June 1772 all his expected resources were coming to him in the form of bills of exchange. Most of the bills on London drawn in Maryland were drawn on and ultimately made payable to the same small circle of firms—Russell, Molleson, West & Hobson, Hanburys, John Buchanan, and Christopher Court, in particular.[45] This concentration was exaggerated for Johnson, who had advised his partners in 1771 not to buy Scottish and outport bills. After the crash of June 1772, he again advised his partners not to touch Scottish bills, even though payable in London.[46] This proved bad advice, for all but one Glasgow firm escaped unscathed, thanks to the liquidity which came from their customary

---

[42] *France and the Chesapeake*, i. 676, ii. 844; U.S. Bureau of the Census, *Hist. Statistics of the U.S.* (Washington, D.C., 1960), 765–6.

[43] HR, p.a. 1507, pp. 77–8, to W. and D., 18 May 1772; to W. Lux & Bowly, 4 June 1772.

[44] Cf. HR, p.a. 1516 (WD&J, London Ledger A), fo. 11.

[45] Cf. HR, p.a. 1513 (WD&J, London Journal, 1771–3), *passim*.

[46] HR, p.a. 1507, pp. 85–7, to W. and D., 22 June, 1 July 1772.

large cash sales to the French.[47] By contrast, there was a high incidence of failure or strained circumstance among the London firms. On the morrow of the crash, prudent firms like the Hanburys started protesting all bills of exchange not fully covered by effects on hand. Others soon followed suit;[48] even the great James Russell, previously most generous in allowing consigners to draw, was forced into this pattern by his creditors' trustees. Since the same small group upon whom the bills were drawn were also generally the firms to whom the bills were payable, the protests soon put a chill on the whole trade. The London bills received by Johnson, seemingly on the most unexceptionable houses, began registering a high proportion of protests: perhaps a quarter or a third in the year from June 1772. With debts falling due and bills being drawn on him, the relatively inexperienced Joshua Johnson soon found himself in straitened circumstances.[49]

A bill of exchange drawn in America on London was commonly payable 'at sixty days sight'—sixty days after presentation to the merchant (addressee, drawee) upon whom it was drawn. If he accepted it, the bill immediately became a negotiable commercial instrument discountable (if good enough) at the Bank of England or elsewhere. It could also be used to pay debts directly.[50] If it was not accepted but merely noted, then the merchant presenting it (the payee) had to hold it for the sixty days to see if the addressee would pay or not. If the latter still refused then, the payee had to 'protest' the bill before a notary public and send the bill and protest back to America to the firm who had sent him the bill. They had recourse against the person from whom they had purchased the bill and in Maryland were entitled to a 15 per cent penalty for compensation. In most cases the claim of the original bill and penalty were settled by the drawing of a new bill. In the difficult times of 1772–3, this might also in turn be protested.

[47] *France and the Chesapeake*, i. 640–1, 665. Johnson did not fully understand this, ascribing Scottish survival to the Ayr Bank's ill-fated scheme of raising money by selling annuities: HR, p.a. 1507, pp. 108–9 to D., 30 Oct. 1772.

[48] HR, p.a. 1507, p. 112, to WD&J, 30 Oct. 1772.

[49] Johnson also had to find cash to meet bills drawn on him: thus his partners authorized their Barbados correspondent, William Potts, to draw on him for rum and sugar they had ordered: ibid., to W. and D., 6 Nov. 1771.

[50] Johnson's journal (HR, p.a. 1513, 1514) contains examples of accepted bills of exchange with less than 30 days to run used as cash to pay debts without discount.

Johnson was in no immediate danger when the bubble burst in June 1772. Most of the goods he had shipped in June–July 1771 had been paid for in cash or settled in the interim; he had relatively few debts outstanding, due, or about to become due. Most of the spring goods shipped in December 1771 and February 1772, worth £8,300, together with autumn goods he was shipping in June–July 1772, worth £8,000, had been purchased on twelve months' credit, creating very specific cash-flow problems for him at precisely foreseeable dates in the future. For him, the twelve or thirteen months following the crash of June 1772 were a time of acute agony. He wrote with frantic frequency to his partners, haranguing them about the necessity of good bills, complaining bitterly about the high proportion of protests among those remitted.[51] He suggested that relief might be obtained if they and William Lux & Bowly of Baltimore exchanged accommodation bills on London on the ill-fated Scottish model.[52] We do not know whether his advice was followed, but his partners were impressed by his straits. They sent him a growing supply of bills of exchange, and even procured letters of credit signed or countersigned by Wallace and other persons of property in Maryland, hoping these would induce Osgood Hanbury to take over their London business or make them a large loan.[53] Though Hanbury refused, Johnson was able to borrow some smaller sums—with or without using the letters of credit, we do not know.[54]

Nevertheless, sums borrowed and bills remitted from the Chesapeake did not pay all his debts outstanding as they came due. At times, Johnson was so desperate that he contemplated giving up and secretly slipping out of London. He did not attempt this, in part from a sense of honour, in part from fear that some suspicious creditor would have him arrested before

[51] HR, p.a. 1507, pp. 88–9, to WD&J, 10 July and *passim* over the next year. On 4 Nov. 1772 Johnson informed his partners that his debts coming due included £1,200 in December, £4,048 in February, £6,707 in June. On 5 Feb. 1773 he advised them of £12,535 in debts to be settled by July. At that time, his Annapolis house owed the London branch £11,020. The balance was due from other correspondents in America. HR, p.a. 1507, pp. 132–5, to WD&J, 6 Feb. 1773. On 17 July 1773 (p. 181) he reported that he would need £9,500 by 1 Jan.

[52] HR, p.a. 1507, pp. 79, 93, to W. and D., 4 June, 17 July 1772.

[53] Ibid., pp. 153–5, 157–8, 172–4, 176, to WD&J, 7 April, 28, 30 June 1773; to W., 10 April 1773.

[54] Ibid., pp. 157–8, 194–5, to W., 10 April 1773; to WD&J, 4 Sept. 1773.

he could get away.[55] In the end, he was saved primarily by the considerate, intelligent forbearance of these creditors. In the prolonged depression following June 1772, the big warehouse-men and linen-drapers who wished to continue trade had to allow extensions of time to the exporting merchants who owed them money, and to go on supplying goods to exporters who had not yet settled their previous year's purchases. Bad though Johnson thought his own position, he must have appeared in relatively sound shape to those experienced lenders. He was thus able to arrange with his largest creditors to extend a good part of his twelve-month credits to fifteen or eighteen months, at 5 per cent p.a. for the extra time. A few of his smaller creditors dunned him unmercifully, but the larger allowed him to pay off some of these small pests preferentially.[56] When one of them, the shoe-dealers Watson & Scott, had him arrested for a small debt, Johnson was out immediately on bail without any real damage to his credit.[57] By August 1773 the worst was over: by the end of the year, 'we are in Top Credit & . . . it is gener-ally said our Payments has been the best by far of any in the Trade'.[58]

Most but not all of his suppliers continued to furnish him even in 1772–3. If the Hanburys' connection, the great Quaker linen merchants Barclays, would no longer serve him, there was always Nash, Eddowes, & Martin ready to oblige.[59] The warehousemen Mauduit, Wright, & Co., from whom Johnson bought woollens, caused unexpected trouble in 1773. They took his order for autumn goods in June and packed them. As the ship was ready to sail in July, they refused to put them on board unless Johnson agreed to have them consigned to Daniel Dulany, a prominent Annapolis lawyer, who was instructed to deliver them to Johnson's partners only after they gave security. Johnson had to agree, though he swore never to deal with Mauduits again.[60]

---

[55] Ibid., pp. 103–4, to WD&J, 2 Sept. 1772; pp. 157–8, to W., 10 April 1773.
[56] Ibid., pp. 165–6, 172–5, to WD&J, 17 May, 28, 29 June 1773.
[57] Ibid., p. 107, to WD&J, 7 Oct. 1772.
[58] Ibid., pp. 214–16, to WD&J, 29 Nov. 1773.
[59] Ibid., pp. 219–20, to WD&J, 22 Dec. 1773. With the dissolution of Nash, Eddowes, & Martin at the end of 1773, the connection was continued by Peter Martin.
[60] Ibid., pp. 186–7, 218–19, to WD&J, 4, 5 Aug., 16 Dec. 1773.

Although Johnson survived the difficult period June 1772–July 1773 without real damage to his firm's earning power or credit-worthiness, it forced him and his partners to review the nature of their business. They had not sought tobacco consignments, but to employ all their resources in exporting goods to Maryland. By returning cash quickly to London, they would enable Johnson to maximize discounts for cash purchases or early payment, as a significant part of their earnings. Turning their capital over quickly, they hoped gradually to raise annual turnover and make it worth while to keep Johnson in London. Things went as expected down to June 1772 but altered radically thereafter. With a glut of goods in Maryland, they had to reduce orders for their winter and summer shipments of 1773.[61] With sales slow and good bills hard to find in Maryland, their remittances to London were slow also. Hence Johnson too ran short of cash and had to borrow and extend the duration of his purchase credits, both of which involved paying rather than earning interest. With the volume of business down in 1773 and the interest account in deficit, the question arose whether the firm would earn enough on their London operations to merit keeping Johnson there. The alternatives were to bring him home or to reconsider their earlier decision not to seek tobacco consignments.

Almost from the start, Johnson had doubted the wisdom of keeping out of the tobacco trade. In November 1771 he had written:

I see, tho now too late, that there was a field opened for our makeing £1500; or £2000. on Tobacco this Year had we excepted [accepted] of the Consignment Business & pushed it, as number was suprized we did not & a number was afraid we should, it is expensive here but the Business Just as easy managed as shiping of Goods— That which is shipped [early] so as to arive here in April May & June will sell well if any ways coloured.[62]

He referred particularly to the 'bright' leaf of the Patuxent and Patapsco valleys in Maryland, much in demand in Holland and

61 Johnson's shipments in February 1773 came to only £2,120. 16s. 7d. compared to £8,295. 19s. 11d. in Dec. 1771–Feb. 1772; his shipments in July–Aug. 1773 were only £5,594. 1s. 1d. compared to £8,082. 11s. 1d. the previous summer. Ibid., to WD&J, 2 Dec. 1771, 25 Feb., 1, 10 July 1772, 16 Feb., 4 Aug. 1773.
62 HR, p.a. 1507, to W. and D., 6 Nov. 1771.

Germany, easily sold for cash. Johnson understandably kept his partners and their friends informed about tobacco prices in London. He sometimes went further. Without consulting his partners, he wrote to the Baltimore merchant, Darby Lux, that his correspondent James Russell was doing a poor job and 'should you ever have occasion to send [a ship] this way again, I dare say my Partners will readily consent to my serveing you'.[63]

Wallace and Davidson, on their side, were considering ways in which the firm might branch out. Early in 1772 they decided to contract for the building of a ship on their account, intending to send it with tobacco (preferably freighted by others) to London, where both ship and cargo would be sold. Earnings from the freight and the profit expected on the sale of the ship (£500–£600 before the June crisis) made this a remunerative way to remit money to London provided the London shipping market remained firm.[64] Inevitably, immediately after the panic of 1772, ship sale prices were not as attractive as they had been a few months before or were to become later.[65] By early 1773, however, Johnson was again optimistic about shipbuilding.[66]

With his firm already attracted towards speculations in ship-building, the panic brought opportunities as well as dangers. With so many tobacco houses breaking, and still others compromised in the eyes of potential consigners because they were known to have called in their creditors, all was in confusion and a spendid opportunity presented itself for new firms to enter the trade. In the first weeks of the crisis, Johnson wrote to his partners that if many Scots firms failed '& you have spirit to Borrow & confidence in me there must be an opening for us to push in the Tobacco [consignment] Trade especially as all [tobacco] purchase [for export] will be at an end with you'. The difficulty of obtaining good bills in Maryland now made tobacco shipments a more attractive form of remittance.[67]

At first the partners were held back by the unattractive ratios between tobacco prices in Maryland and London in the months following the June crash.[68] (Even those receiving consignments

[63] Ibid., to D. Lux, 1 Dec. 1771.
[64] Ibid., to W. and D., 4, 22 June 1772.
[65] Ibid., p. 100, to WD&J, 20 Aug. 1772.
[66] Ibid., pp. 143–5, to same, 3 March 1773.
[67] Ibid., pp. 86–7, to same, 1 July 1772.
[68] Ibid., pp. 98–101, to same, 20 Aug. 1772.

sometimes had to buy in the country in order to fill their ships expeditiously.)[69] However, as the gap between these prices widened in 1773, the firm's interest quickened. They knew that, as prices in Maryland declined, planters who had recently been 'selling in the country' would become interested in shipping to London on consignment.[70] Given their local standing, the temptation to venture was great.

The partners were reluctant to enter the consignment trade in a petty way; economical shipping required chartering whole vessels, dabbling would attract the suspicion of the trade without earning much. Nevertheless, their first venture in tobacco came somewhat unwillingly. In the slack period following the panic, Wallace and Davidson bartered part of their Annapolis surplus of goods for tobacco. When they could not resell the leaf advantageously, they chartered space on a new ship built for the Annapolis merchants, Galloway and Stewart, and consigned 104 hogsheads to Johnson early in 1773.[71] Although the quality was poor and sale necessarily disappointing, Johnson after much hesitation was finally convinced by March 1773 that they should go into tobacco on a large scale.

To his partners, Johnson explained that accepting consignments would mean taking cash out of their general merchandise business and tying it up in payment of freight (due within sixty days of a ship's arrival) and in deposits on Customs duties. Yet in the end they would make more on the commissions of 1,000 hogsheads consigned (about three shiploads) than on £8,000 worth of goods sent to Annapolis—and with less risk.[72] He envisaged reducing their merchandise business to only about £5,000 p.a. and using the resources so freed to procure two ships and make about £3,000 available to the London branch for use in paying freight, duties, and other charges on about 1,000 hogsheads p.a. When his partners appeared 'fearfull our Capital is too inconsiderable to enter into the Consignment Bussiness', he reminded them that 'very few of the Gent: in the Trade began with more Money than we had . . .' Later in the year, Johnson urged his partners to get him 2,000 hogsheads

      [69] HR, p.a. 1507, pp. 106–8, to same, 7 Oct. 1772.
      [70] Ibid., p. 111, to D., 30 Oct. 1772.
      [71] Ibid., pp. 132–5, 142–5, 159–60, to same, 6 Feb., 3 March, 12 April 1773, to James Gibbs, 2 March 1773.
      [72] Ibid., p. 142, to WD&J, 19 March 1773.

yearly, reminding them that the commission came close to £1 a hogshead and that £2,000 was far more than they had been making.[73]

Johnson wanted consignments only from planters and sought no dealings with provincial merchants, who expected 'cargoes' from London on credit.[74] Nor did he want big planters, who expected to draw bills of exchange against their consignments, but the little 'two, three & four hogshead Correspondents in preference to any others [;] their Moneys are generaly sunk [returned] in Goods on which we have 12 months credit & of course [for] that or more time, the use of their money . . .'[75] However, as his hunger for consignments grew, Johnson asked his partners to let some consigners draw up to £5 per hogshead, if necessary to get their consignments.[76] In Maryland, to attract them, Charles Wallace promised the full value of discounts for prompt payment if the planters left money in Johnson's hands with which to buy goods, and full value of any bounties or drawbacks paid by Customs on goods ordered. This annoyed Johnson, not least because of the book-keeping complexities.[77]

The key to the success of Wallace, Davidson, & Johnson in the consignment trade lay, of course, in their ability to attract the confidence of planters in Maryland. To help in this, Johnson wrote to friends in Baltimore and elsewhere, but he counted most on his partners (particularly Wallace) and on their friends travelling through the best tobacco districts, visiting public warehouses and talking to planters. He approved their projected branch store at Nottingham on the Patuxent, while preferring stores further up the river at Pig Point (Ann Arundel County) or Queen Anne (Prince George's County); he was even more anxious to reach the planters in Calvert County (across from Nottingham) and on Patapsco (particularly Elk Ridge), where Russell's influence had formerly been

[73] The 2½ per cent commission was calculated on the hypothetical full sale price including the duties, even though 85 per cent of British tobacco imports were re-exported and drew back all duties. This made the effective commission on receipts closer to 10 per cent than 2½ per cent.

[74] HR, p.a. 1507, pp. 150–2, 192–3, 207–9, to WD&J, 5 April, 20 Aug., 3 Nov. 1773.

[75] Ibid., pp. 150–2, 157–8, to WD&J, 5 April, to W., 10 April 1773.

[76] Ibid., pp. 200, 203, to WD&J, 28 Sept. 1773, 4 Oct. 1773.

[77] Ibid., pp. 210, 212–14, to same, 5, 29 Nov., to W., 22 Nov. 1773.

paramount.[78] He wanted nothing to do with the inferior Potomac tobaccos from St. Mary's and Charles Counties, but did
not mind receiving the less expensive Eastern Shore tobaccos,
uniform in quality and easy to sell.[79]

The alteration of the London branch from buying agency
to tobacco consignment house raised the whole question of the
scale and costs of the London presence. Johnson in later life
was reputed extravagant and socially ambitious, but started
in London with the most frugal intentions. He had heard that
one could live there for 18*d.* a day (£25 a year), but soon wrote
that life was much dearer; laundry alone would cost him £18–
£20 a year.[80] Shortly after his arrival, he rented for £25 a year
a two-room suite at 126 Fenchurch Street, intending to use the
main room as an office and the 'closet' as bedroom. This was
the least he could do, he wrote, 'to support me, at least in the
character of a Gentleman & a Partner to a house that will export 10 or 12 thousand per Annum'. He soon found it not quite
adequate. During the shipping season, his front room was so
cluttered with packages and bales that he was embarrassed to
find space where a caller might sit.[81] He also entertained,
received mail, and conducted business at the 'Virginia Coffee
House', for which he paid an annual guinea 'subscription' to
the proprietress, Mrs. Powell.[82]

Before six months Johnson acquired more ample accommodation at no. 6 [Great] Tower Street:

> I found that in the manner I lived would not answer[;] it looked
> so . . . mean . . . I therefore resolved to take a Counting House
> which has made me of the Consequence a Merchant merits. I have
> fixed nearly between the Custom House & the Change which makes
> it very high tho that I cant help for it is a maxim with me that I had
> rather sink the profits of my labour than to diminish my Partners &
> self in the Good Opinion of the world . . . It has [also] stript me of
> the appearance of a Trantient Person . . .

[78] HR, p.a. 1507, pp. 200, 201, 203, 212–13, 226, 304–7, to WD&J, 28 Sept.,
4 Oct. 1773, 10 Jan., 5 March 1774; to W. Lux & Bowly, 4 Oct. 1773; to W.,
22 Nov. 1773. Johnson described the tobacco from Pig Point as the best on the Patuxent, but was even more interested in getting that from Elk Ridge on Patapsco.

[79] Ibid., pp. 214–16, to WD&J, 29 Nov. 1773.

[80] Ibid., to D., 22 July 1771.

[81] Ibid., to W. and D., 24 July, to J. Tunstall, 26 Aug. 1771.

[82] HR, p.a. 1514 (Journal), p. 295.

He also explained that living in the City 'has not been without its good effects with the staid Cits', when compared with other of his 'Country Men . . . running to the other end of the Town to lodge . . .'[83] Alas, these arrangements proved too modest once the firm decided to enter the consignment business, with its obligations to entertain visiting planters and ship-captains. He advised his partners that expenses must rise considerably with the New Year:

> I must have a dwelling House, Counting House & Sample House besides proper assistance all of which will come to a good Deal of money & it is the more requisite to have a house of my own that I may be enabled to entertain (when convenient) our Country Men that comes here you know the advantage arising from it & in that case you will Consider the Furniture will cost me no small trifle . . .[84]

Johnson paid for the furniture himself and later wrote that the house rent charged to the firm was only £30 a year.[85]

As Johnson's physical accommodation expanded, so did his staff. He was originally expected to be able to do without clerical help, having nothing to keep him busy except purchases and almost no one to write to except his partners. Almost at once, he found extremely time-consuming the business of making clearances at the Customs House. He tried a broker for such business, but a year later said he could save brokerage fees by employing a boy at £10 p.a. living with his own parents. The only other help he then used was a temporary clerk to copy invoices and the like during the shipping season. However, once the consignment business started at the end of 1773, he found it necessary to add a regular clerk at £40 p.a. and a book-keeper at a higher figure.[86]

Although Johnson once boasted that he could sell tobacco better than any London merchant, having been raised on a plantation,[87] he found, when his consignment business became busy in 1774, that for large transactions he had to use brokers, at a fee of two shillings per hogshead. Among them were the

---

[83] HR, p.a. 1507, to W. and D., 6 Nov. 1771, to J. Gibbs, 13 Nov. 1771.
[84] Ibid., pp. 214–16, to WD&J, 29 Nov. 1773.
[85] Ibid., pp. 434–7, to same, 18 July 1774.
[86] Ibid., to W. and D., 3, 24 July 1771; pp. 93, 200, 434–7, to WD&J, 17 July 1772, 28 Sept. 1773, 18 July 1774.
[87] Ibid., p. 277, to Ignatius Perry, 25 Feb. 1774.

prominent Jewish brokers, Jacob Brandon and Joshua de Fonseca Brandon of Bevis Marks, useful in big sales to Dutch and German export houses and uncles of Abraham Lopez Fernandez, almost the only Anglo-Jewish merchant trading to Virginia and Maryland before the Revolution. When Fernandez went out to Maryland in 1774 to collect some debts, Johnson introduced him to his partners and his brother Thomas, the future Governor: 'they [the Brandons] are the greatest Tobacco Brokers in England . . . I could wish that you would make much of him . . . it may sometime be a farthing per lb. advance to us.'[88]

For his insurance in 1774–5, Johnson used the brokers Theodore Williams and J. Letillier.[89] In 1771–3, he had only had to worry about a little insurance on the goods shipped for Maryland. This could be arranged more easily at Lloyd's than at one of the chartered companies:

I have not made it [insurance] in a Publick Office, [because of] their particularity[;] they must know who you are & a deal of that, then again you are plagued more than little enough before you can get the Money after a loss & every body prefer makeing theirs at Lloyds for that reason. I have got ours done at 2 per cent.[90]

In addition, he soon had some small commissions on insuring shipments from Maryland to the West Indies and some bigger wheat shipments of Lux & Bowly from Baltimore to Cadiz.[91] With the tobacco business, insurance work became much more complex: hence the brokers. It was necessary to insure each consignment of one, two, or three hogsheads separately; he needed full information well in advance of the names of the shippers and the number of hogsheads each was sending. Speed was important if insurance was to be made in time. Johnson frequently used the fast but expensive New York packet, while his more parsimonious partners preferred entrusting letters to a ship-captain bound for London. Johnson warned them that, since their method could be up to three weeks slower, they should put all letters containing insurance instructions or bills

[88] HR, p.a. 1507, pp. 321–3, to WD&J, 6 April, to T. Johnson, 7 April 1774; p.a. 1514 (Journal), pp. 183, 257.

[89] HR, p.a. 1517 (Ledger B), pp. 77–8.

[90] HR, p.a. 1507, to W. and D., 24 July 1771.

[91] Ibid., to Lux & Bowly, 3 March, 7 April 1773.

of exchange into the New York packet; and when they did entrust an important letter to a captain, they should instruct him to put it into the post as soon as he arrived in England, not wait to deliver it personally.[92] His partners ignored this advice—with expensive consequences in one case. A captain to whom a letter had been entrusted waited nine days after arrival to deliver it to Johnson. Finding that it contained instructions to insure a vessel with consigned tobacco, Johnson went to Lloyd's that same day only to find that within the hour word had been received at the Tontine Bell of the loss of the vessel on the Isle of Wight. Johnson felt that the delay in making insurance was the firm's fault and that his partners should compensate all consigners, even though a large sum was involved. We cannot tell whether his advice was taken.[93]

In December 1773 Johnson received his first full shipload of consigned tobacco, on his own firm's new ship, the *Kitty and Nelly*. Although it was intended he should sell the vessel along with its cargo, the trade was then looking up and he decided to spend £500 on refitting her for Maryland. Against this, he saved almost £300 for freight at 2½ per cent of value on the March shipment of spring goods to Annapolis. He also reduced costs by having her take in indentured servants at Gravesend, though he had doubts about the economics of this trade.

The *Kitty and Nelly* proved to be the beginning of a very busy two years for Johnson as a tobacco merchant in London. Although his correspondence with his partners has not survived after August 1774, we can reconstruct his tobacco business from ledgers, journals, invoice and sales books. Between December 1773 and November 1775, Johnson received eighteen shipments of tobacco, ranging from four hogsheads on Captain Thomas Eden's *Annapolis* to 545 hogsheads on his own firm's *Kitty and Nelly*, a total of 4,283 hogsheads—slightly more than the 2,000 hogsheads p.a. which he told his partners he could handle. Most came from Patuxent (2,794 hogsheads) and Patapsco (1,217), the areas he had indicated to his partners; relatively little from Potomac (125) or the Eastern Shore (52 from Chester River, 95 from Wye).[94] One hundred and three of the 104 hogsheads sent as

92 Ibid., pp. 214–26, to WD&J, 29 Nov. 1773.
93 Ibid., pp. 237–9, 308–9, to same, 10 Feb., 2 March 1774.
94 HR, p.a. 1530 (Invoice Book of Sales, or 'Tobacco Book').

an experiment early in 1773 were sold for export, 92 hogsheads to Hamburg. When his consignment business started at the end of 1773, the same sales pattern continued. He received little of the cheap, brown, and mild tobacco of the Potomac and Eastern Shore suitable for the French market.[95] The strong, bright, yellow leaf from Patuxent and Patapsco was in demand primarily in Holland, Germany, and the Baltic. The geographical disposition of his sales during 1774–6, in hogsheads, was as follows:[96]

Rotterdam (the major continental mart)	1,660	
Amsterdam	751	
Friesland	15	
Delfzijl	70	
Dutch Total		2,496
Hamburg	530	
Bremen	388	
German North Sea Total		918
Stettin	29	
Danzig	16	
Stockholm	2	
St. Petersburg	8	
Baltic Total		55
France (territory of monopoly)	323	
Dunkirk	47	
French Total		370
Export destinations unspecified		69
Home Trade		36
GRAND TOTAL		3,944

This heavy dependence on the Dutch and German markets made Johnson equally dependent on a small circle of London merchants who bought for them. Many were of Dutch or German origin; most probably bought on commission for Dutch and German principals. Six firms, taking over 200 hogsheads each, all for export, accounted for approximately three-fourths

[95] *France and the Chesapeake*, i. 667–8.
[96] HR, p.a. 1530 and 1521 ('Sales Bk. No. 1', containing accounts of sales sent to consigners, 1773–5). In some cases, Johnson, short of cash to pay the duty, appears to have sold on arrival with the buyer entering the tobacco, arranging for duties, and immediately re-exporting. When a buyer was a foreigner (e.g. Coldberg), a British merchant (e.g. Christopher Court, Osgood Hanbury) seems to have made the Customs entry for him.

of his sales in 1774–6. His eight leading customers (over 100 hogsheads each) were:

William Davidson, Esq. & Co.	951 hhd.
Samuel Coldberg	816
Sir Robert Herries & Co.	426
Langkopf, Molling, & Rasch	310
Hanael Mendez Da Costa	291
Thomas Littledale	200
Sutton & Schombart	146
Andrew Grote, Son, & Co.	133
	3,273

We know relatively little about most of these. Herries was the French buying agent, a great merchant and banker in his own right.[97] Langkopf, Molling, & Rasch (originally Furstenau, Schroeder, & Co.) and Grote & Son (originally Kruger & Grote) were long-established German firms in London, going back at least to the 1740s. Davidson and Littledale were British merchants at Rotterdam, active in the London market only with the speculative atmosphere of 1775–6 and the onset of the American Revolution; Davidson may have been a kinsman of Johnson's Scottish partner, John Davidson.

Johnson's sales books reveal certain patterns touching tender points of commercial ethics. If we compare the prices of sales shown in his 'tobacco' or 'invoice books' with the 'accounts of sales' returned to planter consigners, we find that they do not always agree. These discrepancies arose in part from the necessity of making bulk sales (of twenty to a hundred hogsheads at a time) at flat prices to big buyers, even though one received one's tobacco in small consignments (usually of only two to six hogsheads each). The small consigner, of course, expected each hogshead to be sold according to its quality. What Johnson (and presumably other consignment merchants in London) actually did was to sell at the 'round price' when necessary and then grade the tobacco and reprice it according to quality. They may have used a specialist broker for this: thus Johnson sold a lot of tobacco on 7 April 1774 to Samuel Coldberg for $2\frac{1}{2}d$. per lb. But prices anywhere from $1\frac{3}{4}d$. to $3\frac{3}{8}d$. were reported to the consigners of these tobaccos. If Benjamin Belt had his

[97] *France and the Chesapeake*, i. ch. 24, ii. ch. 26 *et passim*.

one hogshead reported for $2\frac{1}{4}d$. Mary White Bell had hers reported for $2\frac{3}{4}d$. All five hogsheads of Archibald Buchanan, a Baltimore merchant and a close ally of Johnson's firm, were credited at or below the $2\frac{1}{2}d$. of the sale, while all five hogsheads sent by one Sarah Bateman were credited at $3d$. or above. It would appear that a genuine effort was being made to make prices received reflect quality.

Another phenomenon in the sales books is harder to explain. In November–December 1775, after imports had been cut off by Congress and great further rises in prices were expected, Johnson 'sold' 700 hogsheads of tobacco to William Davidson, Esq. & Co. and to Thomas Littledale, both of Rotterdam, at prices between the $3\frac{1}{2}d$. and $3\frac{3}{4}d$. then prevailing in London. However, in his sales invoice book, he has a second set of prices also entered, ranging from $4\frac{9}{16}d$. to $7\frac{3}{4}d$. These are presumably the prices at which the tobacco was subsequently resold at Rotterdam in 1776 or 1777. The implication would seem to be either that Johnson had consigned and not sold the tobacco to Davidson and Littledale, and that the sales in London were therefore fictitious, or that he had indeed sold the hogsheads in 1775 but retained an interest in them by special arrangement with Davidson and Littledale. The latter explanation seems the more likely, for other consignments to Davidson and Littledale in 1777 are clearly indicated as such in his tobacco invoice book.

Johnson's London tobacco sales were by trade conventions paid for by a bill or note due in sixty days, or in cash with a 1 per cent discount. In some cases, cash meant simply a book clearance. Johnson sold tobacco to three firms from whom he had earlier bought German linens on twelve months' credit: Sutton & Schombart; Langkopf, Molling, & Rasch; and Mee Son & Cassau. The 'cash' tobacco sales thus simply cancelled out the sums due for linens.[98] The 'balanced' trades of these German houses in London must have considerably facilitated collections on their linen sales in the difficult times following the crisis of 1772.

Tobacco and a little iron kept Johnson busy during his last years in London, 1774–7. He had also thought of entering the

[98] Cf. the account of Langkopf, Molling, & Rasch in HR, p.a. 1517 (Ledger B), fo. 73.

grain trade. The early 1770s saw high and rapidly fluctuating wheat prices; the corn laws were liberalized and foreign cereals admitted into Britain for a while free of duty. From his arrival in London, Johnson kept his partners and Baltimore correspondents, particularly Lux & Bowly, informed about grain prices in Britain and southern Europe. When Lux & Bowly sent wheat or flour to Ireland, Cadiz, or into the Mediterranean, Johnson handled the insurance and the proceeds were often remitted to him by bills of exchange. When British ports were thrown open, he tried to interest his partners in flour speculations, but they declined this risky trade. Lux & Bowly and other Baltimoreans, however, sent him wheat, maize, and flour in 1775. For them, he provided information on the credit-worthiness of John Thornton (1720–90), the great Russia merchant, grain speculator, and Evangelical.[99]

We know nothing about the profitability of the total business of the firm of Wallace, Davidson, & Johnson, because the books of the parent firm in Annapolis have not survived. Down to the end of 1773, when the firm's business was primarily shipping goods from London to Maryland, all significant profits would have been from the sale in Maryland of the goods shipped from London. However, after the tobacco consignment business began in December 1773, the London agency began to have substantial earnings of its own from the commissions earned on the sale of tobacco (near £1 per hogshead), on purchases of goods for the tobacco consigners, and on insurance and other services performed for correspondents in America. In addition, speculative profits were probably derived from retaining an interest in some tobacco during the very rapid price rise accompanying the outbreak of the American Revolution. After deducting all expenses, the London branch from these retained earnings accumulated a capital of £3,842. 15s. 3d. by 31 July 1775 and £6,052. 3s. 2d. by 31 December 1776.[100]

Joshua Johnson started out in London as buying agent for his partners. Their business was to be confined exclusively to the export of European and Asian goods to Maryland, with

---

[99] HR, p.a. 1507, to W. and D., 29 Aug. 1771; p. 50, to W. Lux, 1 Feb. 1772; pp. 192–5, to WD&J, 20 Aug., 4 Sept. 1773; pp. 213–14, to Lux & Bowly, 22 Nov. 1773; HR, p.a. 1531 ('Accounts of Sale').

[100] HR, p.a. 1514 (Journal, 1774–5), p. 357; p.a. 1515 (Journal, 1775–7), p. 316.

all returns made in bills of exchange. There were definite economies involved in buying in London directly, rather than through correspondents, particularly when one could buy for cash; but there were costs as well. That these were considerable perhaps explains why few other firms in Maryland or Virginia made similar experiments. That of Wallace, Davidson, & Johnson might have succeeded if the costs of the London agency could have been distributed over an ever-increasing volume of shipments to Maryland. That necessary volume was extremely difficult to achieve with their severely limited capital. Buying on normal commercial credit (twelve months) offered great opportunities, but depended ultimately on relatively rapid sales in, and returns from, Maryland. Prospects for mounting sales and quick returns were destroyed by the depression of 1772–3 and the attendant glut of European goods in America. Forced to contract its merchandise export trade to America, the firm could only bear the costs of the London agency by developing new earnings. Thus it was forced into the tobacco consignment trade, which it had first decided to eschew as too capital-intensive for its resources. With the credit of older firms in the trade shaken by the panic of 1772, this new firm, with its extensive connections in Maryland, found it relatively easy to attract a substantial volume of consignments in 1774 and 1775. With the wild rise in tobacco prices in 1775–6, Johnson may well have made substantial windfall profits in addition to his commissions, before the war forced him to wind up his business in 1777 and go over to France.

IX

The Historians' Quest for the American Revolution

NEARLY two hundred years after the Declaration of Independence historians remain anything but agreed upon the causes or the nature of the American Revolution. The word 'Revolution' has become so embedded in historical terminology that it seems most unlikely it will be abandoned, and ingenious attempts have been made to fit events in the American colonies into the pattern of an 'age of democratic revolution'.[1] Yet it is by no means clear whether this is or is not in fact a misnomer, and whether the events leading up to 1776 should more accurately be classed simply as a colonial struggle for independence,[2] or as a civil conflict ending in secession. There is no consensus upon an initial turning-point. Among recent writers Bernhard Knollenberg has suggested 1759; Edmund S. Morgan, 1754; Alison Gilbert Olson and Richard Maxwell Brown postulate a crucial decade in the 1730s.[3] There is some ground for all these suggested dates. Is one of them (or more than one) more justified than the others? The year 1776 clearly can be regarded for some purposes of analysis as a terminal date. Before that year, the Americans were still striving for a continuation of the British Empire on terms compatible with their inherited British liberties; only after it were they out on their own and faced

[1] R. R. Palmer, *The Age of the Democratic Revolution* (2 vols., Princeton, N.J., 1959–64).

[2] For a summary of arguments favouring the interpretation of these events as a revolution, see W. H. Nelson, 'The Revolutionary Character of the American Revolution', *American Hist. Rev.* lxx (1964–5), 998–1014; and for an opposing view Thomas C. Barrow, 'The American Revolution as a Colonial War of Independence', *W. & M. Qtly*, 3rd ser. xxv (1968), 452–64.

[3] Bernhard Knollenberg, *Origin of the American Revolution: 1759–1766* (New York, 1961), p. 11; Edmund S. and Helen M. Morgan, *The Stamp Act Crisis. Prologue to Revolution* (rev. edn., New York, 1963), p. 19; *Anglo-American Political Relations, 1675–1775*, ed. A. G. Olson and R. M. Brown (New Brunswick, N.J., 1970), pp. 3–13.

with the hitherto unwanted task of devising a new framework of government and polity for themselves. Yet this view is hardly congenial to those who emphasize a continuous sweep of American history, running through from the colonial to the revolutionary period and on beyond. In what light is the Revolution to be represented? Various schools of interpretation have arisen, but the growing flood of scholarship seems to demonstrate flaws and incompatibilities first in one and then in another. Indeed, in the present state of study of the Revolution, historians face an exceptionally complicated and exciting situation. More than ever the processes of discovery and adjustment which are taking place, or which require to take place, involve not only the discarding of disproved assumptions but also the achievement of some synthesis of conflicting conclusions which obstinately decline to disappear by the process of disproof.

This rich diversity and conflict in the scholarship concerning the Revolution is doubtless the reason for what seem to be unusually frequent attempts, during the last twenty-five years, at least to draw attention to the problems it raises, if not to propound some basis for synthesis. Early stages in this process were the chapter on the historiography of the Revolution in H. Hale Bellot's survey, *American History and American Historians* (1952),[4] and the collection of readings and essays edited by John C. Wahlke under the title *The Causes of the American Revolution*,[5] both published in the 1950s. Wahlke's book was republished in 1962, but it has been overtaken by subsequent collections with increasingly elaborate and penetrating introductions and bibliographical essays: Esmond Wright's *Causes and Consequences of the American Revolution*,[6] and two collections edited by Jack P. Greene, *The Ambiguity of the American Revolution* and *The Reinterpretation of the American Revolution*.[7] There have been organized discussions of the subject in the United States among scholars concerned with early American history. These have produced valuable restatements of outstanding questions, including at least one major interpretative essay of extreme distinction, Bernard Bailyn's *The Origins of American Politics*,[8]

[4] Ch. iii, esp. pp. 73–87.
[6] Chicago, 1966.
[8] New York, 1969.

[5] Boston, 1950.
[7] New York, 1968 (both).

and at least one highly suggestive collection of papers—*Anglo-American Political Relations, 1675–1775*, edited by A. G. Olson and R. M. Brown.[9]

To discuss the whole historiography of the Revolution is impossible in a paper of this scope.[10] But a survey of significant elements in the heritage of more recent scholarship would be imperfect without mention of the nineteenth-century Whig school, of which the chief names are Bancroft in the United States and George Otto Trevelyan in Great Britain.[11] To Bancroft North America was the Eden of progress and liberty, its inhabitants a chosen people set apart, and for him the Revolution had something of an apocalyptic quality deriving from the outlook of New England Puritanism. As it unfolded, the forces of progress and liberalism in the American colonies triumphed, as they were predestined to do, over reactionary royal government personified by George III. To Trevelyan, the survival of liberty in Britain itself was linked with the defeat of George III's attempt to impose his policies and his power upon the American colonies. Occasionally in more recent times a historian has cast nostalgic glances in the direction of Bancroft and Trevelyan. About thirty years ago G. H. Guttridge tried to refurbish a modified form of the Whig interpretation of politics under George III.[12] More recently Richard B. Morris has edited an abridged edition of Trevelyan's great work on the Revolution.[13] Edmund S. Morgan, in his well-known revision article published in 1957, 'The American Revolution: Revisions in Need of Revising', has suggested, but perhaps not very seriously, that the inconsistencies then apparently developing between various schools of interpretation might force historians back to a revised version of Bancroft.[14] This is not really on the cards. There

[9] Above, n. 3.

[10] For fuller surveys of the recent literature than can be given below, see Wright, pp. 11–50, and Greene, *Reinterpretation*, pp. 2–74.

[11] George Bancroft, *History of the United States* (10 vols., Boston, 1834–74); George Otto Trevelyan, *The American Revolution* (4 vols., 1899–1907) and *George III and Charles Fox, the Concluding Part of the American Revolution* (2 vols., 1912–14).

[12] *English Whiggism and the American Revolution* (Berkeley, 1942, repr. Berkeley–Los Angeles, 1963). For a criticism of essential elements in this view, see Ian R. Christie, *Myth and Reality in Late-Eighteenth-Century British Politics and Other Papers* (1970), pp. 196–213.

[13] *The American Revolution by George Otto Trevelyan. A Condensation into One Volume* . . ., ed. Richard B. Morris (1965).

[14] *W. & M. Qtly*, 3rd ser. xiv (1957), 3–15.

has been far too firm a revision of our understanding of late eighteenth-century British politics since the first publication in 1929 of Sir Lewis Namier's *Structure of Politics at the Accession of George III*.[15] Nevertheless, historians have been unwise to overlook the fact that Bancroft and Trevelyan gave weight to views which they found to be current at the time of the Revolution. Such evidence can be ignored only at the cost of sacrificing important perspectives. The way in which this feature is now being brought back into the story, though as an illusion rather than as a vision of reality, constitutes one of the significant advances of present-day scholarship.[16]

Towards the end of the nineteenth century the discovery of economic history began to affect writing on the American Revolution, and a flourishing school arose devoted to the economic interpretation of it. These historians tended to anticipate a positive answer to this sort of question: 'Was the Revolution caused by the development of deep and irreconcilable social and economic incompatibilities and rivalries between Great Britain and the American colonies?' Such a thesis took distinctive form in such works as A. M. Schlesinger's *The Colonial Merchants and the American Revolution*,[17] and received perhaps its most forthright expression in the work of Louis M. Hacker, *The Triumph of American Capitalism*, published in 1940.[18] It was the general view of this group of historians that the Revolution was essentially the product of a colonial struggle to break out of the economic strait jacket imposed by the Navigation Acts and the Acts of Trade—a strait jacket which was being steadily tightened up by British governments after 1760 in the interests of British capitalism but was in any case intolerable. Hacker described the Revenue Acts of the 1760s as 'a screen to conceal the work of compressing the economy of colonial mercantile capitalism within even narrower limits and reducing it to an even more dependent status'.[19] The constitutional arguments against parliamentary taxation put forward

[15] Rev. edn., 1957.
[16] Caroline Robbins, *The Eighteenth-Century Commonwealthman. Studies in the Transmission, Development and Circumstance of English Liberal Thought from the Restoration of Charles II until the War with the Thirteen Colonies* (Cambridge, Mass., 1959); Bernard Bailyn, *The Ideological Origins of the American Revolution* (Cambridge, Mass., 1967) and *The Origins of American Politics* (New York, 1969).
[17] New York, 1918.   [18] New York, 1940.   [19] Hacker, p. 162.

by the colonists were brushed aside by these writers as merely a cover for material interest. In Schlesinger's opinion, 'the popular view of the Revolution as a great forensic controversy over abstract government rights' would not 'bear close examination';[20] and Hacker likewise concluded:

> The struggle was not over high-sounding political and constitutional concepts: over the power of taxation or even, in the final analysis, over natural rights. It was over colonial manufacturing, wild lands and furs, sugar, wine, tea, and currency, all of which meant the survival or collapse of English mercantile capitalism within the imperial–colonial framework of the mercantilist system.[21]

The impact of this interpretation down to about twenty years ago is very apparent in Hale Bellot's attempt at a perspective of the then state of knowledge. Bellot was prepared to accept the view that 'the commercial oppression that the colonists suffered . . . was far-reaching', and that the result was to recruit 'very formidable forces' to a political agitation which would not otherwise have been dangerous. Thus in his survey the economic motives for the Revolution were given primacy.[22]

Twenty years after the publication of Bellot's book, few, if any, leading historians of the Revolution would appear willing to accept this view. The economic interpretation has proved peculiarly vulnerable to criticism based on a more careful penetration of evidence. O. M. Dickerson, one of its chief critics, has observed that its foundations lay in 'economic theology', and its crumbling seems to be the natural fate of any attempt to tell the story of the past in terms of dogmas or theories, in the spirit of *logos* and not of *historia*. Writers such as Dickerson and L. A. Harper have made it clear that the colonies were beneficiaries, not victims, of the old imperial commercial system.[23] It is becoming evident that historians may yet have to go further than they have done hitherto in

---

[20] A. M. Schlesinger, 'The American Revolution Reconsidered', *Political Science Qtly*, xxxiv (1919), 76–7.

[21] Hacker, p. 161.

[22] H. Hale Bellot, pp. 86, 80.

[23] O. M. Dickerson, *The Navigation Acts and the American Revolution* (Philadelphia, 1951). L. A. Harper, *The English Navigation Laws* (New York, 1939); 'The Effect of the Navigation Acts on the Thirteen Colonies', *The Era of the America Revolution*, ed. Richard B. Morris (New York, 1939); 'Mercantilism and the American Revolution', *Canadian Hist. Rev.* xxiii (1942), 1–15.

distinguishing imagined from real economic grievances. For instance, colonial pamphleteers alleged in 1764 that they were being victimized in the interests of West India planters by a discriminatory duty against French molasses in the Sugar Act. It has only very recently been pointed out that this 'grievance' was minimal: the planters had only a limited surplus of molasses to send to the continent and were as much affected as the mainland colonists by the new duty, since they themselves bought French molasses.[24] Nor can it any longer be accepted that these duties were unduly burdensome. The capacity of the colonial drink trade to bear the burden of the 1764 duty on its raw material has been forcibly stated; it is not irrelevant to this argument that in 1787 Alexander Hamilton thought perfectly feasible a federal duty on spirits of a shilling a gallon, yielding an estimated annual revenue of £200,000.[25] Apart from openness to such attack on points of detail, the economic interpretation of the Revolution also suffers from the weakness of leaving too much other evidence out of account. It is an act of faith, not a process of historical investigation, which dismisses the enormous, overwhelming masses of contemporary evidence demonstrating the urgency and vital nature of the arguments about constitutional principle as merely a smoke-screen for the operation of economic interest. On the other hand, it is equally inadmissible to deny that economic grievances contributed in some degree to colonial discontent between 1760 and 1776. Not only is it beyond doubt that regulatory and administrative provisions in the Sugar Act of 1764 caused some commercial dislocation and a good deal of sheer trouble with red tape;[26] but furthermore—and here economic and constitutional considerations merge—they cut across the very real degree of commercial *laissez-faire*, particularly in regard to direct trade with the European Continent, which the mainland colonies had established in despite of the Navigation Acts.[27] Finally, even those

[24] Jack M. Sosin, *Agents and Merchants. British Colonial Policy and the Origins of the American Revolution, 1763–1775* (Lincoln, Neb., 1965), p. 46 n. 23.

[25] L. H. Gipson, *The Coming of the Revolution, 1763–1775* (1954), pp. 62–4; *The Federalist*, ed. Jacob E. Cooke (Middletown, Conn., 1961), p. 78.

[26] Knollenberg, pp. 164–8.

[27] On the extensive growth of such trade long before 1763, see Thomas C. Barrow, 'Background to the Grenville Programme, 1757–1763', *W. & M. Qtly*, 3rd ser. xxii (1965), 93–104.

fears of economic consequences which were illusory were among the factors shaping colonial attitudes in the period of revolutionary crisis.

It must remain a matter of speculation how far the swing away from the economic interpretation of the Revolution since 1945 reflects a general disillusionment with economic determinism. Such a disillusionment might arise either out of the natural critical reaction which destroys any dogma after it has attained its apogee, or from the more specific post-war world situation with its polarizations on either side of the Iron Curtain. Again, the increasing concentration by historians upon questions of constitutional principle in the Revolution, and the intellectual background to it, may reflect a subconscious concern to re-examine and reaffirm the validity of the basic principles of constitutional government—those arcana of Atlantic political society which have either been rejected or have never been understood by regimes based on party autocracies of whatever colour, from Madrid and Athens to Moscow and Peking.

Be that as it may, the economic interpretation never monopolized the field, and the main thrust of more recent scholarship has been in other directions. In the study of the Revolution there has always been much preoccupation with constitutional issues, and since the war these have attracted a growing weight of attention. Old evidence has been resifted and new evidence plumbed with ever-increasing richness and profundity. Although various divergent conclusions have emerged, in general these are more congruent with the evidence as a whole than were the views of the proponents of the economic interpretation. The fine study of the Stamp Act crisis by the Morgans and the collection of documents edited by E. S. Morgan both stress, with new abundance of detail, how the emergence of the taxation issue in 1764 and 1765 provoked an immediate universal reaction in the colonies, indicative of an overwhelming preoccupation with constitutional rights.[28] Various recent monographs dealing with political evolution in individual colonies underline the extent to which the colonists had developed a vigorous political machinery and a large degree of control over

---

[28] Above, n. 3; Edmund S. Morgan, *Prologue to Revolution: Sources and Documents on the Stamp Act Crisis, 1764–1766* (Chapel Hill, N.C., 1963).

their own internal affairs. For a long time this quasi-autonomy had rarely been challenged effectively from London.[29]

Recently these conclusions have been brilliantly reinforced from a more synoptic viewpoint by Bernard Bailyn in two works which complement each other—his study of colonial pre-revolutionary pamphlet literature, *The Ideological Origins of the American Revolution*, and his survey of colonial political thought and structure, *The Origins of American Politics*.[30] In these two works the exciting sense of historical discovery is sustained at a high peak of intensity. Bailyn has shown that, long before the Revolution, the American intellectual heritage had absorbed a broad view of politics which derived in some essential respects from John Locke but which was more fundamentally shaped by English oppositionist political writing of the early eighteenth century, topped with a dash of the pessimistic and also messianic strain derived from New England Puritanism. In the American colonies, as also to a lesser extent in Great Britain, political thinking was strongly influenced by a profoundly pessimistic and fearful obsession with the dangers attendant upon political power. The ideas and attitudes which had thus become current in the colonies constituted a great 'hinterland' of belief, from which emerged arguments addressed to specific issues as the American crisis unfolded after 1763. Whilst in Great Britain such beliefs were confined to relatively impotent political dissenting groups, divergent social and political experience brought them much wider acceptance in North America. There almost all the factors which gave stability to politics in the metropolitan state were absent. Bailyn points out: 'If contemporaries were struck by the similarities between the formal structure of government in England and in America, historians have reason to be struck by the differences in the informal

[29] Outstanding titles in a long list are R. E. Brown, *Middle Class Democracy and the Revolution in Massachusetts* (Ithaca, N.Y., 1955); T. J. Wertenbaker, *Give me Liberty. The Struggle for Self-Government in Virginia* (Philadelphia, 1958); Jack P. Greene, *The Quest for Power. The Lower Houses of Assembly in the Southern Colonies, 1689–1776* (Chapel Hill, N.C., 1963). Cf. the sections examining the role of assembly and electorate, in theory and practice, in Massachusetts, Pennsylvania, and Virginia *apud* J. R. Pole, *Political Representation in England and the Origins of the American Republic* (1966), pp. 33–165. For some other titles see Greene, *Reinterpretation*, p. 28 n. 44, and for full bibliography, L. H. Gipson, *The British Empire before the American Revolution* (15 vols., New York, 1936–70), xiv, under individual colonies.

[30] Above, n. 16.

structure of politics.'[31] In the colonies political life was deeply
affected by the pressure of fairly numerous electorates of land-
owning yeomen, by repeated clashes between the legislative
and executive branches of government, by the continued (and
resented) enjoyment by the colonial executives of formal prerogative powers which had been lost by the Crown in Great
Britain, and by the absence of facilities whereby governors and
assemblies might be kept in harmony. Legally the governors
had great powers, but politically they were denied freedom of
manœuvre by the rigidity of their instructions, while the
amount of patronage at their disposal was totally inadequate
to oil the political wheels. The relative brevity of their terms
of office also added to their political weakness. The colonial
assemblies lacked the degree of self-determination enjoyed by
the House of Commons and were driven into self-assertion in
other ways by their sense of insecurity, while at the same time
local conditions impelled them into a more active legislative
role. Novelty, change, development, the rapid fluctuation of
economic and political interests created faction rivalries. Far
more than in London, the postures of legislature and executive
reflected constant conflict. In mid-eighteenth-century Britain
contentious issues had practically disappeared from politics. In
America they were rampant. Abundant patronage smoothed
the course of London politics, whilst the abrasive forces at work
in the colonies lacked this lubricant. The limited and static
franchise operating in a highly deferential society in Britain
contrasted with colonial electorates constantly adjusted to the
growth of population and accustomed to tie down their representatives with instructions. In the unstable and strife-torn
political milieu in the colonies British oppositionist ideas found
fertile soil for growth. Fears of the encroachments of power
and the onset of tyranny were endemic and instinctive. Events
after 1763 created a widespread conviction among colonial
leaders that the constitution was breaking down in face of such
regressive tendencies. However illusory such fears might be,
they were felt with deep intensity, and this is an important
part of the explanation of the coming of the Revolution. Indeed,
Bailyn sees this as the only satisfactory explanation for a colonial
reaction which he describes as out of all proportion to the

[31] *Origins*, p. 66.

impositions enacted in British legislation of 1764–7 and the incidents associated with it.[32]

As the American crisis progressed, and more especially after the passage of the Revenue Act of 1767, such commercial grievances as were being voiced sank more and more into the background, and colonial agitation was increasingly and almost exclusively motivated by the desire to protect constitutional rights and liberties. In general, these were defined by the colonists as the preservation of property by the right to be taxed only through their representatives; the safeguarding of personal liberty against police power by the establishment or the maintenance in all circumstances of an independent judiciary and trial by jury; the securing for the assemblies of full internal legislative competence and the power to control their executives by financial sanctions, as was the case in Britain; and more especially after the experience of the 'Massacre' at Boston in 1770, the preservation of political liberty from the menace represented by a standing army. To the colonists these—not economic interests—were the matters principally at stake. As C. M. Andrews pointed out a good many years ago, out of twenty-seven grievances listed in the Declaration of Independence only one was economic in character.[33]

Recent trends in scholarship thus indicate a fair degree of agreement that the crux of the Anglo-American crisis was a problem of government. But there has been a good deal of divergence over the character of the Revolution within this general framework. For purposes of discussion at this point it seems helpful to adopt some of the categories suggested by Esmond Wright, distinguishing three distinct schools of interpretation under the labels of 'progressive', 'neo-Whig', and 'imperialist'.[34]

The pioneer works of the 'progressive' school are usually taken to be C. H. Lincoln's *The Revolutionary Movement in Pennsylvania, 1760–1776* and Carl L. Becker's *History of Political Parties in the Province of New York, 1760–1776*, both published in the

[32] *Origins*, pp. 159–60.

[33] C. M. Andrews, *The Colonial Period of American History* (4 vols., New Haven, Conn., 1934–8), iv. 427.

[34] Wright, pp. 25–46. Such categorizations of historians are arbitrary and precarious: I apologize in advance if any scholar mentioned below feels wrongly pigeon-holed.

first decade of this century.[35] The distinctive tendency of this school was to stress the role of internal conflict between provincial ruling élites and radical (alias democratic) parties in bringing on the Revolution. As the provincial élites tended to be associated or even identified with the agencies of British control, the Revolution took on the semblance of a popular class struggle. Such a view dovetails to some extent with the tendency to emphasize the 'Americanness' of the Revolution, the extent to which it was rooted in a nascent quality of separate nationhood nurtured by conditions of life on the American continent very different from those in the metropolitan state. This interpretation was still colouring distinguished products of historical scholarship in the years just after the last war;[36] but a considerable number of more recent studies indicate that it is insufficiently supported by the evidence.[37] It now emerges that, except to some extent in Pennsylvania, provincial politics were not polarized along class lines. Political divisions revolved round the ambitions of rival factions among the provincial élites, and one faction usually could and did exploit against the other issues arising out of quarrels with the British authorities. The position of the élites rested partly on habits of deference (in this respect colonial political society is now seen as more akin to that of Britain than the progressives assumed it to be); but because franchises were broad in most of the colonies, the members of the élites had to buttress their positions much more than in Britain by the active cultivation of popularity. Furthermore, despite the presence of wealthy men, there was little distinction of class. The findings of Jackson Turner Main, in *The Social Structure of Revolutionary America*,[38] indicate that there was a great social and economic opportunity in the colonies, a high degree of vertical mobility, and a 'remarkably supple class structure', all elements calculated to minimize any rigidity or friction between classes. These findings leave intact very little of the progressive interpretation of the Revolution.

[35] Philadelphia, 1901; Madison, Wisconsin, 1909. For brief sketches of developments in this school see Wright, pp. 35–40, and Greene, *Reinterpretation*, pp. 8–17.
[36] e.g. Merrill Jensen, *The New Nation* (New York, 1950).
[37] For a list see Greene, *Reinterpretation*, pp. 28–9 nn. 44–7. The impact of the criticism is summarized in B. Bailyn, 'Political Experience and Enlightenment Ideas in Eighteenth-Century America', in ibid., pp. 277–82.
[38] Princeton, N.J., 1965.

In a general view, the works of writers of the 'neo-Whig' and 'imperialist' schools present difficulties arising out of the fact that some at least of the members of each of these groups tend to underestimate the importance of the factors of explanation which are of chief concern to the other. While the argument between them has proceeded with urbanity, it is evident from prefatory protests on occasion that some historians have felt there was no alternative but to defend entrenched positions. These stances underscore the strength and vitality of the scholarship on both sides, but they beg the question whether some other way out of an apparent impasse cannot be found.

The primary object of the neo-Whig historians has been to answer a question which has been phrased in the general form: 'Why were the colonists angry?' The answers which have been given vary greatly in the extent of ground covered and the degree of subtlety of penetration, but all add effectively to our knowledge of the American crisis. O. M. Dickerson's *The Navigation Acts and the American Revolution*[39] lays stress on real or apparent maladministration by Customs officials. Bernhard Knollenberg's *Origin of the American Revolution, 1759–1766*[40] is a fully documented catalogue of everything which was causing concern, irritation, or anger to the colonists. The Morgans' *The Stamp Act Crisis*[41] re-emphasizes the crucial nature of the issue of parliamentary taxation, and this conclusion gains a great deal of support from detail in monographs dealing with particular aspects of colonial discontent by writers not themselves necessarily neo-Whig in outlook, such as John Shy's study of the role of the British army in America,[42] Carl Ubbelohde's *The Vice-Admiralty Courts and the American Revolution*,[43] and B. W. Labaree's very thorough examination of the Boston Tea Party.[44] Taken together, the work of the neo-Whig historians traces out in valuable detail many ways in which the British Government and Parliament provoked the colonists to anger. But, like some of the imperialist historians with whom they do not see eye to eye, they tend in some cases to tell only part of the story. The British Government becomes a lay figure against which the

[39] Above, n. 23.   [40] Above, n. 3.   [41] Ibid.
[42] John Shy, *Towards Lexington. The Role of the British Army in the Coming of the American Revolution* (Princeton, N.J., 1965).
[43] Philadelphia, 1951.
[44] *The Boston Tea Party* (1964).

colonists struggle to preserve their liberties. Its activities are condemned or implicitly written off as wilfully wrong; its motivations and the rationale of its actions are not taken into account or given a proportionate place in the general story. In a fine general study like John R. Alden's *History of the American Revolution. Britain and the Loss of the Thirteen Colonies*,[45] despite prefatory protests of intent to hold the balance even, there are nevertheless overtones of manifest destiny and whiffs of brimstone which recall Bancroft. Very little attempt is made to evaluate imperial policy. Elements of degeneracy, or supposed degeneracy, in the society of the metropolitan state are underlined and the ascription of corrupt motives behind pro-ministerial voting slips out from time to time—but (if any of all this matters) nothing is said, for instance, about the native American abuses and oppression which drove the Regulators of North Carolina to revolt.[46] All this reflects an abandonment, at this point, of the search for historical explanations. An essential dimension of the Revolution is missing.

One defence of this approach has been adduced by Morgan from the general impression of British eighteenth-century politics derived from the work of Sir Lewis Namier and other historians who have been influenced by him. If, Morgan asks, British politics after the accession of George III were so dominated by factions and local interests and personal ambitions as these accounts suggest, how is it possible to maintain that governments at Westminster were concerned with enlightened imperial policies? How could such parochial politicians have enlightened views?[47]

Neither the assumptions nor the questions quite fit the case. Politicians address themselves to many levels of activity and concern. Namier was concerned with certain levels which had hitherto been neglected. His two great books on this subject do not give a complete characterization of British politics in the later eighteenth century. However, it is pertinent to the present

---

[45] 1969.
[46] On the provocations given to the Regulators arising out of the corruption of native local officials, see Elisha P. Douglass, *Rebels and Democrats: the Struggle for Equal Political Rights and Majority Rule during the American Revolution* (Chapel Hill, N.C., 1955), pp. 75–80.
[47] 'The American Revolution: Revisions in Need of Revising', *W. & M. Qtly*, 3rd ser. xiv (1957), 4–5, 8, 12–13.

discussion that he did point out that a number of 'experts' on the colonies were elected to George III's first parliament.[48]

It is a familiar fact that over large areas of the business with which it deals, any representative assembly functions with only a very slim basis of personal experience. Only a few members have expertise in a given field. Their colleagues are bound to depend greatly upon their exposition of as much information on a subject in question as can be placed before them. This was well understood in mid-eighteenth-century Britain and a considerable information service had already come into existence to assist the work of the politicians.[49] In part this worked officially. Government statements were embodied in royal Speeches and Messages. Both Houses could call for papers and examine witnesses, as they did on various occasions during the American crisis. This system worked with a strong pro-ministerial bias, for it was generally ministerial initiative and ministerial majorities that dictated the direction of such investigations. More independent, though sometimes ministerially inspired, was the mass of information in pamphlet form available to members of both Houses on any major political question. Its importance is indicated by the government's full exploitation of the technique. Grenville's American policy was given a virtually official full explanation and defence from the pen of his Secretary to the Treasury, Thomas Whately.[50] But this was a game that Oppositions could also play. A select list of pamphlets for 1766 gives over twenty items on the colonies, many directed to the question of parliamentary taxation and fairly equally divided between the two sides of the controversy.[51] This does not include London reprints of leading colonial pamphlets, nor letters to the press, a business vigorously pursued, for instance, by Benjamin Franklin during his years in London.[52]

[48] Sir Lewis Namier, *England in the Age of the American Revolution* (rev. edn., 1961), esp. pp. 229–73, and *The Structure of Politics at the Accession of George III*, passim.

[49] For a general survey of these practices, as they had already developed forty to fifty years before, see G. C. Gibbs, 'Parliament and Foreign Policy in the Age of Stanhope and Walpole', *E.H.R.* lxxvii (1962), 18–37.

[50] [T. Whately], *The Regulations lately made concerning the Colonies and Taxes imposed upon them considered* (1765).

[51] Gipson, *British Empire*, xiv. 62–5.

[52] B. Bailyn, *Pamphlets of the American Revolution, 1750–1776*, vol. i: *1750–1765* (Cambridge, Mass., 1965), pp. 599, 741–2, 747; *Benjamin Franklin's Letters to the Press, 1758–1775*, ed. Verner W. Crane (Chapel Hill, N.C., 1950)

The distribution of copies of pamphlets to individual Members of Parliament was a well-established practice early in the century,[53] and it can reasonably be assumed that it continued in George III's reign. Political clubs connected with the parliamentary Opposition could provide an initiative for the publication of pamphlets as well as opportunities for the discussion of their contents, and there is evidence that they were eagerly purchased.[54] Indeed it is not credible that all this mass of material would have been printed and marketed were it not being bought by people in public life. The British politicians had ample sources of information about America and the reports of parliamentary debates show that they gave it serious consideration.[55] If the conclusions they reached from it were not 'enlightened' from the colonial point of view and led eventually to disaster, then this fact in itself requires to be fully explained, otherwise another dimension of the Revolution remains unexplored; it does not advance knowledge merely to attribute it to parochialism or original sin.

The strength of the imperialist school of historians lies precisely in their asking the questions which rectify such omissions—questions which historians working from other viewpoints tend not to formulate. It may be the case that some historians of the imperialist school are open to the charges laid by the neo-Whigs, that they are insufficiently sensitive with regard to the positions defended by the colonists, or that they depict the colonists as meanly and unjustifiably opting out of financial responsibility for an empire of which they were a part, and from which they benefited, and as spurning the lead of governments whose colonial policy was necessary and enlightened. Where this is so, there is an omission of just those elements in the story with which the neo-Whig historians are primarily concerned, and this too can lead to an imperfect and distorted view of the Revolution.

Such distortion is an occupational hazard for any scholar who seeks to place the Revolution in its context as an imperial

[53] Gibbs, art. cit., p. 35 and nn. 1, 8.

[54] D. H. Watson, 'The Rise of the Opposition at Wildman's Club', *B.I.H.R.* xliv (1971), 66 n. 3, 67–8.

[55] This has recently become clearer for the poorly reported 1760s thanks to 'Parliamentary Diaries of Nathaniel Ryder, 1764–7', ed. P. D. G. Thomas, *Camden Miscellany*, xxiii (R. Hist. Soc., Camden 4th ser. vii, 1969).

event; but it is one that can be overcome; and the imperialist interpretation has had a long and fruitful history. In the late nineteenth century there were historians who realized that George III's governments could not simply be written off as tyrannical and obtuse. The rationale of British policy in North America in the early 1760s was ably explored over sixty years ago by George Louis Beer.[56] More recently it has been much more fully elaborated in the work of a number of scholars, notably Lawrence Henry Gipson.[57] Their investigations seem to establish beyond challenge that there were real problems of imperial commerce and of frontier defence in America after 1760, which could only be dealt with effectively by imperial agencies and imperial authority. There are historians still inclined to deny this; but it is not clear how they assume that such a disunited body as the old colonies had shown themselves to be at the outset of the great war for the empire in the 1750s was to deal with such major questions as holding the French Canadians to their new allegiance, guarding the Floridas against Spanish intrigue and infiltration, or even effectively resisting a general Indian rising of the kind encountered in 1763, at least till a great deal of massacre and destruction had occurred. Given the existence of such problems, the growing burden of imperial defence costs compared with thirty years before, and the frightening increase in the National Debt since 1754, it seems an error to condemn as without sense and reason government policies which aimed at establishing garrisons, imposing frontier controls, providing some imperial administration in territories outside the jurisdiction of particular colonies, and raising part of the expense by taxation on the colonists. However disastrous the unforeseen consequences, these policies were not adopted with sinister intent. There is nothing in the evidence regarding the evolution of these policies to conflict with the view expressed by Gipson, that in 1764 and 1765 the Grenville ministry acted upon the assumption that the colonists would come to see the fairness of their paying their share and the

[56] *British Colonial Policy, 1754–1765* (New York, 1907).

[57] Gipson, *British Empire*, x, chs. i and ix–xii; Jack M. Sosin, *Whitehall and the Wilderness. The Middle West in British Colonial Policy, 1760–1775* (Lincoln, Neb., 1961), chs. i–iv, and *Agents and Merchants*, chs. i–ii; Thomas C. Barrow, *Trade and Empire. The British Customs Service in Colonial America, 1660–1775* (Cambridge, Mass., 1967), ch. viii and art. cit. above, n. 27; Shy, *Lexington*, chs. ii–iii.

necessity that over-all direction should rest with the central government and its agencies.[58]

The validity of Grenville's way of thinking is apparent from events immediately following the achievement of American independence. Although the old imperial authority had been thrust aside, the imperial problems still remained, and a new imperial authority had to be created to deal with them. Time and again during 1787 and 1788, in *The Federalist*, the champions of American union echoed the complaints and the attitudes of British imperial statesmen a generation before. For instance, John Jay alluded to the problem of Indian relations in terms very like those used to justify the Proclamation of 1763:[59]

Not a single Indian war has yet been occasioned by aggressions of the present Fœderal government, feeble as it is, but there are several instances of Indian hostilities having been provoked by the improper conduct of individual States, who either unable or unwilling to restrain or punish offences, have given occasion to the slaughter of many innocent inhabitants.

The wider issue of defence was handled by Alexander Hamilton in terms very similar to those used to defend the Grenville legislative programme (for 'Britain' read French Canadians of 1764):[60]

The territories of Britain, Spain and of the Indian nations in our neighbourhood, do not border on particular States; but incircle the Union from MAINE to GEORGIA. The danger, though in different degrees, is therefore common. And the means of guarding against it ought in like manner to be the objects of common councils and of a common treasury.

Here is what Hamilton had to say in December 1787 about the practice of raising defence revenues by requisition, which the Confederate States had adopted in accordance with imperial precedents before 1763:[61]

Except as to the role of apportionment, the United States have an indefinite discretion to make requisitions for men and money; but

[58] 'The American Revolution as an Aftermath of the Great War for the Empire, 1754–1763', *Political Science Qtly*, lxv (1950), 86–104, esp. 100.
[59] *The Federalist*, ed. Cooke, pp. 16–17. For comparison with the period before 1763, see the evidence discussed in Sosin, *Whitehall*, pp. 29–33, 39–41, 43–51, and Shy, pp. 59–61.
[60] *The Federalist*, ed. Cooke, p. 158. See the discussion of 'the rationale of an American garrison' in 1763 in Shy, pp. 52–68 (on the French Canadians, pp. 54–5).
[61] *The Federalist*, ed. Cooke, p. 93.

they have no authority to raise either by regulations extending to the individual citizens of America. The consequence of this is, that though in theory their resolutions concerning those objects are law, constitutionally binding on the members of the Union, yet in practice they are mere recommendations, which the States observe or disregard at their option.

British statesmen had noted the same phenomenon during the great war for the empire between 1754 and 1763, and again during the Pontiac rising. Moreover, Hamilton condemned the requisition system as unfair and justified an imperial American revenue in terms precisely similar to those Grenville had used in conversations with colonial agents some twenty-five years before:[62]

There can be no common measure of national wealth; and of course no general or stationary rule, by which the ability of a State to pay taxes can be determined. The attempt therefore to regulate the contributions of the members of a confederacy, by any such rule, cannot fail to be productive of glaring inequality and extreme oppression. . . . There is no method of steering clear of this inconvenience but by authorizing the national government to raise its own revenues in its own way. . . . The system of quotas and requisitions, whether it be applied to men or money, is in every view a system of imbecility in the union, and of inequality and injustice among the members.

James Madison, writing early in 1788, provided a remarkable justification of the policy behind the Currency Act of 1764:[63]

The extension of the prohibition [of money issues by the States] to bills of credit must give pleasure to every citizen in proportion to his love of justice, and his knowledge of the true springs of public prosperity. The loss which America has sustained since the peace from the pestilent effects of paper money . . . constitutes an enormous debt against the States chargeable with this unadvised measure, which must long remain unsatisfied; or rather an accumulation of guilt, which can be expiated no otherwise than by a voluntary

[62] *The Federalist*, ed. Cooke, pp. 133–4, 138. Cf. Grenville's remarks about apportionment reported by Jared Ingersoll in 1765, in Morgan, *Prologue*, p. 29 (b).

[63] *The Federalist*, ed. Cooke, p. 300. This is not to say that either the Board of Trade in the 1760s or Hamilton in 1788 really understood this highly complex and technical subject. See Joseph A. Ernst, 'Genesis of the Currency Act of 1764: Virginia Paper Money and the Protection of British Investments', *W. & M. Qtly*, 3rd ser. xxii (1965), 33–74.

sacrifice on the altar of justice, of the power which has been the instrument of it.

And Hamilton pointed out that the exclusion of juries from revenue cases—a feature of Grenville's and Townshend's legislation bitterly resented by the colonists in the 1760s—was the actual practice in the State of New York within a few years of independence and was generally acknowledged as 'essential to the efficacy of the revenue laws'.[64]

To similar problems the Federalists returned answers similar to those of Grenville. In their writings his arguments are vindicated against many of the criticisms levelled against them at the time and sometimes subsequently by historians. There could hardly be a more cogent warning that any thoroughly satisfactory treatment of the Revolution needs to come to terms with the reasonableness of much of British colonial policy in the 1760s.

For a full understanding of the Revolution the imperial dimension must, then, be taken into account. Historians need to know as fully why British statesmen and politicians acted as they did as why the colonists became angry. Recent studies falling within the imperialist line of approach emphasize this fact with fruitful contributions to our understanding of events.

The seminal concept inspiring the symposium edited by A. G. Olson and R. M. Brown[65] is the gradual decay of what was at first in a real sense a single Anglo-American community, with an informal and loosely articulated but effective political system which helped to steer affairs in the direction of compromise and to check the drift towards conflict. The essays in this volume cover only a small part of the potential ground for investigation. They outline the concept of the Anglo-American community and one or two of the circumstances of disintegration, but have not gone further than pioneering the search for explanations of it. Behind the answers so far given lie further questions. Nevertheless, this book represents a fresh approach with a rich potential. Papers by Thomas C. Barrow, Michael Kammen, and John Shy illustrate the increasing discontent in Whitehall in the mid-eighteenth century with the operation of the imperial system, the growing ineffectiveness of the major formal channel of communication through the colonial agents,

---

[64] *The Federalist*, ed. Cooke, p. 563.   [65] Above, n. 3.

and the conceptual limitations which bound the minds of British politicians. Books by Kammen solidly buttress parts of these investigations.[66]

Bernard Bailyn's *The Origins of American Politics* explores with telling emphasis certain aspects of this Anglo-American community, with particular relation to the ideas and assumptions that lay behind political action.[67] It is hardly an exaggeration to say that in this book those who conducted political dissent against imperial authority in the American colonies emerge as oppositionist Englishmen, closely akin in stances and political attitudes to opposition groups found in the metropolitan state all through the eighteenth century. In the colonies these oppositionist politicians were dominant. But in the colonies, too, could be found minorities who shared the opposing attitude of the dominant ministerial groups in politics in Great Britain. A majority in the colonies and a minority in Britain were hagridden by the same fears of the encroachments of kingly or executive power. A minority in the colonies and in time a significant proportion of the politicians at home were haunted by the converse fear, that the forces of democracy would overbalance and destroy the constitution, at least in the American provinces of the Empire.[68] As Edmund Burke put it in 1769: 'The Americans have made a discovery, or think they have made one, that we mean to oppress them: we have made a discovery, or think we have made one, that they intend to rise in rebellion against us. . . . We know not how to advance; they know not how to retreat.'[69] The quarrel that split the Empire was truly an English quarrel. It is within this context that the listener can fully appreciate the note of desolation that rings through some of the correspondence of revolutionary leaders as they watched the approach of the seemingly inevitable moment for armed resistance.

[66] *A Rope of Sand: the Colonial Agents, British Politics, and the American Revolution* (Ithaca, N.Y., 1968), and *Empire and Interest. The American Colonies and the Politics of Mercantilism* (New York, 1970). For an instance of exceptional inter-imperial political integration, see J. R. Daniell, 'Politics in New Hampshire under Governor Benning Wentworth, 1741–1767', *W. & M. Qtly*, 3rd ser. xxiii (1966), 76–105.

[67] See also above, pp. 188–90.

[68] Even on this point, *The Federalist* a few years later re-echoed the fears of British politicians (ed. Cooke, pp. 333–6, 492–3).

[69] *Sir Henry Cavendish's Debates of the House of Commons . . .*, ed. J. Wright (2 vols., 1841–3), i. 348–9.

To different historians the Revolution has appeared in various guises: as a crusade in defence of liberty; as the triumph of a new nation freeing itself from constitutional or economic bonds; as a colonial struggle for independence; as a democratic revolution against an *ancien régime*; or, as seems implicit in Bailyn's more recent writings, as a civil conflict followed by secession. Not all, perhaps none, of these categories are mutually exclusive, though some of them now appear less conformable than others to the known facts. It may be that the Revolution was to some extent all of these things and that we engage in a futile exercise if we attempt to fit it exclusively into one mould. Or perhaps some of these categories are more truly appropriate than others: in that case it is probable we still have a long quest ahead of us before we are, if ever, in a position to judge between them. In the meantime, in whichever light historians consider the Revolution, the advisability of keeping in mind the alternative viewpoints remains—as also of remembering, while we read the records of the eighteenth century, that then, as now, the future was unpredictable.

X

Changing Attitudes towards Government in Eighteenth-century Britain

STUDIES of government administration that seek to go beyond description of mechanics, and make some more general evaluation of performance, must determine their criteria. Among these it would be unhistorical to exclude some consideration of contemporary attitudes towards government. In the present context[1] such attitudes are taken to mean the expectations entertained of government and the willingness to increase its powers on the part of people, within and without its establishment, who were able to exert some influence upon it. Discussion of the general parameters within which government was felt to operate, or ought to operate, forms a natural counterpart to the substantial body of recent research into the functioning of eighteenth-century government departments. It will be argued here that a significant change in public attitudes occurred in the early 1780s, and indeed that it foreshadows what Professor Parris describes as the nineteenth-century revolution in government.[2]

In this as with almost any other aspect of English eighteenth-century public life, the dominant tone is set by 'the politicians', the figures who dominated Parliament, who formed both the ministries of the day and the focus of any opposition, formal or informal. Movement in or out of office might cause them to change tactics, and among them individuals might, of course, hold strongly differing ideas on such issues as America. On what was expected of government, however, and on what limitations should be imposed upon it, they shared to a great degree a common view.

Once the Protestant Succession had become secure, there was a broad general satisfaction amongst these men with the

[1] I should like to express my thanks to my colleagues Professors John F. Naylor and R. Arthur Bowler for their helpful comments on the preparation of this essay.
[2] H. W. Parris, *Constitutional Bureaucracy* (1969).

prevailing political, social, and economic order. Government
was no longer seen as an instrument of radical change; rather,
its functions were felt to be the maintenance of domestic order,
the handling of public finance, the protection of commercial
interests, the conduct of diplomacy and war. The first of these
required the guarantee of an adequate food supply and some
general public provision for those in most dire need. Food called
for governmental initiative[3] on a number of occasions as,
through a succession of Acts relating to the Assize of Bread,
a satisfactory formula was sought for the provision of a cheap
but wholesome supply. Ultimately, however, these measures
were administered at local level, as was of course the other
main provision designed to prevent extreme distress and thus
possible disorder, Poor Relief. It is true that London was the
exception in the eighteenth century to many generalizations
about the century as a whole: it was beginning to experience
some of the problems that, when more widespread in the
nineteenth century, occasioned the entry of central government
into a much wider field of social legislation. However, even in
London, until after 1800, the bulk of both initiative and
administration was derived from or devolved upon local
authority, the City of London and the parishes.[4] Again, Britain's
economic life was beginning to undergo substantial changes;
yet here, too, government devolved and permitted, rather than
initiated and controlled, and there was no great pressure to
the contrary. Changes in forms of land tenure took place and
the road system was improved, but legislation in these areas
was permissive and rarely initiated by government; it resulted
in no appreciable increase in government's administrative functions. Government did not become involved, nor did the men
who ran government believe it should become involved, in any
direct way in the provocation or supervision of industrial or
technical change. By any standard, and certainly by those
applying in seventeenth- and eighteenth-century France, the
British government's role in the encouragement of industrial
and technical advance was minimal.

---

[3] Such initiative was limited, as most of the deliberation leading to legislation
was undertaken by committees of the House of Commons.

[4] Dorothy George, *London Life in the Eighteenth Century* (2nd edn., 1966), pp.
21–2.

Despite the extent of the overseas acquisitions and the problems they set, Britain's government, certainly until after 1763, had neither the administrative machinery nor the desire to exercise close centralized control. Control there was in terms of a mercantilist system of protection and restriction, but this was rarely exercised with thoroughness; and a great deal of the political and judicial administration of the Empire was devolved upon trading companies or the colonists themselves.[5] It was financial necessity, some might say expediency, rather than a fundamental change of view as to the imperial government's role that moved George Grenville to attempt some tighter control of the American colonies; and it was the American response, not any shift in British theory of government, that pushed his successors into further efforts in that direction. Again, it was the affairs of the East India Company and the condition of India that led Lord North and others after him to extend government control in that sphere.

Protectionism, with the consequent elaborate and confusing codes of fiscal control, gave more power to government and contributed greater numbers to its establishment than any other realm of government affairs. On the other hand, the potential domestic power arising from the application of protectionism was a question of great political sensitivity; on this terrain politicians in office learnt to move very cautiously and those in opposition were very alert, as we know from the Excise Bill crisis of 1733. So this was not likely to prove fruitful ground for any further extension of governmental power. Furthermore, it cannot escape our notice that fundamental changes of attitude towards government and the expansion of its activity were to come at a time when the importance of the Customs and Excise was declining in relation to other government services. Thus one cannot look to the administration of the mercantilist system as a seed-ground for government expansion.

It was war that placed the heaviest demand upon eighteenth-century governments, and led Parliament to expect most from them. But it is questionable whether war drastically affected the general attitude towards government or the particular

[5] For some suggestive remarks on 'the seeds of imperial disintegration' after 1688, see the chapter by P. S. Haffenden in *The New Cambridge Modern History*, vi. (1970), esp. pp. 506–7.

views of politicians in or out of office. In wartime there was, initially at least, a general willingness to grant more revenue, but rarely more direct power to government; nor was this sought.[6] Government had to compete with the private sector of the economy[7] for vital resources, but attempts directly to requisition wartime supplies were confined to subordinates on active service and either disowned or compensated for by central government. Property rights were as jealously guarded in war as in peace and governments were generally reluctant to become involved in their contravention.

Why did politicians, not only in opposition but when charged with the actual conduct of war, remain unwilling, either in a positive fashion or merely by default, to extend the powers of government even though they were often aware of the inadequacy of these powers? In the first place, force of necessity was never sufficient to overcome the deep reluctance to embark on fundamental change. Despite shortcomings, Britain won most of her eighteenth-century wars. Even if one could demonstrate that victory was achieved despite rather than because of the government machine, the element of necessity as a driving-force for change was absent: the machine creaked, but it worked. This argument weighed equally against any major extension of the powers granted to government and any fundamental administrative reform. Success in war bred self-confidence. Neither the '45 nor the reverses early in the Seven Years War dented this self-confidence for any length of time. There was no sustained feeling of vulnerability or national crisis. Wars fought successfully and at a distance, with no apparent threat to national survival, did not provoke fundamental or even substantial revision of the machinery through which they were conducted.

Constitutional theory and political principle served to reinforce the politicians' general satisfaction with a style of government neither over-involved nor over-powerful. Whatever the actual practice of decision-making, the position of ministerial government in constitutional theory remained ambiguous.

---

[6] Impressment could obviously be construed as an exception to the point being made here.

[7] For discussion of this issue in relation to the hiring of ships, see D. Syrett, *Shipping and the American War, 1775–83* (1970), pp. 78, 105.

Although disagreement might exist over the relative powers of King and Parliament and the degree of control, desired or actual, that the one should exercise over the other, there was general agreement that ministers must satisfy both. For politicians in opposition the aspect of constitutional theory that loomed largest was the maintenance or reassertion of limitations on the power of the King's ministers. For those in office, there loomed equally large those aspects of established practice that related to parliamentary management, patronage, and the 'influence' available to government ministers. Some doubt has been cast on the effective utility of government patronage for providing votes in the Commons or winning elections, but as a rule ministers believed it to be important to their continuance in office.[8] As a result, before 1782, no ministry took any serious step that would reduce the amount of patronage available to it. Those who railed against 'corruption' when in opposition, as we know, themselves used the same means of influence when in office. Neither an extension of governmental powers nor a major administrative reform that would have diminished ministerial influence was likely so long as Opposition watched for any signs of the former and Administration quaked at the prospect of the latter.

While politicians formed ministries and ran government, they sought the support of a majority of independents in the House of Commons as a basis for any lengthy tenure of office. Many of the views so far summarized as tending to confine contemporary expectations of government were shared by these men, often in greater measure. A suspicion of 'arbitrary' power emanating from the King's prerogative persisted well into the eighteenth century; and later, when there was a more general willingness to support His Majesty's ministers, this was rightly never taken by any ministry as *carte blanche*. The demands of the independents for cheap government were usually more insistent than those of the politicians, for they saw themselves in essence as the representatives of those who bore the bulk of taxation. Their occasional inconsistency in urging ministers to a more aggressive foreign policy, which might turn out to be expensive, represented no real desertion of their belief in the virtue of

[8] See, e.g., I. R. Christie, 'Economical Reform and "The Influence of the Crown", 1780', *Cambridge Historical Journal*, xii (1956), 144–54.

frugality in government, but rather a developing sense of national self-importance and an exaggerated sensibility over national interests. If the independents in the Commons generally had their reasons for urging cheap government, they had other grounds for resisting any extension of the powers of central government, because these were most likely to expand at the cost of a system of local government which they themselves dominated. In their local judicial capacity, in their administration of Land Tax and Poor Relief, through their role in the county militia, in many ways formal and informal, these were the men whom both contemporaries and modern historians observed to be running England.[9] The representatives of provincial England, permeated as many of them were with suspicions and resentments of London and all therein, would not lightly give up the authority they exercised to a central government which they influenced but did not fully control. Thus any minister who proposed any measure which threatened, or was feared to threaten, an extension of central authority was virtually guaranteed the hostility of the bulk of the independents. Even had there existed a minister set on a deliberate plan for the extension of central power, it is questionable whether he could have progressed far in the face of this almost instinctive type of opposition.

From the early 1760s extra-parliamentary opinion became at times both more organized and more vocal in its criticism of the parliamentary and governmental system through which Britain was ruled. Nevertheless, this embryonic reform movement represented no break with the general philosophy of government so far discussed. Rather, even in its more radical forms, it was founded on the traditional belief in limited government and gained much of its impetus from a conviction that the limitations were being contravened. The goal of reform was the maintenance of those limitations by a Parliament better equipped to perform that task—the improvement to be achieved by a reduction of influence, the representation of a greater number of the people, or both.

But if there was as yet little or no pressure upon eighteenth-century government from outside for it to assume a more

---

[9] H. Perkin, *The Origins of Modern English Society, 1780–1880* (1969), p. 41, citing Defoe, *The Poor Man's Plea, in relation to . . . a Reformation of Manners . . .* (1698).

positive or expanded role, what of government itself? Was there no bureaucratic drive to this end, no desire for more power to get the job done or remove encumbrances that stood in the way of more effective government? The answer must be that there was none, certainly not on any significant scale. What then accounts for the acceptance of their limited role by the bureaucrats themselves?

One factor was undoubtedly the leisured pace of administration, a business rhythm largely determined by simple but often neglected factors of technology, particularly as they related to transport and communication. Especially in wartime, a basic test of government's effectiveness was necessarily its ability to move men, ships, and supplies over considerable distances, a task frequently complicated by the need to converge on a precise rendezvous and always by the dependence of every means of transport, internal and external, upon the vagaries of the weather.[10] The concurrent inability to transmit orders with speed and reliability was equally an obstacle to efficient administration: worse, the difficulties of communication could result in directions based on out-dated or insufficient information. Disasters such as the military campaign of 1777 might well have been avoided if Burgoyne, Howe, and Germain had had available to them a more rapid messenger than the packet-boat. Rather less obviously, one wonders what the effect on their policies towards America might have been had Grenville, Townshend, North, Germain, or King George III been able to obtain more rapid information of the evolving American situation. Such impediments, of course, also told upon the domestic and peacetime operations of government—for example, upon control of the Customs service and revenue-collecting machinery.[11] In the realm of communication, the technical means available to government were closely related to the attitude of those directly in its service. The absence of telegram or telephone, the very remote chance of a snap visit from a minister or even from one of his immediate subordinates, conditioned attitudes towards directives from London quite as

[10] N. Baker, *Government and Contractors: the British Treasury and War Supplies, 1775–1783* (1971), pp. 129–31.

[11] J. E. D. Binney, *British Public Finance and Administration, 1774–1792* (Oxford, 1958), pp. 31–3, 57–66.

much as their tardy transmission. One cannot study any area of eighteenth-century government operations without being impressed by the blissful disregard commonly displayed by provincial and overseas subordinates towards instructions from London.[12] The real control that the head exercised over the parts of the eighteenth-century government machine is itself questionable. Implicit acknowledgement of this situation is reflected in the frequency with which departments of central government resorted to urgent pleas and dire threats, rarely followed through, in the face of their subordinates' disregard of prior instructions. An air of frustrated despair and impotence permeates these attempts to wring obedience from subordinates.

But lax compliance with orders was only exacerbated, not originated, by distance from central authority and problems of communication. The very nature of government employment and of the attitudes customarily adopted towards it were fundamental factors in central government's relative lack of control and the slow pace of its machinery. The system of patronage and influence has been studied extensively in its effects upon parliamentary politics, but one does not have to detract from its importance in that respect in order to lay equal emphasis upon its implications for the attitudes of government employees, whether they held sinecure offices or had obtained 'effective' positions with or without influence. The effect was felt at all levels and in all departments. A successful career depended not so much upon performance in office as upon the connections and influence available to the office-holder. Where these were not decisive, it was longevity rather than ability which counted. These conditions applied whether the position at stake was a clerkship in the Treasury, a command in the army or navy, or a minor post in the dockyards. The prevailing methods of appointment and promotion hardly served to stimulate a full commitment to government service. Nor did the forms of reward in a monetary sense. Because it was either inadequate or irregular, the direct and official payment of government employees was more often than not insufficient to sustain them in the style of the social classes from which they were drawn. Thus the perquisites of office, whether it was the Treasury

[12] Baker, pp. 5–6.

clerk's opportunity to profit during the allocation of government loans[13] or the naval captain's prospects of profit from
inflated accounts,[14] constituted a significant part of the return
from government service. Given the technical difficulties of
control, the slow and inadequate means of governmental
accounting, and the relative inadequacy of official salaries, it
is hardly surprising that the line between the officially recognized
perquisites of office and the opportunities for financial profit
presented by office was for much of the eighteenth century very
indistinct and frequently crossed.[15] The impact upon the cost
of government is obvious, though it will never be possible to
measure it precisely. What is more important for the purpose
of this discussion is the influence of self-service in the government
service upon the general attitudes and thus performance of
large numbers of government employees.

Where energies were expended and loyalties displayed, it was
more often than not *vis-à-vis* the individual patron rather than
the government department or the public service as a whole.[16]
The sources of this preference of course lay deep in the nature
of political and social relationships in general, which even in
England had not yet discarded all traces of feudalism.[17] On
those occasions when government service was given any collective recognition it was almost always spoken of in individual
terms, as 'the King's service'. There were other ways in which
the social values of eighteenth-century England permeated
government service. The dominance of the gentleman, the
amateur, the all-rounder was most obvious at ministerial level,
but it influenced attitudes and practices at all levels, not least
in the army and navy. The specialist, the professional, the
merchant, the government 'man of business' were all accorded
their worth by their superiors, but it was not construed as a
qualification for high office. Even Adam Smith tacitly accepted
the superior political judgement of the country gentleman, on
the grounds that the 'specialist', such as a merchant, was too
preoccupied with his own affairs.

    [13] Binney, p. 102.
    [14] Daniel A. Baugh, *British Naval Administration in the Age of Walpole* (Princeton,
N.J., 1965), p. 396.
    [15] R. A. Bowler, 'Logistical Problems of the British Army in America, 1775–83'
(Ph.D. thesis, University of London, 1971), pp. 237–89.
    [16] Baugh, p. 124.   [17] Perkin, pp. 37–52.

In all these circumstances, clearly, there could be no civil service in the modern sense.[18] Without a collective or institutional identity, without the sense of service that was developed later with the regularization of government employment, one would not expect to find any sustained or widespread sense of bureaucratic ambition. The very attitudes of those in government employment, therefore, as well as the technical limitations which surrounded their work offered a built-in resistance to change. The difficulty of gearing administration to its most formidable eighteenth-century task, the conduct of war, illustrates this inertia. The elder Pitt's ability to accelerate the motions of government, traditionally held to be the outstanding example which other eighteenth-century ministers failed to emulate, has recently been questioned in the light of these factors.[19] Certainly one would not disparage the efforts of others besides Pitt who strove to improve the speed and efficacy of the executive power, but at least as striking is the extent to which such men were obstructed by the prevailing attitudes towards and within government. Thus John Robinson drove himself into recurring illness,[20] rather than the Treasury and its subordinates into efficiency, and Charles Middleton blunted his evangelical rapier on the inertia of naval administration.[21] One might even suggest that some of Chatham's later egocentricity and disdain of government was shaped by his frustration during the Seven Years War. It is certainly significant that such early efforts as were made to produce more efficient performance from eighteenth-century government emanated from individuals, rather than from any broad public change of attitude towards government or expectations of it.

Nevertheless, although from a twentieth-century viewpoint one is able to reveal the deficiencies of British government in the eighteenth century, the facts must be faced that in the period 1715–75 Britain won her wars, avoided major social unrest, expanded her colonial acquisitions, and enjoyed general

[18] Parris, pp. 21–8.
[19] C. R. Middleton, 'The Administration of Newcastle and Pitt: the Departments of State and the Conduct of War, 1754–60, with Particular Reference to the Campaigns in North America' (Ph.D. thesis, University of Exeter, 1969).
[20] Baker, pp. 14–15.
[21] Syrett, pp. 18–24. Cf. R. J. B. Knight, 'Sandwich, Middleton and Dockyard Appointments', *The Mariner's Mirror*, lvii (1971), 175–92.

prosperity, by the standards of pre-industrial society. This was achieved without the assumption of sweeping new powers or the curtailment of the freedoms of Englishmen as conceived by those with any political influence. Government fulfilled much of that which was expected of it, and thus no major impetus was created for a change in attitude towards or within government.

The War of American Independence nevertheless marks a decisive turning-point in both the performance of government and attitudes towards it. The last two decades of the century witnessed many changes in both respects. What provoked them? What forms did they take? What was their influence on future developments?

Many factors contributed to the changes, but the most important was undoubtedly the American war. Britain had lost a war which she clearly should have won.[22] Furthermore, defeat, quite as much as—if not more than—earlier success, had been expensive. In the process of fault-finding, material had been provided for thoroughgoing criticism of most aspects of government administration. Practices and procedures, accepted or tolerated while Britain was successful at war, were thrown into suspicion in the face of failure. In particular, one of the direct products of the costly failure was the creation of the Commissioners for Examining Public Accounts, whose detailed and wide-ranging reports served to open up to parliamentary and public attention, and thus to criticism, many facets of government previously shrouded in mystery, if not secrecy.

Not only had the war increased the burden of taxation, but it was also believed to be responsible for loss of trade and other economic difficulties. Moreover, the harvests of 1780 and 1782 were bad and food prices consequently high. The steep rise in the cost of living, accompanied by a high incidence of bankruptcy, substantial unemployment, and an increasing burden on Poor Relief, which coincided in part with the Gordon Riots, created a sense of governmental failure, extending beyond the misconduct of war to fears for the stability of the economy and even of society itself. As complacency was eroded, a new out-

[22] It is the viewpoint of contemporaries, rather than of historians, which is alluded to here.

look becomes discernible. If it did not set in motion a persistent clamouring for change, it must at least be described as a wider acceptance of the need for it. If Parliamentary Reform stirred only a few adherents, many who were reluctant to tamper with the franchise, or even with the reallocation of parliamentary seats, saw a safer remedy for Britain's malaise in the overhaul of the machinery of government.

The growth of a more critical parliamentary attitude was obviously important, but the initiation of change had almost of necessity to come from within government and at a ministerial level. What evidence is there of a fresh outlook there? The inadequacy of existing practices in conducting the war had been brought home to Lord North himself, well before his fall in 1782, although his response did not take the form of any radical revision. He urged the staff in his own department to be more zealous; from 1780 he permitted an element of competitive bidding for major Treasury contracts;[23] and he instituted, if only in an attempt to forestall an Opposition plan, the Commissioners for Examining Public Accounts. Elsewhere in his administration the drive for more rigorous, more vigorous practice came from men in subordinate places: Robinson, Jenkinson, and Middleton. These were men dealing at first hand with the day-to-day frustration of administering departments. For that very reason, however, while their influence on the details of policy had been growing for some time,[24] their capacity to instigate a major shift in policy was limited. The initiative had to come from above, and for a variety of reasons North did not provide it. In part, this was because of a belief, persisting from 1775, that the war would soon be over and that peace would be the time for change conducted with calm and deliberation. North was in any case preoccupied with the war itself and with other pressing problems, such as Ireland. For sustained periods, his response was to withdraw into irresolution even over these.[25] Furthermore, North held the traditional belief in the importance of patronage and influence to his ministry's Commons majority, the more so as that

---

[23] Baker, pp. 43–56.
[24] F. B. Wickwire, *British Subministers and Colonial America, 1763–1783* (Princeton, N.J., 1966).
[25] I. R. Christie, *The End of North's Ministry, 1780–1782* (1958), pp. 32–5.

majority became less secure, and any substantial measure of administrative reform would have damaged the system on which, rightly or wrongly, he believed his ministry depended. Finally, by the time the conduct of the American war had created an environment of political and administrative crisis, North had been at the head of government for ten years; he was set in his administrative ways, indeed a master of those aspects of government finance with which he was most familiar. In these circumstances, the incentive to embark upon sweeping change was unlikely to be very great.

When the Rockinghams came back into office in 1782, they had behind them a longer period in opposition than any other substantial and organized group had experienced in the century. To a certain extent this had imbued them with the *idées fixes* of Opposition—ideas built upon by Burke's view of a deliberate attempt to reduce Parliament to a submissive dependence upon the Crown. These considerations and the Rockinghams' connection with the Association Movement gave to their reforming efforts, once they were in power, a primarily political focus. Rather than improve the effectiveness of administration, the main intention of this short-lived ministry was to reduce Crown influence in Parliament. Nevertheless, the reforms of the second Rockingham ministry were not without influence upon our subject. First, reform which served to reduce the practice of any kind of influence or patronage in the government service, or to eliminate any source of rewards not open to public scrutiny, contributed to a change in attitude towards government and government employment, from both without and within. In this respect, it was not the actual but the supposed extent of past practice, and of its subsequent reduction, that is significant. Second, any measures which served to reduce the fear (justified or not) of the Crown's influence, and so to increase belief in Parliament's control, would ultimately add to the trust placed in government and indirectly to the sense of public responsibility resting with those in that service itself.[26]

In order to find overt policies directed to more than incidental changes, however, one has to move from Rockingham to Shelburne, for here was the one politician of the time, of prime

---

[26] The choice of the word 'service' is deliberate; it conveys, in contrast to 'place' the essence of the change in attitude beginning to occur.

ministerial status,[27] who was committed, politically and personally, to the direct reform of administration. For all its relative
brevity, Lord Shelburne's ministry marks a clear break with
the administrative style that had prevailed for most of the
century, and it initiated many policies that were further to
change the mode of administration. This is not to claim success
for everything Shelburne did in this field. Not all his innovations
were carried through to completion, nor did he approach every
area of administration where change was desirable. Rather,
Shelburne's significance lies in the fact that he was in office
when the need for change was most apparent, as a result of the
failures in the American war, and that this coincidence resulted
in his initiation of reforms that were to have a major practical
bearing on the future.

Shelburne's view of sinecure offices, unlike that of his
immediate predecessors, was not to see them as confined to
their place in the system of political patronage. To him they
were equally significant, perhaps even more so, because of the
part they played in the working of government and for their
symbolic importance for the general attitude to governmental
employment. Resistance to the attack on such offices was
founded upon their consideration as property and thus on
arguments regarding their sanctity. Since this resistance was
often effective, Shelburne, and more particularly Pitt after him,
had to wait for the death of an incumbent before eliminating
his office. Yet with regard to the reduction of sinecures and
other aspects of reform, Shelburne's ideas were generally in
accord, if they did not always coincide, with those expressed
in the reports of the Commissioners for Examining the Public
Accounts. Both the Commissioners and the minister laid
importance on the replacement of fees by regular salaries.
While his own plans for effecting this change were not well
considered,[28] Shelburne's attempts in this direction were of
great significance, for the fee system alone had a lot to do with
shaping the view of government office as a source of profit,
in the most direct and opportunistic sense. His desire to establish
more rigid principles for assessing the usefulness of government

---

[27] The statement assumes that the younger Pitt could not as yet be included
in this category.

[28] John Norris, *Shelburne and Reform* (1963), pp. 203–4.

offices went beyond fees and the most obvious sinecure positions, moreover. In many ways the counterpart of the abolition of fees was the attempt to establish the fundamentals of a progressive career structure, in which promotion would be a factor of ability and application rather than of seniority or influence. Here again, Shelburne took the first essential step. The celebrated Treasury minute of 1782[29] stressed the punctual performance of official duties and discouraged the employment of deputies. Together with gradual reform of accounting procedures and with the regulations which sought to end the habit of removing government papers upon leaving office, the moves against sinecures and fees and the attempt to institute a new career structure point towards a new conception of service in which responsibility and honesty were given pride of place within a more institutional framework. It would be a gross exaggeration to claim that the foundations of a modern civil service were laid in the aftermath of the American war and under the supervision of Shelburne. Yet the established traditions of government service had been challenged and this was a vital pre-condition for the development of the nineteenth-century civil service.

Of as much significance as these concrete innovations were others of a more subtle kind. One such change was the increasing weight given to professional expertise; and related to this, in many instances, a greater receptivity to new ideas. Both Shelburne and Pitt were clearly more ready to listen to the views of specialists, and indeed theorists, than their predecessors had been. Probably the outstanding single example is the influence of Richard Price on Pitt's Sinking Fund.[30] Although less clearly responsible for any particular enactment, the intellectual 'Bowood Circle' was not without its influence on Shelburne's general policies. The tendency to greater specialization within government itself is borne out at basic level by Shelburne's attempts in 1782 to have each clerk at the Treasury handle a specific type of business. Another example from Shelburne's own Treasury career was his resort in 1782 to the expertise

---

[29] Henry Roseveare, *The Treasury: the Evolution of a British Institution* (New York, 1969), p. 122; cf. Binney, p. 181.

[30] C. B. Cone, 'Richard Price and Pitt's Sinking Fund of 1786', *Econ. H. R.*, 2nd ser. iv (1951), 142–51.

of his friend Francis Baring, whom he not only consulted at length as to the cost-efficiency of previous Treasury provisioning contracts but whom he placed in charge of *all* such supplies for the ensuing year. In the early 1790s when that same department of Treasury business was assigned to the Navy Victualling Board, for military as well as naval supplies, it is legitimate to recognize a further step towards professionalization.[31]

Closely related to this growing specialization was the increasing effort exhibited by government itself to possess more 'expert' information. The substantial increase in the bulk of official records dating from the early 1780s, indeed, reflects this desire to base action on sounder information more than it reflects any real expansion of government activity. Nor was this search for more information simply confined to the accumulation of mere opinions; it was in fact accompanied by a much more pronounced statistical emphasis. The desire to be better informed is apparent from Shelburne's own papers; it is implicit in the work of the Commissioners for Examining Public Accounts, who were but the first in a long line of such bodies. The new statistical emphasis stands out from the records of the Board of Trade and the personal correspondence of its head, Charles Jenkinson.[32] Often in the past erroneous decisions had been decisions based on a paucity of information. Even the most notorious episode of government 'corruption' during the American war, the affair of 'Rum' Atkinson, had to a certain extent arisen out of governmental gullibility, itself the product of the lack of reliable information. Many technical obstacles still stood in the way of government's attainment of adequate information, but from the early 1780s a clear desire is discernible to base decision-making on as much relevant information as was attainable.

In one area, Shelburne found that ideas formulated in opposition could not be sustained in the face of experience in office. Before coming into power he had conceived an ideal situation in which the departments of government would be near-autonomous and central control quite loose. In 1782 he soon reversed that position. He found stronger central control, vested in the Treasury, to be vital for both administrative

[31] Baker, pp. 242–4, 252–3.
[32] Liverpool Papers B.M. Add. MS. 38388.

efficiency and financial accountability.[33] From a different, because more essentially political, standpoint, Burke had come to the same conclusion: he appreciated that only through some central control could a government be held accountable and responsible to Parliament.[34] Here one comes to what, in a generalized and long-term sense, was the deepest significance of the various currents set in motion towards the end of the American war. Without the changes that began to make both government as a whole and individual government officials more accountable, more responsible, honest, and accessible, it is highly unlikely that Parliament would gradually have come to grant more powers to government and accept its expanding role in society. For the conduct of government as a 'tighter ship' had not only administrative but political consequences. Of course, the changes of the early 1780s no more secured honesty or effectiveness in government than Economical Reform or the Reform Act of 1832 eliminated 'influence' in politics. However, just as these measures marked a sharp break with the past and were to exert their increasing influence over a lengthy period, so too did the administrative innovations set a pattern that was to become more and more pervasive.

To attribute so much meaning to the coincidence of Shelburne's tenure of office and the aftermath of defeat in the American war does not do justice to the variety of pressures bearing in the same direction. More striking in its way is the co-operation that Shelburne received from some of his immediate subordinates, themselves eager for change. In revising the establishments of certain departments, he enjoyed the support of their respective heads.[35] Thus the drive towards more regular accountability was carried to America in 1782 by Sir Guy Carleton and his commissary-general, Brooke Watson.[36] The general tone of governmental correspondence from about 1782 reflects a more functional, 'committed' approach towards the service. If earlier in the century attitudes towards and within government mirrored the prevailing manners and morals of society at large, is it unreasonable to expect that changes in that society as a whole should have a bearing upon views of government from the 1780s? No major theorist elaborated a

---

[33] Norris, pp. 100–1, 199–200. [34] Roseveare, pp. 120–1.
[35] Norris, p. 211. [36] Bowler, p. 243.

critique of the old administrative system or offered a model for the future as did Adam Smith for the economy and Jeremy Bentham for the legal system; but the absence of any single major thinker in this field should not lead us to suppose that a parallel revision of ideas was not taking place there too. Since Sir Charles Middleton provides an outstanding illustration of it, one might even suggest that the new morality that was to be the hallmark of the Clapham Sect was itself coming to influence government administration.

At all events, the fresh outlook that begins to emerge under the shock of defeat in the American war was not the possession of any one particular political group or party; nor did it necessarily correspond with the battle-lines of Parliamentary Reform. Some of the forces that helped shape it were traditional, such as an extension of the old style 'country' philosophy. Others were new, as with the tendency for a more rational and at times moralizing view of society as a whole. The name of one politician may most fittingly be identified with the new outlook, William Pitt; and the party of so-called New Toryism which supported him in office was certainly not un-influenced by the new approach to government.

It has not been the intention of this essay to identify yet another 'Revolution in Government'. Its purpose has rather been to suggest that quite substantial transformations occur between such revolutions and, in particular, that the less tangible shifts in public attitudes to government, affecting those in its service or indeed arising from them, are important in preparing the way for the more dramatic changes of practice. The standards by which government was judged for much of the eighteenth century changed after 1782. What had been acceptable earlier was no longer tolerable: and gradually, as expectations rose, practice changed.

XI

Fresh Light on the Character of the Nawab of Arcot

THE revival of interest in the European discovery of Indian culture has enabled historians of the eighteenth-century to piece together portraits of certain individuals and groups, but usually from European sources and in a context relevant to European interests. Only occasionally do we hear Indians speak, know what they think, or even what they look like; of their private lives, their hopes and fears, joys and privations, we are usually ignorant. This is regrettable when we seek the real response of Indians to Europeans, still more so in understanding the relationships of Indians with each other. Some advance in both directions is open to us, however, from the materials available for the middle years of the controversial reign (1749–95) of Muḥammad 'Alī Wālājāh, Nawab of Arcot.

The East India Company archives themselves have not been fully utilized for the years after 1763, although they document in abundant detail the Nawab's changing attitude to his new English protectors, his territorial ambitions, and the growth of his large private debt to Company servants. From 1769, with the dispatch of Sir John Lindsay's plenipotentiary mission to inquire into the compliance of the Madras Council with the eleventh article of the Treaty of Paris, which recognized the Nawab, English contacts with him extend beyond the Company and private correspondence multiplies. There are telling comments about the Nawab in plenty, though few of any scope; in particular, his correspondence with the Madras Council, which was mostly drafted by its members or by European advisers at his court (durbar), cannot be taken at face-value. In all this evidence, much of it contradictory, the Nawab's character remains enigmatic. He is both 'a great character . . . faithful beyond example to the Friends [the Company] his benefactors',[1] and 'a shadow, a dream, an incubus of oppression'.[2]

At first sight, the Persian sources are hardly more rewarding. The stylized histories tell us little about the rulers.[3] One manuscript account, however, is of special interest: Saiyid Muḥammad Ḥusain's *Qaṣr-i Wālājāhī* (n.d.). It is detailed, surprisingly accurate, and was evidently based on a large number of Persian sources contemporary with the events described. These came from the Nawab's own archives, which are now preserved in Madras Record Office and a private library[4] where they have recently been catalogued. Together these two large collections comprise the raw material that complements the Company records, and provide an indispensable basis for the political history of the Carnatic in the late eighteenth century.

Among this varied assortment, most of which yields merely incidental information about the Nawab himself, there are several bundles of the Nawab's own diary (*Rūznāmeh*).[5] In April 1773 Kishan Chand, a *munshī* (writer) in the durbar, was chosen to begin this 'most confidential matter' with these instructions— 'to write down a daily list of the Nawab's special orders, the discussions of every moment, and an inventory of the letters'; when he was not present, an account of discussions was dictated to him by the Nawab or other participants. This continued for a few years, but the entries became briefer in 1777 and 1778 and, as a regular practice, appear to have been discontinued shortly afterwards. During these years, one important feature

---

[1] Laurence Sulivan to Stephen Sulivan, *c.* 6 April 1778, Bodl., Laurence Sulivan MSS., Eng. hist. c. 269, p. 13.

[2] *The Works of Edmund Burke* (Bohn's British Classics, 8 vols., 1854–89), iii. 179.

[3] Besides the printed works, *Tūzak-i Wālājāhī*, ed. Saiyid Muḥammad Ḥusain Nainar (2 vols., Madras, 1934–9), and *Sawānihāt-i Mumtāz*, ed. Saiyid Muḥammad Ḥusain Nainar (2 vols., Madras, 1940–4), there are several manuscript histories and family studies, among which Muḥammad 'Ināyat Ḥusain Khān's *Waqā'i'-yi Amīr al-Umarā'* (1836–7), Ḥaidar Nawāz Khān's *Nishān-i Wālājāhī* (1830–1), and Ghulām Ḥusain Khān's *Tuḥfat al-Akhbār* (1819) are of some use.

[4] Saeedia Library, Dīwān Ṣāḥib Bāgh, Royapettah, Madras. The bundles cited below follow Dr. Muḥammad Ghauś's classification. I am very grateful to him for much help.

[5] Besides the nine volumes of the *Rūznāmeh* in Madras Record Office (Persian bundles 65, 66, 67, 68, 33 D, 33 E, 33 F, 33 F (a), 33 G), there are several loose papers in Saeedia Library: some were evidently drafts for the version in the Madras Record Office or for the few excerpts taken to England, translated, and printed in some of the pamphlet literature, e.g. *Original Papers relative to Tanjore* (1777), pp. 11–14.

of the diary was the record of the Nawab's interviews with Europeans; indeed Kishan Chand was told particularly to note these down. Unlike the other kinds of sources mentioned, therefore, the bald factual reporting of the *munshī* tells us more faithfully, in successive interviews over a limited period, what the Nawab said, how he acted, and what else happened at the durbar in his immediate environment.

The value of these diaries is considerably increased, their accuracy and authenticity vindicated, by a comparison with another personal record covering part of the same years. This was kept by George Paterson, who played a major role in durbar politics between 1770 and 1774. Initially he had come to India as secretary to Sir John Lindsay, the plenipotentiary minister, and he threw himself energetically into the task of collecting information and winning his way into the Nawab's confidence. When Lindsay was recalled after a year, the Nawab was persuaded to take on Paterson as a durbar adviser with a regular salary and allowance. For the next three years he saw the Nawab almost daily and was consulted on every matter of importance; he mediated in the complex financial negotiations with Benfield, and even intervened in the delicate rivalries of the durbar and the Nawab's family.

In addition to his energy, other qualities won Paterson this position of trust. He came to India with an open mind, prepared to judge Indians dispassionately but with sympathy. Although his view of Indian politics soured in time, he was always considerate in his personal relationships.[6] Moreover, he was surprisingly outspoken, even when he realized that his advice was contrary to the Nawab's views. Unlike many Company servants he did not have large sums tied up in the Nawab's debts, and though never forgetting his own financial advantage, was not afraid to say what he honestly felt was in the Nawab's best interests. Uncommon, too, was a real curiosity in his surroundings; nothing seemed too insignificant for his observant eye: the workings of a dolphin's heart, the descent of the Cochin Jews ('in the hope that it might throw some light on the curious enquiry about the distinction of colours in men or whether it be owing to climate or not'), the temples at Elephanta, the types of rice grown in the Carnatic. Yet there were certain

[6] Paterson MS. diary i. 221, 234; ix. 51, 192. This is in private hands.

limitations, both of mind and temperament. Once at Madras, his main preoccupations were necessarily with durbar politics, which he pursued with a rigour that sometimes made him hot-tempered and forced him to ignore many other aspects of Indian society that he would perhaps have explored, given more leisure, as his tour through the Carnatic at the end of his stay suggests.

Throughout these years, whatever engaged his interest he recorded accurately and at length in the small pocket-notebooks that he carried with him, and afterwards copied into the large leather-bound volumes that have survived.[7] Rightly he had no literary pretensions, nor did he consider his work 'in any other light but a private diary of my own and which I never mean should see the publick eye'. He wrote down verbatim accounts of his durbar interviews to provide a useful reference for later discussion and correspondence. Where they coincide with the Nawab's diaries, there is a remarkable consistency. But this awkward, unembellished account reveals a great deal more about other aspects of the durbar, the Indian servants and advisers, and the Nawab himself. That it never was reworked into a polished statement adds to its value. Together with the Nawab's own diary, it may help to explain a little of the personality of the Nawab during these years and the traditional milieu in which he lived, which for the most part escape us from the other sources.

Although Paterson, in common with others who lived for a length of time on the Coromandel Coast, left no good physical description of the Nawab, it is not difficult to imagine the immediate and compelling impression the ruler made. In the portraits that now hang in the Company's garden-house in Madras and the old India Office, one glimpses the mannered ease, the quiet dignity and grace that captivated those who met him briefly.[8] When Paterson was in Madras, the engaging

[7] The third of the nine volumes, which cover the voyages to and from India and his four years there, is called the Admiral's Diary: it was kept for Sir Robert Harland, Lindsay's successor, from material provided by Paterson. His observations formed the basis for much of the official dispatches sent in Lindsay's or Harland's name (I.O.L., Home Misc. Series, 103–14).

[8] Edward Ives, *A Voyage from England to India in the year MDCCLIV* (1773), p. 71; Alexander Dow, *The History of Hindostan* (2nd edn., 1770), ii. 396–8. John Macpherson claimed credit for inserting this into Dow's second edition.

simplicity of the Nawab's earlier years, seen in the travellers' accounts, had given way to a measure of personal and public ostentation. On formal occasions, like the presentation of letters from the King or Company, he dressed magnificently, 'jewels on the head, bound to the turban and from which a fine feather sprung up on one side, jewels on the arms, and several strings of very fine pearls, with diamonds pendant, particularly one large square diamond of immense value'; on visiting the haram, he was 'very richly dressed in a complete sett of exceeding fine emeralds'.[9]

His immediate surroundings had also been dramatically transformed in the years before Paterson's arrival. Arcot, the nominal capital, had little to commend it: 'the buildings are mean, scarce the appearance of a good house being in the whole capital . . . the Nabob's palace is in the city. Nothing can be further from any idea of grandeur or magnificence.' When he moved nearer to his political protectors, a site within a mile of Fort St. George was found, adjoining the Company's garden on one side and facing the Indian Ocean on the other. This 'little spot of sandy ground', as he described it, was called Chepauk, and during these years several palaces were in process of construction. Although incomplete, the main building, an attractive amalgam of colonial and 'Moorish' styles, was already in use. At formal ceremonies, the large durbar hall looked splendid, 'covered all over with rich carpets', 'an immense number of the officers of the durbar arranged in order', and in the centre an ornate throne (*masnad*). Outside, in the gardens, there were large tents, illuminated at night by lanterns hung among the trees, firework displays, feasts for three or four hundred, processions of elephants, camels, the Nawab's cavalry, and dancing-girls with the 'country musick'. With all this went the usual courtesies and conceits, presents of attar, rosewater, and court-dresses to his servants and guests, the reception of foreign envoys (*vakīls*), the display of a sumptuously prepared treasury (certainly mortgaged), and the interchange of gifts with other Muslim rulers—cloth, a candelabra, and an elephant, for example, were sent as far as Persia to Karīm Khān Zand.[10]

[9] Paterson, ii. 25; vii. 113; *Rūznāmeh*, 65, 30 April 1773; 66, 9 Sept. 1773.
[10] Ibid. 33 D, 6 March 1775.

Against this background, the more intimate record of the diaries shows us something of the personal appeal the Nawab held for contemporaries. The strongest impression of most European visitors to the durbar was of his unusual politeness. In this Paterson was no exception; after his first meeting he wrote, 'I could not help being exceedingly well pleased with the polite and affable manners of this Prince', an impression forcibly if uncomfortably confirmed when the Nawab, anxious for the latest European news, called him up into his own palankeen, which caused Paterson to comment on 'the great condescension of the Nabob upon this occasion, especially when I consider the great distance between him and me'.[11] Occasionally, too, we have glimpses of him hovering in the background at a feast given for Lindsay's mission, to see if everything was in order, garlanding his guests, or apologizing for the fireworks.

Much later, when a degree of confidence was established between the Nawab and Paterson, this courteous exterior revealed a warmer personality. In conversation he used to good effect proverbs or poetry, drawing morals from classical literature and folklore with an ingenuity that amused his audience.[12] Often, he would interrupt an argument with a laughing aside, turning thus to Paterson, when bargaining with Benfield over his assignments, with the remark that both were very good merchants or that Benfield's head was like a cannon-ball, or illustrating to Paterson how Benfield's demands always increased, 'taking me by the hand and gradually gripping all the way up the arm, till he took my whole body in his arms, "that", said he, "is Mr. Benfield." '[13] He would mimic, too, 'stroking his beard' to suggest sadness, mischievously feign deafness to avert questions that he did not want to answer. With good humour, he would laugh at some of the stranger presents sent back to him by those whom he had rewarded handsomely— sweets from Lindsay that had gone bad on the voyage, tobacco sent by Eyre Coote, 'a very extraordinary present to him who never smokes'. Sometimes he showed real affection. At the end of a long argument with Paterson, he took his head and rubbed

---

[11] Paterson, ii. 182–3.
[12] *Rūznāmeh*, 33 D, 23 July 1775; *Qaṣr-i Wālājāhī*, ii. n.p.; Paterson, v. 18–19.
[13] Ibid. ix. 84.

it against his own, saying, 'There were several things in my head and his that could not agree; we must therefore mix them together.'[14] He wept when Boswall, his private doctor, said he wanted to return to England; and when Paterson left, 'the Nabob embracing me with great warmth wished me all happiness, put a ring on my finger which he told me had been valued at a thousand pagodas, and immediately he left the durbar'.[15]

As Paterson saw and understood more of the durbar, he began to record some of the Nawab's defects. At first he may have interpreted his spontaneity as polite condescension, but later he saw it more as impulsiveness, 'that natural vivacity of disposition which hurries the Nabob to run rather too precipitately into any scheme which at first strikes him'. Several incidents in the diary confirmed his unpredictable temperament. During the first Mysore war, when a raiding party of Hyder Ali was close to Madras, the Nawab had 'got a horseback himself, and a parcel of sepoys about him to each of which he had ordered a dram to encourage them'.[16] In disappointment or anger, 'he pulled off his turban, put it on his knee and scratched his head'; at a time of bad news, he was found 'on the terrace, walking with his turban in his hand almost in a fit of distraction'; in contrast, on receiving good news, for example a successful cavalry engagement at the second siege of Tanjore, he immediately hurried into his palankeen to tell the Governor, shouted 'Great news, great news' to those he passed on the way, met the Governor coming from the fort, left his palankeen and 'pushed himself into the Governor's chariot'.[17]

More serious was the Nawab's 'finesse and dissimulation'. In some interviews, the watery eye and subdued voice, 'in such words and in so humble a manner', could be interpreted as another example of the Nawab's mercurial nature; but there was often an element of stage-management in these scenes. Sometimes a little clumsily, he tried to deceive Paterson over trifles, over letters, the presentation of *nazr* (an offering to someone of higher status), the significance of his titles from the Mughal Emperor; but sometimes also over major issues the Mahratta alliance, Macleane's visit, and Paterson's own role as

---

[14] Paterson, v. 146.   [15] Ibid. ix. 190.
[16] Ibid. ii. 124.   [17] Ibid. vi. 96.

his confidential adviser. What the Nawab did to Paterson, he did to everybody else, as his public actions towards the Madras Council amply demonstrate. He was, it seemed, in his personal and public lives, compulsively fickle, exchanging one policy for the next, one adviser for another in the hope of any immediate, short-term gain. Boswall, the European who probably knew him best, summed it up in this way:

> The Nabob never times things well; but runs at anything, and pursues it with obstinacy for some time 'till he can no more; then he falls off as suddenly again without any reason . . . [he] wants steadiness . . . No, says he, I never will; I'll sooner give the flesh off my bones, yet he agreed to it. The people here come to him and talk him over, and ask it as a favour, then he gives it.[18]

There Boswall touches another basic flaw, the Nawab's susceptibility to flattery. It needed only a few well-timed compliments for Europeans to be rewarded generously, at least in promises which were less frequently fulfilled. This kind of praise could also lead him to make exaggerated claims, as that only he had the ability to organize the Northern Circars, or that he could settle the revenue problems of Bengal in an hour whilst others would take a hundred years.[19] 'Vanity', confided Paterson in exasperation to his diary, 'seems to be one of the Nabob's ruling passions, please him in this, give him titles, tell him he is the greatest and wisest of men and he will do anything to serve the man who studies to please him in that manner.'[20] Yet, occasionally alone with Paterson, he would reveal an attractive modesty which suggests that beneath this view of a courteous, affectionate, amusing man, at once deceptive, capricious, and vain, there were contradictions and complexities that ought to be seen against some of the circumstances of his life.

The Nawab's connection with the English had several effects. One curious characteristic of his was an attempt to adopt some English customs and manners. In most Indian courts, 'hydraulic machines' and 'curious mathematical instruments' were popular exhibits and Chepauk was no exception. He asked Company servants to send back fashionable presents from England.[21] The

---

[18] Ibid. v. 58, 60.   [19] *Rūznāmeh*, 65, 14 June 1773.
[20] Paterson, vi. 65.
[21] R. Palk to L. Sulivan, 5 Nov. 1762, Laurence Sulivan MSS., Eng. hist. b. 191, fo. 113ᵛ.

décor of Chepauk was entrusted to Nicholas Morse, a bankrupt ex-Governor, who ordered settees, chairs, lamps, and mahogany card-tables from England. European painters were also patronized, and among the usual commissions of family portraits there were others of European scenes and faces.[22] But this went beyond the usual interest in the latest inventions and fashions. Not unreasonably, he tried to follow the exact pattern of the English receptions he attended when he gave his own to the settlement, but he also was eager to use them as models for private ceremonies, like the marriage of his sons. He began to copy English eating habits, taking tea in the afternoon according to the brief entries of his own diary for August 1773; coming one morning to the gardens at Chepauk, Paterson was surprised to find the Nawab 'in the chateau at the corner of his gardens at breakfast with his family quite in the English manner. Tea, cakes and several sorts of salading on [the] table, a cloth laid and all on chairs.'[23] He allowed his second son, Amīr al-Umarā', to be a Mason and appear publicly dressed as one (at a time when Paul Benfield was Master of the Lodge).

Much of this was light-hearted and followed inevitably from his nearness to Fort St. George, but there are indications of a more serious bewilderment. From an early point, he had realized the necessity for English advisers, to help in interpreting and translating letters, and especially in negotiating with the Company once the period of co-operation against the French had ended. At first he found them from among his European doctors and incorporated them, in what might have seemed a bizarre fashion, into his durbar; the two or three Europeans watched stiffly on chairs while the Nawab, 'upon his little carpet', pressed petitioners or *vakīls* to sit closer to him. Communication was always a problem; he kept his own Indian translators, even learning a smattering of English himself,[24] but it was still important at this stage for his closest advisers to know Persian or Urdu. Of this group, Alexander Boswall had the highest position of trust; he alone could give medicines to the Nawab, and speak to him in a way no one else did, sometimes

---

[22] Saeedia, bundle 27. With six family portraits, George Willison, in May 1775, included a 'sleeping woman—Venus'.   [23] Paterson, vi. 57.

[24] Ibid. i. 293. Paterson said he seemed to 'have a pretty good notion of English and spoke several words in that language very distinctly'.

'storming at him like an emperor' or pursuing him to the haram quarters in anger.[25] Yet this strange, taciturn man was genuinely devoted to the Nawab, defended him spiritedly against others, and advised him honestly according to his lights.

Although Boswall continued to hold this position for many years, it was plain that as the Nawab's affairs became more complicated he needed more sophisticated and experienced advice. The first sign of this was the appointment of James Johnson, a bankrupt merchant, in what was grandiloquently called the 'English office'; his main task was to act as accountant for the Nawab's debts, but his own financial mismanagement, 'indolence and inattention' only added to the Nawab's problems.[26]

The significant change came with the arrival of Lindsay's mission, which encouraged the Nawab to take a more independent attitude towards the Company. But when he did this, it was plain that he was only escaping from one set of masters to submit to the influence of another. Paterson, moreover, was not content simply to draft his letters and plan his strategy with the Council; he tried to impress upon him his own views of how a ruler ought to behave. After seeing the Nawab's impulsive reaction to good news from Tanjore, he primly noted in his diary, and said openly, that 'it is not proper in a prince to behave so';[27] upset at the Nawab's reward for the bringer of the news of the Tanjore victory, he remarked, 'the prince should always be the prince and never descend to meanness'; he even interfered in the conduct of the durbar, advising that the Nawab 'never should make a practice of writing an answer to every chitt himself'. The Nawab, for his part, often seemed to want and expect this kind of advice, particularly if the problem impinged at all on English interests. With disarming candour, when discussing military arrangements with four of his close advisers, he said, 'Come my four friends . . . sit down and settle this business for me.'[28]

As long as he relied on relatively scrupulous men, like Boswall or Paterson, to help him with the complexities of his

[25] *Rūznāmeh*, 33 D, 11 Aug. 1775; Paterson, vii. 104–5; viii. 26.
[26] *Rūznāmeh*, 66, 2 Oct. 1773; Paterson, iv. 49; viii. 46.
[27] Ibid. vi. 96–7, 187.
[28] Ibid. ii. 190.

relations with the English, no great harm could be done to his permanent interest, which lay in co-operation with the Company. But by the mid-1770s he had thrown himself whole-heartedly into the schemes of a new group of more daring, less reputable adventurers—John Macpherson, Lauchlin Macleane, and John Stewart. Of these, only the first remained for any length of time in Madras; but contact was maintained with the durbar through James Johnson, a *munshī* Bogue Chand, and the Nawab's second son, Amīr al-Umarā'.[29] Under their influence the Nawab seized on ideas that had lain dormant a number of years: to send one of his sons to rule in Bengal, to buy East India Company stock to establish an interest in the Company's direction, to have an agent in England, or to wrest the lands bordering on the Ghats from Hyder Ali.[30] Other ideas were more chimerical, like a vast increase in the size of his army which his finances could never support, or a conquest of Ceylon from the Dutch; but some had enough plausibility, like the future succession of the Carnatic, embodied in his will,[31] to enthral him for several years.

The ease with which he could be manipulated by these men illustrates his ignorance of the realities of English and Company politics and the absurdity of many of his dreams. Yet he was by no means unaware of the precariousness of his position in the Carnatic. A note of desperation frequently breaks through in the record of both the diaries, and with a force and directness far more striking than in the formal letters to the Company, the ministry, or his friends in England. Sometimes he expressed his fears in the form of a fable, that of the cat helping the bird on to the tree and finally eating it, or of the tiger and the sheep, at the end of which he explained, 'these people are the tyger and I am apprehensive that sooner or later they will eat me up';[32] or he used vivid similes, a stone hanging above his head by a thread, or a mother killed for not giving enough milk to

---

[29] Paterson, viii. 44–5.

[30] Nawab to his Bengal *vakīls*, 9 June and 3 July 1765, Saeedia, bundle 4; Nawab to Call, 1 Sept. 1766, *Vikālat-nāmeh* (power of attorney), ibid. and Paterson, iv. 210; Memorandum of requests, c. Feb. 1777 (sent through Macpherson to Macleane), Saeedia MS., Register of European letters, p. 47.

[31] Saeedia MS., the Nawab's will, 7 Feb. 1777; another copy is in I.O.L., Persian MS., 4364.

[32] Paterson, viii. 26; *Qaṣr-i Wālājāhī*, ii. n.p.; *Rūznāmeh*, 33 E, 25 March 1776.

her child.[33] He constantly looked at the fate of other Indian rulers, Shāh 'Ālam and Shujā' al-Douleh,[34] and feared his would be the same.

These fears crystallized around the threat that the Company would seize the *dīwānī*, and that his descendants would be reduced to pensioners, ideas that had been in the minds of several Company servants since the 1750s.[35] Whenever he suspected this, his reactions were bitter. In one especially heated discussion with Francis Jourdan in April 1775, he cried out, 'You want to blame a little on both father and son, say we are not fit to rule, and then take the country. Why prolong it? Take it now.'[36] In these moods, Paterson accused him of 'an unconquerable jealousy', 'so ready to believe everything against Europeans, altho' perhaps from disposition, or perhaps from necessity he puts a favourable face upon these matters'.[37] This resentment was never expressed in any positive action, beyond an angry outburst, quickly followed by contrite abjectness. He might tremble, which according to Paterson he always did when 'exceedingly anxious', threaten to return to Arcot or, more exceptionally, after abusing everyone, exclaim, 'I am no longer fit to govern this country—get the Governor and [the] Admiral and Mr. Paterson and Mr. Benfield and all together make a new Subahdahr, for I must give it up.'[38] But such scenes were usually excused by his plea that 'he would do anything thro' friendship; but he would not be forced', or by a characteristic aphorism, '. . . it is hard to pull a sugar cane from the mouth of an elephant, meaning the sweets of independency and free will were not easy to give up.'[39]

The anger and frustration that underlay his contact with Europeans can, to some extent, be explained by the insecurity of the political tradition from which he had come. To those who knew the Nawab in his youth, the claims he pretended to

---

[33] Ibid. 33 D, 5 April, 4 May, 16 June 1775.
[34] Paterson, vii. 178, 181; *Rūznāmeh*, 67, 15 July 1774.
[35] Morse to Benyon, 20 Oct. 1755, Berkshire Record Office, Richard Benyon MSS., D/EBy bundle 5; Hastings to L. Sulivan, 1 Feb. 1770, B.M., Add. MS. 29126, fos. 10ᵛ–11; Paterson, iii. 164. The *dīwān* was the head financial minister, with civil and judicial powers, and his office was called the *dīwānī*.
[36] *Rūznāmeh*, 33 D, 9 April 1775.
[37] Paterson, vi. 100, 186; vii. 16.
[38] Ibid. viii. 95–6; *Rūznāmeh*, 66, 20 Aug. 1773; 33 E, 11 May 1776.
[39] Paterson, v. 190.

with the encouragement of his later English advisers must have seemed preposterous. He belonged to a dynasty of very recent and unpretentious origins. His grandfather was the first to hold any office of importance, a *qāḍī* at Aurangzeb's court; his father, Anwār al-Dīn, held a variety of posts: the last of several provincial governments was that of the Carnatic, conferred on him by Āṣaf Jāh, the *ṣūbahdār* of the Deccan. When the Nawab, his third son, with English support inherited this enormous tract of land stretching from the river Kistna to Cape Comorin, he found himself in a bitterly divisive feud with the previous Muslim rulers (the Navāits) whom his father had replaced, with very few supporters of his own, in a milieu totally different from North India where he was born and brought up, and only very recently and imperfectly brought under Muslim administration. Robert Orme, who lived through these early years on the Coast, was not exaggerating when he said, 'in my private character I pity no man on earth so sincerely as I do this Nabob.'[40]

When his position as ruler of the Carnatic was assured, he tried to extract some political significance out of a nominal attachment to the Mughal Empire as a counterweight to his dependence on the English. *Sanads* (grants) were obtained for the Carnatic for himself and his eldest son;[41] Aurangzeb's letters were consulted for legal judgements; and not infrequently all the Emperor's correspondence with the Nawab was displayed at the durbar and read out with great pomp.[42] But these gestures could not disguise the rudimentary nature of the durbar and administrative structure. Sometimes he tried to introduce order in durbar proceedings by preventing Europeans wandering in whenever they wanted, or laying down as a principle that the treasury (*khazāneh*) and the *dīwānī* must be held in different hands,[43] but these efforts soon failed. The general impression of the provincial, military, and financial organization is that there was no established pattern and few experienced administrators on whom he could rely.

The personal implications for him of this can be seen in his attitude towards the three main Indian advisers at the durbar.

[40] Orme to J. Payne, 17 Nov. 1757, I.O.L., Orme MS. O.V. 28, p. 218.
[41] Memo. given by the Nawab to Clive, 18 April 1765, Saeedia, bundle 27.
[42] *Rūznāmeh*, 66, 6 Dec. 1773; Paterson, iv. 60.
[43] *Rūznāmeh*, 66, 16 Aug. 1773.

In the Nawab's own diaries they are little more than names; their own contributions to the discussions are recorded, but with little information about personalities. Paterson gives a much more detailed account of them and their relations with the Nawab. 'Abdul Rashīd Khān, the *dīwān* for several years, came from the only family associated with the Wālājāhī dynasty for any length of time—his father-in-law had come to the Deccan with Anwār al-Dīn; his brother-in-law, Muḥammad Najīb, and other relations held important offices too.[44] Paterson usually described him as 'artful' or 'cautious', and never really established any rapport with him, but he remained the most trusted and respected of the Nawab's advisers until his death in 1777. In contrast, Saiyid 'Āṣim Khān, the other important *dīwān* during these middle years of the Nawab's reign, was less aloof to Europeans involved in durbar affairs;[45] he had a reputation for cunning and considerable ability, especially in diplomacy. He was not brought up in the Nawab's service, had none of the family connections of his great rival, 'Abdul Rashīd Khān, but skilfully relied on the Nawab's favour by flattery for many years until his dramatic fall in 1788.[46]

The last of this trio was Avanighadali Venkatachellum, a Brahmin who had been *dūbāsh* (interpreter) to several Europeans, including Eyre Coote and Monson, before he entered the Nawab's service in the 1760s. Although he held no formal position beyond that of interpreter at the durbar, his real influence was probably as great as that of the others, for he had more contact with Europeans in Madras. Paterson relied on him more than anyone else to pass on advice to the Nawab, and for a time a genuine friendship developed between them. The 'little Braminey', as Paterson affectionately called him (to distinguish him from 'fat' Venkatachellum, another durbar interpreter), did 'a great deal for very little', and emerges from the two diaries as a sensible, practical, and usually loyal servant of the Nawab.[47]

Yet there was never any genuine co-operation between the

---

[44] Saiyid Shāh 'Abdul Laṭīf Ẓauqī, *Najīb-nāmeh* (1771–2), *passim*; Ḥaidar Nawāz Khān, *Nishān-i Wālājāhī* (1830–1), *passim*. Both these manuscripts are in Saeedia Library.

[45] R. Sulivan to Hastings, 6 March 1783, Add. MS. 29158, f. 360.

[46] *Ḥaqīqat-i 'Āṣim Khān* (2 Feb. 1789), Saeedia MS., n.p.

[47] Paterson, v. 237; *Rūznāmeh*, 65, 27 June 1773.

three advisers, and they were unable to provide the Nawab with the administrative competence he needed. No less than he, they were often lost in the complex negotiations with Europeans, especially in Benfield's financial affairs; they relied on Paterson's advice, for (as 'Abdul Rashīd Khān admitted) 'we are unacquainted with European manners, and we must trust to you for information'. They could always be bribed; Benfield, for example, as Paterson only gradually discovered, had them in his pay or bribed them over important issues.[48] This added to their rivalries; temporary conspiracies were formed and as quickly broken up. Paterson urged unity on them but it was never possible.

Moreover, even if it had been, nothing could have been achieved without the Nawab's wholehearted support. They felt themselves unable to speak openly to him. 'Abdul Rashīd Khān lamented to Paterson, 'You may say anything . . . because you are not dependent upon the Nabob, and will soon leave this country; but our mouths are shut, for we must remain here our whole lifetime.'[49] Occasionally the Nawab pretended to encourage more candour in discussion, but he never really treated them seriously; councils were suddenly convened and broken off unpredictably, the Nawab bursting into the room with a set of entirely different questions, or expecting agreement with whatever he suggested. At most they gave him a kind of moral support, because, as he said, 'If I do wrong the world shall not only laugh at me, but at all these people also.'[50]

Everything, in effect, depended on him. He intervened in all departments; he tried to conduct the Tanjore sieges from Chepauk; nothing could be done without his authority. He could never trust any of his advisers sufficiently, nor was he himself able to oversee and reorganize the administration of the Carnatic. He had, in many ways, developed since Orme's damning description of the early 1750s: 'a man of very moderate talents, of less resolution and of no application.'[51] During the years that Paterson knew him, he did in fact work tirelessly; the amount of business he did each day is clearly seen from his

[48] Paterson, v. 67–8, 224; vi. 9–10; viii. 169–70, 179. Venkatachellum contrived to take from both Benfield and Comaroo, his *dūbāsh*, without either knowing of the other's bribe.   [49] Paterson, ix. 91.   [50] Ibid. vi. 197.
[51] *Reflections on the disputes subsisting between the Companies of France and England trading to the East Indies*, 24 Nov. 1753, Orme MS. O.V. 17, p. 99.

diary entries.[52] Paterson, who worked with him almost daily for four years, was genuinely impressed with 'the multiplicity of his attentions', and told him an 'undoubted truth, that very few heads would be equal to the business he was constantly engaged in'.[53] But his quick observation and alacrity in discussion were scarcely sufficient against the problems that faced him. As Orme remarked, 'he has cunning, but no sense. Cunning to make shifts, not sense or courage to form a plan.'[54]

The jealousy that marked all his relationships within the durbar was particularly extreme towards his brothers and sons. In the case of one of his elder brothers, Maḥfūẓ Khān, this was fully justified. Eccentric to the point of madness, rebellious, even in old age he was regarded by the Nawab as a political threat. 'Abdul Wahāb, a younger brother, was also held in suspicion: a kind word to him from the Governor was enough to throw the Nawab into the greatest anguish.[55] Any European contact with his close relatives made him intensely nervous, as when, at the height of the Pigot crisis, Khair al-Dīn Khān, a son-in-law, slipped over the wall one night from confinement in one of the Nawab's palaces to seek asylum from the Governor.[56] This was less the fear of rebellion, or replacement, than of European attempts at interference in the succession.

Although 'Umdat al-Umarā', the eldest son, had been formally recognized in the Mughal *sanads* as the heir apparent, the Nawab deliberately kept the issue open. He would not admit that it was an immediate problem, saying, 'I am by no means pleased with the conduct of any of my three eldest sons. And it is not my intention that either of them should succeed me. But I am not old as yet, I may live 20 or 30 years please God and I may have more children.'[57] By stressing that in Islamic law

[52] *Rūznāmeh*, 67, 16 March, 13 July 1774; Nawab to Macleane, 24 June 1775, Saeedia MS., Register of European letters, p. 187; Burhān ibn Ḥasan, *Tūzak-i Wālājāhī*, ed. Saiyid Muḥammad Ḥusain Nainar (Madras, 1939), ii. 11.

[53] Paterson, v. 164.

[54] To J. Payne, 17 Nov. 1757, Orme MS. O.V. 28, p. 218. Paterson's view was rather more favourable: 'Truth however told makes an impression on the Nabob and altho' he may not be pleased at the time, yet it often makes him think and may prevent him from doing a foolish thing, if it should not be able to lead him to what is best; but if smoothly told and suited to his genius and circumstances, it may have the best effects: for the Nabob has good sense and would do much better if left to act by himself' (Paterson, ix. 184).

[55] *Rūznāmeh*, 33 D, 28 March 1775.

[56] *Qaṣr-i Wālājāhī*, ii. n.p.   [57] Paterson, vi. 55.

everything depended on his choice, he tried to keep them dependent on him, upbraiding them for what he regarded as their unfilial acts, publicly reading out letters that exemplified the proper behaviour of a son, or contrasting them with his own actions when young. The effect was the reverse of his intentions; the uncertainty led to greater European interference in the succession, and to the creation of two factions around the rivalry of his two eldest sons.

Paterson was in a privileged position to watch the development of hostility between the two sons and the effect it had on the father. He tells us much more than do the bleak entries of the Nawab's own diary on this subject.[58] He had learnt how to extract delicate information from his durbar sources, and conveys unconsciously the atmosphere of suspicion at the durbar that enveloped this theme. Talking furtively once to 'Umdat al-Umarā', he noted: 'altho' this was a stolen conversation, yet I could observe several at the durbar taking notice of us . . . everyone here has spies placed to observe the motions of every person of the least consequence about the durbar.'[59] He recognized the difficulty of separating truth from gossip, but tried to check what he heard. His revelations, sensational in some respects as they are, allow us to see an aspect of the durbar usually shuttered, and another facet of the Nawab himself.

To most Europeans, the characters of the two sons were quite unambiguous. 'Umdat al-Umarā', the elder, was praised for his good sense, frankness, 'his mildness and sweetness' of disposition.[60] The English doctors, who had known him well for several years, attributed to him more sterling qualities, never vindicated by his subsequent career.[61] In one long durbar interview with Pigot, he makes a favourable impression with modest, sensible remarks and pertinent questions.[62] The second son, Amīr al-Umarā', on the other hand, had never been trusted. It was admitted that he had abilities, had been a competent administrator of Trichinopoly, and had (like his father) 'the capacity of mixing allegorical stories with business in such a way

[58] The durbar knew that Paterson wrote what he heard in his notebooks, and perhaps at the Nawab's request he tore two pages out (*Rūznāmeh*, 66, 10 Oct. 1773).
[59] Paterson, viii. 64.
[60] Hastings to L. Sulivan, 1 Feb. 1770, Add. MS. 29126, fo. 13; Paterson, vi. 84.
[61] Ibid. iv. 73; viii. 110–12.
[62] Saeedia, *Rūznāmeh*, 12 Jan. 1776.

as to please'; but he was not liked in the durbar or by Europeans, except by those who saw their self-interest in his succession. He was usually described as 'cunning, active, vain and industrious', arrogant and overbearing,[63] and in the Persian sources there are indications of a cruel, vicious trait.[64]

After the death of their mother, Khadīja Begum (who favoured the elder son), and the unsuccessful first siege of Tanjore in 1771, the first durbar stories began to circulate openly against 'Umdat al-Umarā'. The charge and counter-charge continued intermittently for the next five or six years, until the Nawab's will sealed 'Umdat al-Umarā''s hopes. What Paterson heard of these events usually came from the Nawab, and is therefore some guide to what his reactions were. In the course of this long campaign, there were the usual allegations of disrespectful behaviour, listening silently while Europeans mimicked the Nawab, taking bribes, and passing on durbar secrets.[65] But three accusations levied against 'Umdat al-Umarā' were new. The first was improbable—that he had tried to persuade his brother to join in a plot to imprison the Nawab and divide the Carnatic between them;[66] the second, more astonishing, was that he had even tried to murder his father. The Nawab described, more than once 'without one single circumstance of variation', how his son had instigated 'a black doctor' to kill him, or a private tutor who always 'slept at the bottom of a small private staircase which came up by the side of the Nabob's cott at Chepauk', or a woman servant who mixed the blood of the 'cockee' bird into his drinking-vessel to make him die or go mad.[67] The third accusation was an even more extraordinary attempt to undermine 'Umdat al-Umarā''s reputation. He was accused of murder, cutting off a wounded man's head 'out of sport and wantonness', and of beating his servants. Through many of these charges there ran a recurrent sexual theme, that he sadistically mistreated his favourite dancing-girl, or that he

---

[63] Paterson, iv. 36.

[64] Muḥammad 'Ināyat Ḥusain Khān, *Waqā'i'-yi Amīr-al-Umarā'* (1836–7), Saeedia MS., n.p.

[65] *Rūznāmeh*, 66, 30 Aug. 1773.

[66] Ibid. 10 Aug. 1773; Paterson, v. 64–5.

[67] Ibid. 65–6; vi. 60–1. The Nawab admitted that 'he had always been accustomed to drink his water out of a guglet without looking at it; but since, he always poured it into a basin first'.

had slept with a woman of the Nawab's haram and claimed that, should anything happen to the Nawab, he would take all the Nawab's women for his own use; he even accused his father of keeping strange women and 'that it was not proper'.[68]

From all these stories that the Nawab told Paterson, one stands out, as it is verified by 'Umdat al-Umarā''s own supporters and is said to have prejudiced the Nawab against his eldest son for ever. This is how the Nawab himself told the story:

> Omdat al Omrah had fallen in love with a dancing girl in the year 1768 while the Nabob was at Colar, which gave the Nabob great uneasiness. That after he had solemnly promised by letter never to see her more and sworn to it, he had brought her to his house in St. Thome and kept her there, where she lived with him amongst the women; and nobody durst give information against her. That the Nabob had at last found it out, and had threatened her with death. That he ordered everything to be prepared for her execution; and as the manner was to be to enclose her in a wall and build her up with bricks, he ordered everything to be got ready; and went there himself to see it done. The whole family were collected, and when she was brought out for execution, the Nabob said, there was but one condition on which he would forgive her: that she should swear never to come near his son any more, and that he Omdat al Omrah would promise never to see her again; both solemnly promised and swore to whatever the Nabob desired. His Highness then sent some of his people to conduct the woman out of the country, who saw her across the Chrystna [Kistna]. However on his setting out on the expedition to Tanjore he sent for her again, and she has lived with him ever since. She had been very ill of a consumption for a long while past, and was attended by Dr. Gordon, but she is now dead, and Omdat al Omrah has expressed great sorrow for her, and had her buried in a very honourable manner.[69]

What really angered the Nawab was less the sexual licence of his eldest son than the careless disregard for his father's wishes. The friends of 'Umdat al-Umarā' believed that the first was not serious, or if it was, was grossly unfair, 'as the whole Carnatick can give living proofs of the Nabob's gallanteries in his youth'. Though the Nawab more than once stressed the difference between the two sons in these terms, 'the one is

---

[68] Paterson, vi. 53–4, 73–4, 117; *Rūznāmeh*, 66, 29 Aug. 1773.
[69] Paterson, iv. 72–3.

constantly in pursuit of other women, while the other is attached to his wife only',[70] it is difficult to believe this weighed as heavily with him as 'Umdat al-Umarā''s disobedience. Sometimes even this seemed over-played, and once or twice he confided to Paterson that it was much less the fault of 'Umdat al-Umarā' than of those who had interfered in his family affairs. He genuinely wanted a reconciliation, and when his son wrote penitent, submissive letters, the Nawab turned to Paterson with a gesture and phrase that showed his irresolution: 'What to do said his Highness, must say sweet words.' When the crisis in their relationship was past its worst, the Nawab admitted 'that he only meant to bring his sons to themselves, that is, to make them sensible of their dependence on him'.[71]

Nor did Amīr al-Umarā' find it always easy to retain his father's favour. Although he had written a fulsome account of the Nawab's virtues,[72] and appeared to be his father's favourite, the Nawab was deeply suspicious. If he spoke to the Governor alone, he was publicly reproved at the durbar; on one occasion he was banished, shut himself up in his house, and swore he would leave the Carnatic. A dramatic reunion followed this disgrace.[73] Even after the intervention of Macleane had strengthened Amīr al-Umarā''s hand, the Nawab still was watchful and resentful, ready to interpret every 'stolen conversation' as a plot against himself.

These fragmentary insights touch the raw nerve of a problem that racked his peace of mind over several years; but, in these diaries, there is unfortunately little else of his inner life we can hope to reach. At one level, he drew his inspiration, such as it was, from traditional Islamic values and patterns of rule. Paterson, among others, was slow to recognize this, reproving the Nawab for actions wholly within his own tradition; only later did he realize that 'he is much less acquainted with European manners than what is commonly believed and which might have been imagined'.[74] When, for example, he had in 1772, for the first time, a real opportunity of reorganizing his finances, he

[70] Ibid. v. 64; vi. 55.
[71] Ibid. 78–9, 139; viii. 32.
[72] *Taḥrīk al-Shifā' bi Auṣāf-i Wālājāhī*, written between 11 Dec. 1772 and 25 March 1773, Saeedia MS.
[73] *Rūznāmeh*, 65, 14 June 1773; Paterson, v. 129, 162, 196–7.
[74] Ibid. vi. 90.

made a traditional gesture of sending out orders for the care of the sick and the poor.[75] Throughout the *Taḥrīk al-Shifā'*, a mirror of how he wanted to be seen, and in many of his letters to his revenue officials in these years, the same image of the merciful, munificent ruler is upheld. Similarly he acted the part of a great patron, to Indian painters, scholars, dervishes, and poets. With the founding of a famous *madraseh* at Vellore and encouragement to scholars and *ṣūfīs* to come from North India, the Carnatic under his patronage became for the first time a distinguished centre for Muslim culture.

At a deeper level, it would seem that this tradition still held real meaning for him. At critical moments like the siege of Tanjore, and even at more ordinary times, astrologers crowded into the durbar and 'were received with respect by his Highness, seated on the same carpet with himself, their idle dreams heard and listened to with attention and money given them in abundance'.[76] He might laugh with Paterson about them, or excuse himself by saying that they were good people and must be given charity, but he consulted them before any important decision.[77] He had a strong belief too in the power of dreams and in his own *karāmat* (spiritual grace), which was demonstrated, at least to his own satisfaction, on several occasions.[78] Not only was he a patron of *ṣūfīs* but he appears to have taken a serious interest in the Qādirī order,[79] as his grandfather had done. One element in his preference for the second son may have been Amīr al-Umarā''s attachment to the same religious order, while 'Umdat al-Umarā' was, like his mother, probably *shī'ī*. The second son characteristically lost no chance of impressing his piety on the Nawab, writing to him after the capture of Nagore that his first act was to 'prostrate himself at the tomb of

---

[75] *Taḥrīk al-Shifā' bi Auṣāf-i Wālājāhī*, n.p.; Paterson, iv. 56.

[76] Ibid. vi. 28.

[77] *Rūznāmeh*, 65, 8 and 17 July 1773; 67, 5 March 1774. Paterson, vi. 124, 269; vii. 231.

[78] *Rūznāmeh*, 66, 17 Aug. 1773; Paterson, vi. 65–6, 219–20. Paterson wrote, 'This appears to me a very curious circumstance, and in explaining it, I read to them Dr. Johnson's definition of the second sight, which they said answered exactly their idea of Carōmet.' James Johnson, who knew how to play on the Nawab's susceptibilities, rushed into the durbar one morning and proclaimed that he had dreamt of the fall of Tanjore (*Rūznāmeh*, 66, 27 Aug. 1772).

[79] *Taḥrīk al-Shifā' bi Auṣāf-i Wālājāhī*, n.p. This *ṣūfī* order was called after Abdul Qādir Jīlānī (d. 1166).

a famous dervish who lies buried there to thank God and pray for long life to his father'.[80]

However, without the Nawab's own writings on these themes, or an account more particular in this respect than Paterson's, it is impossible to enter these recesses of his mind. There are occasional suggestions of a genuine goodness—a debt repaid to the *ra'iyats* of Trichinopoly for money contracted many years earlier,[81] the care he took in dispatching at considerable annual expense a ship for the *ḥajj* pilgrimage. Paterson described the scene on the beach on one of these occasions:

> There we saw about 300 of these fellows, all ready to go on board. In a small choultry [resting-place for travellers], there were about twenty or thirty Arabs, who had come from Mecca last year, and were to return; all these came up to the Nabob, kissed his hands and put them at the same time to their eyes. His Highness then sat down upon a step at the edge of the choultry, and with great patience received the rupees by the handful (about 20 or 30 at a time) from his mootasadies [accountants], and gave to each of the faquiers who were going, some more, some less, according to their rank and station. It was now about 11 a.m., and he said it would last perhaps to 4 o'clock in the afternoon.[82]

In these instances, we glimpse a conviction and steadiness of purpose that few Europeans on the Coast, who saw this enigmatic, perplexed man only in his relations with the Company or in the durbar, could have appreciated.

[80] Paterson, vi. 296.
[81] *Rūznāmeh*, 33 D, 15 June 1775.
[82] Paterson, vii. 118.

XII

Warren Hastings as Scholar and Patron

THE growth of British awareness of the civilization of their conquered provinces in India in the late eighteenth and early nineteenth centuries has attracted considerable attention in recent years.[1] Apart from the intrinsic interest of any study of one society's efforts to come to terms with what it regards as an alien culture, there are good reasons for this attention. It was largely through British scholarship that European intellectuals and artists in the nineteenth century acquired knowledge of India, especially of Hindu India. It was also largely from the same source that the new Indian intellectuals were to become aware of the full extent of what their past had to offer them. Finally, the history of oriental scholarship and that of British administrative policy are not unconnected; the assumptions with which administrators approached contemporary Indian society were to some extent influenced by their assumptions as to what it had been like in the past.

The rise of modern Indology has generally been dated to the last two decades of the eighteenth century: the period of Sir William Jones's arrival in India in 1783, of the founding of the Bengal Asiatic Society in 1784, of the publication of Charles Wilkins's translation of the *Gītā* in 1785, and of the beginning of Henry Thomas Colebrooke's studies. But the new Asiatic Society had roots in the past. Jones was able to add his talents to those of a group of men already engaged in oriental scholarship in India for some years, some of whom had considerable achievements to their credit. This was a situation which had not existed at any previous period in the East India Company's history. Even fifteen years before the founding of the Asiatic

---

[1] e.g. R. Schwab, *La Renaissance orientale* (Paris, 1950); S. N. Mukherjee, *Sir William Jones* (Cambridge, 1968); R. Rocher, *Alexander Hamilton* (New Haven, Conn., 1968); D. Kopf, *British Orientalism and the Bengal Renaissance* (Berkeley, Calif., 1969); J. S. Grewal, *Muslim Rule in India: the Assessments of British Historians* (Calcutta, 1970).

Society, it would not have been possible to find a group of Englishmen in India with any serious interest in their surroundings or, by strict standards, to name any single individual who had made a significant contribution to European knowledge. That there was a coterie of potential scholars and a foundation of knowledge, which made the feats of the 1780s and 1790s possible, was largely the achievement of Warren Hastings, Governor or Governor-General of Bengal from 1772 to 1785.

This essay will try first of all to describe what Hastings did to promote oriental learning, and will then attempt to offer some sort of explanation of why he undertook these activities, why he became (in Dr. Johnson's words) something new, a Governor of Bengal who cared for scholarship,[2] and why an admirer of his could regard his administration as a golden age for orientalists compared with that of Lord Cornwallis which followed it.[3]

Hastings was only seventeen when he first went to India in 1750, but in some respects he was already a formidably educated young man. He had been a distinguished pupil of Westminster, a school which, if it was yielding some of its outright supremacy to Eton, still provided a most rigorous classical education.[4] He had entered Westminster in 1743, had become a King's Scholar in 1747, and was Captain of the School in 1749, the year in which he left because of the death of the uncle who had paid for his schooling.[5] His years at Westminster seem to have given him a 'relish . . . for classical studies' which was to last for the rest of his life;[6] what one of his younger contemporaries rightly called 'a fine style of language' in writing English prose;[7] and the habit which he never lost of composing verses, either in Latin or more frequently in English imitations of Latin metres. On the evidence of the verses surviving in Hastings's papers,

---

[2] *Boswell's Life of Johnson*, ed. G. Birkbeck Hill, rev. and enl. L. F. Powell (6 vols., Oxford, 1934–50), iv. 70.

[3] F. Gladwin to Hastings, 15 Feb. 1790, B.M., Add. MS. 29172, fo. 47.

[4] M. L. Clarke, *Classical Education in Britain 1500–1900* (Cambridge, 1959), pp. 46–60.

[5] I am extremely grateful to Mr. L. C. Spaull, the School's archivist, for information about Hastings at Westminster.

[6] S. Pechell to Hastings, 3 Aug. 1779, Add. MS. 29144, fo. 4.

[7] *Narratives of the Mission of George Bogle to Tibet and of the Journey of Thomas Manning to Lhasa*, ed. C. R. Markham (1876), p. cxxxvii.

Macaulay was no doubt justified in comparing him with other men of action who have shown 'all the little vanities and affectations of provincial blue-stockings'. But Hastings's persistence in versifying is perhaps an indication of a concern for literature which in India was to take him far beyond the limits of the conventional European classics. Judging by his booksellers' accounts, he had acquired the habit of wide reading early in life. Voyages and travels, theology, history, poetry, and plays seem to have been the staple of his reading, but he also took two volumes of Diderot and Hume's essays with him when he returned to India in 1769.[8] Whatever defects it may be customary to ascribe to more traditional eighteenth-century educational institutions, individuals like Hastings, who combined a very considerable literary knowledge with a wide-ranging curiosity about the world, should be set against these defects.

When Hastings began his Indian service in 1750, European awareness of Indian civilization was largely confined to such knowledge of Islamic culture as could be gleaned through an ability to speak Urdu (commonly called 'Moors' or 'Hindoostan' in the eighteenth century) or was accessible to the small number of Englishmen who had mastered Persian. In course of time Hastings became an Urdu speaker[9] and learnt to read Persian.[10] His linguistic attainments evidently gave him a taste for Islamic art and literature and he became an enthusiastic collector. As early as 1762 he was being sent 'some pictures and some Persian history' from Patna,[11] and rare books were still being sent to him after he had finally left India.[12] When he eventually sold his collection to the East India Company, it contained 190 volumes in Persian and Arabic as well as

---

[8] Add. MS. 29227, fos. 63, 210–11. Hastings's library at his death is listed in Farebrother, Clark, and Lye, *A Catalogue of the Valuable Contents of . . . Daylesford House* (1853), pp. 25–45.

[9] See his account of his methods of negotiating with the Wazir of Oudh in 'The Benares Diary of Warren Hastings', ed. C. C. Davies, *Camden Miscellany*, xviii (R. Hist. Soc., Camden 3rd ser. lxxix, 1948), 25–6.

[10] He and Henry Vansittart were said to be the only Englishmen in Calcutta in the early 1760s who 'understood a little Persian' (*A Translation of the Seir Mutaqherin* (4 vols., Calcutta, 1902–3), i, translator's preface, p. 1). John Shore later wrote that Hastings had 'a proficiency' in Persian (Lord Teignmouth, *Memoirs of the Life, Writings, and Correspondence of Sir William Jones* (2nd edn., 1807), p. 297).

[11] W. Fullarton to Hastings, 10 Aug. 1762, Add. MS. 29132, fo. 242.

[12] G. N. Thompson to Hastings, 1 March 1786, Add. MS. 29169, fo. 471.

Sanskrit and Hindi items.[13] The Persian and Arabic manuscripts included many works on history, grammar, and medicine, and an extensive collection of poetry, graced by a magnificent illuminated *Shāh-nāmeh* copied in 1560 and a sumptuous *Kulliyāt-i Saʿdī*.[14] A collection of over 250 Mughal and Persian drawings and paintings, together with a volume of 'Chinese drawings of matchless beauty' and an *Akbar-nāmeh*, remained in his family's possession until 1853.[15] That his interest in Persian poetry was a serious one is suggested by his willingness to comment on poems sent to him,[16] and by his being acknowledged as patron by the poet Minnat (Mīr Kamar al-Dīn), who came to Calcutta from Lucknow.[17] Ultimately, however, his interests died. 'Candidly confessing' in 1809 that his manuscripts 'are of no use to me now, but in the pecuniary profit which I may derive from the disposal of them', he parted with them for £759.[18]

Between the ending of his first service in India in 1765 and his return in 1769, Hastings made an attempt to spread his interest in Muslim culture at home. Apparently acting in conjunction with Henry Vansittart, the former Governor of Bengal, he drafted a *Proposal for Establishing a Professorship of the Persian Language in the University of Oxford*. The Professor would both teach Persian to young men going to India and do his best to interest educated Englishmen in general in a civilization still largely unknown to them.[19] Both Dr. Johnson and the Chancellor of the University approved of the project, but (Hastings wrote many years later) 'it met with no other encouragement

---

[13] [P. Gordon], *The Oriental Repository* (1835), p. 4.

[14] I.O.L., Persian MSS. 863, 1124. The Persian MSS. are listed in I.O.L., MS. Eur. D. 543, p. 7.

[15] Farebrother, Clark, and Lye, *Daylesford Catalogue*, pp. 48–51; forty of the miniatures are described in greater detail in Sotheby and Co., *Catalogue of Persian, Turkish and Arabic Manuscripts, Indian and Persian Miniatures*, 24, 25 Nov. 1968, pp. 110–40.

[16] *Letters of Warren Hastings to his Wife*, ed. S. C. Grier (Edinburgh, 1905), pp. 251–2.

[17] H. E. Ethé, *Catalogue of Persian Manuscripts in the Library of the India Office* (2 vols., Oxford, 1903–37), i. 934. Minnat was a *ṣūfī* who began his career as a poet at Delhi. He was introduced to Hastings by Richard Johnson, deputy to the Resident at Lucknow.

[18] *Oriental Repository*, p. 3.

[19] There are copies of the *Proposal* in the Bodleian (8°. Z. 459. Th.) and in I.O.L., MS. Eur. B. 77.

and therefore dropped'.[20] Proposals to raise money in India for 'Hastings's scheme of a Persian Professorship' evidently also came to nothing.[21]

Hastings's return to Bengal as Governor in 1772 gave him a new incentive for encouraging the study of Muslim India. He believed that one of his most urgent tasks was to overhaul the judicial system of the province and to place it under some measure of British supervision. A new hierarchy of courts was created over which Europeans would preside or whose decisions they would review. Hastings was, however, totally opposed to any suggestion that British involvement should mean the introduction of British law. It was neither practical nor desirable to tamper with traditional Hindu or Muslim law, which were 'consonant to the ideas, manners and inclinations of the people for whose use it is intended' and thus were 'preferable to any which even a superior wisdom could substitute'.[22] If Europeans were to administer Indian law, Hastings believed that the law must be made accessible to them by the establishment of authoritative texts which would then be translated into English. Rapid progress was made on a code of Hindu law,[23] but the translation of Islamic texts went much more slowly. The two most important sources for the *Ḥanafī* law used in India were the *Hidāya*, a commentary written in the twelfth century, and the *Fatāwā al-ʿĀlamgīrī* compiled for the Emperor Aurangzeb.[24] By July 1774 Hastings had acquired an Arabic text of the *Fatāwā al-ʿĀlamgīrī*, which was being translated into Persian by *Maulavī* Ghulām Yaḥyā and three assistants (whose wages were paid in the first instance out of Hastings's own pocket); the Persian version was rendered into English by David Anderson, a young Company servant.[25] By 1776 the same team was working on the *Hidāya*, a much longer task. Anderson was replaced by his brother James, who produced a section of an

---

[20] W. H. Hutton, 'A Letter of Warren Hastings on the Civil Service of the East India Company', *E.H.R.* xliv (1929), 640.

[21] G. Vansittart to H. Vansittart, 6 Jan. 1768, Bodleian MS. Dep. b. 100, p. 35.

[22] M. E. Monckton Jones, *Warren Hastings in Bengal 1772–1774* (Oxford, 1918), pp. 337–8.   [23] See below, p. 248.

[24] Asaf A. A. Fyzee, *Outlines of Muhammadan Law* (3rd edn., Oxford, 1964), pp. 80–1.

[25] See accounts in *Minutes of the Evidence taken at the Trial of Warren Hastings* (11 vols., 1788–94), iii. 1122–3; Anderson to Hastings, 8 Sept. 1774, Add. MS. 45431, fo. 336.

English translation which was sent home in December 1777.[26] The translation was finally finished by Charles Hamilton of the Company's army in 1783,[27] appearing in print in 1791. Ghulām Yahyā wrote a preface to the *Hidāya* which was translated by Henry Vansittart, the son of the Governor and as enthusiastic a Persian scholar as he had been,[28] but unfortunately no copy of this appears to have survived. Hastings also commissioned a work which came to be known as the *Ẕakīreh-i Governor Hastings*, a series of answers to legal questions provided by one Muhammad Wasīl Jaisī.[29]

Hastings was interested in historical investigations as well as legal texts.[30] He gave every possible encouragement to Francis Gladwin's translation of the *Ā'īn-i Akbarī*, believing that 'it comprehends the original constitution of the Mogul empire' and would enable the Company to model its administration 'on first principles . . . most easy and most familiar to the minds of the people'. He proposed that the Company should subscribe to 150 sets of the translation.[31] Financial difficulties led to the proposal being withdrawn, but Hastings's accounts show that he personally paid for twelve sets.[32] The office of personal Persian translator to the Governor-General was also used by Hastings as a reward to historians: William Davy, who had already completed a translation to be published after his death as *Institutes political and military . . . by the Great Timour*, and Jonathan Scott, who was to publish works on Mughal history.[33]

Hastings's desire to endow Muslim scholarship, frustrated at Oxford, was eventually to be fulfilled at Calcutta. In September 1780 he was presented with a petition from 'a considerable number of Mussalmen of credit and learning' asking him to found a *madraseh*, or college, where Mujīd al-Dīn, said to be a distinguished *maulavī* (legal scholar) who had recently arrived in Calcutta, could teach. The petition, with its appeal

---

[26] I.O.R., B[engal] R[evenue] C[onsultations], 2 Dec. 1777, Range 50, vol. 5, pp. 124–8.

[27] I.O.R., B.R.C., 23 Jan. 1784, Home Miscellaneous, 207, p. 439.

[28] Hastings to G. Vansittart, 7 Jan. 177[7], Add. MS. 29128, fo. 29.

[29] I.O.L., Persian MSS. 2614, 2615.

[30] Grewal, *Muslim Rule*, pp. 23–42.

[31] I.O.R., B[engal] P[ublic] C[onsultations], 2 June 1783, Range 2, vol. 61, fos. 187–8.   [32] Add. MS. 29089, fo. 147.

[33] Grewal, *Muslim Rule*, pp. 34–6. For Scott's own account of his career and of Hastings's patronage, see his letter of 11 Sept. 1809, I.O.R., E/1/119, no. 220.

to Hastings's reputation as a patron and to the duty of every 'well regulated government' to promote learning, was superbly drafted, raising the presumption that its eventual recipient drafted it himself. It produced its effect immediately.[34] Mujīd al-Dīn was able to open his college with forty boarders in October 1780. His own stipend, his pupils' fees, and the cost of acquiring the site were all at first met by Hastings out of his own resources, until he was able to persuade the Company to endow the college with a grant of lands and to obtain reimbursement for himself by unfortunately devious means.[35] The early years of the Calcutta *madraseh* were generally unsatisfactory and reforms had to be imposed on it, but in 1785 an inspector found ninety-five students of 'decent and orderly' appearance, who were studying philosophy, eloquence, logic, law, grammar, and 'the sciences in general', under Mujīd al-Dīn and three other teachers.[36]

The legal reforms which Hastings had undertaken in 1772 had created the need for Hindu as well as Muslim legal texts which would be available to Europeans. The compiling of these texts seems to have been the beginning of Hastings's serious interest in Hinduism. At his request, a group of pandits undertook to produce a Sanskrit code from leading Hindu treatises, which was then rendered into Persian. The work was begun in May 1773 and finished in February 1775. In a legal sense the code proved to be of limited value;[37] but it was a contribution of the utmost importance to European inquiries into Hinduism, which for obvious reasons of linguistic ignorance and comparatively limited contact had lagged far behind inquiries into Islam. In promoting the study of Hinduism, Hastings's role was again to be that of patron, stimulating the work of both Europeans and Indians by his own enthusiasm, trying to obtain financial rewards from the Company or appropriate offices for those capable of making contributions, and even digging into his own pocket. In choosing the English translator for the

---

[34] For the petition, see *Cal[endar of] Persian Corr[espondence]* (10 vols., Calcutta, 1919–49), vi. 89; see also Hastings's minute, 18 April 1781, printed S. C. Sanial, 'History of the Calcutta Madrassa', *Bengal Past and Present*, viii (1914), 105–6.

[35] P. J. Marshall, *The Impeachment of Warren Hastings* (Oxford, 1965), pp. 149–52.

[36] Report by J. Evelyn, 31 July 1785, I.O.R., Home Miscellaneous, 487, pp. 12–25.

[37] J. D. M. Derrett, *Religion, Law and the State in India* (1968), pp. 239–42.

Persian text of the pandits' code, Hastings made what was perhaps the most far-sighted of all his acts of patronage. The man whom he chose was Nathaniel Halhed, who had come to India rather older than most Company servants, having already studied Persian at Oxford. The preparation of his translation clearly aroused in Halhed an intense curiosity about Hinduism which went far beyond matters of law, and he provided the code with a remarkable preface in which he discussed religion, the Hindu view of the history of the world, and the Sanskrit language and its literature.[38] The code and its preface, Hastings was assured, were received by 'the educated world' in Europe 'with the greatest satisfaction',[39] while in India Halhed was able to attract another young servant of extraordinary ability, Charles Wilkins, to the study of the Hindus. Wilkins and Halhed produced in 1778 a grammar of the Bengali language, Wilkins's contribution being the astonishing feat of personally making the Bengali characters to enable the book to be printed and then going on to make a fount of Persian characters as well.[40] Hastings took a keen interest in the publication of the Bengali grammar, persuading the Company to purchase 500 copies and creating the salaried office of Printer to the Company as compensation for the money laid out by Wilkins in producing the types.[41]

Whereas Halhed made only limited progress in Sanskrit, Wilkins mastered it, being the first European to have done so for several generations. From the Bengali grammar he went on to compile his own Sanskrit one and to begin a translation of the *Mahābhārata*. In December 1783 Hastings induced the Supreme Council to give Wilkins leave of absence on full salary to continue his studies at Banaras.[42] A year later Hastings persuaded him to make a separate translation of the *Bhagavad Gītā* and to send it to London for publication, the first scholarly translation of a Hindu classic to appear in print in any European

[38] The preface is reprinted in *The British Discovery of Hinduism in the Eighteenth Century*, ed. P. J. Marshall (Cambridge, 1970), pp. 140–83.

[39] R. Orme to Hastings, 14 Jan. 1775, Add. MS. 29136, fo. 17.

[40] K. S. Diehl, 'Bengali Types and their Founders', *Journal of Asian Studies*, xxvii (1967–8), 335–8.

[41] I.O.R., B.R.C., 9 Jan., 20 Feb., 13 Nov. 1778, Range 50, vols. 7, 8, 12, pp. 115, 948–53, 558–61.

[42] Ibid., 9 Dec. 1783, Home Miscellaneous, 207, pp. 169–80.

language. The translation was accompanied by an explanatory letter written by Hastings himself, a glowing expression of his own enthusiasm for a literature which 'will survive when the British dominion in India shall have long ceased to exist'.[43] In the preface to his *Gītā* Wilkins described his relations with Hastings as those of 'a pupil to his preceptor and patron',[44] later calling Hastings his 'Gooroo' and assuring him that he would seek his approval for every line of his translation of the *Mahābhārata*.[45]

Eighteenth-century Europeans had generally found Hindus intensely secretive and unwilling to divulge information to Christians. Hastings's success in persuading pandits to impart their knowledge was thus seen by his contemporaries as a remarkable triumph for his charm of manner and obvious sincerity, an opinion which Hastings himself was inclined to share. Be that as it may, Hastings certainly established fruitful contact with a number of learned Hindus, beginning with the pandits who compiled the code and who refused all offers of reward beyond a meagre subsistence allowance.[46] He was later able to persuade Rādhākanta Sarman, 'a Brahmen of distinguished abilities, and highly revered by the Hindus in Bengal for his erudition and virtue',[47] to produce an exposition of Hindu history based on the *Purāṇas*, which was translated into Persian.[48] Rādhākanta was given a grant of lands worth 1,200 rupees before Hastings left India.[49] Another treatise on Hindu learning, translated from Sanskrit into Persian and compiled by one *munshī* Karparam at Hastings's direction, survives in the British Museum.[50]

The shortage of reliable information in European languages, at least until the 1780s, together with his own inability to read Sanskrit, placed obvious limitations on what Hastings could learn about Hinduism. But his introduction to Wilkins's *Gītā* and an account of Hindu beliefs which he wrote in 1800[51]

[43] Repr. in *Discovery of Hinduism*, pp. 184–91.   [44] Ibid., p. 192.
[45] Letter of 4 May 1787, Add. MS. 29170, fos. 418–19.
[46] *Discovery of Hinduism*, p. 191.
[47] *The Letters of Sir William Jones*, ed. G. Cannon (2 vols., Oxford, 1970), ii. 802.
[48] There is an English translation in Add. MS. 5657.
[49] *Letters of . . . Jones*, ii. 762.
[50] C. Rieu, *Catalogue of the Persian Manuscripts in the British Museum* (3 vols., 1879–83), i. 63.
[51] Letter to E. B. Impey, 16 Feb. 1800, Add. MS. 39872, fos. 4–10.

suggest that he had made serious inquiries and was familiar with certain concepts. Thomas Maurice, a littérateur who aspired to being thought of as an orientalist, claimed that he had learnt from a conversation with Hastings 'to entertain more just conceptions of the great triad of deity, Brahma, Veeshnu and Seeva and the ten Avatars, than any books could impart to me'.[52] Hastings also seems to have had some slight acquaintance with more secular Hindu learning, even if it was probably solely at second hand. In 1783 Reuben Burrow, a very accomplished British astronomer recently arrived in India, presented him with memoranda on Hindu astronomy, suggesting that there was much that the West could profitably learn from it.[53] Hastings quoted Burrow as his authority for the claim that Hindu learning 'comprises many of the most obstruce sciences, and those carried to a high degree of perfection many ages even before the existence of the earliest writers of the European world'.[54]

Dr. Johnson once told Hastings that Europe would expect to learn from him not only about 'the arts and opinions' of Indians, but also about the 'natural productions, animate and inanimate' of India.[55] This refusal to separate human from physical science was entirely characteristic of the eighteenth century. The equal advancement of geographical, botanical, geological, and ethnographical knowledge was accepted as the objective of all the great enterprises of exploration, and Hastings's interests were also many-sided. At his new house at Alipur, near Calcutta, he created a garden for 'curious and valuable exotics from all quarters', such as cinnamon trees from Ceylon. He was acknowledged to be the inspirer of the botanical garden established in Calcutta just after he had left India.[56] From England, he made frequent requests for seeds and plants to be sent to him, at various times apparently hoping to establish the Bhutan turnip, lychees, custard apples, and even

---

[52] *The Indian Antiquities* (7 vols., 1793-1800), i, p. xcvii.

[53] On Burrow see *Historical Records of the Survey of India*, ed. R. H. Phillimore (4 vols., Dehra Dun, 1945-58), i. 155-7, 162-3, 316-20. His memoranda for Hastings are in Add. MS. 29233, fos. 237 sqq., 263 sqq.

[54] I.O.R., B.R.C., 9 Dec. 1783, Home Miscellaneous, 207, p. 172.

[55] *The Letters of Samuel Johnson*, ed. R. W. Chapman (3 vols., Oxford, 1952), i. 363.

[56] S. Turner to Hastings, 10 Feb. 1788, Add. MS. 29171, fo. 104; I.O.R., B.P.C., 16 June 1786, Home Miscellaneous, 799, fo. 13.

mangoes in Britain.[57] Yaks and what he called shawl goats were sent to Bengal from Tibet to be reared at Calcutta, and numerous unfortunate animals were sent after him to England, one yak and a number of goats actually surviving the voyage. He befriended the great surveyor and cartographer James Rennell. But perhaps the most striking examples of the full range of Hastings's quest for knowledge are the expeditions to Tibet which he promoted. George Bogle, who went on the first one in 1774, was told to find out about forms of government, laws, religion, the effects of polyandry, Tibetan 'diversions and entertainments', and Tibetan cooking, to take bearings, and to collect animals, walnuts, and rhubarb.[58] Samuel Turner, who made the second journey in 1783, was accompanied by a 'draftsman and surveyor', as well as by a surgeon who produced an account of 'the Vegetable and Mineral Productions of Bootan and Tibet'.[59]

Hastings's enthusiasm for oriental scholarship has long been noted by his biographers and by historians of contacts between Asia and the West, and thus the listing of his achievements presents few problems. But any attempt to explain why he undertook so much involves an inevitably speculative assessment of his character and qualities of mind. Most attempted explanations have begun by stressing Hastings's appreciation of the practical value of oriental scholarship for the future of British rule in India. The point is repeatedly made that he was convinced that the Company's provinces must be ruled in ways that conformed as closely as possible to traditional Indian methods; British administrators should therefore be well versed in the languages, laws, and customs of the people they administered.[60] This emphasis on practical advantages has much to commend it. Considerations of utility were undoubtedly powerful ones in Hastings's patronage. Thus the Professor of Persian at Oxford would help to prepare men for the Company's

[57] Letter to G. N. Thompson, 18 July 1786, Add. MS. 29170, fo. 133; Thompson to Hastings, 31 Aug. 1786, ibid., fo. 178.
[58] G. R. Gleig, *Memoirs of the Right Hon. Warren Hastings* (3 vols., 1841), i. 412–14; *Narratives of Bogle and Manning*, pp. 3–13; I.O.L., MS. Eur. E. 226, no. 55.
[59] S. Turner, *An Account of an Embassy to the Court of the Teshoo Lama in Tibet* (1800).
[60] For recent statements see Mukherjee, *William Jones*, p. 79; Grewal, *Muslim Rule*, p. 24; Kopf, *Bengal Renaissance*, p. 17.

service; the Calcutta *madraseh* would train Muslim law officers for the Company's courts;[61] the Hindu code and the translation of the *Hidāya* would be used by the courts; the *Ā'īn-i Akbarī* would be a valuable guide to Mughal precedents for the Company's government; Wilkins's Bengali and Persian types would be used to print official papers for the Company; the Tibet expeditions were intended first and foremost to promote trade with Bengal; Hastings hoped through his botanical and zoological experiments to introduce valuable new products into Bengal and Britain—for instance, the cinnamon plantations were intended to break the Dutch monopoly based on control of Ceylon, and he genuinely believed that Cashmere shawls could be made in England if his goats flourished.[62]

But strong as the argument is for believing that Hastings pursued oriental learning for its practical benefits, no single explanation of the motives of so complex a personality is likely to be complete. Indeed, there is abundant evidence in his writings to suggest a wide variety of motives: arguments for the practical utility of any specific project can be matched at every point by arguments supporting it for other reasons. The Persian Professorship would train future Writers for the Company, but Hastings also insisted that the study of 'the manners of the various inhabitants of the earth' should be undertaken for its own sake, since it 'cannot fail to open our minds, and to inspire us with that benevolence which our religion inculcates'.[63] The *madraseh* would train Muslim lawyers, but it would also 'promote the growth and extension of liberal knowledge' in general.[64] He was fully aware that the translations of the *Hidāya* and of the code of Hindu law were not just legal texts, but also objects of 'literary curiosity';[65] even those sections which were of 'little real utility' should be translated to gratify 'the curiosity of the public'.[66] He reiterated the point in commending Gladwin's translation of the *Ā'īn-i Akbarī*: 'every branch of Indian literature' should be added to 'the stock of European knowledge'.[67]

[61] *Cal. Persian Corr.* vii. 2.
[62] Letter of Sir J. Sinclair, 17 Sept. 1790, Add. MS. 29172, fo. 125.
[63] *Proposal for a Professorship*, p. 8.
[64] Letter to Directors, 30 April 1781, I.O.R., E/4/39, p. 322.
[65] Gleig, *Memoirs*, i. 404.
[66] Letter to [D. Anderson], 3 May 1776, Add. MS. 29137, fos. 181–2.
[67] I.O.R., B.R.C., 2 June 1783, Range 2, vol. 61, fo. 187.

He believed that the success of Bogle's mission to Tibet could not be judged by its practical results alone: 'Remember that every thing you see is of importance', he wrote.[68]

From these and many similar statements it is apparent that any explanation of Hastings's energy as a patron must at least begin by recognizing the genuine pleasure which he derived from gratifying the literary tastes and intellectual curiosity implanted in him at Westminster. When sending home Wilkins's *Gītā*, he urged one of his friends to 'defend me if you hear me reproached with lavishing my time on these levities, as they may be termed by many, to the neglect of business. . . . I neither drink, game, nor give my vacant hours to music, and but a small portion of my time to the other relaxations of society. These are my relaxations, and I presume that they are not such as I should be ashamed of, for it is only from the most cultivated understandings that I can derive the means of indulging myself in them.'[69] Even if he eventually disposed of his collection of Persian poetry in a rather summary way, he would hardly have acquired it in the first place if he had not derived real pleasure from it. He admired such Hindu literature as he was acquainted with. He called the *Mahābhārata* a 'work of wonderful fancy',[70] rendering parts of Wilkins's translation into English verse.[71] The *Gītā* he considered to be 'almost unequalled' in its 'sublimity of conception, reasoning, and diction', and he was fond of quoting its 'many precepts of fine morality' in letters to his wife.[72]

Even if Hastings had not been a person of genuine intellectual curiosity, the temptations for a man in his situation to have simulated such curiosity would have been strong. In the 1760s and 1770s respect for what has been felicitously called 'the Gentleman Amateur of Science' was at its height.[73] Joseph Banks is the obvious example, but there are many others, such as Daines Barrington, the correspondent of Gilbert White, or the Scottish peers, Kames, Monboddo, and Hailes. While Hastings lacked the cruder urges to social advancement of Clive and certain other 'nabobs', he was keenly aware of what he

[68] Gleig, *Memoirs*, i. 416.

[69] Letter to J. Scott, 24 Nov. 1784, Add. MS. 29129, fo. 270.

[70] I.O.R., B.R.C., 9 Dec. 1783, Home Miscellaneous, 207, p. 172.

[71] Add. MS. 29235, fos. 50–5.   [72] *Letters to his Wife*, pp. 365, 387.

[73] *The Endeavour Journal of Joseph Banks*, ed. J. C. Beaglehole (2 vols., Sydney, 1962), i. 3.

thought was due to him and to his family; and the prestige of being ranked with other patrons obviously attracted him. His concern for public recognition for his efforts is most apparent over the first Tibetan expedition. Bogle set out in 1774, shortly after the return to Britain of the *Endeavour* (which had earned even more publicity for Banks than for Cook)[74] and of James Bruce from Abyssinia. In one of his letters to Bogle, Hastings wrote:

I feel myself more interested in the success of your mission than in reason perhaps I ought to be; but there are thousands of men in England whose good-will is worth seeking, and who will listen to the story of such enterprises in search of knowledge with ten times more avidity than they would read accounts that brought crores to the national credit, or descriptions of victories that slaughtered thousands of the national enemies.

He believed that if Bogle's journal was published it would surpass in public acclaim John Hawkesworth's edition of Cook's journals.[75] The founding of botanical gardens, as at Alipur, had become extremely fashionable since the recent development of the Royal Gardens at Kew. In sending home animals, Hastings was following the lead of Clive[76] and of the Royal Society, which had applied in 1770 and 1771 to the Hudson's Bay Company for specimens of the fauna of the Canadian North.[77] Even in commissioning translations of Persian or Sanskrit works, Hastings could not be altogether oblivious of an applauding public. He was, Robert Orme assured him, 'amongst the foremost' of philosophy's disciples and his name would not be forgotten for 'the valuable present you are making to learning and reason' in Europe by the code of Hindu law.[78] When threatened with impeachment in 1787, Hastings asked defiantly 'Whether I have shown a disregard to science; or whether I have not, on the contrary, by public endowments, by personal attentions, and by the selection of men for appointments suited to their talents, given effectual encouragement to it.'[79]

[74] Ibid. 51–2. [75] Gleig, *Memoirs*, i. 415–16.
[76] e.g. E. Crisp to Clive, 15 Oct. 1767, I.O.L., MS. Eur. G. 37, box 58, and account in ibid., box 52, fo. 78.
[77] R. Glover's introduction to *Andrew Graham's Observations on Hudson's Bay 1767–91* (Hudson's Bay Record Society, xxvii, 1969), p. xv.
[78] Letter of 14 Jan. 1775, Add. MS. 29136, fo. 17.
[79] Gleig, *Memoirs*, iii. 322–3.

Thus in patronizing learning in India Hastings was indulging his own tastes and curiosity, and acting in a way that he believed a cultivated gentleman ought to act, as well as performing a useful service to the Company and his country. But there is evidence suggesting a deeper and more systematic design behind his patronage, apparent in his writings for some years but becoming explicit in letters written in 1784 in connection with the publication of Wilkins's *Gītā*. He himself called this design a plan for 'reconciliation', the reconciliation 'of the people of England to the natives of Hindostan'.[80] Indians were to be reconciled to British rule by finding that Englishmen respected and admired their laws, their religion, and their institutions. Englishmen in India and, even more important, the British public at home were to be reconciled to Indians through a true understanding of Indian law, religion, and institutions: 'Every instance which brings their real character home to observation will impress us with a more generous sense of feeling for their natural rights, and teach us to estimate them by the measure of our own.'[81] The task of scholarship was to spread knowledge of the 'real character' of Indians and thus to educate Englishmen to rule with benevolence—a word repeated over and over again in Hastings's writings. Indians would then submit with gratitude, and reconciliation would be achieved.

There was, of course, a strong element of practical utility in Hastings's design for reconciliation. A policy of tolerating and preserving Indian traditions and customs seemed to him to be the only way of effectively prolonging British rule. Innovations would provoke opposition, which would shatter the fragile power of the Company. Nevertheless, Hastings's plans seem to have transcended the merely practical and to have been based on a genuine relativism. Indian institutions were not to be tolerated solely to avoid discontent; they were to be respected as good in themselves. He never appears to have been willing to concede the absolute equality of Indian and European civilization. On the other hand, he believed that Indian institutions were well adjusted to Indian conditions, and that there was much in them which Europeans could admire for its own sake. 'There is perhaps no country in the world possessed of

---

[80] Letter to Scott, 9 Dec. 1784, Add. MS. 29129, fo. 275.
[81] *Discovery of Hinduism*, p. 189.

fewer national vices, with a larger proportion of national virtues, than our own'; and yet 'It is not unreasonable to suppose that the powers of the mind are distributed in equal perfection to the whole race of mankind, however differently cultivated and variously applied'.[82]

Hastings's relativism, which led him to advocate an empire based on toleration and respect for differences between rulers and ruled, was in accord with many trends in contemporary European thought. Greatly increased knowledge of the non-European world, the cult of the simple, the extension of natural law concepts to take in the whole of humanity, or their gradual abandonment for standards based on utility, were all tending towards relativism. But the particular inspiration for Hastings's design for reconciliation seems partly to have been his religious beliefs and partly his classical education.

There is very little evidence about Hastings's religious beliefs during his Indian service, the prayers which survive in his papers all having been composed during his retirement.[83] But there is no reason to doubt that he had been a convinced Christian throughout his life, even if the indications are that he was what can loosely be called a 'liberal' Anglican—that is, that he was more concerned with moral conduct and with comparatively limited fundamentals than with strictness of dogma.[84] Christians of this kind were usually prepared to be indulgent in their judgement of non-Christian religions when they found their ethical teaching satisfactory and could be convinced that they accepted certain basic tenets, such as the immortality of the soul and the unity and singleness of God. Hastings evidently judged Hinduism by these standards. He thought that the *Gītā* contained 'a theology accurately corresponding with that of the Christian dispensation, and most powerfully illustrating its fundamental doctrines'.[85] Some years later he wrote that it was possible to show 'how reconcileable the true and original principles of the doctrines of Brahma are to the lights of Christianity'.[86]

[82] *Proposal for a Professorship*, pp. 5–7.
[83] Add. MS. 39891.
[84] R. N. Stromberg, *Religious Liberalism in Eighteenth-Century England* (Oxford, 1954), pp. 92, 169.
[85] *Discovery of Hinduism*, p. 187.
[86] Letter to E. B. Impey, 16 Feb. 1800, Add. MS. 39872, fo. 10.

Not only did Hastings believe that Hinduism was an object worthy of toleration, he also thought that Christians were morally bound to be tolerant. The growth during the eighteenth century of the belief that Christians had a duty to be benevolent to non-Christians has been illuminatingly studied in connection with the rise of the anti-slavery movement.[87] Hastings's writings strike the same note. In his *Proposal* for the Persian Professorship he wrote of that 'benevolence which our religion inculcates, for the whole race of mankind', which should be cultivated by learning to revere the virtues of other peoples and 'to view their errors with indulgence'.[88] In the introductory letter to the *Gītā*, he again stressed the 'obligation of benevolence'.[89] In 1800 he still hoped that a comparison of Hinduism with Christianity, if 'touched with delicacy, and with that awe with which such disquisitions ought to be accompanied', would provide 'strong arguments . . . in favour of universal philanthropy'.[90]

In Hastings's mind the Christian duty of benevolence and toleration seems to have been reinforced by the Roman example, whose influence on him has been noted by Sir Keith Feiling.[91] Any moderately attentive Westminster boy would in the eighteenth century have acquired a very considerable knowledge of Roman history, and Hastings seems to have shared in the admiration for a tolerant, cosmopolitan imperial system which was very widely held in contemporary Europe.[92] In 1763 he wrote that the 'wisest and most permanent states have ever left to conquered nations the exercise of their own laws'.[93] Halhed began the preface to his translation of the code of Hindu law with the observation that 'much of the success of the Romans' could be attributed to 'a well-timed toleration in matters of religion'.[94] When Gibbon paid his homage to the Empire of the Antonines he perfectly reflected the aspirations of men like Hastings for the empire of the East India Company: 'The magistrates could not be actuated by a blind, though

---

D. B. Davis, *The Problem of Slavery in Western Culture* (Penguin edn., Harmondsworth, 1970), chs. x, xi, xii.
[90] Letter to Impey, 16 Feb. 1800, Add. MS. 39872, fos. 8–9.
[91] *Warren Hastings* (1954), p. 236.
[92] P. Gay, *The Enlightenment: an Interpretation* (2 vols., 1967–70), i. 160–71.
[93] H. Vansittart, *A Narrative of the Transactions in Bengal* (3 vols., 1766), ii. 356.
[94] *Discovery of Hinduism*, p. 142.

honest bigotry, since the magistrates were themselves philosophers', while 'in the exercise of the religion which they derived
from their ancestors' the subject peoples of the empire 'uni-
formly experienced the indulgence, and even protection of the
Roman conquerors'.[95]

It was easier to write about reconciliation of peoples than
effectively to bring this about. Some Englishmen in India undoubtedly did accept Hastings's point of view. Attracted by the
stories of great fortunes made in Bengal in the 1760s, rather
more young men of intellectual promise and an education
similar to Hastings's own were coming to India than in previous generations. Such men might not share all Hastings's
enthusiasms, but some of them clearly appreciated that proficiency in languages and a knowledge of India were the way
to win the Governor's favour. Halhed, Wilkins, and the younger
Henry Vansittart are obvious examples, as are a number of
highly educated and extremely able and ambitious young
Scotsmen such as George Bogle, Alexander Elliot, and David
Anderson and his brother James. David Anderson was typical
of the others. He believed that the way to a fortune lay not in
private trade but in 'studying the different branches of the
Company's affairs' and 'gaining the friendship of my superiors
by assiduity and diligence'.[96] Finding that a 'perfect knowledge
of Persian' could not be 'obtained in the common way', he
tried to learn Arabic.[97] Elliot agreed that a young Company
servant should spend his time learning Persian and studying
'the business and history of the country in which I live'.[98] By
1784 Hastings could write with some truth that the Company's
service 'abounded with men of cultivated talents, . . . and liberal
knowledge'.[99] But such men were still a small minority among
Englishmen in India, most of whom no doubt remained largely
oblivious of their surroundings and personally antipathetic to
the 'blacks' among whom they lived.

Hastings's pleas for reconciliation to the Company and the
British public at home fell on even stonier ground. The Directors

[95] *The History of the Decline and Fall of the Roman Empire* (ed. J. B. Bury, 7 vols.,
1896–1900), i. 34–5.
[96] Letter to Sir L. Dundas, 12 Oct. 1772, Add. MS. 45438, fo. 85.
[97] Letter to D. Anderson, Sr., 14 March 1771, ibid., fos. 41–2.
[98] Letter to G. Elliot, 7 Sept. 1772, National Library of Scotland, Minto MSS.,
M 14.   [99] *Discovery of Hinduism*, p. 189.

were certainly sympathetic towards 'every application that may enlarge our servants in general to liberal and useful inquiries',[100] and were not ungenerous in rewarding projects. During Hastings's period in office, no frontal assault was launched on Indian susceptibilities through new policies initiated at home. But it has to be added that such policies had no serious supporters in the Company at this time, and that the motive for tolerance was almost certainly awareness of the practical difficulties involved in change rather than any acceptance of Hastings's advocacy of the virtues of Indian civilization. Towards the end of his life opinion began to shift, and he found himself drawn into controversy on issues such as the opening of the Company's territories to Christian missions, a proposal which he very much disliked.

It would be unrealistic to suppose that the writings of the early orientalists or the portrayal of India which they sought to propagate reached a very wide audience beyond those immediately connected with the Company. In literary circles, however, publications such as Halhed's preface to the code of Hindu law and Wilkins's *Gītā* were received with respect.[101] With the appearance of Jones's essays and translations, interest spread from Britain to continental Europe.[102] Thus, if Hastings had not achieved reconciliation between Europe and India, he had at least helped to ensure that awareness of Hinduism would develop into a minor theme of European art in the nineteenth century.

The reverse of the coin, the reconciliation of Indians to European rule, presented even more intractable problems. Early British administration was remote and isolated, with very limited means at its disposal for making any sort of impact on the millions it ruled. The tiny handful of Indians who came into personal contact with the Governor-General might well be charmed and beguiled, as a group of Banaras pandits later claimed to have been, by his 'kind wishes and agreeable conversation, expressions of compassion for the distressed, acts of politeness, and a readiness to relieve and protect everyone alike without distinction'.[103] A series of brief character-sketches which

[100] Dispatch to Bengal, 16 March 1777, I.O.R., E/4/623, p. 507.
[101] *Discovery of Hinduism*, pp. 11–12, 38–40.
[102] Schwab, *Renaissance orientale*.
[103] P. Moon, *Warren Hastings and British India* (1947), p. 332.

he wrote in 1785 suggests that he had been able to form friendships with Indians, such as the Mughal emperor's eldest son or
the ministers of the Wazir of Oudh, in a way that his nineteenth-
century successors would neither desire nor be able to imitate.[104]
Such men were, however, a microscopic proportion of a population whose only contact with the new administration was the
payment of revenue or occasional glimpses of marching armies
or of the entourage of an official. Lack of means was not, moreover, the only obstacle to reconciliation. Benevolence and the
exigencies of empire did not always go together, as Hastings
himself was painfully aware. He might believe that a conquest
over minds was 'the most permanent as the most rational of
dominion',[105] but even in the introduction to the *Gītā* he wrote
of 'the right of conquest' and of 'the chain by which the natives
are held in subjection'.[106] Even the advancement of oriental
learning could sometimes take place in distinctly unbenevolent
circumstances: after the overthrow of Chait Singh, Raja of
Banaras, in 1781, Hastings asked to have any part of the Raja's
'curious and valuable collection' of 'Shamscrit manuscripts'
which might come to light in the looting of Bijaigarh, the last
of Chait Singh's fortresses to surrender.[107]

Whatever Hastings may have intended, practical difficulties
meant that the design for reconciliation existed in his mind
rather than in actual achievements. Thus it should be judged
as a literary exercise and an effort of the imagination rather
than as an administrative blueprint.

It was probably easier for an eighteenth-century European
to accept and respect an Asian civilization than it was for him
to come to terms with any other non-European civilization.
Asia, with a frontier pushed further and further to the east, had
been part of the European experience for centuries. There are
frequent accounts of Asia in Greek and Latin literature which
would have been familiar to anyone with Hastings's education,
even if he would also have acquired some very bizarre opinions
about India in particular. Recent speculation, such as the essays
of William Jones on the affinity of Sanskrit and European

---

[104] Letter to John Macpherson, 6 Feb. 1785, Add. MS. 29116, fos. 148–51.
[105] Memorial to Augustus Clevland, cited Feiling, *Hastings*, p. 237.
[106] *Discovery of Hinduism*, p. 189.
[107] *Impeachment Minutes of Evidence*, i. 289.

languages, had strengthened theories that Europe and Asia were historically one world. Hastings, for instance, later came to believe that discoveries about Druidic practices were 'strong evidence, that the tenets of Brahma extended over the continent of Europe to the extremity of Gaul'.[108]

If a sense that Europe and Asia had a common past made it easier for Europeans to assimilate new knowledge of Asia, there was an obvious danger that Asia would come to be regarded simply as an extension of Europe, to be understood solely in European terms. In this respect, Hastings is not guiltless. His India is not some imaginary, 'philosophical' China, constructed entirely in the image of Europe and used as a weapon in European controversy; it is based on a solid stratum of knowledge. But it is still a civilization to be measured against Europe. For instance, Hastings denied that he would try to judge Hindu literature by European criteria, but this is precisely what he did in the introductory letter to the *Gītā*. He may have disapproved of 'comparisons between the absurdities of other religions and the purity of our own',[108] but it was inevitable that he should judge Hinduism by his own Christian standards. Thus his view of India is still a Eurocentric one. But verdicts so favourable and advocacy so enthusiastic, based on genuine knowledge, suggest that he had taken at least a few steps along what he himself called the 'new and most extensive range for the human mind beyond the present limited and leaden field of its operations'[109] which knowledge of India was presenting to the West.[110]

[108] Letter to Impey, 16 Feb. 1800, Add. MS. 39872, fo. 8.

[109] I.O.R., B.R.C., 9 Dec. 1783, Home Miscellaneous, 207, p. 172.

[110] This essay has benefited greatly from the comments and suggestions of Mr. Simon Digby, Dr. J. D. Gurney, and Dr. Rosane Rocher.

XIII

Horace Walpole and King George III

LORD HOLLAND, the first editor of Horace Walpole's memoirs, wrote about their author: 'He was . . . during the whole of his public life, too much under the guidance of personal feelings.'[1] There are two kinds of truth in Walpole's memoirs—the truth of fact and the truth of feeling. He took pains to ascertain facts, but before these were incorporated into a narrative of events they were filtered through the sieve of personal feeling. Walpole was aware of this process and expected his readers to make allowances. 'I paint what I felt', he wrote, 'and I warrant my veracity, of which my feelings were the symptoms. If they misled me, let my judgment be blamed—if they misrepresented facts to me, or if I have been misinformed, let better authority and future evidence be preferred to my narrative of what I saw, knew, or believed.'[2] There can be no doubt that Walpole's feelings misled him with respect to several of his great contemporaries. No one, for example, will accept as fair his character-sketch of Lord Chancellor Hardwicke ('In the House of Lords he was laughed at; in the Cabinet, despised');[3] or of Lord Shelburne ('His falsehood was so constant and notorious, that it was rather his profession than his instrument').[4] These are not impartial assessments but the reflection of political prejudice and personal dislike. Before we can use Walpole's memoirs as source material for history we must do as he advised: strip from them the husk of personal feeling and reveal the kernel of objective truth. Walpole himself is the most important character in his memoirs and possibly the least understood.

[1] *Memoirs of the Last Ten Years of the Reign of King George the Second* (2nd edn., 3 vols., 1847), i, p. xxi.

[2] These sentences are from a passage on the Chevalier d'Éon, which is omitted from the published text of Walpole's *Memoirs of the Reign of King George the Third*, ed. G. F. R. Barker (2nd edn., 4 vols., 1894), i. 314.

[3] *Memoirs George II*, i. 160.

[4] *Journal of the Reign of King George III, from the Year 1771 to 1783*, ed. Doran (1st edn., 2 vols., 1859), ii. 566. Usually known and cited below as *Last Journals*.

Next to Walpole, the most important character is King George III, the only character apart from Walpole himself who appears throughout from 1751 to 1791.[5] It is the purpose of this essay to discover Walpole's sources about the King and to account for his prejudices.

The need for a careful scrutiny of the memoirs will be clear if we examine what is almost the first mention of the King (then Prince George). After recounting the events which followed the death in 1751 of Frederick, Prince of Wales, Walpole writes: 'The Princess, finding that Prince George, at eleven years old, could not read English, though Ayscough [his tutor], to make amends, assured her he could make Latin verses . . .'[6] One wonders who told Walpole this extraordinary story or how he came to believe it. It is obviously ridiculous to assert that the boy could not read English but could write Latin. In fact there is abundant evidence to show that he could read and write English (and also French and German) long before the age of eleven. His first extant letter, thanking George II for the Garter, is dated 23 June 1749.[7] Frederick's letters to his son show that Prince George had been writing to his father since at least 1747, when he was nine years old.[8] Yet this passage is frequently cited as evidence that George III was slow to learn and even mentally retarded. When Walpole wrote it he knew little of Prince George beyond common gossip. As he tells us that he never went to court, we must conclude he rarely saw the Prince.[9] But before he began his memoirs of George III's reign he had acquired what must have seemed a reliable source of information about the King. It was, however, a suspect and tainted source.

In 1759 Walpole's favourite niece Maria, illegitimate daughter of Sir Edward Walpole, married James, 2nd Earl Waldegrave, a marriage arranged by her uncle Horace. From 1752 to 1756

[5] For a history of the MSS. and a bibliography of Walpole's memoirs, see A. T. Hazen, *A Bibliography of Horace Walpole* (New Haven, Conn., 1948), pp. 93–7.

[6] *Memoirs George II*, i. 80. The Prince was in his thirteenth year when his father died.

[7] B.M., Add. MS. 32684, fos. 78–80, printed in Bonamy Dobrée, *The Letters of King George III* (1935), p. 1. There is also a covering letter in German to Baron Münchausen.

[8] The Prince of Wales's letters, in the Royal Archives, are printed in Averyl Edwards, *Frederick Louis, Prince of Wales* (1947). None of Prince George's letters to his father appear to have survived.

[9] *Memoirs George II*, ii. 170.

Waldegrave had been governor to Prince George, but had not made a success of the appointment. He was not the man to win the confidence of a shy, lonely, and inarticulate youth; and he was intensely disliked by the Prince. In later years George III remembered Waldegrave as 'a depraved, worthless man'.[10] Waldegrave was high in favour with George II, and on the formation of the Prince's household in 1756 expected to be appointed Groom of the Stole. He was taken aback when he learnt that the Prince had demanded this office for Lord Bute— a clear indication of where favour would lie in the coming reign.

In recording Waldegrave's death in his *Memoirs of George III*, Walpole writes:[11]

Lord Waldegrave . . . had been so thoroughly fatigued with the insipidity of his pupil the King, and so harassed and unworthily treated by the Princess and Lord Bute, that no one of the most inflammable vengeance, or of the coolest resentment, could harbour more bitter hatred and contempt than he did for the King's mother and favourite. This aversion carried him to what I scarce believed my eyes when he first showed me, severe satires against them. He has left behind him, too, some memoirs of the few years in which he was governor to the Prince, that will corroborate many things I have asserted; and will not tend to make these anecdotes be reckoned unjust and [un]merciful.

Among other things, Walpole learnt from Waldegrave what appeared to be confirmation of a story which had long been current in London—that Bute was the lover of the Princess Dowager and that this was the explanation of his influence over the King.[12]

Walpole's first impressions of George III's character are based on what he learnt from Waldegrave. His first character sketch of the King in the memoirs of George III reads like a paraphrase of Waldegrave's.[13] His account of the King's education is not based on personal knowledge but simply reflects Waldegrave's dislike of Bute:[14]

A few pedantic examples were the sum of Lord Bute's knowledge; yet his partisans affected to celebrate the care he had taken of the

---

[10] *The Diaries and Correspondence of George Rose*, ed. Leveson Vernon Harcourt (2 vols., 1860), ii. 187–8.   [11] *Memoirs George III*, i. 212.
[12] James, Earl Waldegrave, *Memoirs from 1754 to 1758* (1821), pp. 38–9.
[13] Compare Walpole's sketch (*Memoirs George III*, i. 16–17) with Waldegrave's (*Memoirs*, pp. 8–10).   [14] *Memoirs George III*, i. 42.

King's education. . . . It proved indeed that His Majesty had learned nothing, but what a man, who knew nothing, could teach him.

Far from being ignorant, Bute had a knowledge of history and literature comparable to that of Walpole himself and an interest in science unusual for a man of his rank and time. It was through Bute's teaching that the King developed his love of the arts and sciences which so enriched his life. The indolent boy whom Waldegrave had known became the cultured monarch who patronized Herschel and collected the King's Library. But Waldegrave knew nothing of this. He could only think of Bute as the man who had supplanted him. Hence the 'bitter hatred and contempt' he felt for Bute and the Princess.

Thus Walpole began his *Memoirs of George III* on the wrong foot. He believed he had a reliable source of information about the King when he had nothing but Waldegrave's insinuations and inventions. From these materials he constructed a Gothic romance, about a 'passionate domineering woman' and a 'favourite without talents', who took advantage of the young King's inexperience to engage him in a plot against the constitution.[15] The romance ends with the death of the Princess in 1772, an event of no importance in George III's reign but obviously significant to Walpole. The final paragraph of the *Memoirs* consists of reflections on 'this unfortunate mother's fate'.[16]

Everything that Walpole writes about the King's personal life during the first twelve years of the reign is coloured by his belief that the Princess was 'all powerful over the mind of her son'.[17] Thus he tells us that the King and Queen were kept in seclusion at Buckingham House, 'a damp unwholesome spot', because the Princess wished to isolate them from their courtiers.[18] He did not know that the King disliked St. James's Palace, that the decision to buy Buckingham House was his alone, and that he preferred to live in private rather than with his court. Similarly, in his account of the King's marriage, Walpole writes: 'So complete was the King's deference to the will of his mother that he blindly accepted the bride she had chosen for him.'[19] He then tells the story of how David Graeme was sent by Bute 'to visit various little Protestant courts' in Germany 'and make report of the qualifications of the several unmarried

[15] *Memoirs George III*, i. 4.   [16] Ibid. iv. 242.   [17] Ibid. ii. 68.
[18] Ibid. i. 125; ii. 59.   [19] Ibid. i. 48–50.

princesses'. Again we see how little Walpole really knew. The facts are that the King's choice of a bride was entirely his own and was made without consulting his mother, and that Graeme's mission was simply to prepare the Duchess of Mecklenburg Strelitz for the dispatch of a formal embassy.

Walpole made these mistakes because he was subject to the limitations which apply to every historian. He did not know the whole truth, and the part he did know he interpreted according to preconceived ideas. His partiality led him to accept Waldegrave as a reliable witness. But there is this to be said for Walpole: he knew his limitations and repeatedly urged his readers to take account of them. The first pages of his *Memoirs of George III* are full of such warnings: 'How far I have been in the right or in the wrong, I leave to the judgment of posterity'; 'these are memoirs, not history'; 'Remember, reader, I offer you no more than the memoirs of men, who had many faults, written by a man who had many himself.' Walpole believed he had arrived at the truth, but basically he was a humble man. He expected to receive correction from posterity. It is posterity's duty to supply that correction.

Walpole's peculiar contribution to the mythology of the early years of George III's reign is the emphasis he placed on the role of the King's mother. His description of the Princess as 'passionate' and 'domineering' does not agree with what he had previously written about her or what we know of her from other sources. As far as it is possible to prove negative facts in history, it can be proved that the Princess was not Bute's mistress and that she exercised no political influence during her son's reign. Events would have taken the same course had she died ten years earlier. There would still have been the Peace of Paris, the Stamp Act, the Townshend duties, the expulsions of Wilkes. Yet as late as 1768, in writing of the riots in London, Walpole describes the Princess as 'the authoress of all these calamities'.[20]

Namier had an explanation of Walpole's obsession with the Princess, which he used to give to his friends in private though not sufficiently sure of it to commit himself in print. He referred to the story that Horace Walpole's real father was not Sir Robert but Carr, Lord Hervey. According to Namier, Horace

[20] Ibid. iii. 136.

half believed this story, and to convince himself and posterity that it was not true described himself on the title-page of his *Memoirs* as 'youngest son to Sir Robert Walpole, Earl of Orford'. He developed an unconscious dislike of his mother who had deprived him of his rightful father, and transferred this dislike to another mother—the Princess Dowager. In effect, he interpreted the early years of George III's reign in terms of his personal life. Romney Sedgwick, who distrusted what he called 'speculative psychologising', laughed at this explanation. He pointed out that the story of Walpole's doubtful paternity was retailed only after his death, and that it was the sort of story in which the nineteenth century delighted. Sedgwick believed that Walpole's dislike of the Princess arose from his dislike of Bute, who had given away the reversion of a sinecure held by Walpole in the name of his elder brother. Neither explanation is wholly satisfactory. I offer no explanation of my own, but merely point to the importance of Waldegrave in supplying information about George III to Walpole.

In July 1765 Walpole's political friends came to power, with his cousin Henry Seymour Conway as Secretary of State and Leader of the House of Commons. Walpole's account of the first Rockingham ministry suffers from his being out of the country most of the time. It is not until Chatham takes office in July 1766 that the most authentic part of his *Memoirs* begins. Walpole now had for the first and only time reliable information about George III—from Grafton and Conway, who saw the King regularly in the Closet. He was still obsessed by the idea that Bute and the Princess governed the King, but at one point—during his account of the ministerial negotiations of July 1767—he makes what he describes as 'a remarkable observation'.[21] The King agreed to Grafton's suggestion, made in the Closet, to renew the offer to Rockingham—from whence, writes Walpole, 'it was plain he did not always consult the Princess or Lord Bute'. If he did not consult the Princess and Bute about a proposal to change his ministry, then when did he consult them?

Even more remarkable in Walpole's account of these negotiations is how he identified himself with the King's purpose. For the first and only time in his life he played a decisive part in

[21] *Memoirs George III*, iii. 63.

history—and on the side of the Crown. George III's aim was to avoid having to capitulate to the Opposition, and Walpole told Conway that 'there were many independent men who would not sit still and see the Closet taken by storm'.[22] And again: 'That all sober men, not ranked in any faction, would not bear to see the King taken prisoner . . . that all danger of arbitrary power was over.'[23] Was every man to depend on King Rockingham and nobody on King George? Was the power and influence of the Crown to be usurped by a faction? And here is Walpole's final observation on these negotiations:[24]

In all my experience of the King or knowledge of his measures, he never interfered with his ministers, scarce took any part in his own business (I speak of the past years of his reign) unless when he was to undo an Administration. Whether hating or liking the persons he employed, the moment he took them, he seemed to resign himself entirely to their conduct for the time. If what they proposed was very disagreable to him, at most he avoided it by delay. How far he had entered into his mother's and Lord Bute's plans while they were all-powerful at the beginning of his reign, cannot be known.

At last we begin to learn something of the real George III. From 1766 to 1768, the only period when Walpole had access to authentic information about the King, he no longer appears as a tool in the hands of his mother and Bute but as a truly constitutional monarch, accepting the advice of his ministers and giving them his full confidence.

The concluding section of Walpole's *Memoirs of George III*, which deals with the Grafton ministry and the first two years of North, was not begun until 1771. By then Walpole was out of Parliament and Conway and Grafton had left the Cabinet. Walpole no longer had first-hand information about political affairs at the top, and was weary of writing memoirs.[25] His narrative suffers accordingly. Yet his interest in politicians and their doings was unabated. He had always been more interested in politicians than in politics, in personalities rather than in principles. For the years 1772 to 1791 he kept a journal, hitherto published only as far as 1783. This is greatly inferior in historical value to the memoirs but is still an important source of information about Walpole himself.

[22] Ibid. 41.   [23] Ibid. 55.
[24] Ibid. 66.   [25] Ibid. 107.

In 1772 it was no longer possible to believe in the influence of Bute and the Princess. Bute had spent most of the last two years on the Continent and the Princess was dying. Walpole was reluctant to abandon these long-cherished objects of his hatred, but the need to construct a new myth was obvious. Though he criticized Burke, he leant towards Burke's theory of a secret junto. The aim of this junto, so Walpole believed, was to continue the work begun by Bute and the Princess, to increase the personal power of the King, and to 'establish a despotism that may end in tyranny in his descendants'.[26] But this myth was too anonymous to suit Walpole. At the end of his *Memoirs of George III* he reverted to the ideas with which had had begun his *Memoirs of George II* twenty years earlier. The real cause of the 'present discontents' was the education George III had received in arbitrary ideas, instilled into him by Jacobites and quasi-Jacobites; and the real villains were Andrew Stone and Lord Mansfield, Viscount Bolingbroke and the Earl of Hardwicke.[27]

At this point we should recall Walpole's own words, written at the time he was expounding this latest myth:[28]

> However, instead of seeing with my eyes, I recommend to posterity to use their own discernment. Abandon the author, accept what truths he has delivered, correct his mistakes, condemn his prejudices, make the best use you can of any wholesome lessons he had inculcated, avoid such errors as he has pointed out.

Walpole's delusions about George III's education have been exposed by Romney Sedgwick.[29] It remains to explain the increased bitterness Walpole showed towards the King from 1772 onwards. In part this was the result of the displacement of Bute and the Princess Dowager as villains of the story. So long as they were active the King could be seen as the tool of his mother and his favourite, more sinned against than sinning. But after Bute's voluntary exile and the Princess's death the King was clearly acting on his own. And just at this time he committed an offence for which Walpole never forgave him.

---

[26] *Memoirs George III*, iv. 90.   [27] Ibid. 88–96.   [28] Ibid. 85.
[29] Introduction to Romney Sedgwick, (ed.) *Letters from George III to Lord Bute, 1756–1766* (1939), pp. xix–xliii. For details of the King's education, based on material in the Royal Archives, see my book *King George III* (1972), pp. 40–4, 55–8, 64–6.

In September 1766 the Duke of Gloucester, the King's favourite brother, secretly married Maria, dowager Lady Waldegrave. Their intimacy had long been the talk of London society, and Walpole had advised his niece to break off the relationship. He knew that the King would object to their marriage and feared it would bring unhappiness to both parties. Yet when the marriage was declared in September 1772 Walpole felt bound to take his niece's part. His character was such that he could have done no other.

As Macaulay pointed out, Walpole had an ambivalent attitude towards royalty. Although he described himself as 'a quiet republican',[30] his republicanism was not based on principle and he had no liking for radicalism. The only two royal personages who emerge with credit from his memoirs are William, Duke of Cumberland and Frederick the Great, both of whom carried high the concept of monarchy. Though he laughed at the foibles and follies of kings, he was eager to learn about their personal lives; and at least two of his friendships (with Madame du Deffand and Lady Suffolk) may have owed their origin to his curiosity about royalty. Secretly, he was proud that his niece had won the love of a Royal Duke and that the great-grandchildren of Sir Robert Walpole would be in remainder to the throne of Great Britain. But not even to posterity would Walpole admit his pride. Like many people who profess to despise royalty and its trappings, Walpole was disposed to be a good courtier and yet was secretly ashamed of his royalist leanings.

There was another aspect of Walpole's character which led him to take the part of his niece. One of the difficulties about appreciating Walpole is that his faults are all on the surface while his virtues are not so easily recognized. It must also be admitted that he does not appear at his best in his memoirs. Hence the reason why Macaulay, a superficial observer of human nature, failed to understand Walpole. One of the greatest of his virtues was his sympathy for those whom he saw— whether rightly or wrongly does not matter—as the victims of oppression. This led him to try to save Byng in 1757, to engage in politics on behalf of Conway in 1763, and to sympathize with the Americans after 1775. His feeling for the oppressed

[30] *Memoirs George II*, i. 377.

was heightened when the oppressed was a woman and a close relation. George III's refusal to recognize the Duchess of Gloucester as a member of the Royal Family roused Walpole's chivalry. 'I was now to determine what part to take', he wrote, 'and, as the Duke was now disgraced and my niece oppressed, I chose the handsome part, and resolved to incur the King's prohibition and pay my court to them.'[31]

It was a corollary of Walpole's sympathy for the oppressed that he imputed the worst motives to those whom he had cast for the role of the oppressors. In 1756, for example, he alleged that Newcastle and Hardwicke had hounded Byng to death to preserve their political position. While seeking to remedy the injustice to Byng, he himself committed an act of even greater injustice on Newcastle and Hardwicke. Once Walpole had become emotionally attached to a cause he could see it only in terms of a victim and a villain. There is a touch of melodrama in Walpole's interpretation of history.

Thus George III is cast for the role of villain in Walpole's journals. In politics he is depicted as a potential tyrant, in private life as cruel and unfeeling. Those attached to him are described as his tools or are concerned only for their private interests. Even had Walpole known all the facts about George III (which he did not), he would have been incapable of sympathizing with the King's feelings about his brother's marriage. Yet there is much to be said for George III. Gloucester was the man he loved best, the one man to whom he could confide everything. But Gloucester had not treated the King with an equal degree of confidence. Not only had he concealed the fact of his marriage for six years but he had written to the King in a manner to suggest that the rumour was untrue.[32] Walpole shows scant sympathy for the Duke of Cumberland, who had also incurred the King's displeasure by marrying a subject. One wonders if he would have been sympathetic to Gloucester had not Gloucester married Maria Waldegrave.

Though Walpole never married and is not known to have had a mistress, his closest relations were with women. Yet they were all women of a peculiar type—old enough to be his grandmother (Madame du Deffand) or young enough to be

[31] *Last Journals*, i. 135.   [32] Brooke, *King George III*, p. 277.

his granddaughter (Mary Berry), wives of close friends (Lady Upper Ossory) or near relations (the Duchess of Gloucester)— women whom he could adore but could not be expected to marry. Yet his adoration was never uncritical. It is surprising how closely Walpole and George III agreed in their views of the character of the Duchess of Gloucester. Walpole wrote that her passions were 'ambition and expense' while the King described her as proud and vain.[33] Despite his knowledge of her character, Walpole felt towards her as a knight towards his lady. Yet mixed with his chivalry there was a practical concern for her financial security. In a character-sketch of himself written in 1759 Walpole claims that he possessed one virtue in a singular degree—'disinterestedness and contempt of money'.[34] In this he deceived himself. He had a common-sense appreciation of the importance of money in life, but no desire to amass money for its own sake. He liked comfort but despised avarice. He was concerned for the future of a sinecure he held for the life of his elder brother, but would not barter his political independence in exchange for that sinecure. Perhaps he did not always appreciate that he was able to indulge his political independence only because of the financial security provided for him by his father.

The Duchess had a jointure of only £1,000 a year from her first husband.[35] Having married without the King's consent, she could expect no jointure on her second marriage. She had three children by Lord Waldegrave and was to have three more by the Duke of Gloucester (one of whom died in infancy). Gloucester was in bad health and twice in the 1770s seemed about to die. What would become of the Duchess, Walpole asked himself, should she again become a widow?

Had Gloucester married with the King's consent, he would have received financial provision from Parliament for his family. It was therefore to the interest of the Duchess to have the marriage recognized by the King, and in this she was supported by her husband and encouraged by her uncle. Although the King had no doubt of the legality of the marriage, he yielded to the Duke's request to have it authenticated by the

---

[33] *The Correspondence of King George III, 1760–1783*, ed. Sir John Fortescue (6 vols., 1927–8), iii. 165; *Memoirs of George III*, iii. 268.
[34] *Memoirs George II*, iii. 163.   [35] *Last Journals*, i. 143.

Privy Council. But he made a distinction between the position of the Duchess and that of her children. He refused to recognize the Duchess as a member of the Royal Family. But the children, having been born in wedlock, were in succession to the Crown and were entitled to a parliamentary provision. In 1775 the King informed Lord North that should Gloucester die he would take care of the children.[36] And when in 1778 he asked Parliament to provide for the younger branches of the Royal Family, even Walpole admitted that he made a 'handsome provision' for the children of the Duke of Gloucester.[37] In 1787 he gave the Duke a further £4,000 a year to pay for the education of his children; and when the allowances to the King's children were increased in 1805, those to Gloucester's children were increased in the same proportion. The King treated Gloucester's children as he did his own, and Gloucester's son subsequently married one of the King's daughters.

Had Walpole really understood George III's character, he would have known that, though the King could be harsh, he was rarely unjust. However much he may have disliked the Duchess or thought the Duke was weak in contracting such a marriage, he would not visit the sins of the parents upon the children. Walpole's fears for the Duchess's financial security were without foundation and arose from the ill-informed opinion he had of the King. George III provided for the Duchess of Cumberland after her husband's death, and he would have done the same for the Duchess of Gloucester had her husband died. A little more direct contact with the King would have assuaged all Walpole's fears and softened the harsh portrait he gives of George III.

Walpole learnt from the Duchess many stories about George III which she had learnt from the Duke. How far they were true, or whether they had been distorted by the Duchess before being retailed to her uncle, we shall perhaps never know. At the height of Gloucester's dissatisfaction with the King, when he was most under the influence of his wife, he talked indiscreetly not only to Walpole but also to the Duke of Richmond, one of the leaders of opposition. Walpole was even allowed to make copies of Gloucester's correspondence with the Secretary of State (writing on behalf of the King), which he reproduces in

[36] *Correspondence of George III,* iii. 165.   [37] *Last Journals,* ii. 249.

his journals. Though Gloucester had little interest in politics, he was persuaded by his connections to vote against the Quebec Bill. It is not difficult to understand why George III disliked his brother's marriage.

In 1780 Gloucester and the King were reconciled. For some time Walpole maintained his connection with the Duke, and had this continued longer he would have had (what he had not had since 1768) a reliable source of information about the King. But Gloucester could no longer bear his wife's imperious temper, and in 1787 he confessed to the King that he regretted his marriage.[38] The details of the estrangement between the Duke and his wife do not appear in Walpole's journals and there is little about it in his correspondence. He could not admit to posterity that his niece was a shrew who had made her husband unhappy.

Any man who undertakes to write memoirs must reveal more about himself than he does of other people. Walpole's memoirs are a record of his enmities and feuds: for his friendships we must go to his correspondence. His portrait of George III is interesting, not for what it tells of the King, but for what it tells of Walpole.

[38] Brooke, *King George III*, p. 281.

XIV

James Sharp: Common Councillor of London in the Time of Wilkes

THE importance of the City of London in the politics of the eighteenth century is well known, and much has been written to explain the causes and character of London radicalism. A primary difficulty, however, in studying the affairs of London has so far been the lack of personal records of those participating in them. The City itself has preserved excellent archives, but very few even of the leading City politicians have left any private papers behind them. An exception is James Sharp, by profession an ironmonger in Leadenhall Street, and a member of the Common Council of London from 1765 to 1783: though even in his case, his activities are illuminated as much by the correspondence of his brothers and sisters as by the surviving letters he wrote or received. One of the most interesting items in Sharp's surviving papers is a report of two long conversations with George III in 1770, parts of which are reproduced below.[1]

James Sharp was one of the five sons of Thomas Sharp, Archdeacon of Northumberland, and a grandson of John Sharp, Archbishop of York. Since the Archdeacon could only afford to provide a university education for his two eldest sons, the three younger were apprenticed in London, William becoming a surgeon, James an ironmonger, and the most famous of them, Granville, starting out as a draper before becoming a clerk in the Office of Ordnance. The three brothers in London always acted as a unity, and in considering the remarkable career of Granville Sharp one must remember how dependent he was throughout most of his career upon the encouragement and financial support of William and James. When, with the out-

---

[1] The Sharp MSS. are owned by Miss Lloyd-Baker of Hardwicke Court, Gloucester, and I am much indebted to her for permission to use them.

break of the American Revolution, Granville felt that he would
have to give up his post in the Ordnance, James and William
hastened to reassure him about the future. On 5 October 1775,
while Granville was in Northumberland on leave of absence,
James wrote to him from London:

We very much approve, *here*, of your asking a farther leave of
absence. It will give you a little leisure, which you so very much
want; and it will let you have a little enjoyment of the friends you
see so seldom; and, above all, it may give some chance for a turn
in public affairs; and of this I do not at all despair; but if it should
be otherwise, and you should think it proper to give up your
employment—I will now speak for my brother William as well as
for myself—we are both ready and willing, and, God be thanked,
at present *able*, to take care that the loss shall be none to you; and
all that we have to ask in return is, that you would continue to live
amongst us as you have hitherto done, without imagining that you
will, in such a situation, be burthernsome to us, and also without
supposing that it will then be your duty to seek employment in some
other way of life; for, if we have the needful amongst us, it matters
not to whom it belongs—the happiness of being together is worth
the expense, if it answered no farther purpose. But I will go farther,
I have no doubt but the mutual assistance we are of to each other,
and the consequence we acquire by it, is more than adequate to
any third employment we might reasonably hope could be obtained;
and, in case of the death of either party, much more would be lost
to the family by your absence than perhaps might be produced by
other means.[2]

James had already been directly involved in Granville's
struggle against slavery in England, and he pressed his brother's
argument upon that wealthy slave-owner, Alderman William
Beckford, who before he died acknowledged that there could
be no slave property in England.[3] Similarly, it was no doubt
because William Sharp had been an assistant surgeon at St.
Bartholomew's Hospital that James became a governor of that
institution.[4] William and Granville for their part put their own
money into James's business.[5]

[2] Prince Hoare, *Memoirs of Granville Sharp* (2nd edn., 2 vols., 1828), i. 189–90.
[3] G. Sharp to Alleyne, 1772 (Sharp MSS.).
[4] Journal of St. Bartholomew's Hospital, 12, 15, 19 Jan. 1779; Benefactors
Book, 19 Jan. 1779 (both in possession of St. Bartholomew's Hospital).
[5] G. Sharp to John Sharp, 3 Nov. 1783 (Sharp MSS.).

James Sharp had been born in Durham on 14 January 1730/1, and baptized in the cathedral on 2 February.[6] Nothing is known about his education, but he may have briefly attended Durham School. In 1746 he was brought to London and apprenticed to Samuel Southouse, of the firm of Southouse & Chapman, ironmongers in Leadenhall Street.[7] Southouse was a member of the Drapers' Company. The business was situated at 15 Leadenhall Street, next door to the East India Company's headquarters. James served out his apprenticeship and got his freedom in 1755. In 1759 he bought a partnership for £1,000, the money being provided as a loan by his cousin, Mrs. Elizabeth Prowse, wife of Thomas Prowse, M.P. for Somerset. His former masters in fact retired, and he became ultimately the sole owner of the business, and eventually built himself a new house there.[8] His sister Elizabeth was his housekeeper until she married in 1762.[9] In 1764 James married Catherine Lodge, daughter of John Lodge, packer in St. Helen's, Bishopsgate Street. Announcing his intention of marrying Miss Lodge, if she would have him, he wrote:

> The thought of this has occasioned me to look more narrowly into my circumstances and I have the happyness to find them such that I need not be afraid to sett out with my coach and live in such a manner as will be agreeable to me; making my grand point in view, the continuation of our present happyness in one another, for what do we now enjoy that have not been the effects of our mutual affections and assistance of each other! and while this continues amongst us what can hurt us?—In every respect Miss Lodge seems to be a person that will continue those blessings to us as well in publick as amongst ourselves, and should I meet with success I think I bid fair for being made the happyest man living.[10]

The following year William Sharp married Catherine Barwick (daughter of Thomas Barwick, merchant of Friday Street), whose brother was already married to Mrs. James Sharp's sister. As so often in the history of the Sharp family, marriages strengthened existing connections. From the financial point of

6 Family Bible at Hardwicke Court.
7 Elizabeth Prowse's Family Chronicle (Sharp MSS.).
8 A plan of this house is among the Sharp MSS.
9 Elizabeth Prowse's Family Chronicle.
10 James Sharp to John Sharp, 23 Feb. 1764 (Sharp MSS.).

view, James Sharp's marriage was presumably not profitable in the long run because that branch of the Lodge family went bankrupt, but it was certainly a very happy marriage. There were two children: John, who died young, and Catherine.

James Sharp's business interests can be discovered from the catalogues which he issued.[11] His trade, at least before the American Revolution, as he told George III in 1770, was chiefly to America and the West Indies. The King, knowing that New York had decided to import from Great Britain again, asked if he were not therefore full of business.

J.S. Not more so than usual. Indeed I have had as much business as I could well manage ever since the late war; and I do not trade so far to the north as New York or Boston.
K. I suppose the American trade is a very great trade?
J.S. It is a great trade indeed; tho' it had been the opinion of many it would not be found of much use to England, because it produced nothing but what England did, and it proved so for some time, till the bounty upon corn was taken off which att once releivd our poor manufacturers at home, and opend a return from America which had never been thought of before; corn being sent from America to Spain and Portugal which is now remitted in hard money to England, and will continue unless an unatural bounty should ever again be putt upon corn, in trade I believe either bounty's or restrictions are generaly wrong.
K. My ideas of trade are that in the first place strict justice should be persued, and freedom in trade incouraged as much as possible—but when once a plan is adopted it ought never to be broke through.[12]

James Sharp's catalogues show that he concentrated on the production of agricultural machinery, and sold a remarkable variety of goods. For example, he manufactured many types of plough: a drill plough, a turnwrest or Kentish plough, Mr. Ducket's trenching plough, Mr. Arbuthnot's draining plough. His manufactory was at 133 Tooley Street in Southwark, where apparently forty men were regularly employed.[13] Late in his career he patented an improved version of the Franklin

[11] A collection of these catalogues survives in the Sharp MSS.; the British Museum has an excellent specimen.
[12] Conversations with George III, pp. 16–17 (Sharp MSS.).
[13] James Sharp obtained protection from impressment for forty men at Tooley Street during the American War (P.R.O., Adm. 7/373).

stove.[14] In his autobiography Franklin wrote that he himself had declined to patent his invention, and added: 'An Ironmonger in London, however, after assuming a good deal of my Pamphlet, and working it up into his own, and making some small Changes in the Machine, which rather hurt its Operation, got a Patent for it there, and made as I was told a little Fortune by it.'[15] Franklin is almost certainly referring to James Sharp, but is also exaggerating. The Franklin stove was invented in 1739–40. James Sharp took out his patent in 1781, but could hardly have made a fortune in the two years before his death. His stoves certainly had some success: they were used, for example, in a number of public buildings, such as the Common Council Room in Guildhall and Drapers' Hall. The other major business adventure of James Sharp was the manufacture of what he called 'rolling carts and wagons'—vehicles on which wheels were replaced by rollers which would smooth out the ruts in the terrible eighteenth-century roads.[16]

Despite the American war, James Sharp's business remained prosperous. Although his trade had been mostly to America and the West Indies, his family found that there were few bad debts which could not be collected.[17] Occasional references can be found in the accounts of public bodies to the purchase of substantial quantities of goods from James Sharp: the East India Company purchased from him, and so did the Thames Navigation Committee of the Common Council and the Oxford Canal. No general estimate, however, is possible of the extent of his trade.

James Sharp worked hard and successfully at his business career, but he also found time for relaxation. All the Sharp family were keen musicians and their concerts were among the

[14] B. Woodcroft, *Alphabetical Index of Patentees of Inventions* (1854); James Sharp, *An Account of the Principle and Effects of the Air Stove-Grates* (10th edn., n.d.), copy in the British Museum. Various editions, with slightly different titles, are in the Sharp MSS.: some are in both French and English.

[15] L. W. Labaree, R. L. Ketcham *et al.* (ed.), *The Autobiography of Benjamin Franklin* (New Haven, Conn., and London, 1964), p. 192.

[16] For these also he produced printed advertisements (copy in the British Museum). On the general controversy on wagon wheels see S. and B. Webb, *The Story of the King's Highway* (1963), pp. 83–4. James Sharp was also responsible for making the iron brazier on Brizlee Tower at Alnwick.

[17] G. Sharp to John Sharp, 3 Nov. 1783 (Sharp MSS.); one bad debt is recorded in G. Sharp to J. Coles, 30 June 1797 (P.R.O., T. 79/21).

chief musical events of London life. By the 1780s the Sunday concerts—held alternately at James's house in Leadenhall Street and William's house in the Old Jewry—had become very large affairs indeed. A record survives of those who attended William's concerts between 1773 and 1783. Performers and guests numbered usually about ninety, but on two occasions more than 320 people were present. Most of the best professional musicians of the day were glad to play at these concerts. The family concerts had begun when the brothers first settled in London; from the same early period dates the family habit of voyaging on the Thames. They had two boats in the 1750s: the *Apollo* and the *Griffin*. In 1771 the *Proa* was built, and the *Union Yacht* was added in 1777. All the boats—like the music and the musical instruments—were owned by the brothers collectively. It was the musical 'water-schemes' which attracted the notice of George III, and led no doubt to the monarch's willingness to see James Sharp at a personal interview. The basic reason for the two meetings with the King which James records was the improvement of the river Thames, but George III was probably more interested in the Sharps' music:

The King.   Pray which of your brothers plays upon the two flutes?
J.S.   My youngest brother Granville . . .
K.   Dont you think he has a very fine voice, tell me impartialy dont you think he has the best voice in England? Speak impartialy now.
J.S.   He is my brother. I cant help being partial. I realy think he has.
K.   What instrument do you play?
J.S.   I play the serpent, may it please your Majesty.
K.   Oh—tis you that play the serpent is it? I admire it much. What sort of mouth peice do you use?
J.S.   It is of the shape of the trumpett mouth peice only bigger. I will shew your Majesty (pulling it out and presenting it to him, which he took into his hand).
K.   I fancy you will think me very singular in musick, for I love the trumpett the most of any instrument whatever. I wonder they are so little used in concert.
J.S.   Your Majesty shews great judgement in this, for the trumpett is certainly one of the finest instruments in the world; the dissuse of it arises from the great labour in blowing it, and the great practice necessary for a good performer

K.   Do you play any other instrument than the serpent?

J.S.   I have formerly play'd the bassoon and the French horn, but the serpent being of most use generaly I keep to that.[18]

In Zoffany's famous picture of the Sharp family on their barge on the Thames, painted in 1779 and 1780, James Sharp is holding his serpent. William Shields, the composer, records his surprise at James's ability to play the 'cello part in trios on that instrument.[19]

K.   I am very fond of old musick, particularly of Corelli. I don't like the present compositions. They are too quick and hurrying. Don't you think so?

J.S.   The present style of musick is certainly of a very rapid kind, but we have many fine compositions mixed with those movements. Your Majesty mentions Corelli's musick, my brother with his flutes can play the first and second fiddle parts of all Corelli's sonatas.

K.   Both att once?

J.S.   Yes.

K.   That's very extraordinary . . .

They then discussed church music and the way in which the services were performed in the Chapel Royal and in St. Paul's Cathedral:

K.   I am surprized to see so few subscribers to Dr Boyce's publication of anthems—it is the finest work I have ever seen—and I am told their [*sic*] are many choirs have not subscribed.

J.S.   I have been informed upwards of eleven choirs have not subscrib'd, tho' it is not only the most usefull but the noblest thing of the kind that has ever been done.

The King was also interested in the boats, for some points in the design of which James Sharp was himself responsible. He had seen the house on top of one of the barges hastily extended during a sudden shower:

K.   I like the contrivance in your own barge of lengthening out the house. How came you to think of such a thing?

J.S.   Necessity obliged us to have something of this kind; for our musick has the best effect in the open air; and it was not possible

---

[18] Conversations with George III, pp. 11–13.

[19] The picture is reproduced in E. C. P. Lascelles, *Granville Sharp and the Freedom of Slaves in England* (1928), opp. p. 122. William Shields is quoted in P. Hoare, *Memoirs of Granville Sharp*, ii, Appendix, xix.

to remove the harpsicord and instruments so soon as was necessary in hasty showers, but this contrivance answers our purpose extreamly well.[20]

The musical talents of the Sharps were hereditary, and Catherine, James's daughter, from her earliest years took part in the family concerts. She told a cousin, who described her musical powers as of the highest order, that at four or five years old she was placed on a table to sing to the Duke of York, and one song was always required of her at each concert, which destroyed the pleasure of the evening for her. Her cousin added: 'Few ever had the power of giving so much pleasure in that way—I shall never forget her rich, clear voice and the exquisite taste of her performance vocal and instrumental—often extempore.'[21]

The Sharp family tended to regard their chief barge as a kind of substitute country-house. When the *Union Yacht* was sold in 1786 Christie 'happily said of it, that it comprehended all the advantages of the most finished country villa, besides many which were peculiar to itself. It had all the accommodations of a house, and was free from the inconveniences of bad neighbourhood, for its site could be changed at pleasure; it had not only the richest, but also the most various prospects; and it was a villa free from house-duty and window lights; it paid neither church tythe nor poor's rate; it was free both from government and parochial taxes; and it not only had a command of wood and water, but possessed the most extensive fishery of any house in England.'[22]

The ironmonger's business in Leadenhall Street, taken over by James Sharp, was in the parish of St. Andrew Undershaft, on the vestry of which in later life James occasionally played his part, and in the ward of Lime Street, at the wardmote of which James produced a copy of his freedom on 6 January 1757.[23] Samuel Southouse was a member of the Common Council of London for over twenty years and his apprentice must inevitably have become familiar with City politics long

[20] Conversations with George III, pp. 14, 29–30.

[21] 'Reminiscences of Barwick Lloyd Baker' at Hardwicke Court.

[22] Newspaper cutting in the Sharp MSS.

[23] Vestry Minute Books of St. Andrew Undershaft (Guildhall Library, MS. 4118/3); Lime Street Ward Wardmote Inquest Minute Book (ibid., MS.1169/1).

before he felt able to take an active part in them. James Sharp was elected to the Common Council in December 1765 and remained a member until his death in 1783. The only evidence available suggests that he was popular with his constituents.[24] As far as the ward of Lime Street was concerned, James Sharp appears only infrequently in its surviving records, apart from his annual election to the Common Council. In 1771 the ward presented an address to the imprisoned Lord Mayor, Brass Crosby, and to Alderman Oliver, who had defied the House of Commons on the question of the printing of its debates. This address was written by Granville Sharp.[25] In 1780, just before the Gordon Riots, James persuaded his ward to adopt his views on the Catholic question, which he probably himself took over from Granville. Neither of the Sharps wished Catholics to be persecuted, but they maintained that the Catholic Relief Act of 1778 had been wrong in two respects: in allowing to Catholics the establishment of seminaries and the purchase of land. The views of Lime Street ward were adopted by the Common Council. When the Gordon Riots broke out the ward organized itself for self-protection and James played a full part in that organization.[26]

On the Common Council itself James Sharp did his full share of the work. He served on many committees, both standing committees and special committees. There is no point in listing in detail his multifarious committee appointments, since only occasionally is it possible to trace the influence of an individual in committee work. James was, for example, on the committee appointed in March 1771 to support the imprisoned Crosby and Oliver, but no information appears to be available as to his personal attitudes to its activities. On the other hand, he was on the committee to celebrate the acquittal of Admiral Keppel in 1779 and dined with the Admiral—but it is no surprise to find that the 'grand band of martial musick on horseback' was provided by James Sharp.[27] He was consistently

[24] See the voting figures at the election of 21 Dec. 1769 (Guildhall Library, MS. 1169/1).

[25] Lime Street Ward Wardmote Inquest Minute Book, 21 Dec. 1771 (ibid., MS. 1169/1); P. Hoare, *Memoirs of Granville Sharp*, ii, Appendix, x–xii.

[26] Lime Street Ward Wardmote Inquest Minute Book (Guildhall Library, MS. 1169/2); G. Rudé, *Hanoverian London, 1714–1808* (1971), p. 179.

[27] Journal of the Common Council, 67, fos. 209–12 (Corporation of London Record Office).

on the radical side in City politics, which could not have been predicted from his conservative and clerical background. The poll-book of the general election of 1768 in London shows that James Sharp voted for Sir Robert Ladbroke, William Beckford, and Barlow Trecothick: since he could have voted for four candidates, it was therefore a matter of deliberate choice that he avoided voting for a court candidate; nor did he vote for John Wilkes—but, after all, Wilkes was not yet the symbol of the radical movement. In the preliminaries of the election of Lord Mayor in 1771, James was asked to take the chair at a meeting in support of James Townsend and John Sawbridge, being described as 'an ironmonger, (a Gentleman well known and much esteemed in the city)', but modestly declined the honour. In the succeeding elections of chief magistrate he voted for Wilkes and Townsend.[28] In the parliamentary by-election of 1781 he voted for Sir Watkin Lewes.[29] Similarly, when his attitudes to the exciting events within the Common Council can be ascertained during both the Wilkes and Wyvill periods of radicalism, he is always found on the radical side. He voted on 5 May 1769 for the summoning of a Common Hall on the decision of the House of Commons to seat Luttrell in place of Wilkes. He voted again on 1 March 1770 for the summoning of another Common Hall. He voted and spoke for the Remonstrance which the Common Council adopted on 14 May 1770, calling upon the King to dissolve Parliament and to dismiss his ministers, and indeed was on the committee which drew it up and on the committee appointed to present it.[30] When James Sharp saw the King on 15 September 1770, the King made some remark to the effect that if he showed himself in favour of the canal which the City was supporting, the canal would be opposed. James at once asserted: 'I have great reason to believe, nay I can take upon me to say that I am very sure the City of London will rejoice to do every thing in their power, that may any way contribute to your Majestys pleasure or convenience provided it does not interfere with the publick

[28] *The Poll of the Livery of London . . . March . . . 1768* (2nd edn., n.d.); newspaper cutting, dated Sept. 1771, in material relating to William Nash in the Noble Collection at the Guildhall Library (C. 78); *A list of the persons who have polled for Messieurs Wilkes and Townsend* (Guildhall Library).

[29] Guildhall Library, MS. 1583, vol. 2, p. 2.

[30] *Public Advertiser*, 8 May 1769, 5 March, 16 May 1770.

8223781 U

good.'[31] Meeting James Sharp appears to have slightly softened the attitude of the King towards the City; at any rate George III talked about how pleased he was with the music of the Sharps on the river, and described James 'as a very sensible clever man, and sayd he did not think that there had been such a worthy sensible man, among the citizens of London, but then sayd, he is a *bill of Rights man* with the Address, yet he is satisfyed he did it from principle, and does not take it amiss.' Another Remonstrance, however, was adopted on 15 November 1770. James Sharp again was on the committee which drew it up and was among those who presented it to the King; it was noticed that the King 'changed countenance' when James came to kiss hands.[32]

Since the bulk of James Sharp's trade was with America and the West Indies, he could hardly fail to be deeply concerned at the outbreak of the American war. He was almost certainly the 'Mr. Sharp' who attended and spoke at the meetings of American merchants in January 1775.[33] He was responsible for moving resolutions on 21 February 1775 in the Common Council against the Intolerable Acts.[34] In 1778 he spoke in the Common Council in support of an address for conciliation with the colonies.[35] When the Wyvill movement got under way, he became a member of the City Committee of Correspondence, and afterwards of the Livery Committee of Correspondence. At Granville's insistence he persuaded the City Committee to stand by the principle of annual parliaments and reject triennial parliaments.[36]

For many years James Sharp's chief interest in City affairs was in the development of communications. His interest in communications had already been shown in his propagation of 'rolling carts and wagons'. It was also shown in his devotion to the improvement of the Thames and the construction of canals. When the Common Council took note of attendances at its committees in 1781, James Sharp had attended no meet-

---

[31] Conversations with George III, p. 3.
[32] Elizabeth Prowse's Family Chronicle, quoting letters of Thomas Sharp.
[33] *Public Advertiser*, 13 Jan., 10 Feb. 1775.
[34] Memorandum of Granville Sharp, containing notes on a volume of City petitions (Sharp MSS.).
[35] *St. James's Chronicle*, 3–5 March 1778.
[36] I. R. Christie, *Wilkes, Wyvill and Reform* (1962), pp. 109–10.

ing of the Commissioners of Sewers out of forty-one, no meeting
of the committee on imprisonment, five out of thirteen meetings
of the City Committee of Correspondence; but he had attended
all twelve meetings of the Thames Navigation Committee.[37]
The Thames Navigation Committee had been set up in 1770,
largely as a result of James Sharp's own efforts.[38] Originally its
plans had been ambitious. Canals were virtually to replace the
Thames. One canal was to be built from Reading to Monkey
Island; another was to be built from Monkey Island to Isle-
worth. Various links were to be established between these canals
and the Thames. James Sharp also believed that a canal should
be built from Moorfields to Waltham Abbey on the river Lea.
To further the building of canals James Sharp published two
pamphlets: *An Address to the Right Honourable the Lord Mayor . . .
on the Importance and Great Utility of Canals in General* (1774) and
*Extracts from Mr. Young's Six Months Tour through the North of
England* (1774). But the more ambitious schemes fell to the
ground, and the City was restricted in its jurisdiction to the
Thames below Staines. The Thames Navigation Committee
therefore concentrated on three tasks: the purchase of private
tolls in order to establish a single, moderate toll, the construction
of an uninterrupted towing-path (which included preserving
the banks of the river by the use of wooden piling), and the
dredging of the river to deepen and narrow the channel. In
these more modest tasks, James Sharp was as active as he had
been in the more ambitious original schemes. He still, however,
remained a believer in the benefits of canals, and took an eager
interest in their construction all over England: he was particularly involved in the affairs of the Oxford Canal, of which he
was an original shareholder.[39]

The development of canals brought together James Sharp's
three major interests: the pleasures of travelling by water, of
playing music, and of helping in the development of communications. It is no surprise to find the Thames Navigation
Committee frequently on the water in their own barge, but

[37] Journal of the Common Council, 68, fos. 113–19 (Corporation of London
Record Office).
[38] The minute books of the Thames Navigation Committee are in the possession of the Port of London Authority.
[39] Committee Minute Books of the Oxford Canal (British Transport Historical
Records).

accompanied by the Sharp family on the *Union Yacht*. And, of course, there was music. As canals began to be constructed all over England, the Sharp family began to take holidays on them. The ever-ingenious James Sharp had a 'house' constructed which he could carry on his post-chaise and attach to any coal barge on any canal he wished to explore. The most extensive of the Sharps' canal trips appears to have been undertaken in 1774. Eight brothers and sisters and James's daughter, Catherine, went on it. The total distance they travelled was 454 miles, of which 170 were on land and 284 on water.[40]

In August 1783, while still as full of activity as ever, James Sharp was struck down by a 'paralytic disorder'. Granville Sharp took over his business concerns, and James was taken to Weymouth. But his health got no better, and he disliked being separated from his brothers and sisters, so that he began to long to return to London. Granville and William met him on the road and brought him back to Leadenhall Street. He was so weak that Granville had to carry him into the house. Three days later, on 5 November, he died. On 12 November he was buried in St. Andrew Undershaft: 'A very full congregation' and 'the funeral psalm solemnly performed' by Dr. John Worgan.[41]

[40] Elizabeth Prowse's Family Chronicle.
[41] Diary of Granville Sharp (Sharp MSS.).

XV

Johnson and Burke

In the spring of 1783 Dr. Johnson gave some serious advice to his friend Edmund Burke. At least it was almost certainly to Burke, although the editors of the *Life of Johnson* and not Boswell himself supplied the name. Burke perfectly fits the passage in which the advice occurs. He was in office in 1783 and under fierce attack. He offered to resign if the House of Commons condemned his official acts, and for many good reasons he must have longed to do so. The harassments he had been enduring since the death of Lord Rockingham in the previous summer had all but distracted him.

A gentleman [says Boswell's discreet passage] talked of retiring. 'Never think of that,' said Johnson. The gentleman urged, 'I should then do no ill.' JOHNSON. 'Nor no good either. Sir, it would be a civil suicide.'[1]

If the gentleman was Burke, it was obviously sound advice. In 1783 Burke was still in his early fifties, almost in the middle of his career. He had been in Parliament for seventeen years and was to remain there for eleven more. His reputation was still high, in spite of many vocal opponents; the period of his greatest influence—during the French Revolution—was still ahead. It would have been a major blunder to retire at just that time.

Still, it is interesting that Johnson was the man who gave the sound advice—because about twenty years before, when *he* was in his early fifties, he had made a choice of his own which was one of the most questionable acts of his life. It was when he

[1] *Boswell's Life of Johnson*, ed. G. Birkbeck Hill, rev. and enl. L. F. Powell (6 vols., Oxford, 1934–50), iv. 223. Boswell does not date this passage, except by placing it immediately after an entry for 17 May 1783; it probably belongs to the period between 24 and 28 May for which his Journal fails entirely. In the Commons debate of 2 May, Burke had defended his reinstatement of the Pay Office clerks John Powell and Charles Bembridge. He returned to the defence on 19 and 21 May.

was harassed and almost distracted by the pressures of his own career. A small pension which was offered to him at the age of fifty-two gave him for the first time the chance of a kind of half-retirement. Johnson took that chance. Whether he later thought of his choice as a 'civil suicide' one cannot, of course, be sure, but there is no doubt that he was deeply unhappy in the years that immediately followed. He, like posterity, must have made some comparisons between his literary productivity before and after he took the pension. In the fifteen years before, he had worked as few men of letters have ever worked. He had proposed, planned, and published his *Dictionary*, done most of his edition of Shakespeare, brought out the *Rambler*, the *Idler*, *Rasselas*, *The Vanity of Human Wishes*, and his usual large number of prefaces, dedications, sermons, essays, brief lives, and book reviews. He had shown what Samuel Johnson performing at full strength could do as an active writer. Small wonder if such a harvest had left even him exhausted! But in some curious way it had, and he was in a mood for retreat. For the time, he wanted ease more than glory. In the fifteen years *after* the pension, the record is rather different. He produced what for most men would be a creditable list of publications, but it was a few pamphlets, the Shakespeare edition (completed under a real threat of public censure), some poems, a book of travels, a few book reviews, and the usual miscellanea. For Johnson in the prime of life—his fifties and early sixties—that was almost inactivity. His main occupation, once he had the pension, turned out to be talking. He met Boswell and knew he had found an ideal reporter; he went to live with the Thrales, took frequent vacations, did what was for him a remarkable amount of travelling, blamed himself for his idleness—but did not regain the momentum of his early career. Until the late 1770s, with the *Lives of the Poets*, he made no major use of his literary powers. The King himself, when the occasion offered, urged him to return to serious writing. Johnson fully appreciated the compliment implied, and made a clear promise;[2] but it took him nearly a decade to get himself back into harness.

[2] As Boswell relates it, the famous interview in the King's library in February 1767 ended with a request and a promise: 'His Majesty expressed a desire to have the literary biography of this country ably executed, and proposed to Dr. Johnson to undertake it. Johnson signified his readiness to comply with his Majesty's wishes' (*Life of Johnson*, ii. 40).

Now every reader of Boswell should be extremely grateful for just this state of affairs. We would not have the *Life of Johnson* in its present fullness without those later years of inactivity. We would not have Mrs. Piozzi's *Anecdotes*, or some of the most interesting entries in Fanny Burney's *Diary*, or half the other glimpses of Johnson in the journals and memoirs of his time. For us it is ideal that, having shown his full strength and nearly killed himself under the strains of his early days, he was able to lie back and digest the experience of his life and pour it out for us in the years of talk.

But could Johnson himself see things in this encouraging way? He was conscious of his powers, and had a most religious sense of his duty to use them. He knew the appalling state of the world, and how much it needed the help of its natural leaders. He knew how few men there were in England or in Europe who were his intellectual peers, and that in a sense he was turning his back on their world of public action. Surely fifty-two is early for a great cultural hero to take himself out of the battle! He blamed his own sloth—read sporadically—talked in private companies—ate some good dinners and enjoyed society. This is not the life to which heaven is promised.

It is, of course, easy to overstate his perversity. Johnson probably made no single deliberate decision to retire and write less. He only let himself drift into a particular state of mind. The pension was granted in 1762; perhaps four or five years passed before he and his friends fully realized how great its effects were to be. In the spring of 1766 Goldsmith and Boswell were still assuming that nothing was radically changed. They wondered at any shift in the Doctor's normal habits. Why, Goldsmith complained, did he now go less often to the theatre?

'You give yourself [he said] no more concern about a new play, than if you had never had any thing to do with the stage.' JOHNSON. 'Why, Sir, our tastes greatly alter. The lad does not care for the child's rattle, and the old man does not care for the young man's whore. . . . as we advance in the journey of life, we drop some of the things which have pleased us; whether it be that we are fatigued and don't choose to carry so many things any farther, or that we find other things which we like better.' BOSWELL. 'But, Sir, why don't you give us something in some other way?' GOLDSMITH. 'Ay, Sir, we have a claim upon you.' JOHNSON. 'No, Sir, I am not obliged to do any more. No man is obliged to do as much as he can do. A man is to have a part of his life to himself. If a soldier has fought a good many campaigns, he is not to be blamed if he retires to ease and tranquillity. A physician, who has practised long in a great city, may be excused if he retires to a small town, and takes less practice. Now, Sir, the good I can do by my conversation bears the same proportion to the good I can do by my writings, that the practice of a physician, retired to a small town, does to his practice in a great city.' BOSWELL. 'But I wonder, Sir, you have not more pleasure in writing than in not writing.' JOHNSON. 'Sir, you *may* wonder.'[3]

Johnson was fifty-six at the time of that conversation. He was to live on to seventy-five.

His *invalide* existence, if that is what it should be called—in any event his existence withdrawn from the main fields of exertion—is the chief fact to remember in any discussion of Johnson's relations with Burke. For most of the period of their friendship Burke was *in the world* and Johnson half out of it. Indeed Burke came on to the national stage at almost exactly the time when Johnson was acknowledging the extent of his own withdrawal from it. Burke entered the House of Commons in January 1766, at the age of thirty-seven. Until that time he had been immensely hard-working, had impressed a few friends and a widening circle of acquaintances, but he was a relatively obscure figure. His first session was meteoric. As Johnson himself expressed it, he 'gained more reputation than perhaps any man at his ⟨first⟩ appearance ever gained before. He made two speeches in the house for repealing the Stamp-act, which were publickly commended by Mr. Pit, and have filled the town with wonder.' Burke, he added, was a 'great man by Nature, and is expected soon to attain civil greatness'.[4]

For once the Doctor erred on the side of optimism. Burke was to hold a leading place in the House of Commons for nearly three decades, but he never reached 'civil greatness' if that meant a peerage or a seat in the Cabinet; the post of Pay-master-General was the highest he ever held. And in time he, like Johnson, was to grow sick of the battle and ready for retreat. But that—in the 1760s—was still far ahead, and mostly

[3] *Life of Johnson*, ii. 14–15.
[4] *The Letters of Samuel Johnson*, ed. R. W. Chapman (3 vols., Oxford, 1952), i. 185.

beyond Johnson's death. In the first part of his parliamentary career Burke had as much success and applause as a realistic statesman had a right to expect. Johnson, well placed on the side-lines, could watch his Eminent Friend lead the kind of full committed life that he himself had resigned.

He was not long in finding that Burke was in one respect a kindred spirit. He enjoyed 'good talk' in private company more than almost anything else. The two men became famous rivals. When they met, at the Club, or in the Thrales' library, or in other social settings, they were expected to square off for a conversational contest. The other persons present, who may have come with some hope of talking themselves, accepted the humbler fate of being an attentive audience. As Johnson described one occasion when he and Burke began talking around midnight: '. . . the Ladies listened . . . and said, as I heard, *there is no rising unless somebody will cry fire.*'[5]

The rivalry, which all agreed was close, never becomes very real in the pages of the *Life of Johnson*. It is one of the few disappointments of that magnificent work. The book, of course, is about Johnson, and understandably Boswell does not present Burke at full length. We are told he is Johnson's Mighty Opposite; we do not learn it first hand. Johnson himself we see in action hundreds of times, tossing and goring all conceivable opponents with a marvellous variety of fighting styles. He wins every bout, and most of us close the book convinced that he was the greatest talker that ever lived. When we have experienced all this first hand, it is not enough for Boswell to *say* that in certain other encounters, which took place off stage, Burke was a worthy antagonist and ran Johnson hard. We do not see him run Johnson hard, and the only Burke we meet does not look as if he could. He seldom talks at all, and the few sayings of his we are given hardly demonstrate powers much above the mediocre.

Well, this is an artistic problem of the *Life of Johnson*, and it is not easy to see how Boswell could have solved it. At the time his book was published few readers had to be told of Edmund Burke's powers. Even his enemies granted him genius, however deranged. The *Reflections* had been out six months, being eagerly debated, and the famous break with Fox in the Commons came in the same month as Boswell's book. Burke was

[5] Ibid. ii. 359.

one of the most conspicuous persons in England, or even in Europe, in May 1791.

His conversational style was not much like Johnson's, and perhaps it was bound to be less vividly recorded. As Coleridge explained the matter half a century later:

> Dr. Johnson's fame now rests principally on Boswell. It is impossible not to be amused by such a book. But his *bow-wow* manner must have had a good deal to do with the effect produced; for no one, I suppose, will set Johnson before Burke, and Burke was a great and universal talker; yet now we hear nothing of this, except by some chance remarks in Boswell. The fact is, Burke, like all men of genius who love to talk at all, was very discursive and continuous; hence he is not reported; he seldom said the sharp short things that Johnson almost always did, which produce a more decided effect at the moment, and which are so much more easy to carry off.[6]

Contemporaries who heard the two champions were never perfectly sure which one deserved the palm. Burke had some partisans among the most competent judges. Goldsmith argued for him (with certainly little hope of changing Boswell's mind). Langton after one performance complained that Johnson talked too much: he would rather have heard more from Burke.[7] Sir Joshua, according to Northcote, when praising Burke's abilities, said he thought 'even Dr. Johnson felt himself his inferior'.[8]

It is obviously too late now to settle the question of precedence. If Johnson really did feel inferior, it must have been extremely hard on his peace of mind. Every reader knows the Doctor's competitive theory of 'talk'. In his view it was always a contest, which somebody had to win. As he told Boswell, '. . . it cannot be but one or other will come off superiour. I do not mean that the victor must have the better of the argument, for he may take the weak side; but his superiority of parts and knowledge will necessarily appear . . .'[9]

That was not an easy ethic to live by if you argued with Edmund Burke. Indeed, it was not a very sensible one for Johnson to maintain. Surely, it is more important for conversation to excite and delight its audience than for it to demonstrate

---

[6] *The Table Talk and Omniana of Samuel Taylor Coleridge*, ed. T. Ashe (1896), p. 239.

[7] *Life of Johnson*, ii. 260; iv. 26–7.

[8] James Northcote, *Life of Sir Joshua Reynolds* (2nd edn., 2 vols., 1818), ii. 211.

[9] *Life of Johnson*, ii. 444.

anyone's personal ascendancy; and to tell the truth, Johnson's own special excellence was of a rather undisciplined kind. What he sometimes lacked in knowledge or even in cogency, he easily made up in wit, drama, vigour, unexpectedness, and personal style. With any normal audience he had no reason to fear comparison with Burke or with anyone else. Perhaps Socrates, who had Plato for his Boswell, might have vanquished him, but it is hard to think of others. For Johnson to insist that nothing mattered but 'parts and knowledge' was to throw away his aces. In 'parts and knowledge' Burke was at *his* best, and serious controversy was the business of his life. It was no accident that in the great national struggles which tore political Britain in the late eighteenth century—over taxing America, over governing India, over the principles of the French Revolution—Burke in all three cases held centre stage. He was also an Opposition statesman, which meant that he had infinite practice in marshalling his facts and reasons under the least favouring conditions of public debate. For Burke, to move from the House of Commons to the relative calm of a private argument, even with Johnson, was almost relaxation. It must be remembered, too, that he was the younger man by twenty years.

Still, Johnson had to do things his own way. He habitually 'talked for victory', and sometimes pretty unscrupulously, in the opinion of his friends. As Goldsmith put it, he was for making a monarchy of what should be a republic; and in the unavoidable struggles, if his pistol missed fire, he knocked you down with the butt end of it.[10]

Some have gone so far as to suggest that Johnson's competitive habit was in fact something more than a habit: was a kind of mental compulsion, of which he himself might have been only partly aware. One of the most devoted of modern Johnsonians was willing to accept this hypothesis after he had tried the experiment of taking Johnson to a psychiatrist (that is, after he—the Johnsonian—had spent several hours with a specialist, pouring out for him a vast number of facts about Johnson's early life, feelings, and problems).[11] The specialist rose to the

[10] Ibid. 257; iv. 274.
[11] Mr. Herman Liebert, now the Editorial Chairman of the *Yale Edition of the Works of Samuel Johnson*, made this interesting experiment several years ago. It is discussed briefly in his essay 'Reflections on Samuel Johnson: Two Recent Books and Where They Lead', *Journal of English and Germanic Philology*, xlvii (1948), 84–6.

occasion and offered a diagnosis. Was not Johnson driven by a
need for compensation? In his childhood he must have felt a
good deal of shame and resentment at having so ugly, diseased,
and awkward a body. What more natural than to find his
remedy in exalting the powers of his mind? Once such a pattern
of compensation was established in his psychic system, he really
would have to win all his arguments, for he was always (unconsciously) proving something to himself. 'Talking for victory'
was then not merely a matter of bad manners or of intellectual arrogance; it was the working out of a deep psychological
need.

One passage in the *Life of Johnson* should have attracted the
attention of these two enthusiasts. It is a somewhat oblique
passage, for Boswell had its facts from Langton and Langton
from Johnson:

> He related, that he had once in a dream a contest of wit with
> some other person, and that he was very much mortified by imagin-
> ing that his opponent had the better of him. 'Now, (said he,) one
> may mark here the effect of sleep in weakening the power of reflec-
> tion; for had not my judgement failed me, I should have seen, that
> the wit of this supposed antagonist, by whose superiority I felt
> myself depressed, was as much furnished by me, as that which I
> thought I had been uttering in my own character.'[12]

No psychiatrist perhaps would be much impressed by Johnson's concluding remarks, which were all too clearly designed
to reassure himself as to the powers of his conscious mind. The
dream itself would count with a psychiatrist and, of course,
primarily for what it revealed of the unconscious mind. It may
have revealed a good deal. In the dream, as Johnson said himself, he was 'mortified by imagining that his opponent had the
better of him'; '. . . my judgement failed me', he said; and the
opponent obtained a 'superiority' by which he felt himself
'depressed'.

Well! If Johnson was the man whom we all suppose we know,
the word 'dream' hardly seems to be strong enough for the
case. That was a most appalling nightmare!

The question is, was it a nightmare that could tell us anything about Johnson's feelings towards Burke? Burke was his

best-known antagonist, and as likely as any to have disturbed his slumbers. A 'contest of wit' with Burke might not have worried Johnson. He always treated Burke's wit with elaborate scorn.[13] But wit was hardly the most fundamental experience of that dream, which was about a contest the Doctor was losing. In the dream he met a rival whom somehow he could not cow.

Like a great many other people, Johnson occasionally had vain wishes that he could live a part of his life over again and manage things better. Most readers remember his regret that he had not been bred to the law. In his seventieth year he was still insisting to Boswell: 'Sir, it *would* have been better that I had been of a profession. I ought to have been a lawyer.' Sir William Scott wrung his heart by reminding him of the legal honours he might have won. It was after Lord Lichfield died and his title became extinct, and Scott said to Johnson: ' "What a pity it is, Sir, that you did not follow the profession of the law. You might have been Lord Chancellor of Great Britain, and attained to the dignity of a peerage; and now that the title of Lichfield, your native city, is extinct, you might have had it." Johnson, upon this, seemed much agitated; and, in an angry tone, exclaimed, "Why will you vex me by suggesting this, when it is too late?" '[14]

He had a similar but no doubt less passionate regret that he had not become a Member of Parliament. At one time his friend William Strahan did seriously propose in a letter to one of the Secretaries of the Treasury that Lord North's Government might welcome such a recruit. Could he be brought into a safe seat? That was in 1771, when Johnson was sixty-one. Nothing came of the proposal, and even Boswell never seems to have asked questions about it, though he says, somewhat vaguely: '. . . at a later period of his life, when Sir Joshua Reynolds told him that Mr. Edmund Burke had said, that if he had come early into parliament, he certainly would have been the greatest speaker that ever was there, Johnson exclaimed, "I should like to try my hand now." '[15]

---

[13] He contrasted it sharply with his more solid gifts: 'When Burke does not descend to be merry, his conversation is very superiour indeed. There is no proportion between the powers he shews in serious talk and in jocularity. When he lets himself down to that, he is in the kennel' (ibid. 276).

[14] Ibid. iii. 309–10.   [15] Ibid. ii. 137–9.

There were few fields in which Johnson could not have tried his hand, and politics stirred him deeply. He undoubtedly argued politics with Burke, even though it is just as certain that he sometimes resolved not to.[16] An unshakeable Tory and a bottomless Whig, they were almost sure to turn up on opposite sides of any question; and in the nature of things Burke had all the advantages when politics were discussed. Once at least they came close to a public confrontation. It was Johnson who challenged, though without naming Burke as his opponent or showing any signs of open hostility to him. In April 1774 Burke had made his famous speech in the Commons on American Taxation. He delayed printing it, but finally brought it out in pamphlet form on 10 January 1775. On 21 January Johnson announced to Boswell: 'I am going to write about the Americans.'[17] He had been prodded into it by the Ministry but, of course, he must have agreed to making the attack. *Taxation no Tyranny* came out on 8 March.[18] It dealt with the same problem as had Burke's speech and—in 1775—was addressed to the same audience, the British reading public. For once Johnson allowed himself to show some concern over the reception of a pamphlet of his. He wished this one had had more replies. ' . . . I never think I have hit hard,' he said, 'unless it rebounds.'[19] Burke did not reply to Johnson, but exactly two weeks after *Taxation no Tyranny* came out he spoke again in the House, this time making his famous Speech on Conciliation with the Colonies.

The rivalries of great men are sometimes full of bitterness, and no doubt this one could have been, with a little less careful management. Johnson never lost his violent feelings about the

---

[16] Johnson saw very well both the danger and the solution. ' . . . I can live very well with Burke', he told Boswell and Goldsmith in 1772: 'I love his knowledge, his genius, his diffusion and affluence of conversation; but I would not talk to him of the Rockingham party' (*Life of Johnson*, ii. 181). Mrs. Thrale in a dramatic sketch she wrote in 1779 made him say to Burke: ' . . . we have long ago agreed not to talk about publick affairs' (*Bulletin of the John Rylands Library*, xvi (1932), 100).

[17] *Letters of Johnson*, ii. 4. He was, of course, challenging a wide field of opponents, including Lord Chatham and the American Congress. But Burke's was the best-organized and most impressive argument he had to answer.

[18] Boswell's editor suggests that the Ministry was admirably prompt in rewarding it: 'Sixteen days after this pamphlet was published, Lord North, as Chancellor of the University of Oxford, proposed that the degree of Doctor in Civil Law should be conferred on Johnson' (*Life of Johnson*, ii. 318 n. 1).

[19] Ibid. 335.

Americans. It was a subject on which even Boswell had no comfort to give him. Boswell sympathized with the colonists. When he recklessly said so to Johnson, more than two years later, he was horrified by the result: '. . . the violent agitation into which he was thrown, while answering, or rather reprimanding me, alarmed me so, that I heartily repented of my having unthinkingly introduced the subject.'[20] Johnson's denunciations extended to Sir George Savile, whom he called a 'little dirty scoundrel, like the rest of his party'.[21] The subsequent course of the war—which was fought very much on Johnson's principles—must have strained his temper to the limit.

One naturally wonders, did it also strain one of his principal friendships? If the psychiatrist's guess was a valid one, Burke must have had a reasonably important role in Johnson's psychic life. He was *the* man most able to disturb that peace of mind which depended on winning all arguments. Should not such a man when he appeared have aroused some degree of hostility? If, as Reynolds thought, Burke did more than pose a vague intermittent threat—if he actually gave Johnson persistent feelings of inferiority—why did not that destroy his hard-won security and plunge him into deep anxieties, mixed with envy and fear of the man who embodied the danger?

Boswell is not a profound analyst, but he gives the main facts about the friendship of Johnson and Burke, which apparently continued happily for twenty-six years. There were no great (visible) crises, and only the faintest signs of any real bitterness. There were, granted, some facts about the friendship which Boswell did not supply. Its beginning is recorded by Arthur Murphy if it is recorded at all. Murphy describes a meeting of the two men over a Christmas dinner at Garrick's in 1758. It might have been their first.[22] What most impressed Murphy

---

[20] Ibid. iii. 206.

[21] *Boswell in Extremes*, ed. Charles McC. Weis and Frederick A. Pottle (1971), in the *Yale Editions of the Private Papers of James Boswell*, pp. 183–4. In the following year Boswell described *Taxation no Tyranny* to Robert Orme as 'a piece of magnificent sophistry' (ibid., p. 282).

[22] Murphy unluckily mentions no date, but only says: 'He met him for the first time at Mr. Garrick's several years ago' ('An Essay on the Life and Genius of Samuel Johnson', in his edition of the *Works of Samuel Johnson* (12 vols., 1792), i. 98). But there *was* a meeting on Christmas Day 1758, and no earlier meeting is known. For a full and able discussion of the problem, see Donald C. Bryant, *Edmund Burke and his Literary Friends* (Washington University Studies, St. Louis, 1939), p. 16.

about the occasion was that he heard Johnson submit to contradiction by a younger man. Burke was still in his twenties in
1758; the subject was Bengal. When Johnson saw Murphy the
next morning, he made his own comment: 'I suppose, Murphy,
you are proud of your countryman; *cum talis sit, utinam noster
esset.*'[23] It is the first of the many tributes which over the next
quarter-century he paid to his favourite antagonist.

Boswell preserves the tributes rather better than he preserves
a full record of the talk. To tell the truth, Boswell probably did
not see the two men together a very large number of times.
For almost ten years of his friendship with Johnson he did not
see them together at all: he and Johnson discussed Burke
occasionally, but Boswell was collecting notes on a man he had
not yet met. His first-hand records of encounters began in April
1773 when he himself became a member of the Club. In the
next dozen years they depended on the frequency of his visits
to London, which were sometimes widely spaced.

This makes it all the more necessary to pay attention to the
tributes, since they are the best evidence we have to illuminate
a long friendship. There are two minor questions about them
which perhaps ought to be raised. First, why do they so often
strike us as *deliberate* tributes? Johnson was somewhat deliberate,
no doubt, in most of his talk, and revolved things well in his
mind before bringing them out. His sayings were small works
of art. But were not the tributes to Burke unusually studied?
The Latin sentence to Murphy is an example. It is a kind of
motto. When Johnson visited Burke at Beaconsfield in 1774 he
again made his comment in Latin: '*Non equidem invideo; miror
magis.*'[24] That too sounds like a motto, for either the house or
its master. And, of course, there is that well-remembered verbal
vignette which Johnson kept throwing into his conversation
for at least a decade: the one which always ended with his
pronouncing Burke 'an extraordinary man'. It has recently
been given to us in a new form by Professor Waingrow. When
Boswell shortly after Johnson's death was collecting accounts of
his doings and sayings from scores of people, he wrote to
Johnson's (and Burke's) physician Dr. Richard Brocklesby. In

---

[23] 'If this be the kind of man he is, would he were ours.'
[24] 'Yet I do not envy; I rather marvel' (Virgil, *Eclogues*, i. 11; *Life of Johnson*,
iii. 310).

his letter of reply Brocklesby recalled a high compliment Johnson had paid to Burke:

Sir, if you were driven by a storm of rain to take shelter under an oak tree in company with Burke, he would describe the shower of rain though a very common thing—he would describe it in so animated and lively a picture that to hear him go on you would be content for the pleasure he gave you to be wet to the skin.[25]

Boswell never made use of Brocklesby's version, but he recorded the compliment itself in four other forms. The first, an extremely odd one, he entered in his Journal but never printed. When he and Johnson were in Edinburgh in 1773, just before starting off on their tour of the Hebrides, they had a social evening with some Scottish friends and Burke was discussed. Said Johnson:

'Burke Sir is such a man that if you met him for the first time in a street where there was a shower of cannon bullets and you and he ran up a stair to take shelter but for five minutes, he'd talk to you in such a manner that when you came down you'd say this is an extraordinary man.'[26]

Boswell himself must have thought that odd, for he did something quite out of character. He altered it. In 1785, when he was preparing copy for the printer of his *Journal of a Tour to the Hebrides* he deleted the 'cannon bullets' which he had written down a dozen years before (they can still be discerned, however, beneath his marks of deletion) and inserted a different metaphor before sending the page to the printer. In the *Tour* as published the passage reads:

'Burke, Sir, is such a man, that if you met him for the first time in a street where you were stopped by a drove of oxen, and you and he stepped aside to take shelter but for five minutes, he'd talk to you in such a manner, that, when you parted, you would say, this is an extraordinary man.'[27]

[25] *The Correspondence and Other Papers of James Boswell Relating to the Making of the Life of Johnson*, ed. Marshall Waingrow (vol. 2 of the Research Edition of *The Yale Editions of the Private Papers of James Boswell*, New Haven, 1968), pp. 93–4.

[26] *Private Papers of James Boswell from Malahide Castle, in the Collection of Lt. Colonel Ralph Heyward Isham* (privately printed, 1928–34), vol. vi. Boswell's sheet with its imperfect deletion is reproduced (opp. p. 178) in this volume and fully discussed by its editor, Geoffrey Scott.

[27] *Journal of a Tour to the Hebrides with Samuel Johnson* (1785), p. 26. It is not necessary to believe that Boswell himself composed the alternative form. As

Indeed Boswell ultimately gave it two further forms. The *Life of Johnson* describes an interchange in the last year of Johnson's life:

> BOSWELL. 'Mr. Burke has a constant stream of conversation.' JOHNSON. 'Yes, Sir; if a man were to go by chance at the same time with Burke under a shed, to shun a shower, he would say—"this is an extraordinary man." If Burke should go into a stable to see his horse drest, the ostler would say—we have had an extraordinary man here.'[28]

One cannot help being a little curious about all this. Why did that particular compliment have to be varied with so much art and delivered so frequently?[29] Was Johnson again trying to prove something to himself?

The other minor question to be asked about the many tributes is: Why did Johnson make them so *excessive*? He was

---

Geoffrey Scott suggests (p. 173), he may have 'done no more than substitute an equally authentic phrase used on some unrecorded occasion'. Even so, his un-Boswellian crime did not pay. Before the Malahide Papers provided final proof, the keen editorial eye of Dr. R. W. Chapman had seen that there was something wrong with the emended passage. He pointed out in a perceptive note that 'People do not *take shelter* from droves of oxen' (see his edition of *Johnson's Journey to the Western Islands of Scotland and Boswell's Journal of a Tour to the Hebrides* (Oxford 1924), p. 463).

[28] *Life of Johnson*, iv. 275–6.

[29] There is no lack of evidence for the variation and repetition. Mrs. Piozzi alludes to the compliment—indeed applies it herself to Johnson: 'Of him it might be said, as he often delighted to say of Edmund Burke, "that you could not stand for five minutes with that man beneath a shed while it rained, but you must be convinced that you had been standing with the greatest man you had yet seen"' (Hester Lynch Piozzi, *Anecdotes of the Late Samuel Johnson, LL.D.*, ed. S. C. Roberts (Cambridge, 1925), p. 135). Arthur Murphy declares that Johnson's 'constant observation was, "That a man of sense should not meet Mr. Burke by accident, under a gateway to avoid a shower, without being convinced that he was the first man in England"' (*Works of Johnson*, i. 96). Robert Bisset slightly changes the cast of characters: 'Dr. Johnson, while he declares his opinion, that if Burke were to go into a barn, the threshers would think him the wisest man they ever saw, testifies that he himself was never in Burke's company without departing the wiser' (*Life of Edmund Burke*, 1798, p. 134). James Prior again insists on the frequency: 'Often did he [Johnson] repeat "That no man of sense could meet Mr. Burke by accident under a gateway, to avoid a shower, without being convinced that he was the first man in England"' (*Memoir of Edmund Burke*, 1824, p. 64). Half a century after Johnson's death the *Quarterly Review* in its notice of Coleridge's *Table Talk* was still reminding its readers that 'Johnson's eulogy of Burke is in every body's recollection', and quoting a fresh version. In the *Quarterly* a 'barber's boy' rather than a thresher, an ostler, or a man of sense was making the discovery that Burke was extraordinary (*Quarterly Review*, liii (Feb. and April 1835), 80).

not a man lavish of praise: certainly not to his contemporaries. But he made Burke an exception. 'Burke is the only man whose common conversation corresponds with the general fame which he has in the world.' He is the 'first man in the House of Commons'. He is the 'first man every where'.[30] Burke's friend and protégé Dr. Thomas Campbell records an even more emphatic—because less general—judgement: '. . . Dr. Johnson . . . has been heard to say, that during his acquaintance with life, he knew but two men who had risen considerably above the common standard: the one was Lord Chatham, the other was Edmund Burke.'[31] Lord Chatham was the Winston Churchill of his day; one sees how far the Doctor was willing to go in praise of his own rival.

His ultimate and no doubt highest tribute will not come as a surprise to anyone who has worked long on Burke and known him well. It was paid on a day when Johnson was ill and not quite up to his usual exertions: '. . . Mr. Burke having been mentioned, he said, "That fellow calls forth all my powers. Were I to see Burke now, it would kill me." '[32]

[30] *Life of Johnson*, iv. 19–20; v. 269.
[31] *Strictures on the Ecclesiastical and Literary History of Ireland* (Dublin, 1789), p. 297. Boswell knew of this judgement, and mentioned it to Burke himself in 1778 (*Boswell in Extremes*, p. 272).
[32] *Life of Johnson*, ii. 450.

XVI

Edmund Burke and the Enlightenment

I T would be difficult to find anywhere in the eighteenth century a more powerful denunciation of 'this enlightened age'[1] than in the later works of Edmund Burke. Indeed, his writings on the French Revolution are still considered to be the most complete and most damaging attack ever made on the Enlightenment. It is hardly surprising that his own political ideas should be seen as the antithesis of all that the Enlightenment stands for or be interpreted in terms of a 'revolt against the eighteenth century', a revolt which older critics saw as an anticipation of Romanticism, but which it is more fashionable nowadays to see as a return to the Natural Law doctrine of Thomas Aquinas.[2]

However, while this kind of interpretation is well established, there are good reasons for doubting whether it is entirely accurate. If there is a black and white distinction between Burke and the Enlightenment, how are we to account for his lifelong admiration of Montesquieu ('the greatest genius which has enlightened this age'[3])? How are we to understand his affinities with the Scottish Enlightenment, and particularly his enthusiasm for the moral and economic theories of Adam Smith?[4] Even Burke's 'scholastic' interpreters have drawn attention

---

[1] The term 'Enlightenment' was not in use in English until the nineteenth century (see *O.E.D.*). Burke frequently uses the verb 'to enlighten' and the adjectival form 'enlightened'. His references to 'this enlightened age' in his later writings (e.g. *Works*, iii. 359) are usually ironic. All references to Burke's works are to *The Works of Edmund Burke* (Bohn's British Classics, 8 vols., 1854–89).

[2] For the 'Romantic' interpretation of Burke, see C. E. Vaughan, *The Romantic Revolt* (1923) and A. Cobban, *Edmund Burke and the Revolt against the Eighteenth Century* (1929). For the 'scholastic' interpretation, see especially P. J. Stanlis, *Edmund Burke and the Natural Law* (Ann Arbor, Mich., 1958).

[3] *Works*, vi. 297.

[4] On Burke and the Scottish Enlightenment see B. T. Wilkins, *The Problem of Burke's Political Philosophy* (Oxford, 1967), pp. 50–71. On Burke and Adam Smith see C. B. Macpherson, 'Edmund Burke', *Transactions of the Royal Society of Canada*, lii (1959), 19–26.

to an aspect of his thought which suggests an eighteenth-century affinity: his belief in an aprioristic Natural Law. Some of these same critics, by stressing his interest in sentiment and natural feeling, have brought him surprisingly close to Rousseau and the *sensibilité* of the period.[5] Besides, one can hardly overlook the obvious fact that Burke, especially in his early literary career, was in touch with the intellectual life of his age, and that most of his active political life was devoted to the working and defence of that most eighteenth-century phenomenon, the English constitution. When all this is taken into account, and when it is remembered that Burke professes to believe in government by consent, toleration, free trade, and (as he tells us himself) rational moral and political principles,[6] it seems rather absurd to suppose that it is possible to understand him only by pushing him forward to the Age of Romanticism or back to Aquinas. This is not to deny that he has affinities with earlier and later traditions of thought; nor is it to deny that there are important differences between Burke and (say) Voltaire or Rousseau; but it seems obvious that he should be studied in the context of his own age.

It was his increasing awareness of the eighteenth-century aspects of Burke's thought that led Alfred Cobban, in the Preface written in 1960 for the second edition of his *Edmund Burke and the Revolt against the Eighteenth Century* (originally published in 1929), to confess that he had serious reservations about the main thesis of his book, and that he now believed that 'Burke and the Lake poets, though in a sense they were in revolt against the aridity, the lack of poetry, of the eighteenth century, represent also not so much a denial as an enlargement and liberalisation of its ideas'.[7] But although there have been hints of a not dissimilar view from at least one distinguished Enlightenment scholar,[8] Cobban's brief and provocative remarks seem to have had no repercussions on recent Burke criticism.

---

[5] Stanlis, pp. 168 sqq., and F. P. Canavan, *The Political Reason of Edmund Burke* (Durham, N.C., 1960), pp. 54–81.

[6] *Works*, vi. 113–14.   [7] Cobban, p. xiv.

[8] Lester G. Crocker, reviewing L. I. Bredvold's *The Brave New World of the Enlightenment* (Ann Arbor, Mich., 1961) in *Journal of Modern History*, xxxiv (1962), 331–2, writes: 'The author would be astonished (and hurt) to know how many of Burke's ideas are also found among the *philosophes* (including Rousseau), and how many *philosophes* opposed the positions he [Bredvold] attributes to them.'

It can hardly be doubted, however, that Cobban rendered an important service to scholarship in suggesting that it is time Burke's relation to the Enlightenment was re-examined. There is no reason to suppose that, because he rejected some currents of Enlightenment thought, he rejected them all; and it is worth asking, for example, whether his disagreement with the *philosophes* was not in essentials an eighteenth-century quarrel, a divergence within the Enlightenment itself, rather than supposing that it must have been a case of Burke–Aquinas, or Burke the Romantic, standing aloof from his century and denouncing an age to which he so manifestly belongs.

It is extremely misleading to think of the Enlightenment in terms of a fixed ideology or a united band of philosophers with a clearly formulated programme of reform. Such alliances as we find were no more than temporary; and the leading thinkers of the period were, on many fundamental issues, deeply divided. It is more helpful to think of the Enlightenment as an intellectual movement which is the continuation of the rationalism and scientific inquiry of the seventeenth century, absorbing the empiricism of Locke and remaining open to new developments in philosophy, science, history, and geography. The Enlightenment is not merely a questioning of accepted beliefs; it is essentially a quest for values in an age when it was felt that, with the help of reason and experience, it would be possible to discover the truth about man and nature. In the first half of the eighteenth century—which is all we need consider for the moment—the example of Newton's brilliant success in the natural sciences was felt as an encouragement in this quest, and it was generally believed that there was a congruence between the world of experience and man's intuition of moral values. It was a period when, in England and France, there were many deists or deistical Christians, but few atheists; much faith in empiricism, but little materialism; and plenty of enthusiasm for civil liberty, but no serious call for revolution. This was, on the whole, a period of optimism, when Leibniz and Pope were influential, and when, if not everyone believed that 'whatever is, is right', at least it was generally agreed that there was a rational providential order behind the empirical order. The most representative work of these years is Montesquieu's *Esprit des lois* (1748), which was greatly admired for its concern with facts as well as for its attempt to demonstrate that behind the facts there was an order intelligible to the human mind.

It would be interesting if we could give a full account of the young Burke's reactions to the English and French thinkers of this period. However, this is not possible, for our information is fragmentary, especially for the important formative years between 1750 and 1756. It would appear, at least, that he may have been interested in works like Bayle's *Dictionnaire*, which he mentions in an early letter,[9] for he was 'of an inquisitive and speculative cast of mind',[10] and in religion was sceptical of both the Roman Catholic and Protestant claims to truth.[11] He was attracted to the English deists, studied them in some detail, but was dissatisfied with their rationalistic approach to revealed religion.[12] He found that rationalism led to scepticism, and seems, at least for a time, to have had an extreme reaction and taken refuge in 'enthusiasm'.[13] It is this same reaction against critical rationalism that is the inspiration of *A Vindication of Natural Society* (1756), where, parodying the style of Bolingbroke, he hopes to show that this kind of criticism, which is destructive of religion, is equally destructive when applied to society, and therefore inapplicable to both.

It is customary to see in the *Vindication* evidence, even at this early date, of Burke's rejection of the Enlightenment, and particularly of the French Enlightenment, for it has been supposed that Rousseau's *Discours sur l'inégalité* (1755) was one of the works he was attacking.[14] However, this is an oversimplification, for rejection of rationalistic systematizing is a major theme in France at this time, and if Burke is attacking Rousseau he is doing so for the same reasons as Voltaire.[15] Even if Burke is doing no more than attacking the sceptical implications of

[9] *The Correspondence of Edmund Burke*, ed. T. W. Copeland *et al.* (9 vols., Cambridge and Chicago, 1958–70), i. 72 (letter of 29 Nov. 1746 to R. Shackleton).

[10] A. P. I. Samuels, *The Early Life, Correspondence and Writings of the Rt. Hon. Edmund Burke* (Cambridge, 1922), p. 402.

[11] Ibid., p. 404.

[12] J. Prior, *Memoir of the Life and Character of the Right Hon. Edmund Burke* (2nd edn., 2 vols., 1826), i. 19.

[13] H. V. F. Somerset (ed.), *A Note-book of Edmund Burke* (Cambridge, 1957), pp. 68, 71.

[14] R. B. Sewall, 'Rousseau's Second Discourse in England from 1755 to 1762', *Philological Qtly*, xvii (1938), 97–114.

[15] For the French context of the debate see H. Roddier, *Jean-Jacques Rousseau en Angleterre au XVIIIe siècle* (Paris, 1950), pp. 33 sqq.

critical rationalism, he has close affinities with the French writers of the period. Indeed, the *Vindication* reads like the development of an idea he may have found in the *Esprit des lois*:

C'est mal raisonner contre la religion, de rassembler dans un grand ouvrage une longue énumération des maux qu'elle a produits, si l'on ne fait de même celle des biens qu'elle a faits. Si je voulais raconter tous les maux qu'ont produits dans le monde les lois civiles, la monarchie, le gouvernement républicain, je dirais des choses effroyables.[16]

However, Burke's attitude to the evils of society is not quite the same as Montesquieu's. Montesquieu's aim was, indeed, to refute scepticism by showing that 'dans cette infinie diversité de lois et de mœurs, [les hommes] n'étaient pas uniquement conduits par leurs fantaisies',[17] and this he does by showing that behind 'diversité' there are various moral and psychological factors which, along with 'causes morales' and 'causes physiques', shape man's life in society. Burke, morover, does not share Montesquieu's gloom about the evils present in society,[18] and simply explains them away by asserting that it is an abuse of reason to be over-critical and that, as we do not understand God's ways to man, we must meekly submit to Divine Providence.[19] His theme, in fact, is that of the various *contes* which Voltaire had been publishing since the mid-1740s: Voltaire's usual technique is, like Burke's, to produce a catalogue of human woes (through which, unlike Burke, he conducts a hero) and then, in the last chapter, to counsel submission to a Providence which man does not understand. However, nothing is more striking than the difference in tone between the two writers: for Burke the woes are a joke, or at least the subject of an amusing parody; but for Voltaire (and for many of Burke's readers, who did not see his joke until it was explained)[20] they are a grim reality. In his Preface Burke brushes the problem of evil aside, and appears to believe that in this life, as well as

---

[16] *Esprit des lois*, Book XXIV, Ch. 2.   [17] Ibid., *Préface*.
[18] Montesquieu notes sombrely that most of the inhabitants of the world live in despotic states (ibid., Book V, Ch. 14).
[19] *Works*, i. 4.
[20] The explanatory preface was added to the second edition (1757): see T. W. Copeland, 'Burke's *Vindication of Natural Society*', *The Library*, xviii (1938), 461–2.

in the life hereafter, the wicked are punished and the virtuous rewarded.[21] Voltaire is less optimistic in his conclusions: he hopes that the wicked will be punished in the life hereafter, but has no doubt that in this life they flourish, and when he counsels submission it is with a growing awareness, culminating in *Candide* (1759), of man's helplessness in a universe he cannot understand. In the *Vindication* Burke is preaching that kind of naïve optimism which Voltaire had accepted in his earlier works, but which he had learned, through bitter experience, to distrust.[22]

The French thinkers of the middle of the century who rejected rationalistic speculation turned to empirical investigation as a more promising form of inquiry—or at least such was their professed intention, for in fact they never freed themselves entirely (any more than did Burke) from metaphysics. Burke likewise shows a preference for empirical inquiry in his other works of this period. The *Sublime and Beautiful* (1757), in which he examines the origin of our aesthetic ideas by tracing them to the operation of the senses, is an application of Locke's sensationism comparable to what we find at about the same time in Condillac and d'Alembert. That Burke was in favour of extending this same empirical method to other areas can be inferred from his enthusiastic reception[23] of Adam Smith's *Theory of Moral Sentiments*, which was published two years later; here moral experience is explained in terms of sympathy, in much the same way as Rousseau, at the same time, was relating moral virtue to the sentiment of pity.[24] Burke's other major work of these years, the *Abridgment of English History*, is an attempt, largely inspired by Montesquieu, to explain historical events by the operation of physical and moral causes.[25] Burke the historian is by no means uncritical: he is convinced of the intellectual progress that has been made by civilization since

[21] 'Do they think to enforce the practice of virtue, by denying that vice and virtue are distinguished by good or ill fortune here, or by happiness or misery hereafter?' *Works*, i. 3.

[22] On Voltaire and eighteenth-century optimism see W. H. Barber, *Leibniz in France: from Arnauld to Voltaire* (Oxford, 1955), and I. O. Wade, *Voltaire and Candide* (Princeton, N.J., 1959).

[23] In a review of the work in the *Annual Register*, 1759, and in the letter of 10 Sept. 1759 to Smith (*Correspondence*, i. 129–30).

[24] Sewall, art. cit., and Roddier, pp. 41–2.

[25] C. P. Courtney, *Montesquieu and Burke* (Oxford, 1963), pp. 46–57.

barbarous times,[26] and one suspects Voltaire would have been delighted, for example, with his account of the naïve credulity which lay behind the organization of the Crusades.[27]

While Burke, in these works, seems to consider himself a thoroughgoing empiricist, and disclaims man's ability to unravel by reason the ultimate cause of things, he has no doubt that behind the welter of sensations and facts of experience there is a rational order and a Divine Providence. In aesthetics he believes there is an immutable standard of taste which, in the last resort, is a matter of rational judgement.[28] In ethical thought he believes, with Adam Smith (and Rousseau), that man has morally good impulses implanted in him by God. In history he believes that the master-mind of God is never far distant, and that Divine Providence places in man guiding impulses which emerge at the appropriate time and place.[29] His views on religion are not clear, but he seems to have been broad-minded and tolerant. He is eager to acquire knowledge, and, as editor of the *Annual Register*, plays an active part in disseminating knowledge. He is impatient with obscurantism, and he takes to task, for example, legal historians who refuse to examine in detail the growth of English law.[30] In all this Burke is obviously very much a man of the Enlightenment; his ideas are a mixture, characteristic of the period, of rationalism and empiricism. No doubt, like every educated man of the time, his outlook owes much to the traditional Christian and classical heritage; but his masters are Locke and Montesquieu, and his affinities are with the empirical thinkers of the period. Nevertheless, the young author is in some ways out of tune with the enlightened thought of the 1750s: his rather facile recourse to Divine Providence, his robust confidence in a rational order behind the empirical order, looks rather dated—something more often to be found in the earlier and more optimistic years of the century than at the time when he was writing. Nor does he appear to have any inkling of the directions in which his ideas might lead: he pursues empirical inquiry without any awareness that it might result in materialism; he studies history without suspecting that his faith in a providential order might be belied by the facts; and he admires the sentimental morality

[26] *Works*, vi. 195.   [27] Ibid., p. 336.   [28] Ibid. i. 66.
[29] Ibid. vi. 193, 248.   [30] Ibid., p. 414.

of Adam Smith without seeing that it might lead to a naturalistic reduction of ethics to psychology. In France[31] all these implications had been clearly grasped, and enlightened thought had started to develop along a line which makes Burke seem slightly old-fashioned.

Before Burke had time to catch up with these recent intellectual developments, he had entered politics, first in 1761 as private secretary to W. G. Hamilton, and then in 1765 as a member of the House of Commons. It is not possible here to study in any detail his parliamentary career, nor indeed would it be entirely relevant to the present purpose, for his primary concern during these years was with practical problems rather than with philosophical debate. It can safely be said, however, that on most of the major political issues of the period Burke was on the side of enlightened opinion. It is perhaps on the problem of Catholic emancipation in Ireland that he is most unequivocally enlightened, and his views on the subject were fixed by the middle 1760s, when he wrote the *Tracts on the Popery Laws*. Here he condemns the penal laws in the name of Natural Law and natural rights,[32] quotes Bayle as an authority on toleration,[33] condemns the persecution of the French Protestants,[34] and outlines reforms which make it clear he prefers civil liberties to the dogmatic claims of any revealed religion.[35] His position on America is equally liberal, and in his analysis of the colonial problem he makes a brilliant use of Montesquieu's technique of sociological analysis. His record on India is somewhat tarnished in the light of modern scholarship, but there can be no doubt that his heart was on the side of the Indian masses whose rights, he believed, had been trampled underfoot by Hastings. In the same way Burke's views on Economic Reform, relief for the Dissenters, reform of the laws on libel and homosexual offences, the slave trade, and many other topics must in the final analysis be deemed liberal and enlightened. Even when

---

[31] And, of course, in England by Hume, although it would appear that he had relatively little influence on the thought of the period.

[32] Ibid., pp. 24, 29.   [33] Ibid., p. 29.

[34] Ibid., pp. 25–7.

[35] 'For the Protestant religion, nor (I speak it with reverence, I am sure,) the truth of our common Christianity, is not as clear as this proposition; that all men, at least the majority of men in the society, ought to enjoy the common advantages of it.' Ibid., p. 30.

we consider such a minor matter as his enthusiasm for agricultural experiment, our conclusion will be the same. Unlike Dr. Johnson, he did not refuse to shake hands with free-thinking Frenchmen, was a generous host to Raynal and Mirabeau at Beaconsfield,[36] and, when he visited France in 1773, was ready to have lengthy discussions with the *philosophes* he met in the *salons* of the French capital.[37] It has been supposed that he was horrified at the atheistical views of some of the writers he met,[38] and the speech denouncing atheists which he made shortly after his return to England is often quoted as an important piece of evidence in support of the view that he was totally opposed to the Enlightenment.[39] However, this is to assume that Enlightenment and atheism are synonymous, whereas Voltaire and Rousseau would have agreed with Burke when he described atheists as 'outlaws . . . of the human race'[40]—in the *Contrat social* it is envisaged that it might be necessary to inflict the death penalty on unbelievers.[41] Burke's declaration, 'Have as many sorts of religion as you find in your country, there is a reasonable worship in them all', would have been considered the purest deism in France, and is perfectly in keeping with the main tradition of enlightened thought. In fact, it is probably fair to say that the only issue (which was, however, an important one) on which Burke appears to be un-enlightened was parliamentary reform. It might be argued that in the context of eighteenth-century England opposition to such reform was perfectly reasonable, and it could be pointed out that even Voltaire was uneasy about any suggestion that political power should be lodged anywhere but in the hands of an élite. On the other hand, it cannot be denied that demands for political reform were growing in both France and England, and that new economic, social, and intellectual developments pointed to the need for a greater measure of reform than Burke thought desirable. His defence of the English constitution in terms of 'prescription', his rigid refusal to contemplate any

[36] Courtney, p. 36; *Correspondence*, iii. 363–4.

[37] Courtney, pp. 32–5.

[38] *Yale Edition of Horace Walpole's Correspondence*, ed. W. S. Lewis, xxxii (1965), 103.

[39] *Works*, vi. 102 sqq. [40] Ibid., p. 112.

[41] *Du Contrat social*, Book IV, ch. 8. For Voltaire's views on atheism see the *Dictionnaire philosophique*, art. ATHÉE, ATHÉISME.

extension of the franchise, and his dismissal of any attempt to judge existing constitutional arrangements in the light of natural rights form a curious contrast (never satisfactorily explained by the casuistry of his interpreters) to his liberal and open-minded attitude to most other political issues of the period. However, his views on the English constitution will be best discussed in connection with the French Revolution.

There is no evidence that Burke, during the period 1760–89, had much detailed knowledge of intellectual developments in France. Indeed, it is probable that he had little interest in most of the topics that the *philosophes* and Rousseau were discussing. Confident that the basic principles of the English constitution had been settled once and for all in 1688, content with the religion of his country, and free (at least to outward appearance) from any serious doubts about man's place in the general scheme of things, Burke can hardly have shown much enthusiasm for the French writers' endless discussions on the fundamental problems of metaphysics, epistemology, ethics, and politics; nor can he have had much sympathy with their violent anti-clericalism. However, what was at issue in all this mass of philosophical writing, and what was often obscured by its polemical tone, was a basic problem which is by no means irrelevant to the study of Burke: the problem, which we have already had occasion to mention, of whether there was a transcendent order behind the empirical or natural order of things.

We have seen how Voltaire, in his *contes*, finds a bewildering discrepancy between his deistical notion of God's Providence and the apparent chaos of man's empirical existence. In Diderot, Helvétius, and d'Holbach this problem is solved, or explained away, by denying God's existence, dismissing the belief in a transcendent order, and seeing man simply as part of physical nature. This was the logical outcome of a thoroughgoing empiricism; unlike Voltaire's Newtonianism, it was compatible with recent developments in the biological sciences. It is with the implications of these ideas that much of the intellectual debate of the second part of the Enlightenment is concerned, Voltaire and Rousseau taking up a defence of the moral dimension in man against what they consider the immoral implications of materialism. It was essentially a debate about moral values, and Burke had some inkling of this when he wrote, 'Rousseau is a moralist, or he is nothing'.[42] Burke, too, is a moralist or he is nothing, and he was soon to enter, rather belatedly (as usual, one is tempted to add), the great moral debate of the Enlightenment.

Burke's reactions to the French Revolution are not quite like those of anyone else in England at that time. He sees it not simply as one of those political upheavals of which history affords so many examples, but as something new and unprecedented: 'the most astonishing [revolution] that has hitherto happened in the world',[43] a phenomenon which is 'out of nature', a 'monster', a 'spectre', a 'moral earthquake'.[44] It is 'a revolution in sentiments, manners, and moral opinions'[45] which, by perverting 'the natural order of things',[46] flies in the face of the laws of God. What Burke means by 'the natural order of things' is perhaps most concisely summed up when he speaks of 'that action and counteraction, which, in the natural and the political world, from the reciprocal struggle of discordant powers, draws out the harmony of the universe'.[47] However, at a less mystical level, what 'the natural order of things' means is exhibited, for Burke, in the English constitution, which is 'placed in a just correspondence and symmetry with the order of the world',[48] where past, present, and future are smoothly continuous, the different interests of society harmonized and balanced, self-interest and social reconciled, reason and 'the untaught feelings'[49] blended, and the laws of commerce (which Burke sees as 'the laws of God')[50] respected. Just as there is harmony in the natural and moral worlds, so is there harmony in the English constitution, which is at once natural, rational, prescriptive, and providential. The old French constitution, he believes, could easily have been improved in order to conform to a similar harmonious pattern.[51]

To analyse the elements which make up Burke's defence of traditional values and his ideas on natural order, one would have to take account of many strands of thought which could

---

[42] *Works*, ii. 535–6.   [43] Ibid., p. 284.
[44] These terms occur throughout Burke's writings on the Revolution. See, e.g., ibid., pp. 284, 532; iii. 8; v. 155, 373, 410.
[45] Ibid. ii. 352.   [46] Ibid., p. 322.   [47] Ibid., p. 308.
[48] Ibid., p. 307.   [49] Ibid., p. 359.   [50] Ibid. v. 100.
[51] Ibid. ii. 308.

be traced back to the Renaissance and ultimately to medieval and classical sources. His basic notion of the harmony of the universe is essentially the classical *concors discordia rerum*, which is familiar to every reader of Shakespeare and Milton, and which was given memorable expression in the eighteenth century in Pope's *Essay on Man*, where it was adapted to the optimistic outlook of the period.[52] Burke takes up the familiar theme, and (like Pope in this respect) grafts on to it such typical eighteenth-century ideas as *laissez-faire* liberalism, the theory of the balanced constitution, the harmony of sentiment and moral values. The result is a vigorous restatement of that optimistic providentialism which is characteristic of the first part of the Enlightenment, and if Burke does not quite believe that this is the best of all possible worlds, he certainly does think that England has the best of all constitutions. Indeed, he becomes almost Leibnizian when he analyses the mathematics of 'the whole scheme of our mixed constitution', which is so constructed as 'to prevent any one of its principles from being carried as far as, taken by itself, and theoretically, it would go'.[53]

It is interesting to compare Burke's alarm at the 'moral earthquake', which in 1789 threatened to shatter the cosmic harmony in which he so sincerely believed, with the despair of one of his elder French contemporaries on the occasion of a literal earthquake. Voltaire's reactions to the Lisbon earthquake of 1755 have often been analysed: he now abandons his faith in Leibniz and Pope, ridicules optimism, and in *Candide* asserts that all man can do in a universe which he does not fully understand is to cultivate his garden and cope with such empirical problems as arise. However, he does not abandon his belief that there is a transcendent order, he clings to his belief in God and Natural Law, and asserts that reason is still a guide to action in a wicked world. The crusade against religious fanaticism (*l'Infâme*) which he undertakes at about this time is something of an emotional reaction following the psychological and moral crisis of these years. It is not unlike Burke's equally frenzied crusade against political fanaticism, inspired by a similar crisis. In the same way both writers single out for special loathing atheists and materialists, who, as they understand

[52] See, on this general background, Alexander Pope, *An Essay on Man*, ed. Maynard Mack (1950), pp. xxiii sqq.   [53] *Works*, iii. 110.

them, are aiming at nothing less than to legitimize chaos and disorder by denying transcendence. Also, Voltaire's scathing attack on rationalistic systematizers, caricatured so mercilessly in the figure of Pangloss, is not dissimilar to Burke's denunciation of the prophets of natural rights: the main charge levelled against both Pangloss and 'smugglers of adulterated metaphysics'[54] is that they are so much obsessed with abstract theory that they have forgotten empirical reality. It is on empirical reality that both thinkers profess to base their philosophy; but whereas Voltaire, when he looks around at the European societies of his day, is appalled at what he can only describe as disorder and chaos, Burke is convinced that the harmony of the cosmos is revealed not only in the English constitution, but also (short of a few easy adjustments) in the old French constitution, and boldly trumpets forth what, at least in the more lyrical passages of his writings, amounts to a new version of the old optimism.

Burke's sudden awareness in 1789 that there were some things which were 'out of the order of nature' would have been no news to Diderot forty years earlier. Diderot was something of a specialist in abnormalities and monsters; hence his studies of the blind (*Lettre sur les aveugles*), the deaf mutes (*Lettre sur les sourds et muets*), and such 'moral monsters'[55] as Rameau's nephew and Jacques le fataliste. Diderot believed that nothing was to be gained by pretending that everything in the empirical world revealed an order which was rational or providential, or that a deistic or Christian God was necessary to explain such natural phenomena as matter and motion. For Diderot, as for Helvétius and d'Holbach, the only order was the empirical order—which indeed was orderly only in the sense that there was a rigid chain of cause and effect. This rejection of faith in an ordered cosmos opened a new line of inquiry which the eighteenth-century materialists explored ruthlessly and, in Diderot's case, with a penetration and genius which has brought him close in some respects to the twentieth-century exponents of the 'absurd'. Diderot can find no solution to his search for values in this chaotic, though fascinating, world; but he states

---

[54] *Works*, ii. 362.
[55] This term is used by Lester G. Crocker, in *Nature and Culture: Ethical Thought in the French Enlightenment* (Baltimore, 1963), pp. 379 sqq.

the problems with unrivalled honesty and insight. His vision of an apparently meaningless universe, where matter unfolds without divine intervention, is no less inspired and poetic[56] than Burke's most majestic descriptions of the ordered cosmos: a reminder that the subject of primeval chaos has always been found by poets and musicians a theme no less inspiring than that of the Creation. It is here, in the materialists' awareness of a blind and purposeless universe, that we have one of the extremes of the thought of the Enlightenment; it is at the other extreme (but not outside the Enlightenment itself) that we find the thought of Edmund Burke. In this perspective Voltaire and Rousseau are closer to Burke than to the materialists. Diderot's place in the spectrum is difficult to determine, however, for, in spite of his atheism and materialism, he believes sincerely in the intrinsic value of moral experience and rejects the crude and immoral implications of the kind of materialism developed by Helvétius.[57] If he never succeeds in reconciling his ethical ideas with his materialism, it is because he cannot accept that convenient Providence which, though apparently belied by the facts of experience, makes it possible for a thinker like Burke to harmonize all antinomies.

In Rousseau we find a thinker who, like Burke, rejects with horror the implications of materialism, any hint of a denial of Divine Providence and cosmic harmony. Man, he believes, becomes truly human and fulfils his potentialities only when a similar harmony is reproduced in his life as a moral being. Like Burke he distrusts rational abstractions and vague cosmopolitanism, in place of which he recommends 'les premiers mouvements de la nature'[58] (Burke's 'untaught feelings'), which, however, must be controlled by rational judgement. Indeed, like Burke, Rousseau believes that the foundations of man's moral life lie in a harmony of reason and sentiment, and there are many passages in the *Reflections on the Revolution in France* which are in agreement with, for example, the following:

Si c'en était ici le lieu . . . je ferais voir que *justice* et *bonté* ne sont point seulement des mots abstraits, de purs êtres moraux formés

---

[56] See especially the *Lettre sur les aveugles*, ed. R. Niklaus (Geneva and Lille, 1951), pp. 40–4.

[57] In the *Réfutation suivie de l'ouvrage d'Helvétius intitulé* l'Homme (1773–5).

[58] *Émile* (Paris, Éd. Garnier, 1961), p. 81.

par l'entendement, mais de véritables affections de l'âme éclairée par la raison, et qui ne sont qu'un progrès ordonné de nos affections primitives.[59]

However, as soon as Rousseau proceeds beyond this point to elaborate his ideas on education or on politics, his divergence from Burke is clearly marked. The divergence takes place not, as is often supposed, because Rousseau confuses the rights of natural man and the rights of the citizen (which, in fact, he distinguishes in much the same way as Burke),[60] or because he preaches a 'return to nature' (which he does not), but because he could not assume, as Burke did, that harmony and perfection were already embodied, in essentials, in any existing political constitution. Like Voltaire, when he turns to look at human societies, he is filled with despair:

> Le tableau de la nature ne m'offrait qu'harmonie et proportions, celui du genre humain ne m'offre que confusion, désordre! Le concert règne entre les éléments, et les hommes sont dans le chaos! O sagesse, où sont tes lois? O Providence, est-ce ainsi que tu régis le monde? Être bienfaisant, qu'est devenu ton pouvoir? Je vois le mal sur la terre.[61]

In truth, Rousseau is much more extreme than Voltaire in this respect, and one of the reproaches he levels at the *philosophes* is that they are on the whole satisfied with the civilization of the period, whereas he holds that civilization, as we know it, is corrupt at its very roots. Hence, he believes, the necessity to reconstruct society *de novo* and the need to begin with a moral regeneration of man, whom existing society has corrupted. Thus, changing our perspective, we might say that it is in Rousseau rather than in the materialists that we find the opposite pole of the Enlightenment from Burke. And yet there is the curious similarity of their ethical ideas at the most basic level, Rousseau holding out as an ideal something that Burke sincerely believes is already embodied in the old way of life.

It is customary to discuss Burke's relations with the Enlightenment in terms of his attack on the ideology of the French Revolution and his rejection of the extreme radicalism of Price and Paine. However, in such an approach there is a danger of

[59] *Émile*, p. 278.
[60] See A. Cobban, *Rousseau and the Modern State* (2nd edn., 1964), pp. 158–63.
[61] *Émile*, p. 337.

confusing Enlightenment and Revolution, of neglecting what men like Voltaire and Rousseau actually said, and of supposing that it is only in the political radicalism of the 1780s that one finds the true milk of the Enlightenment. In reality, the major thinkers of the Enlightenment were hostile to revolution, and on practical matters were usually as pragmatic as Burke himself. Voltaire rejects as absurd the notion that people have a right to make what laws they please; he admires the English constitution and the English attitude to religion; and his ideas for reform in France are a version of the *thèse royale*, based not merely on his idea of what is right, but on an interpretation of history.[62] The most daring political article in the *Encyclopédie* is probably REPRÉSENTANTS, written by d'Holbach, which recommends for France nothing more than the kind of structural reforms which even Burke admitted were necessary, and envisages that there should be a property qualification for voters. As for Rousseau, it is well known that he made a careful distinction between what was ideally right and what was expedient, and in his treatment of practical problems takes Montesquieu as his model.[63]

And yet, if the French thinkers of the period are not revolutionaries, it would be a distortion to treat them as conservatives: what most of them wanted for their country was a reformed monarchy, and their ideals—liberty, the rule of law, toleration, and representative government—are in essentials no different from Burke's. But there was a difference in their respective situations. As Voltaire had noted in the 1730s, these ideals had already been realized in England; what Burke is defending in his later writings is essentially that constitution which, to the first part of the Enlightenment, was one of the wonders of the world—and he goes on using precisely those arguments of harmony and mechanical balance that had been so dear to the mind of the early eighteenth century. There can be no doubt that Cobban was right in suggesting that he was, after all, a man of the Enlightenment. On the other hand, he is a man whose affinities are with the early Enlightenment, so that by the end of the century he becomes something of an anachronism,

[62] On Voltaire and politics see R. Pomeau, *Politique de Voltaire* (Paris, 1963).
[63] On Rousseau and 'utopianism' see J. Fabre, *Lumières et romantisme* (Paris, 1963), pp. 101–30.

defending an old-fashioned constitution with old-fashioned arguments. It is hard to see that he in any way stands for a 'liberalization' or 'enlargement' (to use Cobban's terms) of the Enlightenment. On the contrary, his attitude in his later works of opposition to almost any change in existing constitutional arrangements had the effect of contributing to the delay of reforms which were becoming more and more overdue. However, the nagging doubt of his consistency remains: at the very time when he was writing impassioned descriptions of the harmony of the universe and the English constitution, he was fighting for the rights of the Indians against Warren Hastings and taking an active part in the movement for Catholic emancipation in Ireland, which implied a modification in the coronation oath of the sublime and unalterable English constitution.

There is something paradoxical about the usual interpretation of Burke, which celebrates his superb grasp of 'circumstances' and yet cannot deny that his most important philosophical works were written in response to circumstances which he did not understand. He did not see that if most of the writers of the French Enlightenment were violently anti-clerical it was because their Church was intolerant; nor that if they were hostile to the political establishment it was because there was nothing in France to correspond with the British Parliament or the British rule of law. It is customary to speak of Burke as a political realist and of his French contemporaries as visionaries: yet it is to the French writers that we must turn for an accurate analysis of what was rotten in the state of France, and it is Burke, with his admiration of the 'age of chivalry', who is the visionary. Indeed, there is something of the visionary in Burke from the very beginning, as is seen in his idealization of the Rockinghams; and later, it would be hard to think of a more utopian scheme than his efforts to take war into Europe in order to restore the *émigrés* in France. On the other hand, what he did see, and with uncommon insight, is that once historical continuity is broken the individual will be alienated from the community, that men will be lost in a universe without any compass to guide them, and will lose all sense of time, becoming like 'flies of a summer'.[64] The fundamental

[64] *Works*, ii. 367.

point that Burke missed in this superb analysis is that historical continuity had already been broken many decades before he was writing on the subject—not by wicked philosophers, but by the failure of political and social institutions to obey 'the great law of change'[65] and to keep pace with the moral and psychological needs of the community. The established way of life was becoming an anachronism, and the leading writers in France in the eighteenth century were already tormented by that anguish and estrangement which Burke prophesies will follow the Revolution. In works like Voltaire's *Candide* and Rousseau's *Confessions* we see today an analysis of the anguish of modern man; Burke sees in them nothing but obscenity and wickedness, not realizing that in their own way they deal with the very same moral problem as his works on the Revolution.

One wonders whether Burke's violent reaction against the atheism and materialism which he sees as the cause of the French Revolution is not, in the last analysis, the result of a deep psychological insecurity, a need to believe in a set of values which, in his earlier years, had already been threatened by sceptical doubt. In one of his darkest moments he wonders whether the Revolution might not, after all, be the result of the workings of Divine Providence,[66] and he experiences an anguish which is paralleled in the eighteenth century only by that of Voltaire, who, likewise, draws back in horror at the possibility of the existence of what today we would call an 'absurd' universe. Although Burke may at times speak like Pangloss (for example, when he idealizes Marie-Antoinette and the 'age of chivalry'), he is in the end more like Voltaire, for he cannot deny the existence of evil; his frenzied restatement of the old arguments of providentialism and the harmony of the cosmos is similar to Voltaire's clutching at old-fashioned Newtonian deism. Burke's refusal to consider the Revolution of 1688 as a real revolution, his contention that the constitution had existed 'time out of mind', is not dissimilar to Voltaire's refusal to take seriously scientific discoveries which were incompatible with a universe created by a Divine Clockmaker: if Voltaire is a 'fixiste'[67] with regard to the creation of the universe, Burke is a 'fixiste' with regard to the English constitution, and what both

---

[65] Ibid., p. 439.   [66] Ibid. iii. 393.
[67] See R. Pomeau, *La Religion de Voltaire* (Paris, 1956), pp. 400 sqq.

writers reject is any argument which would undermine the immutability of moral values. Burke's political philosophy often comes close to the optimistic providentialism of the early eighteenth century. However, it is not the optimism of Shaftesbury or Pope: it is a providentialism under enormous pressure from events which is struggling to survive as a guide to man's moral life in an age of unprecedented crisis.

In the present paper attention has been focused mainly on Burke's relations to the French Enlightenment. His relation to the English Enlightenment (and not merely to Price and Paine) is a large subject which has never been adequately explored,[68] so that it is permissible to wonder whether many of his leading ideas do not come from reflection on (not necessarily agreement with) writers like Shaftesbury, Hutcheson, Pope, and the English deists. It was certainly not from Aquinas that he learnt that the laws of commerce were the laws of God or that the 'untaught feelings' were a source of virtue; nor did Aquinas provide him with a doctrine of religious toleration or a theory of the English constitution. At the same time, there is no need to make him a Romantic, since he is simply expressing, in his own incomparable way, ideas that were familiar to eighteenth-century readers.

[68] There is little on this important subject apart from M. Einaudi, 'The British Background of Burke's Political Philosophy', *Political Science Qtly.*, xlix (1934), 576–98.

XVII

The Legacy of John Wesley:
The Pastoral Office in Britain and America

THE Wesleyan doctrine of the Pastoral Office, a closely articulated exposition of Wesley's legacy, had a hectic heyday in England in the second quarter of the nineteenth century. Theologically it has fallen upon hard times,[1] but it remains an interesting problem in the transmission of ideas, more particularly in the respective roles of ideas and events in shaping institutions. The doctrine appealed to history as well as to scripture, and assumed *a priori* that every body politic possessed sovereign legislative power.[2] The Methodist legislature was Conference, in which Wesley had chosen to exercise his plenitude of power with the preachers, and to which he had ultimately bequeathed his power to station them in their respective 'circuits' or preaching rounds by the Deed of Declaration. His general superintendence over the whole Society had been vested in each circuit in what had been known as his Assistant (that is the general overseer of the circuit) and Helpers (the other itinerants), and were now known as the Superintendent and ordinary preachers; and his daily oversight had passed to District Committees acting on behalf of Conference. This concentration of spiritual authority, it was claimed, was rooted in

---

[1] For a theological treatment, see John Kent, *The Age of Disunity* (1966), pp. 44–85, and J. C. Bowmer, 'Church and Ministry in Wesleyan Methodism from the Death of Wesley to the Death of Jabez Bunting' (Ph.D. thesis, University of Leeds, 1967).

[2] The following outline is based on J. Beecham, *An Essay on the Constitution of Wesleyan Methodism* (3rd edn., 1851), pp. 2–6, 42, 46–9, 81 sqq., 117, 120. This, the first major text (originally published in 1829 and republished in 1850 and 1851, when the Wesleyan Reform secessions were in full flood and Beecham as President had to act up to his doctrine), spans the entire active history of the doctrine. Cf. Richard Watson, *Theological Institutes* (1829), iii. 361–9.

the New Testament. Christ had filled the whole Pastoral Office, and transmitted his authority to his ministers. The pastor, wholly given up to the work, must feed and also rule the flock; his authority, which included ordination, legislation, the power of admission into the Church, and of reproof, exhortation, and excision from it, was *sui generis*, and could not be shared with those who were not pastors, even if, like local preachers or class leaders, they performed valuable spiritual functions; and the fullness of his power was held to afford the best safeguard 'that our doctrines shall be preserved in their purity'.

In the heyday of Jabez Bunting, from about 1825 until the 1850s, the polemical intent of this skilful double appeal to what must *a priori* be, and to the practical upshot of Methodist history and scripture, was betrayed by a certain smoothness, even slickness. For the striking feature of Methodist theological literature in the generation following Wesley's death in 1791 was its total silence on the whole matter.[3] The biblical commentators of the immediate post-Wesleyan period, too, who had to make something of the whole range of texts to which the later expositors of the Pastoral Office appealed, made very modest claims. Indeed they altogether undermined that pillar of ministerial authority, Heb. 13: 17—'Obey them that have the rule over you . . . for they watch over your souls as they that shall give account'[4]—and put their polemical energy into expounding texts which rebuke the abuse of pastoral power.[5] In this they maintained the tradition of Wesley himself, whose *Notes on the New Testament* were among the authoritative standards of the Connexion. Wesley asserted for the minister 'a power of inflicting and remitting ecclesiastical censures', but his desire to justify the ministrations of his helpers led him to talk as if pastoral authority might be divided, and he was often brusque with the official shepherds of parishes, his fellow

---

[3] This negative conclusion, first reached by the most careful student of the whole matter, Dr. J. C. Bowmer, 'Church and Ministry', pp. 307–9, is fully borne out by my own studies. The literature produced for, and about, the ministry even shows occasional tendencies to lapse into the very low view that the minister was simply a 'speaking brother'.

[4] T. Coke, *Commentary on the New Testament* (1803), *sub loco* (cf. commentary on Acts 20: 28 and 1 Cor. 4: 21); J. Sutcliffe, *A Commentary on the Old and New Testament* (2 vols., 1834–5), ii. 417, 426, 620. Text quoted in Wesley's version.

[5] e.g. Adam Clarke, *The New Testament . . . with a Commentary and Critical Notes* (1817), *sub* 1 Pet. 5: 3.

Anglican clergy.[6] Nor could the high Wesleyans of the Bunting era ever agree in their appeal to history, though they understood that if the itinerant were truly a full pastor of the Church of Christ, he must be shown to have exercised his authority independently of the Church of England at the earliest possible date. Richard Watson insisted that the preachers, while lacking the imposition of hands, had been 'virtually' ordained from the time of and by virtue of their summons to Wesley's first Conference in 1744.[7] This ran into historical difficulties: Wesley had always distinguished between the prophetic office (the right to preach and exhort), which he believed his itinerants possessed, and the priestly office (the power to administer the sacraments, etc.), which they did not; this was powerfully argued in his famous Korah sermon. Furthermore, the theory of 'virtual ordination', from 1744 onwards, failed to explain why Wesley had ordained several men in and after 1784, quite independently of their reception into full connexion. The Methodist historian George Smith went so far as to date the origin of the Methodist Pastoral Office back to 1739, when Wesley began field-preaching, and thought that denominational status was complete when Wesley separated his United Society in London from the Moravians on Sunday, 20 July 1740. Methodism, he believed, had undergone no further change 'except from small to great'. But this too encountered logical obstacles. By 1740 Wesley's Society could hardly be distinguished from earlier religious societies, like those associated with Horneck and Woodward, which had never become a denomination. Moreover, this argument undercut Smith's second line of defence that, after Wesley's death, Conference regarded reception into full connexion 'as equivalent to real or formal ordination'.[8] Uncertain as Smith was, however, he never rivalled the confusion of the American historian Nathan Bangs, who claimed that when Methodism

[6] e.g. on 1 Thess. 5: 13 ('Esteem them very highly in love for their work's sake'), *'For their work's sake* . . . But how are we to esteem them that do not work at all?' Even Heb. 13: 17 required obedience not in conscience or judgement but in 'your own will in things purely indifferent'. John Wesley, *Explanatory Notes upon the New Testament* (1958 edn.), pp. 387, 761, 762, 853, 886.

[7] *Life of John Wesley* (12th edn., n.d.), pp. 203-5, 372-6; A. B. Lawson, *John Wesley and the Christian Ministry* (1963), p. 111.

[8] *History of Wesleyan Methodism*, i (5th edn., 1866), 162, 164, 171; ii (4th edn., 1863), 235. Taking men into full connexion every year, Conference in 1792 forbade ordination without its special consent.

first entered the American colonies in 1766, it 'had received a regular shape [and] was known as a distinct denomination, though still adhering to the Church of England'.[9] On neither side of the Atlantic would the untidy ways of the eighteenth-century Church of England dovetail with the stricter categories of nineteenth-century churchmanship.

Wesley himself persistently refused to admit that he had separated, and in most respects was more comfortable in the Church of England at the end of his life than at the beginning. His field-preaching and other early arrangements led to clashes with Church authority at various levels, and had to be justified by necessity. Necessity had to be reinforced by casuistry. A tacit dispensation from the rubrics and canons, Wesley concluded in 1755, had the same force as an explicit dispensation—and the connivance of the Church authorities at what they could not but know amounted to a tacit dispensation.[10] The enthusiasm with which he embraced the arguments of Lord King and Stillingfleet, that bishops and presbyters were of the same order and that Christ and the Apostles prescribed no particular form of church government, betrayed Wesley's apprehensiveness about a new move. The Conference minutes of 1744 promised obedience to bishops 'in all things indifferent'. As Wesley became embroiled with the hierarchy on matters doctrinal and practical, however, a certain desperation began to colour his pledges of loyalty. In the summer of 1755 the game seemed almost up: 'My conclusion (which I cannot give up) that it is lawful to continue in the Church stands, I know not how, almost without any premises that are able to bear its weight.'[11] Moreover, the Wesley whom the nineteenth-century orthodox remembered as the hammer of Arians and Calvinists gave vent to much eighteenth-century weariness with the entrenched theological positions of the past. The Rules of Society required of members only a desire 'to flee from the wrath to come, to be saved from their sins'. Like the pioneers of revival in America, Wesley stressed the New Birth, the conditions of vigour and energy in the faith, and yet shrank from allowing even this

[9] *A History of the Methodist Episcopal Church* (10th edn., 4 vols., New York, 1857), i. 44–5.

[10] *The Journal of John Wesley*, ed. N. Curnock (8 vols., 1938), iv. 120.

[11] *The Letters of John Wesley*, ed. J. Telford (8 vols., 1931), iii. 145; cf. ibid., pp. 131, 151.

primitive Christianity (as he believed it to be) to become a test, a means of sifting the sheep from the goats, a process ruinous ever since the Reformation. At the end of his life, Wesley was still claiming that Methodists

do not impose, in order to their admission, any opinions whatever. Let them hold particular or general redemption, absolute or conditional decrees; let them be Churchmen or Dissenters, Presbyterians or Independents, it is no obstacle. Let them choose one mode of baptism or another, it is no bar to their admission. The Presbyterian may be Presbyterian still; the Independent or Anabaptist use his own mode of worship. . . . They think and let think. One condition and one only is required,—a real desire to save their soul.[12]

Looseness to old orthodoxy as well as to old discipline might have compounded Wesley's discomfort in the Church. In fact, the Church's very inability to generate policy enhanced in it a capacity for absorption which enabled it to cope with later movements much more prickly than Methodism. After twenty years Wesley began, indeed, to enjoy a real 'tacit dispensation'. As early as 1758 he found that 'controversy is now asleep, and we in great measure live peaceably with all men, so that we are strangely at leisure to spend our whole time in enforcing plain, practical, vital religion'.[13] If from Richard Green's bibliography of *Anti-Methodist Publications* (1902) are removed the titles produced by the Arminian controversy (a bout of evangelical infighting) and those evoked by the expulsions from St. Edmund Hall in 1768 (which did not concern Wesley's Methodism), it appears that the number of anti-Methodist publications diminished with every decade, and by the end of Wesley's life was very small indeed. At a popular level too, 'where the movement pushed into new terrain it still encountered violence, but not on the scale of the 1740s and 1750s. In many once troubled places Methodism was soon tolerated and even welcomed'.[14] 'Prejudice seems now dying away', noted Wesley contentedly.[15] He himself became a popular public institution. At one time he

---

[12] *The Works of John Wesley* (Zondervan edn., 14 vols., Grand Rapids, Mich., n.d.), xiii. 266. Cf. John Wesley, *Sermons on Several Occasions*, ed. J. Beecham (1872), iii. 182–3.

[13] Wesley, *Works*, viii. 225–6.

[14] J. Walsh, 'Methodism and the Mob in the Eighteenth Century', *Studies in Church History*, viii (1972), 227.

[15] Wesley, *Journal*, vi. 390.

had justified field-preaching by the fact that pulpits were closed to him; from 1774 onwards he peppered his *Journal* with invitations to preach, and sometimes celebrate, in the parish church, especially in Yorkshire, and occasionally with the explicit approval of the bishop. Even in the Isle of Man, where in 1776 Bishop Richmond 'for the prevention of schism' had banned Methodist preachers from communion, Wesley in 1781 (after George Mason succeeded to the see) found 'no opposition . . . from the Bishop (a good man) or from the bulk of the clergy . . . we have now rather too little than too much reproach'.[16]

While Wesley's faith in the Church seemed gradually vindicated, formal Dissent, moving deeper into rationalism, became steadily less palatable to him. Moreover, Wesley's mission was to the nation, and especially to the lower classes, whereas on both sides of the Atlantic the old Dissent became increasingly élitist, aware not merely that the populace did not take to its new liberal rationalist views, but that it might become highly dangerous if it did. It was Dissenting ministers, rather than the parish priests of legend, who excommunicated Methodists in England, and still more in America.[17] America, indeed, was calculated to confirm Wesley's antipathy to Dissent. He mishandled the ideological conflict created by colonial revolt, advising the Government of the justice of the American cause, and yet pamphleteering so strongly against it as to leave a tradition in the connexional management that he 'had like to have ruined Methodism there'.[18] American Methodism was indeed painfully rent. In 1779 the Virginia Methodists joined with the Baptists to overthrow the Anglican establishment in the colony.[19] Deprived of their legal provision, the Virginia clergy stopped work, and a hectic Methodist expansion created a case for Methodist ordination, so that the people might receive the sacraments no longer available from the clergy. The Fluvanna Conference of 1779 introduced presbyteral ordination, and administration began. The one English preacher remaining in America, Francis Asbury (1745–1816), then

[16] L. Tyerman, *Life and Times of Rev. John Wesley* (6th edn., 3 vols., 1890), iii. 229; Wesley, *Journal*, vi. 151, 321.
[17] Ibid. iii. 70, 73.
[18] M[ethodist] C[hurch] A[rchives], R. Pilter to Jabez Bunting, 23 Oct. 1819. Cf. *History of American Methodism*, ed. E. S. Bucke (New York, 3 vols., 1964), i. 164.
[19] W. W. Sweet, *Methodism in American History* (New York, 1933), p. 101.

confined in Delaware, called a small group of northern preachers to what can only be called a schismatic Conference, established his sole authority over them, and extracted a promise that they would allow the sacraments to be received only from Anglican clergy. Asbury wrote coolly 'to our dissenting brethren in Virginia hoping to reclaim them'.[20] The Conference at Manakintown, Virginia in 1780 was critical; to the end it seemed that Asbury, representing a link with a fallen establishment and an English connexion now out of reach, must fail to convince the majority party. Yet somehow—Asbury suppressed the minutes—he got an agreement to suspend administration till Wesley could be consulted; and so the breach between a northern Methodism, over which Asbury had informally made himself bishop, and a southern Methodism which seemed to have taken the decisive step into presbyterianism was bridged over. Wesley could hardly have had a sharper warning against the perils of a dissenting Methodism.

Could Wesley cope with the American disputes and still provide for the continuance of the English movement after his death within the now congenial limits of the Church, and within his own not very singular views of church and ministry? The most recent scholarly opinion holds that 'if ever there was a year when Wesley could be said to have irrevocably severed himself and Methodism from the Church of England it was in 1784 when, by his ordinations and by the Deed of Declaration to take effect upon his death, he sought a settlement for the societies on both sides of the Atlantic'.[21] Yet more than one view of even that well-documented year is possible.

Wesley was resolved that 'no Methodist Trustees, if I can help it, shall after my death, any more than while I live, have the power of placing and displacing the preachers';[22] and by the Deed of Declaration (1784) he bequeathed his stationing power to Conference. The dispute in Virginia showed the inadequacy of a simple reference to Conference, and so the Deed named 100 preachers to constitute the Conference, and maintain their numbers by co-optation. They became known

---

[20] *The Journal and Letters of Francis Asbury*, ed. E. T. Clark (3 vols., 1958), i. 307; cf. ibid. iii. 22.

[21] F. Baker, *John Wesley and the Church of England* (1970), p. 218.

[22] Wesley, *Works*, xiii. 727.

as the Legal Hundred. As John Pawson, one of the preachers keenest to administer the sacraments, put it:

. . . the principle of this Deed was to identify the meaning of the word Conference, so that it might be ascertained & acknowledged by the law of the nation, & by that means to secure all the chapels. But there certainly was no more design of paving the way for ordination, or separating from the church by anything that was then done than of flying up into the clouds.[23]

For the chapels 'situate in Ireland, or other parts out of the kingdom of Great Britain', Conference might appoint delegates armed with its full powers, whose acts, signed and entered into the Conference Journal, should be deemed to be Conference acts. Of late years Wesley had held Irish Conferences every other year, presiding alternately with Thomas Coke, and after his death Coke became virtually perpetual President of an annual Irish Conference. Irish preachers were also named among the Legal Hundred. How this provision might be extended to 'other parts out of the kingdom of Great Britain' speedily transpired.

In September 1784 a presbytery of three Anglican priests— John Wesley, Thomas Coke, and James Creighton—ordained two itinerants, Whatcoat and Vasey, as deacons and elders, and Wesley made Coke General Superintendent of the American work. They took supplies of the *Sunday Service in North America*, Wesley's reformed and abbreviated version of the Book of Common Prayer, which contained forms of ordination, closely modelled on those of the Church, for a threefold ministry of deacons, elders, and superintendents. They were to make Asbury joint general superintendent, and to ordain selected American preachers to administer the sacraments. Wesley had long believed he was 'as real a Christian bishop as the Archbishop of Canterbury',[24] and his clandestine transaction with Coke (also a presbyter) makes sense in the light of the provisions of the Deed of Declaration for 'parts out of the kingdom of Great Britain'. All Wesley could give (and this Coke knew he could not do without) was his explicit blessing upon the remodelling of American Methodism. He seems to have envisaged an extension of the system operating in Ireland, with the American Methodists linked notionally with the Church of

---

[23] M.C.A., Tyerman MSS. iii, fo. 66.   [24] Wesley, *Letters*, vii. 262.

England by the superintendency of Thomas Coke, and substantially by a modernized prayer-book; like the Irish, the
Americans were also given a toehold in the sovereign legislature
of Methodism (which also operated in an Anglican context) by
the stationing of three members of the Legal Hundred among
them. There have always been allegations that Wesley was here
pushed into schism by the ambition of Thomas Coke. Certainly
his outburst against the assumption of the title of bishop by
Coke and Asbury is famous.[25] Yet the American arrangements
were entirely consistent with Wesley's wider disposition of his
affairs, and Coke's weakness was not ambition, but the thickest
vein of personal silliness ever disclosed by a Methodist leader
of the first rank.[26] Coke multiplied the criticism Wesley must
inevitably encounter by treating the American preachers to a
slashing attack upon the Anglican clergy. John Wesley's bitterest
critic was his brother Charles; he had always held straiter views
of church order and for thirty years had imagined himself to
'stand in the way of [his] brother's violent counsellors, the object
of both their fear and hate'; nor was he sweetened by John's
willingness to act behind his back:

> Lord Mansfield told me last year [he wrote to Dr. Chandler] that
> ordination was separation. This my brother does not and will not
> see; or that he has renounced the principles and practice of his
> whole life; that he has acted contrary to all his declarations, pro-
> testations, and writings, . . . and left an indelible blot on his name
> . . . our partnership here is dissolved, but not our friendship.[27]

Yet this letter to an Anglican priest bound for America itself
suggests that the dispute between the Wesley brothers was not
so much the end-product of a long course of ecclesiastical
irregularity in England, as part of a larger disagreement in the
Anglican world about the unprecedented situation across the
Atlantic.

[25] Asbury, *Journal and Letters*, iii. 65. As a weary old man, Asbury himself echoed
Wesley: 'A Bishop, oh that it had never been named. I was elected and ordained
a superintendent as my parchment will show' (ibid. iii. 378).

[26] Coke never grew up; towards the end of his life his colleagues rescued him
on the brink of matrimony with a woman whose record of business fraud was so
bad that 'if one of our travelling preachers were to marry such a woman he would
be censured, if not excluded from the Connexion. The woman's creditors were
exulting in the prospect of arresting the Doctor immediately on his marriage with
her.' M.C.A., Tyerman MSS. i, fos. 349–50.

[27] Tyerman, *Wesley*, ii. 247; T. Jackson, *Life of Charles Wesley*, ii (1841), 391.

'By a very uncommon train of providences', as Wesley put it in the understatement of the century, the jurisdiction exercised by the Bishop of London in America had been ended by the peace settlement of 1783. The English bishops could not ordain citizens of what was now a foreign power, men unable to take the oaths of allegiance and supremacy. The rump of episcopalian clergy in America could neither look to them for salvation, nor replace them by any ordinary procedure. William White, rector of Christ Church, Philadelphia, recommended in 1782 that the episcopalians, lay and clerical, should make a sort of social contract with each other, declaring themselves an episcopal church, and together elect 'a superior order of ministers . . . they both being interested in the choice'.[28] 'In an emergency in which a duly authorized ministry cannot be obtained', the first duty was to maintain public worship and preaching. White's programme, which entered deeply into the final constitution of the Protestant Episcopal Church of America, was far more republican than Wesley's; but its assumption that 'the duty and office of a bishop differs in nothing from that of other priests, except in the power of ordination and confirmation, and in the right of precedency in ecclesiastical meetings' was the same.

Like Wesley, White was immediately challenged. A small group of Connecticut clergy, maintaining that 'an episcopal church without an episcopacy, if it be not a contradiction in terms, would . . . be a new thing under the sun',[29] secretly chose Samuel Seabury to be their bishop, and dispatched him to England for consecration. The issue between White and Seabury could hardly be isolated from the issue between the brothers Wesley. White was kind to Coke in America, tried to promote a union with the Methodists on his own platform, and attempted to negotiate with Wesley in England in 1787.[30] Charles Wesley collected evidence of clerical alarm from New York

[28] W. White, *The Case of the Episcopal Churches in the United States considered* (Philadelphia, 1782), reprinted in *Hist[orical] Mag[azine of the] Prot[estant] Episc[opal] Ch[urch]*, xxii (1953), 435 sqq. 'Never had so strange a sight been seen before in Christendom, as this necessity of various members knitting themselves into one by such a conscious and voluntary act': Samuel Wilberforce, *History of the Protestant Episcopal Church in America* (2nd edn., 1846), pp. 195–6.

[29] *Hist. Mag. Prot. Episc. Ch.* xxii. 479.

[30] E. J. Drinkhouse, *History of Methodist Reform*, i (Baltimore, 1899), 267–8 n.; J. Vickers, *Thomas Coke, Apostle of Methodism* (1969), pp. 90–1.

and Seabury's correspondence with the S.P.G., and wept that the American 'poor sheep' had 'been betrayed into separation from the Church of England' by not waiting for Bishop Seabury. Two Methodist preachers were ordained by Seabury, one of whom kept Charles Wesley supplied with backstairs gossip.[31]

John Wesley's low estimate of Seabury's prospects was borne out by the result. For some years the knowledgeable had been pressing the Americans to seek 'legitimization' by ancient ecclesiastical authority from Catholic Rome to Lutheran Scandinavia, or to take direct presbyteral action: 'If the British islands were sunk in the sea (and the surface of the globe has suffered greater changes)', counselled Franklin, 'you would probably take some such method.'[32] The Primate's view that Seabury's consecration by the nonjuring Scottish bishops 'would create jealousies and schisms in the Church' was dismally fulfilled. It was held that the Scottish bishops required a *congé d'élire* from the Pretender (who must absolve Seabury from allegiance), that Seabury remained in canonical subjection to them, even that his orders were invalid. Efforts were made to exclude Seabury from the convention of his church on the grounds that he was still receiving half-pay as a former British army chaplain, a charge quaintly parried by White with the doctrine that 'an ecclesiastical body needed not to be over-righteous'.[33] Still worse, Seabury had promised to introduce the Scottish communion office with its primitive un-Anglican devotions, while White's party were as keen as Wesley to bring the Prayer Book up to date; they produced a form which omitted the Athanasian and Nicene creeds and the descent into hell. And lest anyone but Charles Wesley thought the Bishop of Connecticut more palatable to American Methodists than he was to American episcopalians, Seabury called on them to 'return to the unity of the Church which they have

---

[31] MS. copies of the letters collected by Charles Wesley are in M.C.A. Cf. Jackson, *Charles Wesley*, ii. 392; Baker, p. 275.

[32] Prince Hoare, *Memoirs of Granville Sharp* (1820), pp. 207 sqq.; E. J. Beardsley, *Life and Correspondence of Samuel Seabury* (Boston, 1881), pp. 97–161; Wilberforce, pp. 199–207; R. D. Middleton, *Dr. Routh* (1938), pp. 48 sqq.; W. White, *Memoirs of the Protestant Episcopal Church in the United States of America* (Philadelphia, 1820), pp. 88, 91; *The Private Correspondence of Benjamin Franklin*, ed. W. T. Franklin (1817), pp. 57–8.

[33] Beardsley, p. 160; Hoare, pp. 212, 231 n.; *Hist. Mag. Prot. Episc. Ch.* xxii. 484–6; White, *Memoirs*, pp. 124, 166, 172–3.

unreasonably, unnecessarily and wickedly broken, by their separation and schism'.[34]

The American latitudinarians were more skilful. They got their own State governments to press the ministry in England for legislation to enable sympathetic English bishops to consecrate three Americans, who might thus create an English succession independent of Seabury. This Bill 'to enable the English Bishops to consecrate [three Socinians] for foreign countries, viz. the overthrow of Bishop Seabury of Connecticut',[35] introduced by the Primate in 1786, was frustrated in its original intention by the failure of the bishop-elect of Virginia to raise the fare to come for his consecration. White and Provoost, the new Bishops of Pennsylvania and New York, had now to take Seabury seriously, and in 1789 they brought Connecticut, still making no concessions to the synodal rights of the laity acknowledged in every other diocese, into a national Protestant Episcopal Church. The discomforts of this uneasy diplomatic combination of theological opposites soon made themselves felt. In April 1791 Thomas Coke, confessing that 'I went further in the separation of our church in America than Mr. Wesley . . . did intend', proposed a reunion to Bishop White, involving the reordination of the American preachers. This astonishing volte-face was probably due to the fright Coke received from the explosion of militant conservatism in England. English Methodists, it seemed, could only be safe as a religious society unequivocally within the Church, and by the same token they should make overtures to the Protestant Episcopal Church on behalf of the American Methodists; the latter, moreover, were in serious constitutional trouble, which might be salved by a fresh legitimization of the management.[36] Coke had characteristically gone behind Asbury's back; and on receiving news of Wesley's death, he scampered off to England in the hope of succeeding to Wesley's monarchical authority. White, however, responded kindly, suggesting that Coke and Asbury be consecrated bishops for the Methodists in a united Church. Seabury made no reply at all, and by 1791 the tongues of angels could hardly have

[34] Wilberforce, p. 215; Beardsley, p. 230.

[35] Wilberforce, p. 216.

[36] M.C.A., Thomas Coke to Joseph Benson, 15 July 1791; J. J. Tigert, *A Constitutional History of American Episcopal Methodism* (2nd edn., Nashville, Tenn., 1904), p. 317.

united a Protestant Episcopal Church whose present energies were entirely consumed by the problem of survival and the incalculably aggressive machine being constructed by Francis Asbury. The two vehicles of the Anglican tradition in America had, therefore, already diverged decisively in style, orientation, and power.

In 1791 Coke seems to have sought an American settlement in the general interests of a Methodism in which England was the senior partner, a *coup* which had eluded him even in 1784. In that year the Christmas Conference, a specially summoned gathering of the American preachers, had undertaken to obey Wesley 'in matters belonging to church government', and after his death 'to do everything . . . to preserve and promote our union with the Methodists in Europe'. But Asbury knew that on the sacrament question he had driven Wesley's authority to the limit; his future usefulness turned on securing a vote of confidence from the American preachers which would tie their hands and might deter Wesley from stationing him out of the country, or from sending him on roving commissions as he had sent Coke and tried to send Freeborn Garretson. Asbury insisted on election by his brethren, thus creating a precedent by which future ordinands would be nominated by the Superintendent and elected by the Conference. In 1786 Wesley summoned a General Conference to meet at Baltimore the following year which was to make the Englishman, Richard Whatcoat, a Superintendent and the American, Garretson, Superintendent for missions in Nova Scotia, Newfoundland, and the West Indies. The Americans, however, had long made their own arrangements for Conferences, and were incensed. They refused to appoint the new Superintendents, extracted a written undertaking from Coke never to exercise his episcopal functions outside the United States, expunged their undertaking to accept Wesley's authority, left his name out of the minutes, and held that even he had no power to move Asbury to Europe. Moreover, they treated the proceedings, not as a General Conference, but as the Baltimore Annual Conference brought forward.

Herein lay a second problem. The Christmas Conference had been a constitutional convention: once it dispersed, the Americans lacked the sovereign conference which existed in England, the continuance of which after Wesley's death had been prescribed by the Deed of Declaration. The General Superintendent had to conduct local Annual Conferences as Wesley conducted the Irish Conference. Three were required in 1785, but as early as 1790 fourteen were needed, two beyond the Alleghenies. In 1789, in a desperate effort to secure common policy and legislation, Asbury created a Council of Bishops and presiding elders (*anglice* chairmen of districts, or assistant bishops) to safeguard the general welfare of the church. He appointed the members and retained a veto; yet this Council could not, any more than Wesley, bind any district without the support of the District Conference. The hopelessness of expecting the sovereign legislature in England to control the separatism of American district conferences was poignantly illustrated by the one modification of the American Discipline carried by the Council on its own authority, an article against dealing in slaves:[37] the most divisive moral issue they must face was outside the experience of almost all the English preachers. Assailed by James O'Kelly, a hell-raiser deeply entrenched in Virginia, and opposed by Coke, the Council was dropped in 1791.

One resort remained. Wesley was scarcely in the grave when, in July 1791, the Americans buried his scheme of government and summoned a General Conference for the following summer. This Conference led to considerable constitutional development. A great campaign by O'Kelly to allow the preachers an appeal against the stations appointed by the bishop was defeated at the cost of a substantial secession; but the whole body of preachers agreed to meet every four years, and established their power over the discipline and government of the Church; bishops were to be elected by and be responsible to them. On the other hand, the executive was strengthened by the formal recognition of the order of presiding elders, appointed by the bishops. The plenitude of power formerly exercised by Wesley was being divided among various hands; indeed, the westward march of American Methodism made some formal federalism increasingly desirable. In 1808 New York obtained the support of the 'fringe' New England, Western, and South Carolina Conferences in an effort to break the grip upon the General Conference established by the central Conferences of Baltimore, Philadelphia, and Virginia. After a deadlock which brought the

[37] Tigert, p. 252.

church to the point of break-up, the General Conference replaced itself by a quadrennial 'Delegated Conference', composed of one-fifth of the membership of each district Annual Conference. The Delegated Conference was not to be in practice sovereign; except under stringent conditions, certain reserved matters including standards of doctrine, the system of representation and of itinerant episcopacy, and the general Rules of Society were beyond its reach. A peculiar and independent American Methodism was now in being. Coke was not present, but had to bear the odium of the revelation of his private negotiations with Bishop White in 1791. The General Conference, in effect, politely sacked him. It elected its first native-born bishop, William McKendree. But nationalism and sectionalism went hand in hand. With Asbury's support, each Annual Conference was authorized to form its own regulations relative to dealings in slaves. A pastorate untrammelled by formal lay influence, and yet constitutionally debarred from enforcing a common ethic, was a thing undreamt of in the English apologetic for the Pastoral Office.

Europe was as full of surprises for church government as America. Having ordained for America, Wesley had begun to ordain for the West Indies and elsewhere in the overseas mission field (a practice Conference continued after his death) and, in a few cases, for Scotland, where he was becoming too old to celebrate in person.[38] So far Wesley had not trespassed upon the jurisdiction of the Church of England; but at the very end of his life he ordained Rankin and Moore, who neither left the country nor themselves ordained, though Moore was to survive till ordination by imposition of hands began in Methodism in 1836. Wesley also ordained Alexander Mather, thought likely to be his successor, and was alleged to have made him a bishop. Conference became increasingly concerned with the question of separation from the Church, but Wesley himself remained adamant against it. He produced his famous Korah sermon to show that the itinerants' call to preach did not include a priestly vocation,[39] and he is said to have given Coke a fearful

---

[38] M.C.A., Tyerman MSS. iii, fo. 150.

[39] This sermon was suppressed after Wesley's death, and when in 1829 it was republished as Sermon no. cxv, it bore a footnote suggesting that it was not to be taken seriously.

dressing-down when that enthusiast talked boldly of introducing the sacraments in England.[40] Not until his eighty-sixth birthday in 1789 did Wesley admit (what his preachers already knew) that he was ageing; and when he died in 1791 the constitutional future for Methodism was so obscure that the strident factions among the preachers each claimed him for themselves.

In 1787 James Creighton had tried to secure the support of the English hierarchy for Wesley's original scheme of episcopal management; he now, after Wesley's death, reported that a pale shadow of this was in favour—the Connexion to be governed by chairmen of districts appointed annually.[41] The party eager to separate from the Church and introduce the sacraments avowed that Wesley intended such a system, quite independent of regular ordination, and that he had made Mather a bishop to set it going. Their case was not helped by Mather's losing his nerve and joining the pro-Church party. John Pawson exploded:

> Wonders never cease. Would you think it after all their clamour about the church, & their quoting Mr. W[esley's] authority, this self-same Mr. W. ordained Mr. Mather Bishop just after the London Conference [in 1788]. This was in order that he might support the Church of England. Is it possible that Mr. W. could intend this? No it is not. It is rank nonsense . . .[42]

And there were those to whom the whole hierarchical principle was an un-Methodist abomination. Joseph Bradford, who claimed to know Wesley's mind, held that 'if Mr. Wesley told Messrs. Moore & Bradburn that he was determined that the Methodist[s] should after his decease become an Episcopal Church, he left the world with a lie in his mouth'.[43] Certainly Wesley was said to have declared: ' "As soon as I am dead, the Methodists will be a regular Presbyterian Church" . . . [and] he meant, that *his death would make us such*. While he lived, he was the head, the Bishop; but as soon as he died, all his power

[40] M.C.A., Tyerman MSS. iii, fos. 142, 133 (cf. fos. 150–1); Tyerman, *Wesley*, iii. 443.
[41] Lake Junaluska, N.C., United Methodist Church Archives, Creighton MSS., 4 July 1791. Cf. Smith, *Wesleyan Methodism*, ii, Appendix E.
[42] M.C.A., Tyerman MSS. iii, fo. 204. Cf. S. Bradburn, *The Question, 'Are the Methodists dissenters?' fairly examined* (n. pl., 1792), p. 14. Mather had declined ordination at short notice in 1785 (Tyerman MSS. iii, fo. 54).
[43] M.C.A., Tyerman MSS. i, fo. 139.

died with him.'[44] Whatever the form of government, no one supposed that taking a preacher into full connexion was virtual ordination. John Pawson held explicitly that

we must have ordination among us, were it only to preserve order & to keep up a proper esteem in the minds of the people for that most sacred ordinance. Observe with regard to the far greater number of preachers now in Connexion, ordination was not so much as thought of, much less was it intended either by themselves or by those who recd. them into Connexion. Therefore these men cannot be ordained. Ordination among us was never thought of when we were admitting preachers till the last London Conference [1788]. And although at Leeds [1793] we had a most solemn and blessed time when the preachers were admitted, yet there were some among those 24 that I would not ordain on any account . . . & we have some others in full connexion who pass along in some poor Circuits who are by no means fit to be ordained.[45]

It was soon obvious that a President changing annually and a yearly Conference session of two or three weeks could not manage the Connexion. The critical problem, however, was not administrative but political.[46] The campaign against the Test and Corporation Acts in the late eighties raised a spirit of militant resistance in the Church of England; the French Revolution raised it still further, and for a time provided the Church with sufficient mob force to nullify the guarantees of the Toleration Act. The chief victims of the mob were the old Dissenters, especially the Unitarians; but prudence conspired with the rising conservatism of the Methodist grandees, laymen and preachers, to stop the drift from the Church, and it was reinforced by resentment towards the élite among the preachers on the part of all those itinerants considered unfit to administer the sacraments. Rational and hysterical by turns[47] but always a weathercock, Coke went with the tide, and for two Conferences after the death of Wesley the conservative coalition was on top. In the autumn of 1792, however, the response of English artisan opinion to the movement of the Parisian *sans-culottes* loosed a

[44] Bradburn, *Are Methodists dissenters?*, p. 19.
[45] M.C.A., Tyerman MSS. iii, fo. 242. Cf. ibid. i, fo. 128; iii, fo. 145.
[46] For a fuller discussion, see W. R. Ward, 'The French Revolution and the English Churches; a Case Study in the Impact of Revolution upon the Church', *Miscellanea Historiae Ecclesiasticae*, iv (1972), 55–84.
[47] M.C.A., Thomas Coke to Joseph Benson, 15 July 1791.

torrent of anti-establishment opinion which in Methodism took the form of an uncontrollable clamour for separation. After pitched battles in all the Methodist urban centres, the preachers were left with no option but to follow the flock or lose it, and in 1795 they made a compact with the trustees of the Connexion. It was called the Plan of Pacification. Forbidding the general administration of the sacraments, the Plan contained escape clauses which permitted administration on condition of lay and Conference consent, and so enabled Methodists to move rapidly and overwhelmingly into practical Nonconformity. Thus an entirely unforeseeable outburst of lay anti-clericalism had thrust ministerial functions upon the preachers in conditions that made selective ordination impossible.

Moreover, administrative hierarchy also suffered defeat. In 1794 President Pawson made a serious attempt on pragmatic grounds to establish episcopacy, starting from Wesley's bishops, Coke and Mather. A small secret conclave of preachers, held at Lichfield, prepared to divide the English and Scottish work into eight districts, each with a bishop to ordain: six of these should come from the conclave. A storm was raised against this plan by William Thompson, who ascribed it to 'love of power' and bitterly assailed the coalition of Coke and his personal enemies which had promoted it. At the next Conference he defeated the scheme,[48] together with Mather's last attempts to establish himself as 'king in Israel', and thus destroyed an opportunity for a degree of institutional decentralization which Methodism later badly needed.

The Plan of Pacification, indispensable to internal order, put the Connexion in political jeopardy. The year 1795 saw the worst of a severe subsistence crisis and opened the door to an unprecedented wave of itinerant preaching—Methodist, Baptist, Congregational, and indeed undenominational—which shook the Church in its rural strongholds. With the old mobs now impossible to raise, the Church authorities called for fresh legal powers, particularly the withdrawal of legal protection from Sunday Schools and itinerant preaching under the Toleration Act. From 1795, when Coke was given to understand that some pledge of loyalty was required from the Connexion,

[48] M.C.A., W. Thompson to R. Rodda, 9 May 1794; W. Thompson to J. Benson, 8 May 1794; Tyerman MSS. iii, fo. 249.

Methodism was in danger. Coke's reply was to campaign for the exclusion of Alexander Kilham, a preacher seeking to reform Methodism by increasing lay influence, and to try once more to strengthen the Anglican connexion by obtaining episcopal ordination for a number of Methodist preachers. The rising tone of Anglican churchmanship, and its new predilection for political solutions, made this cause hopeless; but Kilham was expelled in 1796, and a great race for support between him and Conference began. In 1797 he offered extensive lay participation in the government of a New Connexion, while the old Conference made substantial concessions to the local authorities of circuit and Society, the Quarterly and Leaders' Meetings. When in 1829 and subsequent years the high Wesleyan doctrine of the Pastoral Office was formally expounded by John Beecham (1787–1856) and his successors, it was held that these concessions were purely procedural and in no way abridged the connexional principle or the authority of the Pastoral Office; at the time it was said that ministerial authority had been surrendered.[49] Moreover, in an astonishing confession, John Pawson, who had pressed so hard for the sacraments, held that 'Church hours & the sacraments have not by any means answered the expectations of either preachers or people', and should be surrendered to save the itinerancy from the government. Alas, 'the Plan of Pacification stands in the way'.[50] The idea that the rights secured by the Plan to laymen to solicit the sacrament from the preachers inhibited the latter from abandoning the Pastoral Office was not a notion entertained in the age of Jabez Bunting. Was it, however, surprising that the *Form of Discipline* of 1797 required the minister to feed and guide, but not to teach or govern the flock?[51] Or that the generation which took the torch from Wesley, and surrendered successively his scheme for an international episcopacy, ordination, and unfettered preachers' rule as they had been kept up in America,

[49] J. Crowther, *The Methodist Manual* (Halifax, 1810), p. 31.

[50] M.C.A., Tyerman MSS. iii, fos. 319–20.

[51] The *Form of Discipline* defined the office of a minister as 'to watch over souls as he that must give account; to feed and guide the flock'. Both these phrases came from the minutes of Wesley's first Conference (1744), where the first had applied to the ordained clergy of the Church and the second derived from his commission to his lay Assistants 'in the absence of the minister, to feed and guide, to teach and govern the flock'. On the latter powers, which the ministry most needed in the 1820s, the *Form of Discipline* was characteristically silent.

preserved a deafening silence on the question of the Pastoral Office?

Yet a change was at hand. In 1799 a young Manchester revivalist, Jabez Bunting (1779–1858), began his probation as a Wesleyan preacher. He united force of personality with force of circumstances to effect a wholesale change in English Methodism. Faced with disorderly revivalists at Macclesfield in his second circuit, in 1803, Bunting developed a stern view of church order and discipline. From this preoccupation circumstances never permitted him to escape. Revivalism, class conflict in the flock, difficulties in the agencies of religious action, such as the Sunday Schools, related to the Methodist Societies but often imperfectly controlled by them, the dreadful financial crisis which set in after the war[52]—all, in Bunting's view, called for the determined exercise of discipline locally, reinforced by the collective action of the pastorate in Conference. Bunting inspired a vigour of central executive activity unseen since Wesley. His central administration stiffened the Methodist executive as episcopacy might have done. Zealous for the conversion of the heathen, Thomas Coke had had no conception of the elaborate logistics of modern missions: the Methodist Missionary Society, one of the great nineteenth-century charities, was Bunting's answer to that need. His Theological Institution preceded Anglican attempts to provide seminary training for the ministry. There were Conference committees to govern the raising or expenditure of funds, or to break up long-standing constitutional arrangements in the circuits. And there were continual negotiations with Government on the future of emancipated West Indian slaves, on the security of missions, on education.

Bunting published little, but his early Macclesfield letters contained the double appeal to Wesley and the New Testament, together with that exaggerated emphasis on discipline which flowered in the doctrine of the Pastoral Office as expounded by the 'high' Wesleyan party in the second quarter of the nineteenth century. He called on the preachers to return 'to the

[52] On these problems, see W. R. Ward, 'The Religion of the People and the Problem of Control, 1790–1830', *Studies in Church History*, viii (1972), 237–57. I have made a biographical assessment of Bunting in *The Early Correspondence of Jabez Bunting* (R. Hist. Soc., Camden 4th ser. xi, 1972).

spirit & discipline of ancient Methodism, & with that resolve to stand or fall'. The church was constituted by 'that proper ministerial *pastorship* & *oversight* of the flock which the New Testament enjoins as universally necessary'. 'ECCLESIASTICAL DISCIPLINE . . . is to effect and maintain an open and visible separation between *the Church* and *the world*.'[53] Later the Liverpool Minutes, drafted under his presidency at the critical Conference of 1820, compellingly described the new ministry, evangelical yet resolute, and became required study for District Meetings and ordinands. Of the great Methodist authorities Bunting alone supported the lay apologists who replied to the attempts of Mark Robinson of Beverley to revive a Church Methodism in 1825, and asserted 'substantially a good and valid *presbyterian* ordination of our ministers, which every preacher receives when admitted into full connexion'.[54] In 1829, at the end of his second presidential year, Bunting gave a notable ordination charge, setting in the general context of the ministry 'that godly discipline which . . . [is], equally with the dispensation of the word and sacraments, an institution of Christ'.[55] Defeated during his first presidency, he succeeded during his third (1836) in introducing ordination by imposition of hands, instead of reception by simple vote of Conference. The Methodist preacher was now, for all to see, a minister, ordained to an undifferentiated ministry of which Wesley had known nothing. Methodism was now (according to one of Bunting's preacher friends) 'an entire system', what Wesley might have condemned as a sect.[56]

The challenge of the Methodist secessions of 1834–5 and 1850–5 consolidated in the mind of Alfred Barrett, whose works became prescribed texts for Methodist ministers, the doctrine towards which Bunting had been working. Barrett's *Essay on*

[53] M.C.A., J. Bunting to R. Reece, 15 July 1803; Bunting to G. Marsden, 13 Dec. 1803; T. P. Bunting, *Life of Jabez Bunting* (2 vols., 1859–89), i. 430.

[54] M.C.A., Bunting to H. Sandwith, 10 Feb. 1825; H. Sandwith to Bunting, 12 Feb. 1825.

[55] *Sermons by Jabez Bunting*, ed. W. L. Thornton (2 vols., 1861–2), ii. 375, 379.

[56] M.C.A., W. Vevers to Bunting, 13 April 1830; Wesley, *Letters*, viii. 66, 71; *Works*, xiii. 272. It was still an odd system. Missionaries who had returned home after completing their probation were to be examined like the ordinands of the year; having been ordained before going overseas, they were not subject to re-ordination, but were at least theoretically liable to be refused reception into full connexion at this point, four or more years after ordination.

the Pastoral Office explained that Christ had established different orders of ministry for different purposes. The Apostles had been commissioned to found the Church, complete its doctrine, and convince the Gentiles. Prophets had expounded the Christian sense of the Old Testament to the Jews. Pastors and teachers were to govern the settled congregations of the faithful, and had a continuing function when the work of the other two orders was done and they came to an end. Having thus inverted Wesley's order, and made his preachers almost successors of Aaron, Barrett expounded the functional Methodist view of church and ministry. Circuit superintendents were very like the 'primitive angel or bishop of the Church'; what mattered was not the succession of offices but the maintenance of pastoral oversight. English Methodism had no order of deacons, but it did not lack diaconal service.[57] The harrowing débâcle of the Wesleyan Reform secessions, which cost a third of the member-ship, drove Barrett still higher. In some amazing history he held that Wesley's assistants had been genuine pastors, and that this made separation from the Establishment inevitable, though it had in fact been 'compelled' 'by the exclusive acts of the clergy of that day'. But at bottom he wanted to get away from history, and even from his old functionalism, into a symbolic doctrine of the Church, 'the necessary connexion between a definite form of doctrine, and a suitable as well as definite church regimen in which to teach it to all around'. Wesleyan Methodism taught the need to attest justification by a spotless life; it stressed the hazard of losing the heavenly treasure by slothfulness and sin. This state of spiritual *Angst* necessitated 'especially amongst the industrial classes . . . a subordination of one to another, with a putting away of reserve, a mutual watch-fulness among the ministry'.[58] Hearty to a fault, and un-ashamedly regarding their religious institutions as devices for a purpose, the flock could hardly be expected to recognize this inward spiritual essence of which the outward form of the Wesleyan constitution was now held to be the symbol. Symbol-ism, moreover, had painful practical disadvantages, for the

---

[57] A. Barrett, *Essay on the Pastoral Office as a Divine Institution in the Church of Christ* (1839), pp. 10–11, 118–19, 126.

[58] A. Barrett, *The Ministry and Polity of the Christian Church* (1854), pp. 15, 109–10, 31–2.

1830s saw the emergence of a lunatic fringe among the preachers which wanted the legislation of 1795 and 1797 modified or repealed, in order to put the plenitude of pastoral authority beyond all doubt.[59] But conservative revolution was a pipe-dream.

As the Connexion ran into difficulties in the forties, high Wesleyans began to suspect that the vast authoritarian Methodism of America—where 'there is no low Methodism and high Methodism, no *in* and *outs*, no *government* and its partisans to keep in office or to remove, [where] Methodism is one'—embodied Wesley's 'real mind'.[60] In Asbury's comments and sermon notes the familiar Wesleyan words attach themselves to ministry—'to preach the gospel in all its essential points, to administer the ordinances; and to rule the Church of Christ'.[61] In the vast spaces of America, the itinerants much more closely resembled the prime mover described by Barrett than ever they could in England. The frontier from the extreme north to the Gulf of Mexico was mostly opened up by local preachers; but the fact that by 1820 the Methodists, starting from scratch, had overhauled the Baptists, who employed similar lay agencies, and in the next twenty years were greatly to outstrip them must owe much to the co-ordinating, organizing, and evangelistic labours of the itinerants. Asbury's journal witnesses eloquently to the way the hardships and peculiarities of the itinerant life reinforced the preachers' corporate sense, and to his understanding that they were part of a huge migration.[62] Asbury was an entrepreneur in religion, a man who perceived a market to be exploited, one of the most remarkable men of this kind there have ever been. Of limited gifts but infinite toughness, Asbury, from the moment of his arrival in America in 1771, grasped (indeed was obsessed with) the key to the situation—that the American migration could only be won by an itinerant ministry in Wesley's original sense, a ministry not church-based. Finding

---

[59] M.C.A., J. Bicknell to Bunting, 2 March 1835; W. Binning to [Bunting], 10 July 1851; Oliver Henwood to Thomas Clulow, 23 April 1853.

[60] J. Dixon, *Methodism in America* (3rd edn., 1849), pp. 63, 241; J. Dixon, *Methodism in its Origin, Economy and Present Position* (1843), p. 127. Episcopal Methodism had in fact recently become *two*, with the secession of the southern Methodists on the slavery question.

[61] Asbury, *Journal and Letters*, ii. 294; cf. ibid. iii. 183.

[62] Ibid. ii. 410–11, 417; iii. 453.

the preachers settling down in the eastern seaboard towns, he prized them loose and contested their every attempt to settle again. Asbury conceived himself as restoring a New Testament system of itinerant episcopacy; he found the corruption of city life, not in its sin, but in the inertia it opposed to itinerant ministry:

> I wish to warn you [he wrote in his Valedictory Address] against the growing evil of locality[63] in bishops, elders, preachers or Conferences. Locality is essential to cities and towns, but traveling is essential to the country. Were I to name cities such as Jerusalem, Antioch and Rome, with all the great cities, both ancient and modern, what havoc have these made in the Churches! Alas for us! out of seven hundred traveling preachers, we have about one hundred located in towns and cities and small rich circuits. Guard particularly against two orders of preachers; the one of the country, and the other for the cities; the latter generally settle themselves to purchase ministers, too often men of gifts and learning intend to set themselves to sale.[64]

The rural orientation of American Methodism was an entrepreneurial rather than (as in England) a market fact; Asbury's machine opened up new areas, but 'other denominations came [and] took possession of the villages' which grew up later.[65]

Primitive itinerancy and poverty made all the difference to the American ministry. At the Christmas Conference of 1784 the preacher's allowance was fixed at $64 (a sum raised in 1800 to $80), with allowances in proportion for wife and children. But the family allowances were rarely paid, and at the end of his life Asbury reckoned that not more than one-sixth of the preachers, in the wealthiest circuits, received their own allowances in full. There were few preachers' houses outside the great cities. And throughout the period of breakneck expansion from 1800, the whole system was in the financial straits which came upon English Methodism only after the Napoleonic wars. Asbury's power sprang from his willingness to share not merely the labour but the deprivation of the itinerants. Half of those who died in the ministry were under thirty; two-thirds had

[63] 'Locality' or 'location' meant, in Methodist parlance on both sides of the Atlantic, settling in one place.
[64] Asbury, *Journal and Letters*, iii. 475–6.
[65] Bangs, ii. 294.

travelled less than twelve years. Of course, itinerants for whom there were in practice no houses or family allowances were single men. The Virginia Conference of 1809 was attended by eighty-four preachers of whom only three were married.[66] To marry meant normally to 'locate', to find a house and settled work, and it kept terms of service short. Of the fifteen preachers received in 1784, one-third had retired from the itinerancy in less than two years; nearly another third in five. And so it continued for a couple of generations. Between 1792 and 1796, 161 men entered the itinerancy, but there was a net gain of only 27. Deaths, expulsions, and 106 locations accounted for the rest. Up to 1814, 1,616 candidates had been received into full connexion; by 1816, 819 had located, many of them to render yeoman service as local preachers. The Methodist Episcopal ministry was really a militarily organized mission, largely composed of short-service agents who could hardly be pastorally related to the flock in the traditional European sense.[67] Of course the American flock was different, its extreme mobility making the autocratic powers of the itinerants more acceptable, while the rapid turnover of the itinerants in turn created acceptance for the autocracy of the bishops and presiding elders. Asbury understood what he was about, noting from Thomas Haweis's *Church History* that 'the [primitive] evangelists were the chief superintending, episcopal men; aye, so say I; and that they prescribed forms of discipline and systematized codes of doctrine'.[68]

In England, by contrast, the commentators noted from 1800 how much less laborious the circuit rounds had become, and from 1815 how itinerancy in the old sense of sleeping, praying, and preaching with the people in their rural homes and meeting-places was coming to an end, and with it that symbolic institution, the circuit horse. Too many country circuits were

"'Drinkhouse, i. 199. For Asbury's touching account of his preference for celibacy, *Journal and Letters*, ii. 423, 591.

[67] A. Stevens, *History of the Methodist Episcopal Church in the United States of America* (4 vols., New York, 1866–7), ii. 140 and iv. 185; Bucke, *History of American Methodism* (p. 328, n. 18), i. 472. The nearest English parallel was the way the Hull Primitive Methodist Circuit, 1822–7, picked up a scattered mass of popular evangelicalism between the Humber and the Scottish Border, by means of poorly paid temporary agents, regarded by no one as ministers: *Proceedings of the Wesley Historical Society*, xxxvii (1970), 169 sqq.

[68] Asbury, *Journal and Letters*, ii. 488.

neglected, and ravaged by the Ranters.[69] Before long, the comment was that home missions had ceased altogether. And it was a married ministry. In Wesley's time less than a third of the preachers were married; by 1814 it was three-quarters of a total number which had trebled since his death.[70] The cause of the increase was the great proliferation of chapels, especially urban chapels, built on debt, which provided appointments with a minimum of travelling and required no nights away from home. These conditions were congenial to a married ministry, but all sections of the Methodist community, including the adherents who were not members of Society, shared responsibility for the situation which produced them. 'The Meth[odist]s [it was noted in 1802] are now saying, Let us have genteel chapels that we may be like our neighbours';[71] and their version of what Asbury abused as 'locality' called, as he predicted, for a genteel ministry. Fittingly enough, Alfred Barrett, a man of 'particularly chaste and elegant mind', had a successful ministry at the Oxford Road chapel, 'attended by most of the élite of the Methodist body in Manchester'.[72]

The development of a high doctrine of the ministry to support an active central administration, in England, drove together the two causes of religious democracy and local rights. The strains to which American Methodism was subject tended to drive them apart. By 1830 the bishops of the Methodist Episcopal Church had ceased to itinerate over the whole church in Asbury's manner, and had established an informal balance of North and South. The South seemed to have effectively compromised the originally strong Methodist anti-slavery witness.[73] Unlike the supporters of local rights in England, it could appeal to a high or strict interpretation of the constitution of 1808, and especially to the restrictive rule that forbade the Delegated Conference to 'do away [with] episcopacy, or destroy the plan of our itinerant general superintendency'. Yet in the North and West strong feeling arose against appointing

[69] On these problems, see W. R. Ward, *Religion and Society in England, 1790–1850* (1972), pp. 99–101.

[70] M.C.A., W. Myles to Joseph Dutton, 3 June 1814.

[71] M.C.A., Tyerman MSS. iii, fo. 319.

[72] John Evans, *Lancashire Authors and Orators* (1850), p. 30.

[73] On this whole subject, see D. G. Mathews, *Slavery and Methodism* (Princeton, N.J., 1965).

slave-holders to high office. In 1832 James O. Andrew owed
his election to the episcopate to the need to find a southerner
who did not own slaves. 'It is not my merit that has made me
a Bishop', he exclaimed with tears in his eyes, 'but my poverty.'
Fittingly enough, the final crisis was brought on by Andrew's
acquiring slaves through inheritance and marriage, the law of
Georgia forbidding manumission. The North held that it was
the policy of the church not to elect slave-holders to the episcopate, for they could not itinerate in the North. Andrew had
disqualified himself and should resign. A bishop convicted of
immorality might be constitutionally removed, but no proceedings were ever taken against Andrew; the North was exerting naked Conference power over the episcopate in a way the
South had resisted ever since 1808. Cornered at last, the South
virtually abandoned Wesley's doctrine that bishops and presbyters were equal in order and different in office:

It is true that the Annual Conferences select the Bishops of the
Church, by the suffrages of their delegates, in General Conference
assembled; but the General Conference . . . does not possess the
power of ordination, without which a Bishop cannot be constituted
. . . Episcopacy even in the Methodist Church is not a mere appointment to labour. It is an official consecrated station, under the protection of law . . . If the doctrine against which we protest be
admitted, the episcopal office is, at best, but a quadrennial term of
service.[74]

In America, as in England, the hard-pressed 'high' Methodists
were seeking to move from a functional to a symbolic doctrine
of the church. Repudiating the Conference leverage against
episcopacy, the southerners seceded in 1844; the Civil War was
casting its shadow before.

On both sides of the Atlantic the attempt to save the day
for the modern developments in Methodism by asserting their
symbolic status had by 1850 ended in disaster. Not surprisingly,
one notable writer, George Steward,[75] now returned to the view
that the legacy of John Wesley consisted in the empiricism and

[74] G. F. Moede, *The Office of Bishop in Methodism. Its History and Development*
(Zürich, 1964), pp. 84–102.
[75] George Steward, *The Principles of Church Government and their Application to
Wesleyan Methodism* (1853); also George Steward, *The Farewell to Wesleyan Controversy* (1854).

the functional considerations which underlay the institutions he entailed upon his posterity, clearly perceiving that institutional collapse could no longer be remedied by magnifying ministerial authority. But this was a highbrow presentation of the traditions of Methodist reform, a part of the Wesleyan patrimony which falls beyond the limits of this paper.

The Writings of
Lucy Stuart Sutherland

References to *The Brown Book* refer to the annual magazine published by the Lady Margaret Hall Association of Senior Members.

1931

Review of Eleanor C. Lodge, *Sully, Colbert and Turgot: a chapter in French Economic History. Oxford Mag.*, 15 Oct., p. 40.

1932

'Edmund Burke and the First Rockingham Ministry', *E.H.R.* xlvii. 46–72.

'The Accounts of an Eighteenth-Century Merchant: the Portuguese Ventures of William Braund', *Econ. H. R.* iii. 367–87.

Review of D. M. Goodfellow, *A Modern Economic History of South Africa. Econ. H. R.* iii. 441–2.

1933

A LONDON MERCHANT 1695–1774 (Oxford Historical Series).

1934

'The Law Merchant in England in the Seventeenth and Eighteenth Centuries', *T.R.H.S.*, 4th ser. xvii. 149–76.

'Lord Shelburne and East India Company Politics, 1766–9', *E.H.R.* xlix. 450–86.

1935

'The Use of Business Records in the Study of History', *B.I.H.R.* xiii. 69–72.

Review of A. Mervyn Davies, *Warren Hastings. Maker of British India. New Statesman and Nation*, 29 June, pp. 964–5.

1936

'Sir George Colebrooke's World Corner in Alum, 1771–73', *Economic History*, iii. 237–58.

1937

Edited (with May McKisack), M. V. Clarke's *Fourteenth Century Studies* (Oxford, Clarendon Press).

1938

Edited (with Helen M. Cam and Mary Coate), A. E. Levett's *Studies in Manorial History* (Oxford, Clarendon Press).

1940

Review of Sir Philip Magnus, *Edmund Burke, a Prophet of the Eighteenth Century. E.H.R.* lv. 341–2.

Review of D. Wecter, *Edmund Burke and his Kinsmen, a Study of the Statesman's Financial Integrity and Private Relationships. E.H.R.* lv. 505–6.

Review of *The Yale Edition of Horace Walpole's Correspondence, Vols. III to VI: Correspondence with Mme. du Deffand*, ed. W. S. Lewis and Warren Hunting Smith. *Oxford Mag.*, 28 Nov., pp. 110–12.

1946

'Samson Gideon and the Reduction of Interest, 1749–50', *Econ. H. R.* xvi. 15–29.

Review of *Le Journal de Gibbon à Lausanne, 17 août 1763–19 avril 1764*, ed. Georges Bonnard; and of Georges Bonnard, *L'Importance du deuxième séjour de Gibbon à Lausanne dans la formation de l'historien. E.H.R.* lxi. 408–11.

1947

'The East India Company and the Peace of Paris', *E.H.R.* lxii. 179–90.

'The East India Company in Eighteenth-Century Politics', *Econ. H. R.* xvii. 15–26.

1949

Review of H. Butterfield, *George III, Lord North and the People, 1779–80. The Listener*, 10 Nov., p. 821. Not signed.

Review of Holden Furber, *John Company at Work: a Study of European Expansion in India in the late Eighteenth Century. E.H.R.* lxiv. 526–8.

Review of *The Jenkinson Papers, 1760–1766*, ed. Ninetta S. Jucker. *T.L.S.* 20 May, p. 323. Not signed.

Review of Sir Charles Petrie, *Earlier Diplomatic History, 1492–1713. T.L.S.*, 18 Nov., p. 746. Not signed.

1950

'Universities and Schools', *Universities Qtly.*, v. 20–5.

Review of E. H. Carr, *Studies in Revolution. T.L.S.*, 4 Aug., pp. 477–8. Not signed.

Review of Ferdinand Schevill, *The Great Elector. History*, N.S. xxxv. 131.

Review of H.R.H. Prince Chula Chakrabongse, *The Education of the Enlightened Despots. History*, N.S. xxxv. 132.

Review (with E. A. O. Whiteman) of P. A. Scholes, *The Great Dr. Burney. History*, N.S. xxxv. 272–3.

1951

Review of *The Private Correspondence of Lord Macartney, Governor of Madras (1781–85)*, ed. C. Collin Davies (R. Hist. Soc., Camden 3rd ser. lxxvii). *T.L.S.*, 2 Feb., p. 67. Not signed.

1952

THE EAST INDIA COMPANY IN EIGHTEENTH-CENTURY POLITICS (Oxford, Clarendon Press).

Review of *Bibliography of British History. The Eighteenth Century, 1714–1789*, ed. Stanley Pargellis and D. J. Medley. *B.I.H.R.* xxv. 66–8.

Review of *The Private Correspondence of Lord Macartney, Governor of Madras (1781–85)*, ed. C. Collin Davies (R. Hist. Soc., Camden 3rd ser. lxxvii). *Econ. H. R.*, 2nd ser. v. 160–1.

Review of S. McKee Rosen, *The Combined Boards of the Second World War: an Experiment in International Administration. E.H.R.* lxvii. 314–15.

Review of L. B. Namier, *Avenues of History. T.L.S.*, 4 July, p. 431. Not signed.

Review of *Fort William–India House Correspondence and other Contemporary Papers relating thereto (Public Series)*, vol. v, *1767–1769*, ed. N. K. Sinha. *E.H.R.* lxvii. 608–9.

1953

'Two Letter-books of Richard Barwell 1769–73. Letter-book I', *Indian Archives*, vii. 115–45.

'Samson Gideon: Eighteenth Century Jewish Financier', *Transactions of the Jewish Historical Society of England*, xvii. 79–90.

Review of Richard Pares, *King George III and the Politicians. Time and Tide*, 4 April, pp. 454–5.

Review of M. Bellasis, *Honourable Company. Spectator*, 26 June, p. 836.

Review of S. K. Bhuyan, *Anglo-Assamese Relations, 1771–1826. A History of the Relations of Assam with the East India Company from 1771 to 1826, based on Original English and Assamese Sources. Econ. H. R.*, 2nd ser. vi. 97.

Review of *The Correspondence of David Scott, Director and Chairman of the East India Company, relating to Indian Affairs, 1787–1805*, ed. C. H. Philips (R. Hist. Soc., Camden 3rd ser. lxxv, lxxvi). *E.H.R.* lxviii. 286–8.

1954

'Pembroke College' and 'Somerville College' (part), in *V.C.H., Oxfordshire*, vol. iii: *The University of Oxford*, pp. 288–97; 343–5.

'Two Letter-books of Richard Barwell, 1769–73. Letter-book II', *Indian Archives*, viii. 14–42.

'The Hanoverian Kings' (last section with J. H. Rose), *sub* 'English History', in *Encyclopaedia Britannica*, viii. 523–31.

Review of Philip Woodruff, *The Men who Ruled India: The Founders. T.L.S.*, 23 April, pp. 257–8. Not signed.

Review of *Miscellanea Gibboniana*, ed. G. R. de Beer, G. A. Bonnard, and L. Junod. *E.H.R.* lxix. 493–4.

1955

With J. Binney, 'Henry Fox as Paymaster General of the Forces', *E.H.R.* lxx. 229–57.

'The Ostend Company', in *Encyclopaedia Britannica*, xvi. 955.

Review of Philip Woodruff, *The Men who Ruled India: The Guardians. T.L.S.*, 18 Feb., p. 102. Not signed.

Review of Percy Scholes, *The Life and Activities of Sir John Hawkins, Musician, Magistrate and Friend of Johnson. History*, N.S. xl. 165–6.

1956

'The City of London in Eighteenth-Century Politics', in *Essays presented to Sir Lewis Namier*, ed. Richard Pares and A. J. P. Taylor, pp. 49–74.

'A Letter from John Stewart, Secretary and Judge Advocate of Bengal, 1773', *Indian Archives*, x. 1–12.

Review of *Horace Walpole's Correspondence with William Mason* (2 vols.), ed. W. S. Lewis, G. Cronin, jun., and C. H. Bennett. *The Connoisseur*, cxxxviii. 64.

Review of J. H. Plumb, *Sir Robert Walpole, The Making of a Statesman. The Times*, 29 March. Not signed.

Review of Per Fuglum, *Edward Gibbon, his View of Life and Conception of History, E.H.R.* lxxi. 335–6.

Review of Keith Feiling, *Warren Hastings. E.H.R.* lxxi. 462–4.

Review of John Brooke, *The Chatham Administration, 1766–1768. T.L.S.*, 26 Oct., pp. 625–6. Not signed.

Review of G. Giarrizzo, *Edward Gibbon e la cultura europea del Settecento. E.H.R.* lxxi. 655–7.

Review of S. Bhattacharya, *The East India Company and the Economy of Bengal from 1704 to 1740. E.H.R.* lxxi. 673–4.

1957

'New Evidence on the Nandakuma Trial', *E.H.R.* lxxii. 438–65.

'The Resignation on behalf of Warren Hastings, 1776: George Vansittart's Evidence', *Bengal Past and Present*, lxxvi. 22–9.

Review of John B. Owen, *The Rise of the Pelhams. T.L.S.*, 1 March, p. 127. Not signed.

Review of Herbert Butterfield, *George III and the Historians. The Times*, 28 Nov. Not signed.

Review of K. G. Davies, *The Royal African Company. Oxford Mag.*, 5 Dec., pp. 192–[3].

Review of *Studies in Italian Medieval History presented to Miss E. M. Jamison*, ed. P. Grierson and J. Ward Perkins (Papers of the British School at Rome, vol. xxiv (N.S., vol. xi), 1956). *The Brown Book*, pp. 40–1.

1958

Review of R. J. S. Hoffman, *Edmund Burke, New York Agent with his Letters to the New York Assembly and Intimate Correspondence with Charles O'Hara, 1761–1776. E.H.R.* lxxiii. 313–16.

Review of Ian R. Christie, *The End of North's Ministry, 1780–1782. The Times*, 24 April. Not signed.

Review of *The New Cambridge Modern History*, vol. vii: *The Old Regime, 1713–63*, ed. J. O. Lindsay. *Econ. H. R.*, 2nd ser. xi. 368–9.

1959

THE CITY OF LONDON AND THE OPPOSITION TO GOVERNMENT, 1768–1774. A STUDY IN THE RISE OF METROPOLITAN RADICALISM. The Creighton Lecture in History, 1958 (University of London, The Athlone Press).

Review of Jack Lindsay, *1754 T.L.S.*, 16 Oct., p. 590. Not signed.

Review of *Mauritius and the Spice Trade: the Odyssey of Pierre Poivre*, ed. M. Ly-Tio-Fane (Mauritius Archives Publication Fund, Publication No. 4). *Archives*, iv. 120–1.

1960

Edited THE CORRESPONDENCE OF EDMUND BURKE, vol. ii: July 1768–June 1774 (General editor, Thomas W. Copeland: Cambridge University Press and University of Chicago Press).

'Lady Margaret Hall', *American Oxonian*, xlvii. 70–5.

'The New Status of Women', *Oxford*, xvi, no. 3, pp. 72–6.

Obituary of Sir Lewis Namier. *Oxford Mag.*, 20 Oct., pp. 31–2.

Review of J. Steven Watson, *The Oxford History of England*, vol. xii: *The Reign of George III, 1760–1815. The Listener*, 6 Oct., p. 577.

Review of *Fort William–India House Correspondence and other Contemporary Papers relating thereto (Public Series)*, vol. ii, *1757–1759*, ed. H. N. Sinha. *E.H.R.* lxxv. 531–2.

1961

'The City of London and the Devonshire–Pitt Administration, 1756–7'. The Raleigh Lecture on History, 1960. *Proceedings of the British Academy*, xlvi. 147–93.

Biographical introduction to Richard Pares, *The Historian's Business and other Essays*, ed. R. A. and Elisabeth Humphreys, pp. ix–xiv.

'Sir Lewis Namier' (translated into Italian by Pino Fino), *Rivista storica italiana*, lxxiii. 415–18.

Review of J. H. Plumb, *Sir Robert Walpole, The King's Minister. The Times*, 19 Jan. Not signed.

Reviews of B. B. Misra, *The Central Administration of the East India Company, 1773–1834. Oxford Mag.*, 16 Feb., pp. 230–1. *Econ. H. R.*, 2nd ser. xiii. 533–6.

Review of T. H. D. Mahoney, *Edmund Burke and Ireland. Oxford Mag.*, 11 May, p. 339.

Review of C. B. Cone, *Burke and the Nature of Politics: The Age of the American Revolution. History*, n.s. xlvi. 60–1.

1962

THE EAST INDIA COMPANY IN EIGHTEENTH-CENTURY POLITICS (reprint by the Clarendon Press, Oxford).

A LONDON MERCHANT, 1695–1774 (reprint by Frank Cass & Co.).

Edited, with J. Brooke, Sir Lewis Namier's Ford Lectures, 1934, in Sir Lewis Namier, *Crossroads of Power*, pp. 73–117.

'In Memoriam Lucy Barbara Hammond (née Bradby), 1875–1961', *The Brown Book*, pp. 28–9.

Review of Basil Williams, *The Oxford History of England*, vol. xi: *The Whig Supremacy, 1714–1760*, 2nd edn., rev. C. H. Stuart. *The Listener*, 26 April, p. 726.

Review of C. H. Philips, *The East India Company 1784–1834* (new edition). *Journal of Southeast Asian History*, iii. 139.

Review of George Rudé, *Wilkes and Liberty: a Social Study of 1763 to 1774. Oxford Mag.*, 24 May, pp. 328–9.

Review of R. Shackleton, *Montesquieu—a Critical Biography. Oxford Mag.*, 31 May, p. 344.

Review of Ainslie Embree, *Charles Grant and British Rule in India. The Economist*, 28 July, pp. 359–60. Not signed.

Review of P. G. M. Dickson, *The Sun Insurance Office 1710–1960. The History of Two and a Half Centuries of British Insurance. Econ. H. R.*, 2nd ser. xiv. 567–9.

1963

'Sir Lewis Namier, 1888–1960', *Proceedings of the British Academy*, xlviii. 371–85.

Review of *The Later Correspondence of George III*, vol. i, *1783–1793*, ed. A. Aspinall. *Oxford Mag.*, 7 March, p. 236.

Review of George Rudé, *Wilkes and Liberty: a Social Study of 1763 to 1774. W. & M. Qtly.*, 3rd ser. xx. 624–6.

1964

Contributions to *The History of Parliament. The House of Commons 1754–1790*, ed. Sir Lewis Namier and John Brooke.

Review of *The Later Correspondence of George III*, vol. ii, *1793–1797*, ed. A. Aspinall. *Oxford Mag.*, 7 May, pp. 288–9.

Review of P. Mackesy, *The War for America, 1775–1783. Oxford Mag.*, 22 Oct., p. 37.

Review of John Ehrman, *The British Government and Commercial Negotiations with Europe 1783–1793. E.H.R.* lxxix. 864–6.

1965

Review of J. T. Boulton, *The Language of Politics in the Age of Wilkes and Burke. History*, N.S. l. 234.

Review of L. W. Hanson, *Contemporary Printed Sources for British and Irish Economic History, 1701–1750. The Library*, 5th ser. xx. 66–8.

Review of *Calendar of State Papers, Colonial Series. America and West Indies*, ed. K. G. Davies. *E.H.R.* lxxx. 176.

1966

STUDIES IN HISTORY (British Academy Lectures. Selected and introduced by Lucy S. Sutherland. Oxford Paperbacks, No. 111).

With John A. Woods, 'The East India Speculations of William Burke', *Proceedings of the Leeds Philosophical and Literary Society*, vol. xi, part vii, pp. 183–216.

Review of *The Political Journal of George Bubb Dodington*, ed. J. Carswell and L. A. Dralle. *T.L.S.*, 20 Jan., p. 38. Not signed.

Review of Benjamin Woods Labaree, *The Boston Tea Party. W. & M. Qtly.*, 3rd ser. xxiii. 158–60.

1967

'Lewis Namier, and Institutional History', *Annali della Fondazione Italiana per la Storia Amministrativa*, iv. 35–43.

Review of Sir Francis Hill, *Georgian Lincoln. T.L.S.*, 2 March, p. 164. Not signed.

Review of P. G. M. Dickson, *The Financial Revolution in England. T.L.S.*, 20 July, p. 641. Not signed.

Review of *The Complete Letters of Lady Mary Wortley Montagu*, vol. i, ed. Robert Halsband. *E.H.R.* lxxxii. 839–40.

Review of C. B. A. Behrens, *The Ancien Régime. The Brown Book*, pp. 48–9.

1968

'Edmund Burke and the Relations between Members of Parliament and their Constituents', *Studies in Burke and his Time*, x. 1005–21.

Review of Joseph Spence's *Observations, Anecdotes and Characters of Books and Men Collected from Conversation*, ed. James Osborn. *E.H.R.* lxxxiii. 403.

Review of Edward Gibbon's *Memoir of My Life*, ed. Georges A. Bonnard, and of J. W. Swain, *Edward Gibbon the Historian. E.H.R.* lxxxiii. 404.

Review of *The Correspondence of Jeremy Bentham*, vols. i and ii, *1752–1780*, ed. Timothy L. S. Sprigge. *New Society*, 9 May, pp. 683–4.

Review of *The Complete Letters of Lady Mary Wortley Montagu*, vol. ii, ed. Robert Halsband. *E.H.R.* lxxxiii. 616–17.

1969

With W. Doyle and J. M. J. Rogister, 'Junius and Philip Francis: New Evidence', *B.I.H.R.* xlii. 158–72.

'William Miller Macmillan: an Appreciation', *St. Antony's Papers*, no. 21, *African Affairs*, no. 3, ed. Kenneth Kirkwood, pp. 9–24.

Review of M. C. Bradbrook, '*That Infidel Place': a Short History of Girton College 1869–1969. Spectator*, 21 March, pp. 381–2.

Review of S. N. Mukherjee, *Sir William Jones: a Study in Eighteenth-Century British Attitudes to India. E.H.R.* lxxxiv. 587–9.

Review of three pamphlets on Equality for Women, *The Brown Book*, pp. 70–4.

Translation into Japanese of 'The City of London in Eighteenth-Century Politics' (1956) and of THE CITY OF LONDON AND THE OPPOSITION TO GOVERNMENT, 1768–1774 (1959), by Professor M. Iwama, Professor of Western History, Tohoku University (Miraisha, Tokyo, Social Science Seminar, 44).

1970

'Maria Edgeworth's Tree Paeony', *The Brown Book*, pp. 63–4.

Review of G. R. Elton, *The Practice of History*, and *The Future of the Past. E.H.R.* lxxxv. 106–9.

Review of *The Complete Letters of Lady Mary Wortley Montagu*, vol. iii, ed. Robert Halsband. *E.H.R.* lxxxv. 178–9.

Review of Dorothy Marshall, *Dr. Johnson's London* (New Dimensions in History, Historical Cities, ed. N. F. Cantor). *E.H.R.* lxxxv. 618.

Review of *Horace Walpole, Writer, Politician and Connoisseur: Essays on the 250th Anniversary of Walpole's Birth*, ed. Warren H. Smith. *E.H.R.* lxxxv. 618–19.

Review of John J. Murray, *George I, the Baltic and the Whig Split of 1717. T.L.S.*, 9 Oct., p. 1166. Not signed.

Review of M. G. Kammen, *A Rope of Sand. The Colonial Agents, British Politics, and the American Revolution. E.H.R.* lxxxv. 856–7.

Review of E. Longford, *Wellington, the Years of the Sword. The Brown Book*, pp. 48–50.

1971

Review of *The Letters of Sir William Jones*, ed. Garland Cannon. *South Asian Review*, iv. 261–4.

Review of Loren Reid, *Charles James Fox*. *History*, N.S. lvi. 452–3.

Review of R. Rocher, *Alexander Hamilton (1762–1824). A Chapter in the Early History of Sanskrit Studies*. *E.H.R.* lxxxvi. 422.

Review of B. T. Wilkins, *The Problem of Burke's Political Philosophy*. *E.H.R.* lxxxvi. 422–3.

1972

Review of *The Correspondence of General Thomas Gage with the Secretaries of State, and with the War Office and the Treasury 1763–1775*, ed. C. E. Carter. *E.H.R.* lxxxvii. 630.

Review of *Fort William–India House Correspondence and other contemporary papers related thereto*, vol. iii, *1760–1763*, ed. R. R. Sethi. *E.H.R.* lxxxvii. 631–2.

Review of P. Nightingale, *Trade and Empire in Western India, 1784–1806*. *E.H.R.* lxxxvii. 632–3.

Review of Ian R. Christie, *Myth and Reality in Late-Eighteenth-Century British Politics and Other Papers*. *E.H.R.* lxxxvii. 633–4.

1973

THE UNIVERSITY OF OXFORD IN THE EIGHTEENTH CENTURY (Bryce Lecture, Somerville College, 1972).

Index

This index is primarily one of persons and places, but some subjects of particular importance have been included

B b

Index